Russian Eyes on American Literature

Russian Eyes
on American Literature

Edited by

Sergei Chakovsky

and

M. Thomas Inge

PUBLISHED BY

UNIVERSITY PRESS OF MISSISSIPPI

JACKSON AND LONDON

AND

A. M. GORKY INSTITUTE OF WORLD LITERATURE

The essays in this book have been translated from the Russian by Lise Brody.

Copyright © 1992 by the University Press of Mississippi
Manufactured in the United States of America

95 94 93 92   4 3 2 I

The paper in this book meets the guidelines for permanence and durability of the Committee on Production Guidelines for Book Longevity of the Council on Library Resources.

Library of Congress Cataloging-in-Publication Data

Russian eyes on American literature / edited by M. Thomas Inge and
  Sergei Chakovsky.
      p.   cm.
   Translation of Russian essays.
   Includes bibliographical references and index.
   ISBN 0-87805-584-3
   I. American literature—History and criticism.   2. Criticism—
Soviet Union.   I. Inge, M. Thomas.   II. Chakovskiï, S. A.
PS58.R87   1992
810.9—dc20   92-19552
                                                                    CIP

British Library Cataloging-in-Publication data available

CONTENTS

PREFACE

During the days of the Soviet Union, communications about the nature and purpose of literature between Russian and American critics were fraught with inevitable misunderstandings. As Deming Brown explained in his pioneer and still definitive study up to 1962, *Soviet Attitudes Toward American Writing* (Princeton University Press, 1962):

> In the Soviet Union the relationship between literature and politics is direct and intimate. Even literature that refrains from specific political appeals—or attempts to avoid politics altogether—is subject to evaluation of a political nature. Literary activity in the United States, by contrast, is much less civic in its orientation. The writer and the critic are at liberty to accept or reject political responsibility and to seek their own values in literature. . . . The American writer functions under no explicit ideological mandate and . . . need not make explicit social or moral judgments. The Soviet writer, on the other hand, has inherited from pre-revolutionary Russian literature a sense of social duty and a deep concern for the national destiny (p. vii).

The strong commitment to political and social values in the Soviet Union under Communism called for the development of a singular critical theory for the appreciation of literature of all nations in which the value of a work was almost entirely determined by its political and ideological content, the so-called "socialist realism" serving as the highest artistic benchmark. Stalin, one of the creators of this theory, saw writers as engineers of the human soul who lead readers through the correct stages of revolutionary development.

Given these constraints, when critics turned their eyes toward American literature, they found precious little to praise since few writers in the United States have ever committed themselves single-mindedly to Communism or any other political doctrine. The reality of the situation soon encouraged the development of a slightly more flexible critical perspective known as "critical realism" which finds value in the writer who displays "the malfunctioning of capitalist society and . . . the unhappiness, frustrations, and inhumanity that result from its operations" (Brown, p. 11). Even though the writer may embrace the values of the materialistic society, exposures of injustice, corruption, and ugliness will arouse discontent and contribute to the beginnings of revolutionary ferment. Given the tendency of American writers to deal harshly with the failures of the democratic system, such a perspective allowed Soviet critics to discuss and find merit in a greatly expanded list of authors. Once the door was opened ever so slightly, however, critics were soon working toward taking writers at their face value and finding things to admire in their style and artistry aside from political content.

When *perestroika* and *glasnost* arrived and literary criticism was allowed openly to follow its own paths of development, a host of practicing and new critics emerged to assume the task of shaping more balanced ways of interpretation and appreciation. The essays collected in this volume are representative of the new order. While few of them practice any of the latest trends in critical theory that have possessed the West, and they demonstrate no allegiance to any singular perspective or methodology, the authors do reflect some distinctive attitudes and points of view that are shaped by the Russian character and experience.

This volume sets several precedents. To our knowledge, it is the first product of an official collaboration between the Gorky Institute of World Literature in Moscow and an American university press in the area of American literature. It is the first effort to explore many of the major developments in the whole of American writing, from colonial times to the present, by Russian critics free from the rigorous ideological limitations of the Soviet system. Finally, it is the first collection of essays on American letters by Russian critics written specifically for readers in the English-speaking world.

While all of the contributors are fluent in English and could have written their essays in that language, they were requested to write them in Russian on the theory that the flow of thought and style would be richer and freer in one's native tongue. The essays were then translated into English and approved by the authors to assure accuracy. This procedure may have inhibited the practice of individual style, but we hope something has been gained in the fullness and clarity of expression.

This is likely to be but the first of many such collaborative projects as the United States and Russia begin to explore each other's culture in open and free ways until now impossible. Both nations have always been deeply interested in the art and culture of the other with an intensity that not even the Cold War could dampen. If Americans can here see themselves as others see them through the prisms of literature and learn what others find provocative in their cultural heritage, then the book will have fulfilled its purpose.

M. Thomas Inge
Randolph-Macon College
Ashland, Virginia
April 1992

INTRODUCTION

Original as these individual essays may be, this book should also give some idea of the work done lately in and around A. M. Gorky Institute of World Literature, a division of the Russian Academy of Sciences. Founded in 1932, the Institute gradually evolved to become the premier research facility for literary history, theory, textology, and bibliography in what was the Soviet Union. For the last ten years its staff of over two hundred in collaboration with colleagues from other research centers and universities all over the country has been producing an average of twenty books a year on subjects ranging from classical poetics to American mass literature—intended as specialized teaching aids, reference, or intellectual enrichment for the more inquisitive among general readership.

Official focus on the literature of the United States came a decade after the Gorky Institute was founded. In 1947 the Institute published the first volume of *The History of American Literature*. For many years this solitary work remained a lonely cornerstone, but in time it became a monument to the precarious position of American literary scholarship in the Soviet Union. As written by our foremost specialists in the field, most notably Anna Elistratova and Abel Startzev, the *History* was denounced as "anti-scholarly" (read: too lenient on "capitalist" ideology). The sequel to volume one never followed. The project—nurtured, among other reasons, as a contribution to the spirit of the Allied war effort—was scrapped. "Struggle with cosmopolitism" became the slogan of the day in the U.S.S.R. In America the campaign of "red baiting" soon followed. Whoever may have been the original culprit of this standoff, the Cold War years in the U.S.S.R. offered no haven for American scholarship. In the sixties, during Khruschev's "thaw," a study of American literature haltingly started to re-emerge. In the seventies the period of Detente allowed it to attain political, cultural, and scholarly legitimacy. In the mideighties during Gorbachev's programs of *perestroika* and *glasnost* American literary study was given spectacular impetus in the U.S.S.R.

It was during those memorable days in Moscow that the idea for this book, first offered by Hunter M. Cole of University Press of Mississippi, got enthusiastic support from Peter Palievsky, Deputy Director of Gorky Institute, and Yasen Zasursky, Dean of Moscow State University School of Journalism, both leading authorities on American letters. The design as it crystalized in our conversations with M. Thomas Inge was to show the genres of Soviet literary scholarship as they relate to major historical periods and artistic personalities in American literature. No hopes for comprehensiveness were entertained. Such a grand design would have required a much larger volume, or even a series of books like this.

Included here are our attempts to show how Russian scholarly eyes view the literature of America. Ekaterina Stetsenko's piece on colonial literature reflects our search for the roots of American literary mentality beyond the ready-made traditions of the Old World. This impulse, so it would seem to me, is shared by Maya Koreneva and Yuri Kovalev, even if their approaches to what we term the golden age of American letters, the age of romanticism, are quite individual. Next, a leap to the innovative, path-breaking poetics of Mark Twain—rebellious yet legitimate heir to the older masters—is taken in Pavel Balditzin's study of Twain's enigmatic "Autobiography." Dmitry Urnov's reflective polemics with T. S. Eliot—a sample of our "criticism of criticism"—takes us up to a study of twentieth-century American authors, the subject by far the most popular with Soviet literary scholars.

Maya Koreneva, Vasili Tolmatchoff, Natalia Yakimenko, Nickolai Anastasiev, and I myself try out some new approaches to the work of now established American figures we consider to be classics—O'Neill, Fitzgerald, Hemingway, Faulkner, and the expatriot Nabokov. Tatiana Morozova and Tamara Denisova take a more general philosophic view, raising the ever-pertinent theme of man and society as manifested in the American novel. Maya Tugusheva introduces the feminist dimension. Alexandr Muliarchik and Alexei Zverev, reflecting the complexity of the phenomenon as well as the spectrum of existing critical opinion, express somewhat conflicting views of the literature of the eighties.

The idea behind the design of this book was for us to touch bases, not to score a home run of any sort. Compulsive competitiveness between our nations affected our intellectual exchanges for too long. This project, instead, intends to coordinate U.S. and Russian wavelengths, to facilitate productive dialogue, and to foster cooperation between the scholars of our two countries.

Over the years, the words *dialogue* and *cooperation* have often been ideological small change in political transactions between U.S.S.R. and the U.S.A. and hence subject to much abuse. There are no safeguards against this in the future. Politicians will play their games. Yet our genuinely working together professionally is a clear possibility now. Moreover, such an attitude of cooperation is essential if American literary studies are to have any future in the former Soviet Union. The multi-volume *History of American Literature*, a major project at the Institute at present, is one example of our great interest in American letters. It is long overdue, for academic histories of all major European literatures have been available to Russian readers for many years. This American project can be brought to successful completion only in cooperation with our American colleagues. Their bibliographic support is essential, as are the enriching exchanges of ideas, ranging from symposia to joint authorship.

Immediate practical matters aside, the field that lies before us is wide and deep, the challenge both quantitative and qualitative. First, a mass of material still awaits systematic research by scholars in Russia: regional, ethnic, and other minority American authors are examples that readily come to mind. The second challenge is more universal. It questions the validity of our working definitions of literature, calling for the refinement of our analytical skills to match the precious texture of the subject—the work of art.

Aiming for broad historical, cultural, psychological, or psychoanalytic generalizations, and too often attempting to pigeonhole an author within a certain school or tradition, the scholars of the former U.S.S.R. often have lost sight of the basic realities of literature as art form. Indeed, it is normal for an artist to be a loner, and to baffle rigid categorization and preconceived ideological patterns. His or her work is a world unto itself. Springing from the real world and yet intended for it, a novel is an individual work of art. As Eudora Welty stated in *The Eye of the Story*, a work of fiction is "something that never was before and will not be again, *not the same thing as the raw material* of external life, not even of the same family of things" [italics supplied].

In my country, the scholar's new challenge, I believe, is to trace in a consistent way this exciting artistic transmutation that raw materials of life undergo as they become new and artistic entities. Moreover, I believe the scholarly goal should be to marry the idea of such aesthetic uniqueness to the idea of broad historical and artistic patterns, close textual scrutiny, and socio-cultural analysis. Doing so calls for a revitalization of interest in the individual work of art, and for a synthetic approach that is adequate to the artistic work, which in itself is both manifold and whole.

Whatever the vagaries of market economy—a factor to be reckoned with by both American *and* former Soviet scholars—the blending of our methodologies and cultural backgrounds is definitely called for now. One can be reasonably sure that in joining our scholarly insights we will shed new light on this wonderful child of many parents—American literature.

Sergei Chakovsky
Moscow
April 1992

Russian Eyes on American Literature

EKATERINA STETSENKO

The Formation

of the Secular Literary Tradition

in Colonial America

The English discovered America nearly one hundred years after Columbus. Until 1607, when they finally succeeded in establishing themselves firmly in the New World, the lands across the ocean remained for them a strange, mysterious, enigmatic world. Like any unknown, that world concealed possible wonders and dangers and, at the same time, inspired hopes of satisfying desires unattainable in the homeland.

The thrill of this hope led people to believe whichever rumors and stories of the New World they wished to believe and to see in their crossing of the ocean what they wished to see. America seemed to them a fairy-tale land of "milk and honey"—Eldorado, paradise found, a place still in some golden age, an earthly Eden where people, like "birds of the sky," neither "reap nor sow," but merely pluck sweet fruit from eternally green trees and gather the silver and gold scattered at their feet.

The journey "to the end of the world" takes on all the necessary attributes of a fairy tale, in which the eternal battle is carried on between the forces of light and dark. The heroes find a wondrous land after passing through cruel trials, overcoming obstacles, and battling monsters. John

Sparke, who arrived in Florida in 1564, populated America with lions, tigers, unicorns, and snakes with three heads and four legs. David Ingram, who traveled on foot from Mexico to Nova Scotia in 1568–69, claimed to have seen elephants, cannibals with dogs' teeth, and the Devil himself (though this claim is doubted by many historians).

However, the laws of the travel account, demanding authenticity and confirmation either by first-hand experience or by reference to eyewitnesses, forced these authors to balance their fabrications with disclaimers, to include sobering facts in their narratives. Sparke admits that he describes a dragon according to the words of some "French captain," that he himself did not find either gold or silver in America. Arthur Barlowe—who arrived in America in 1584 on a boat equipped by Sir Walter Raleigh, and who considered the aborigines "void of all guile and treason"—tells that, nevertheless, the Englishmen preferred, as a safety measure, to sleep in their own boat rather than on the Indians' land.

The image of America as a primitive paradise changed fairly quickly from an incentive to a deterrent to settling and was replaced by the image of a land, perhaps less wondrous and alluring but more understandable, comparable with Europe. There seemed to be an attempt to convince the reluctant reader, who feared unknown lands, that the move to America would not mean a complete break from everything familiar.

Thus, Thomas Harriot (1560–1621), in *A Brief and True Report of the New-Found Land of Virginia* (1588), presses it upon his countrymen that America is not a waiting paradise where one can live without trouble or care, but an abundant land, which must be turned into paradise through persistent labor. He lists its natural riches, comparing them all, for the most part favorably, with England's. Because one of the deterrents to colonization was fear of the Indians, Harriot tries to present them as innocent and childlike, as peaceful farmers easily converted to Christianity. Somewhat naively Eurocentrist, the author assures us that the Indians gladly submitted to the English, recognizing the latter's superiority, and accepting true religion and civilization. In fact, the picture painted is of something close to utopia, in which everything is founded on a rational social structure and a life in harmony with nature.

Many accounts from the beginning of the 17th century are written in a similar vein. The authors unanimously assert that the American climate is far more beneficial to the Englishman's health than the English climate, the land far more fertile, the rivers deeper, the air fresher, the game fatter.

"Optimism, often irrational optimism, became a dominant quality of restless Americans early in their history."[1] As we see, the propagandistic intentions of early descriptions of America, the authors' optimistic biases, the lack of practical knowledge and experience, and a fairly low level of scientific understanding all led to frequent distortion of facts and to their adornment with fairy-tale and utopian elements. Writings of this sort bore the mark of unwitting or intentional fictionalization, which became a distinguishing feature of the genre.

After the creation of permanent settlements, more and more neutral, factual information began to appear in accounts, openly describing the real hardships of colonization. Many now wrote of severe winters, clashes with Indians, starvation, and discord among the settlers. During the first half of the 17th century, when the settling of America had only begun and life was still taking shape in the colonies (which remained closely tied to England and did not yet recognize their own independence), the main concerns were geography, climate, and daily life, rather than politics or culture; these defined the genre during this period. A defined compositional structure took shape, with logical transitions from one subject to the next. Josephine K. Piercy lists four obligatory components in the canon: a description, according to the requirements of medieval science, of the four elements: earth, air, water, and fire; an enumeration of natural resources; a sketch of the Indians; and propaganda in favor of the colonies.[2] Often, there was also an account of colonial life. Thus, records were a syncretic genre, a combination of scientific treatise, ethnographic essay, propagandistic advertisement, and historical chronicle. Their style was characterized, on the whole, by neutrality. With a few exceptions, nature was described without emotion; data on plants, animals, and useful minerals were catalogued; lists of colonists were included. Yet, at the same time, these records preserved a noticeable inclination to fictionalize. To a certain degree, accounts took on the role of belles lettres, a genre that developed slowly in the early English colonies.

These English subjects, resettled across the ocean, felt themselves part of the English nation and culture; they did not attempt to create their own literature, turning for the most part to those literary pursuits that reflected their practical activities. But America was not merely a fragment of England; it was a new environment in which a particular way of life and a particular social, political, and spiritual culture had begun to form. Documentary genres reflected not only the practical but the spiritual side of existence in the young nation. A large role in this was played by the fairly manifest nature of the views of the authors, who were participants in, and witnesses of, all that occurred. Unlike 20th-century man, the man of the 17th century was not as alienated from nature, society, and government; he was aware of the close ties to his surroundings. Authors treated and commented upon history in their own way—putting themselves at the center, drawing analogies between external events and their own inner world.

This trait became characteristic of written works in various branches of early American literature, which were subject to various cultural influences. In the 17th century there was a blending of the traditions of a dying medieval culture, the Renaissance, Reformation, and approaching Enlightenment. In both secular and religious thought, man was seen as part of a unified whole—a divine plan, the universe, a worldwide brotherhood. There was a tendency to place every real event in a certain general context, to generalize it through a rational, mystical, or artistic view of the world. It is impossible to agree with the opinion of many scholars—in particular, C. Holliday—that colonial literature before 1676 belongs wholly to English culture and that the formation of the American national consciousness occurred later.[3] An analysis of early American literature suggests that the national consciousness began to form at precisely this time—in the 17th century, at a juncture of cultural eras, all of which had a specific influence in the American context.

As Daniel Boorstin observes, "The most fertile novelty of the New World was not its climate, its plants, its animals, or its minerals, but its new concept of knowledge," which consisted in the prioritization of the practical.[4] The wave of Puritan emigration brought with it specific religious world-views. "The most evident, wide-ranging, and long-lasting influence of medieval thought on American development showed itself in the conception of teleological values of existence."[5] But the Puritans fleeing England saw religion as a course of action, as a deed, and pursued a practical goal: to build, in this new place, a "city on a hill." The traits of the Renaissance man grew more pronounced: his energy, individualism, love of freedom, willingness to serve the common good. The Puritans cultivated rationalism and attempted to realize the ideal of a rational, democratic society. These new Americans had a heightened sense of changing reality, of the possibilities for choice, for affecting history.

Thanks to their "openness" and dynamism, accounts, a syncretic genre, reflected all the diversity of early American culture and in many ways contributed to the formation of the national consciousness. Their inclination to portray various sides of life helped overcome the limitations of any one view of surrounding reality; this had its effect on both content and style. Brevity and simplicity were accompanied by Baroque mannerism, precise, factual descriptions by quotations from the Bible and the ancients, sober judgment by mystical commentary. The world of predestination, guided by Providence, blended with a world that was known and transformed by human reason. Real life experience, which the authors tried to explain within the framework of their ideology, was perpetually revising the speculative picture of life.

Depending on the author's conception of the predominance of God's will, the laws of nature, or human reason, the text might be organized around various ideas and subjected to various forms of ideological and aesthetic regulation. As a genre in early American literature, accounts took several forms; what's more, the variation was clearly along regional lines. The populations of the colonies founded in the first half of the 17th century were heterogeneous in education as well as in social and religious affiliation, but each was dominated by one wave or another. The prevailing secular or religious ideology placed its stamp on the cultural life of each colony and determined the direction of its literature.

Among the founders of Virginia were many searching for glory and adventure, undoubtedly people of the Renaissance. As Moses Coit Tyler writes, "As compared with the people of New England, they of Virginia were less austere, less enterprising, less industrious. They were more worldly, self-indulgent; they were impatient of asceticism, of cant, of long faces, of long prayers; they rejoiced in games, sports, dances, merry music, and in a free, jovial, roistering life."[6] The difficulties to be overcome in taming virgin lands and the dangerous expeditions into Indian territory provided endless possibilities for satisfying human inquisitiveness and displaying fearlessness, invention, and initiative.

One of the most colorful figures in early American history is the legendary John Smith (1580–1631), with whose name the birth of the national literature is usually linked. His *Generall Historie of Virginia* (1624), the most interesting of his works, tells of events in which the narrator himself was a participant; this circumstance determines both the structure and the tone of the story. One is struck by Smith's extraordinary egocentrism, his excessive self-glorification and boasting, which are usually explained in a

simple, superficial way: the Captain, leaving America due to an unfortunate event, wished to return to Jamestown, which had fallen into a state of
collapse, and carry out his intended reforms. Therefore, he had to convince people who could subsidize his travels and equip ships for him of his
irreplaceability as leader of the colony, and to prove the uselessness of its
current leaders. These motives, of course, led the author to exaggerate his
worth; but it is necessary to recall that his egoism had not only subjective
causes but deep cultural roots.

Smith was a child of the Renaissance, a whole man, who saw himself as
an active reformer of the world, claiming his right to free self-development.
His disputes with the other leaders of the colony, his unwillingness to
follow orders, and his constant efforts to act upon his own judgment are
evidence of individualism, but individualism of a particular type. The
Renaissance view did not estrange man from society; it recognized his
personal freedom to serve the common good, not to conflict with it.
Smith constantly stresses that all of his actions had a single goal—to help
the colony, settle relations with the Indians, attain unity of aspirations
and actions among the settlers. Strictly speaking, Smith's main complaint
about his companions is their shirking of collective work, their lack of
discipline, their fruitless hopes for easy prosperity, and their greed and
mercenariness—which lay at the base of the vulgar variety of bourgeois
individualism which, in its early stage, opposed egoism to the interests of
society. "There was no talke, no hope, no worke," laments Smith, "but
dig gold, wash gold, refine gold, loade gold. . . ."[7] Smith's open and
candid conflict with his countrymen is the first external evidence of the
contradiction between Renaissance and bourgeois individualism, which
would later move inside American culture and in many ways define both
the national character and the national myth—the "American dream."

The Renaissance attitude left its mark on the author's relationship
to the reality surrounding him. Smith's narrative is focused on events of
importance to the colony rather than his own spiritual world. Smith does
not analyze his own internal concerns or connect events with divine will;
instead, he tries to know and explain perceptible reality. For this reason,
we are shown not only his surroundings but the narrator himself, from an
external point of view.

Smith has an inherent respect for knowledge, experience, and practice;
yet, at the same time, he is an idealist and a dreamer. It is on the basis of
this respect that Everett Emerson calls him the new man—the American.

"He imagined a prosperous America, a place where a man could enjoy nature and its fruits. . . . Above all, Smith was an American."[8]

Smith's efforts to paint the blessings of the New World, to interest and gain the favor of his reader, lead to his failure to maintain a neutral, factual approach. In his account of the life of the colony, Smith tries to stick to strict chronology, to the accuracy of dates and geography. He provides the routes of expeditions into Indian territory and lists the settlers. Descriptions of nature and daily life, however, interest him much less than descriptions of heroic deeds. Smith was writing for future generations, which would have to admire the acts of their fathers, and for history, "a matter of the glories and great deeds of men—not their prosaic daily affairs."[9] The narrative singles out the most vivid and dramatic events—above all, those episodes involving travels to Indian land and captivity there, which contain both adventure and the hint of romantic intrigue. In a certain way, the critic Norman Grabo is correct, though stretching the point, when he refers to the book as a "chivalric romance."[10]

In a certain sense, Smith's books mythologized American history and later served the function of a missing national epic literature. Opinion varies about the artistic merits of Smith's legacy. Everett Emerson places it among the "great glories of literature."[11] Charles Angoff maintains the opposite view: "He wrote atrociously. He knew very little about spelling and almost nothing about English grammar."[12] Perhaps H. M. Jones is right: "vain, mercurial, self-seeking, yet devoted to a cause; dogged and irresponsible; half genius and half charlatan, the only secular Elizabethan in American literature is, by a wild paradox, incarnate proof of the dictum that the style is the man."[13] In Smith's style—colorful, confused, conversational, full of flamboyant rhetoric, with its repeating rhythmic structures—the author's character, pragmatic and idealistic, is revealed; but so is the nature of the genre and its historic mission. During the early period of American colonization, accounts helped introduce new, practical experience and knowledge of the world into the existing system of beliefs, presenting it in the language of European culture. From this come the constant attempts at "literariness," the fictionalization, the historical and mythological parallels, and the mixing of genre forms.

From this point of view, it is interesting to look at the works of William Strachey, an eminent man of letters and a historian, who for several years was secretary of the Jamestown colony. In his book, *The Historie of Travell into Virginia Britania* (1612), Strachey places America's native inhabitants

outside world civilization, justifying the seizure of the land and the enslavement of the Indians on the grounds of their paganism. At the same
time, writing of the Indian leaders, Strachey not only refers to them in
the English manner as kings and queens, but endows them with characters entirely typical of European or Eastern rulers. Description of the
Indians by analogy with whites, with the aid of European clichés and
fictional devices, had a double effect. On one hand, it increased the lack of
understanding and acceptance of the strange culture; on the other, it
associated that culture with the European world, bringing about a peculiar sort of assimilation.

The literature of the Puritan colonists, the "Pilgrim fathers" who
founded New Plymouth, had its own characteristics. Daniel Boorstin calls
Puritan New England a "noble experiment in applied theology."[14] The
realization of Protestant ideals, putting them to the practical test, was
reflected in the secular genre of records and chronicles which, unlike
religious works, dealt with the relationship of the "pilgrims" not only to
God, but to the surrounding earthly world as well. They did not see
turning to "useful," moralizing, factual literature as secularization, since
scientific and historical knowledge aided the comprehension of divine
Providence. The Puritans became the creators of a specific type of account, imbued with the religious consciousness of the Reformist era,
oddly combining medieval mysticism with the New Rationalism.

The Puritans' main historic document was William Bradford's book,
History of Plymouth Plantation, written over the course of twelve years,
beginning in 1630. Bradford mythologizes early American history but on
an entirely different basis than did the "Virginia Cavaliers." His historical
consciousness is inseparable from his religious consciousness, according
to which the fate of the Puritan community and every one of its members
is predetermined by providence and inscribed in "Heaven's Book." The
chronicler's task is to establish facts and events as the revelation of divine
providence, revealing their meaning through a correctly ordered chain of
cause and effect and reporting simply, as is appropriate to the clarity and
logic of higher truth. Since, according to the Bible, history purposefully
unfolds from its beginning point to its inevitable end, Bradford's narrative
also begins with an account of the persecution of the Protestants in the
16th century and advances from year to year, from event to event.

Human history is the realization not only of will but of the struggle of
unearthly forces, the eternal war between God and Satan, who have

chosen it as their battleground. Earthly and eternal worlds enter into one another. Satan is a participant in political intrigues, as real as pagan emperors or Catholic priests. He causes the Protestants bloody torture and cruel trials, imprisonment, exile, and other forms of persecution. The universal fight between good and evil is reflected in the polarization of historical facts in Bradford's accounts, destroying their declared objectivity, making for biased judgments. The religious rift in England led to a dichotomy: God/Satan; Christianity/Paganism; Protestants/Papists. Accordingly, at one pole were the pious, the devout, the true servants of God; and at the other, the unrighteous, given to ignorance, blasphemy, and unbelief, sin and profanity, intrigue and subterfuge. Every event is weighed by an all-encompassing law of morality. The government of earthly life from above has deep ethical meaning, connecting religion and history.

The Puritans' transformation of their own history into a metaphor for biblical history created a certain double, contradictory conception of the historic process, which saw history both as linear and as cyclical, repeating a phase through which humanity had already passed. Analyzing the Puritans' peculiar sense of history, Larzer Ziff wrote that, for them, analogy takes precedence over chronology; the sense of tribal loyalty belonging over the details of historical change.[15] In Ziff's view, the Puritans felt that they belonged to God, not to the world, and therefore excluded themselves from European history.[16] This trait of Puritan consciousness was noted by another of its students, Jesper Rosenmeier, who characterized Bradford thus:

> History, he thought, was not something that just happened *to* him and his fellow Separatists; it lived *in* and *through* them.[17] The Pilgrim fathers considered themselves the chosen people, "sons of Israel" expelled from Egypt (England), crossing the desert to Canaan to build their "city on a hill." Other peoples, the colonists explained, had their land by providence; *they* had it by promise. Others must seek their national origins in secular records and chronicles. The story of America was enclosed in the scriptures, its past postdated and its future antedated in prophesy.[18]

For the colonists at New Plymouth, the settling of America was not only a practical but, above all, a spiritual act; their road to the "Promised Land" was the road of every member's soul to salvation. The histories of the whole world, the chosen people and each individual, were inseparable in the Puritan mind, which in many ways determined the nature of the

American social mythology and national character. The teaching of the Separatists helped form the idea of America as a chosen land as well as America's particular form of individualism, which did not separate personal fate from the nation's historic mission.

In this regard, the very form of the narrative is telling: Bradford writes at times in the first person, at other times from the point of view of the whole community, including himself in the collective "we" or "they." The author is both a participant in events and their chronicler, taking on the roles of both commentator and moralist. Like John Smith, he is characterized by a certain "social individualism"; but his individualism is based not on the secular, Renaissance idea of man, but on the religious.

Bradford does not focus on glorifying his own actions, but on the general affairs of the colonists. Private fate, suffering, feelings, and cares appear in his book as full-bodied facts of history. Furthermore, "material" incidents become part of the general divine plan only when, after human interpretation, they gain a spiritual, metaphorical meaning. Such a crossing from "low" to "high," almost a required component of every section of the text, is always accompanied by a marked change in narrative style. Descriptions of secular conflicts, such as the soldiers' attack on the Puritans as they departed for America, are mostly laconic, short on artistic method, and conversational in tone:

> But after the first boat full was gott abord, and she was ready to goe for more, the master espied a greate company, both horse and foote, with bills, and gunes, and other weapons; for the countrie was raised to take them. The Dutch-man seeing that, swore his countries oath, 'sacramente,' and having the wind faire, waiged his Ancor, hoysed sayles, and away.[19]

People are concerned with their pressing problems—families left behind, the lack of provisions and money. But God sends them a new trial—a storm—and unexpected rescue, to remind them of His strength, of the great mission entrusted to them. "Upon which the ship did not only recover, but shortly after the violence of the storme begane to abate, and the Lord filed their afflicted minds with shuch comforts as every one cannot understand, and in the end brought them to their desired Haven, wher the people came flocking admiring their deliverance. . . ."[20] The rhythm of the sentences becomes more solemn, and a "higher" vocabulary appears—"afflicted minds," "deliverance"—along with images containing a double, metaphoric sense—"desired Haven."

Bradford's book is saturated with biblical symbolism and metaphor, into which are translated images from the real world—above all, the ocean and untamed lands. The Puritans "passed the vast ocean, and a sea of troubles before in their preparation."[21] The actual crossing of the watery expanse is compared to the overcoming of heaven-sent ordeals. America is a severe continent which must be settled, and a biblical desert, on which the road must be laid to Canaan. " . . . what could they see but a hidious and desolate wildernes, full of wild beasts and willd men? . . . For summer being done, all things stand upon them with a wetherbeaten face; and the whole countrie, full of woods and thickets, represented a wild and savage hew."[22] Further: "May not and ought not the children of these fathers rightly say: *Our fathers were Englishmen which came over this great ocean, and were ready to perish in this wilderness . . .*"[23]

However, the implacable logic of earthly events, demanding a practical and rational approach, destroyed the speculative model of reality and weakened the connections between the earthly and heavenly worlds. The line between these worlds often shows up very clearly. *History of Plymouth Plantation* contains an episode in which their juxtaposition even becomes comical. Arguing the unlawfulness of their Massachusetts neighbors' infringement on Plymouth territory, the colonists wrote to them:

> But wheras you say God in his providence cast you, etc., we tould you before, and (upon this occasion) must now tell you still, that our mind is other wise, and that you cast rather a partiall, if not a covetous eye, upon that which is your neighbours, and not yours; and in so doing, your way could not be faire unto it. Looke that you abuse not Gods providence in such allegations.[26]

The switch from mysticism to rationalism is especially frequent in the interpretation of natural phenomena. The raging elements might be seen as God's wrath, as a moral lesson, but the author still remembers to report the strength and height of the waves, the direction of the wind, the duration of the lunar eclipse. An earthquake is explained as God's displeasure at disorder in the Separatist community: "So powerfull is the mighty hand of the Lord, as to make both the earth and sea to shake. . . ."[27] Further on, it is noted that the earthquake was followed by several cold summers: "but whether this was any cause, I leave it to naturallists to judge."[28]

In Bradford's book, not only a high drama—historical and spiritual—is played out, but a low one—political and social—as well. In an effort to preserve the inner integrity of the narrative, Bradford frequently uses worldly events as illustrations of useful moral lessons. Several instructive stories are clearly parables, describing punished evildoers and repentent sinners.

The book includes biographies (written in the style of "lives"), such as the author's recollections of the elder William Brewster, who died in 1643. The hero has all the virtues of a righteous man—he is highly educated, possessed of reason, pious, hard-working, humble, and sympathetic to the poor; his life contains all the necessary landmarks: divine illumination, persecution for his faith, and reward in the form of long life and a peaceful death.

All the same, man's path to God is not easy: In the spiritual and worldly dramas, action is guided by various forces—the hand of the almighty and sinful human nature. Bradford's tale is a chronicle not only of selfless toil and the fulfillment of God's will, but of deceit, betrayal, intrigue, greed, cunning, cruelty, endless quarrels and disputes among members of the community, with the London Company, neighboring colonies, and Indians. "I say it may justly be marveled at, and cause us to fear and tremble at the consideration of our corrupte natures, which are so hardly bridled, subdued, and mortified; nay, cannot by any other means but the powerfull worke and grace of Gods spirite," laments the author.[29]

Bradford's belief in man's basic depravity is revealed particularly clearly in his descriptions of the Indians, who, in his opinion, are naturally power-hungry, crafty, and cruel. Although the Christian ideals of charity and justice toward savages are present, no less so are the gloomy biblical themes of the punishment of pagans by "fire and sword."

> It was a fearfull sight to see them thus frying in the fyer, and the streams of blood quenching the same, and horrible was the stinck and sente therof; but the victory seemed a sweete sacrifice, and they gave the prays therof to God, who had wrought so wonderfuly for them, thus to enclose their enimise in their hands, and give them so speedy a victory over so proud and insulting an enimie.[30]

The Puritans' projection of Old Testament mythology onto American history is evidenced in their perception of the aborigines' strange world as an "unclean" land, the kingdom of Satan, sin, and chaos, in which the true faith must be spread and order established. The colonists saw the fact

that the ancient sons of Israel destroyed the unbelieving tribes and received their land from God in reward as a heavenly sign, a blessing on
their own actions toward the Indians. John Underhill, a participant in the
war against the Pequot tribe, justified the destruction of the Indians in his
memoirs, *Newes from America* (1638): "Sometimes the scripture declareth
women and children must perish with their parents. Sometimes the case
alters; but we will not dispute it now. We had sufficient light from the
word of God for our proceedings."[31] His companion, John Mason, who
published *A Brief History of the Pequot War*, explained the whites' victory
so: "Thus the Lord was pleased to smite our Enemies in the hinder Parts
and to give us their Land for an Inheritance."[32]

In using the Indians' sinfulness to justify forcing them from their ancient lands, and the settlers' sinfulness to explain the colony's many misfortunes, Bradford reasons according to the religious conception of man
as a "vessel of sin" in need of divine admonition, encouragement, and
punishment. In some of his reasoning and judgment, however, he displays
traits of a philosopher and politician, admitting the existence of objective
social laws independent of human will or nature. The history of the
Puritan commune, modeled after the early Christian communes, is evaluated from the point of view of practical reality. Attempting to work their
fields communally and distribute the harvest equally, the colonists found
themselves impoverished and nearly starved. The situation changed radically when the land was distributed to families, each receiving the maize it
grew itself. Families, including women and children, "whom to have
compelled would have bene thought great tiranie and oppression,"
worked from morning till night.[33] "The experience," Bradford instructs
us,

> that was had in this commone course and condition, tried sundrie years,
> and that amongst godly and sober men, may well evince the vanitie of
> that conceite of Platos and other ancients, applauded by some of later
> times;—that the taking away of propertie, and bringing in communitie
> into a comone wealth, would make them happy and florishing; as if
> they were wiser than God.[34]

He continues: "Let none object this is men's corruption, and nothing to
the course it selfe. I answer, seeing all men have this corruption in them,
God on his wisdome saw another course fiter for them."[35]

Perhaps the American approach to the conflict between reality and ideal was already beginning to form itself in logical reasoning such as this. In the extreme conditions of the struggle to survive, any ideals that constrained reality were forced to give way; ideology was formed in accordance with experience. At the same time, the national consciousness was inherently inclined to create stubborn myths. In many ways, this contradiction defines the structure of Bradford's narrative, in which the worldly and the spiritual, fact and ideal, alternate, infiltrate each other, and collide.

Bradford strives for accuracy and objectivity; but, at the same time, his task is that of a propagandist. What's more, he sees his work as instruction for future generations who will need to know "with what difficulties their fathers wrastled in going throug these things in their first beginnings, and how God brought them along notwithstanding all their weaknesses and infirmities."[36] For this reason, strict reporting is combined with a fairly free treatment of facts, which are frequently chosen for their moral message and which serve to illustrate the book's overall ideology. Bradford does not simply list major and minor events in the life of the colony, he uses them to construct an orderly system proving the wisdom of divine providence. To do this, he abandons chronology, putting together in the text facts similar in their significance but relating to different periods; he turns back in time and jumps ahead. He puts the history of the colony into a wide historical and cultural context, filling the narrative with references to the Bible and ancient writers; he skillfully uses the devices of scientific logic and, at the same time, is able to turn separate episodes into short, moralistic novellas. To maintain the necessary pace and interest, insignificant occurrences are left out and sections of cited documents are omitted. In a word, Bradford's work gives witness to the fact that the Puritan belief system aided in the fictionalization of this documentary genre no less than did the Renaissance attitude.

Both Puritan and Renaissance world-views were characterized by the attempt to dramatize history and by their attention to the individual. Both traits show up in the writings of the Virginians and New Englanders. But on the whole, these ideologies did not mix well; where they came into direct contact, sparks often flew. One of the most fascinating pages in early American history is the conflict between the residents of Plymouth and Merry Mount, described in Bradford's book and by Thomas Morton (1575–1646?) in *New English Canaan: or, New Canaan* (1637), and later used by Washington Irving and Nathaniel Hawthorne. The behavior of Morton, who arrived in America in 1622, aroused great indignation among the residents of New Plymouth. Endless orgies, the sale of alcohol and arms to the Indians, and the pagan maypole festival, which finally exhausted the patience of the godly Puritans, led to Morton's arrest and exile from the colony. "Unlike the Puritans," writes M. M. Koreneva, "he lived in an atmosphere of Renaissance culture, of which he carried a fragment to far, wild America."[37] This atmosphere penetrates all three sections of his book, which, as far as genre is concerned, more closely resembles poetic, pastoral, biblical legend and satirical comedy than it does documentary reporting.

D. Connors, who has studied Morton's legacy, gives a true description of the book's first two parts: "He puts aside his factual account of the region's commodities and transfigures by the use of appropriate imagery and mythological allusions, the wilderness country of New England into the golden world of the poet."[38] As Morton portrays it, using ancient and biblical imagery, America is a land of "milk and honey," Canaan, Eden, Arcadia, with an extraordinary abundance of flowers, game, and birds. The author overwhelms the reader with pictures of millions of turtle-doves, pecking at the fruit of lush branches, of crystal streams flowing in green valleys, lulling travellers with their tender babble, "jetting most jocundly where they doe meete and hand in hand runne down to Neptunes Court, to pay the yearly tribute which they owe to him as soveraigne Lord of all springs."[39] He constructs long, complicated sentences, filled with colorful epithets, metaphors, and comparisons, as if trying to convey the richness of the land through richness of expression. His description of the native residents of New England is as idyllic as his description of its nature and is clearly imbued with ideas of the harmfulness of civilization and the blessings of the "natural life."

The third section is written in an entirely different key. Connors calls it a typical Renaissance comedy, containing all the required elements: dramatic conflict, humorous stories, deliberate distortion of facts, caricatures, characters with amusing nicknames, and inserted verses. It is a caustic satire on the Puritans, who are compared to the "natural people" (Indians). If the red folks are good and just, the English are greedy Separatists, inhumane, and tending toward pontification and hypocrisy.

Here the genre of records stretches to include satire, a combination that showed itself in the 18th century to be quite effective. In this way, Morton's book, absorbing the artistic traditions of the Renaissance, to some degree anticipates the genre's further development. Attempting, accord-

ing to the rules of satire, to discover, expose, and ridicule his adversaries'
most vulnerable traits, Morton charges the Puritans with ignorance. He
mocks them for seeing the maypole as a pagan idol, revelry as the Devil's
machinations, and ancient, mythical images in songs praising life and
spring as blasphemy.

Morton's criticisms are undoubtedly exaggerated. Many of the Puritans
were extremely well educated and had a deep knowledge of philosophy
and literature and respect for the natural sciences. The reason for their
refusal to accept the Renaissance world lay not in ignorance but in their
own view of man and of the relation between the physical and the spiritual, between human reason and human sensibility, which, they felt, were
in deep discord. Since the body was thought to be the "vessel of sin" and
the passions to be distractions from the concerns of the soul, the faithful
had to lead a life free from earthly temptations and joys and to maintain
strict rules of behavior.

This ideology had its theoretical base in the speech delivered in court
by John Winthrop (1588–1649), accused of exceeding his vested authority
as lieutenant governor of Massachusetts. Winthrop distinguishes two
forms of freedom: natural and civil. Natural freedom, which belongs to
animals as well as people, allows man to act in accordance with his desires
and to determine for himself the line between good and evil—thus, in
Winthrop's opinion, increasing the amount of evil in the world. Civil
freedom includes moral freedom, founded on a covenant with God, and
political freedom, founded on agreement among people, and leads to the
increase of good. The essence of this independence lies in voluntary sub-
mission to power, something no more onerous than the church's submis-
sion to the dominion of Christ.

John Winthrop was the ideologist of the Puritan Congregationalists,
who arrived in New England in 1630 on the *Arabella* and set about building "New Jerusalem," a theocratic state founded on religious and moral
rigorism. The leader of the colony was also its first chronicler, describing,
in his *History of New England*, events from 1630 to 1649.

Winthrop's accounts are, it would seem, an exemplary model of the
genre. Dry, informative, written in short, simple sentences, all possible
events are listed, by year and day—the arrival of the ships, the attack on
the livestock by wolves, fires; data on the numbers of deaths of people and
animals; the weather. Striving for complete objectivity and personal distance, the author is nonetheless interested in the material world only as

the revelation of divine providence, which no man may fully comprehend. As all events—large and small, significant or insignificant from man's point of view—are directed by God, the chronicler does not consider it his right to select, evaluate, or express his own emotions, as that would be an attempt to pass judgment on providence. Even situations in which impassivity seems unthinkable are described with complete abstraction:

> Friday, 2. The *Talbot* arrived there. The [ship] has lost fourteen passengers. My son, Henry Winthrop, was drowned at Salem.[40]

And not a word more, no hint of a father's grief, complete humility before the higher will. The report is not accompanied by angry tirades, as is the news of Morton's arrest in Bradford's book. The author limits himself to stating the fact and a simple explanation of its reason. In such fragments we feel especially keenly the separation of reason and emotion in the Puritan consciousness, the attempt to subject everything to rational analysis, to suppress the genuine impulses of the soul and, as Kenneth Murdock has noted, to replace them with reactions more appropriate from the religious point of view.[41]

Winthrop allows himself to comment on events, not emotionally but logically, guessing at the symbolic, metaphoric meaning of facts, determining causal links between sin and retribution, misfortune and its foreshadowing. He connects a child's death by drowning to the fact that his father broke the law prohibiting the faithful from working on Sunday. The loss of belongings in a fire is a trial, preparing its owner for heavier misfortune. "But it pleased God that the loss of this linen did her much good, both in taking off her heart from worldly comforts, and in preparing her for a far greater affliction by the untimely death of her husband, who was slain not long after at Isle of Providence."[42]

Facts lose their neutrality, their single meaning, and become confirmation of sin's inevitable punishment and virtue's reward. They may be altogether devoid of earthly meaning and serve as a sort of metaphor, as, for instance, the story of the struggle between the snake and the mouse, which is interpreted as follows: "The snake was the Devil, the mouse was a poor contemptible people, which God had brought hither, which should overcome Satan here, and dispossess him of his Kingdom."[43] And all the same, although, as Koreneva says, "adherence to Puritan Orthodoxy illuminates Winthrop's work in the sinister light of the most dismal form of Calvinism," occasionally they contain a spark of humor.[44] The story of the

two settlers, one of whom intentionally distracted the other with conversation so that his cattle would stray in the field, is quite comical. The
mouse that ate a collection of Anglican prayers in the library, leaving
untouched all the other, more pious books, is described not without
irony. Despite the underlying religious motivation and the didactic tendencies of such stories, there is no doubt that they have a genetic link to
oral folklore.

Even those Puritan accounts that are farthest from any artistic interpretation of reality, and which bear the stamp of fanaticism, contain the
shoots of American national culture. It is worth looking into the depths
of the Puritan consciousness for the sources of such American character
traits as the tendency to self-analysis and self-evaluation, the sense of
personal guilt and responsibility for evil, and the striving to act according
to a higher moral law. In the literature, these traits are reflected as a
peculiar form of psychologism, in the specifics of plot construction, in the
use of a system of symbols, and in the widespread motif of the "search for
the Father."

The main theme of the *Autobiography* (1640) of Thomas Shepard
(1605–1649), written in the form of an instructional address to his son, is
God's fatherly protection, leading man through life and demanding his
respect and obedience. Shepard is full of admiration for the wisdom of
the Almighty, who saves him from persecution, inspires him with the idea
to emigrate, provides him with travel companions, and allows him to
cross the ocean safely. And, when terrible misfortunes befall him—illness,
the deaths of his wife and child, natural disasters—he does not grumble,
but seeks the reason for his punishment in his own weaknesses, sins, and
insufficient religious fervor: "But here the Lord saw that these waters
were not sufficient to wash away my filth & sinfulness & therefore he cast
me into the fire as soone as ever I was upon the sea in the boat. . . ."[45]

Winthrop, who focused on guessing at the higher meaning of external
events, employed what can be seen as the "simple style," which the Puritans thought most appropriate for relating God's—always clear and
accessible—word and design. Shepard portrays the difficult work of the
human mind and soul as they try to grasp the connection between the
individual's inner world, fate, and providence. His thoughts flow from
one complicated sentence to the next, becoming immersed in an endless
flow of speech, tending toward an epic style and grand tone. The style
seems to reflect the inadequacy and confusion of reason in front of heav-

enly powers, as well as the heart's rapture in recognizing its participation in the realization of divine will.

The tendencies of the Puritan chroniclers toward abstract philosophical and religious reflection and universal generalization transformed their works into an odd mixture of historical chronicle and teleological treatise, filling the works with biblical metaphor and complicated rhetoric. These peculiarities of Puritan literature, however, cannot be seen only as evidence of its limitation to Scholasticism and isolation from practical reality. These are undoubtedly zealous attempts to control the barbaric world unfolding before the Europeans' eyes, to master it by means of the system of understanding created by them. From this comes the dramatic tension in both sense and style, which not only does not abate as civilization spreads across the American continent, but, on the contrary, intensifies at the end of the 17th century, perhaps because of the growing contradiction between the Puritan ideals and reality.

Magnalia Christi Americana is a work published in 1702 by the New England religious conservative, Cotton Mather (1663–1728). Mather numbers the discovery of America among the three most important events of the turn of the 15th and 16th centuries, along with "the Resurrection of Literature" and the "Reformation of Religion." All historical facts have religious meaning for him and are part of the vast, epic struggle between God and the Devil, in the center of which was the American continent, with its native and English inhabitants. It was Satan, the author believes, who first populated America with the pagan Indians, thinking to separate a part of humanity "and their Posterity out of the sound of the silver trumpets of the Gospel, then to be heard through the Roman Empire."[46] Indian tribes, according to Mather, are the antipodes of the European peoples, both in the geographical and in the spiritual sense, as residents of the earth's other hemisphere and as the creation of the dark force. But when the appointed hour arrived, God revealed America to Christians and ordered his chosen Englishmen to settle the New World a second time, and spread the true faith there.

In practice, however, colonization proved far more difficult than was promised by the plan of the "Pilgrim fathers" for building a "city on a hill" and converting the pagans. A chasm remained between the anti-worlds of European civilization and the New World—which was difficult to cross with one's thinking locked in religious mythology. Not understanding or accepting their unholy surroundings, the Puritans were forced to live on the border between two hostile cultures; this created serious ethical and moral problems.

The attitude of the colonists toward the native Americans is most fully recorded in literary works that describe whites' experiences living among the Indians. The most popular example of this genre, which was extremely widespread at the end of the 17th and the beginning of the 18th century, was Mary Rowlandson's *The Narrative of the Captivity and Restoration of Mrs. Mary Rowlandson* (1682). The deeply religious Mrs. Rowlandson, a pastor's wife, describes an Indian attack on Lancaster, the deaths of women and children, and the hardships of the journey to Indian territory and of her stay there—all from the somewhat detached position of an observer watching a drama played out before her eyes and trying to guess at its moral lesson. What is striking is the author's ability to notice the details of her surroundings and relate them in simple, vivid language, while at the same time translating all events into a prepared system of biblical metaphor. For Rowlandson, the very fact of captivity, with all its cruel realities, becomes a symbolic crossing into a certain Otherworld, to which a Christian could be sent only to try her spirit. The Indian country is Hell, populated by "packs of devils" and endowed with all the attributes of the netherworld—bonfires and unrestrained orgies accompanied by wild dances and horrible wailing.

The drama in Rowlandson's story lies in the fact that she must live among these "devils" and adapt herself to "Hell," which she involuntarily begins to perceive as human existence. Rowlandson is forced to come into contact with her Indian neighbors, to earn her bread by sewing, to receive food and shelter from her enemies. Like a true Puritan, however, she continues to keep herself removed from the unholy world, striving to resist temptations and earn eternal bliss.

This historical episode from the life of a New England colony is transformed into a history of the human heart subjected to trying ordeals and receiving a moral lesson. Misfortune is seen as fitting, for how can the faithful save her soul without having tested her strength of spirit and devotion to God in an extreme situation? "For whom the Lord loveth He chasteneth, and scourgeth every son whom he receiveth," the author quotes from the Bible.[47] Having lost in one fell swoop her freedom, family, and belongings, Rowlandson learns to know the "extreme vanity of this world"; she survives the trauma and becomes a different person.[48] The road she travels from civilization to "the desert" and back is her soul's road from the chaos of ignorance and pride to the harmony of knowledge and humility. That is the path of all Puritans leaving their homeland, settling on the wild shores of the Atlantic, and creating in the "world of darkness" a "kingdom of light."

Richard Slotkin, who has deeply analyzed the book, writes that Rowlandson uses the biblical legend as an archetype of personal and collective history and that she employs universal mythology to describe the concrete American situation.[49] In severe natural circumstances, surrounded by hostile tribes, the colonists were constantly threatened with ruin and destruction, leading them to ponder the relation between free human will and divine providence.

The captivity narrative, with its adventure component and psychologism, was probably, in the artistic sense, the most forward-looking form of the documentary genre. We may agree with the critic R. B. Nye, who calls it the forerunner of the American novel: "These tales of captivity, witchcraft, and danger furnished in America a base for the Gothic novel, the romance of sensibility, the frontier Indian novel, and the folk tale, and marked as well the beginnings of a native literary tradition. . . ."[50]

The predominance of certain biases over others in Europeans' attitudes toward native culture was largely the result of the needs of their own civilization. Europe and the Indian worlds could be compared as strongholds of Christian faith and a barbaric chaos created by the Devil, or, on the contrary, as the Old World, corrupted by the vices of history, and the primitive paradise, dwelling of the "natural man." Leopold Sea writes in his "Philosophy of American History" that the Europeans, having crossed the ocean, wanted not only to project their culture onto the pagan peoples, whom they saw as "first people," outside history, but also to break free of their own history, not to copy the old society, but to create a new one. In any case, the colonists were pragmatists, focused on utilitarian needs; for them, the Indians were, above all, part of their natural surroundings and objects for exploitation. "This society did not include, but excluded. It was a society of individuals among individuals, each pursuing his own interests. There was no place in it for the Indians with their backwardness and natural refusal to accept alien and incomprehensible customs and laws."[51]

In the colonization process that had begun a century earlier in Latin America, the interaction between European and native cultures took a different path—a complicated path of meeting and parting and, in the final account, assimilation and synthesis. This was made possible, in the opinion of scholars, by the influence of Baroque culture, which tended to combine various sources and which freed human consciousness from medieval narrowness:

> Creatively using such a basic trait of the Baroque aesthetic as the ability to combine and synthesize various influences into an organic whole and a single dynamic, Creole culture and literature found in the Baroque an extremely important means for self-expression and for the development of new traditions, which appeared as Hispano–European and Indian sources united.[52]

Although traces of the Baroque traditions can be detected in the works of North American authors as well—especially in the abundance and variety of tropes, the striving for metaphorical reflection, and the theatricalization of real historic events—on the whole, the Baroque was not inherent to them as an ideological or aesthetic system. The literature of the English colonies absorbed elements, mostly from Renaissance and Protestant culture, relating not to regions of the world but to appropriate stages of European history. It also displayed the tendency, typical of its time, for synthesis, only not, so to speak, "geographical," but "historical" synthesis. In fact, despite the inevitable influence of the Indian world, the literature did not assimilate that world, remaining a branch of European literature transplanted to new soil.

The first signs of the distinctive character of this grafted literature appeared in chronicles and accounts, the most important and widespread genres in the New World. Incorporating elements of empirical description and historical annals, scientific treatise and philosophical essay, biography and autobiography, political lampoon and heroic epic, they were the ideal form for expression and consideration of the colonies' practical and spiritual experience. They reflected the formation of the national consciousness, character, and culture. Many themes, subjects, images, and myths that would later become traditional to American literature can be traced to them.

MAYA KORENEVA

The Romantic Poetics

of Hawthorne

"It is odd enough," wrote Hawthorne in this famous letter to J. T. Field,

> that my own individual taste is for quite another class of novels than
> those which I myself am able to write. If I were to meet with such books
> as mine by another writer, I don't believe I should be able to get
> through them. Have you ever read the novels of Anthony Trollope?
> They precisely suit my taste; solid and substantial, written on the
> strength of beef and through the inspiration of ale, and just as real as if
> some giant had hewn a great lump of the earth, and put it under a glass
> case, with all its inhabitants going about their daily business, and not
> suspecting that they were made a show of.[1]

Contemporary scholars prefer to see this slightly ironic statement as
referring not to Trollope himself, but to the popular book industry of the
time. Perhaps this is true; in either case, Hawthorne's description does not
lose its power. He contrasts his own artistic principles to the realistic
novel, be it in the primitive version of popular fiction or in its more
refined form represented by the works of Trollope. This argument is
strengthened by his double use of the word *novel*, while he always referred
to his own major works as *romances*.

Hawthorne was a contemporary not only of Trollope, but of Dickens, Thackeray, Balzac, and Stendhal. The events that unfolded before the eyes of these writers, for all their national specificities, were similar in many ways, developing as they did from social processes common to all the countries of Europe as well as to the United States. Hawthorne did not share the aesthetic aims of those European novelists, preferring romanticism because it seemed to represent a higher form of expression of the truths of existence. Realism, in his opinion, could offer a lot in the way of reconstructing the external, objective side of reality; but that was the limit of its possibilities.

Hawthorne sets forth his views on art and the task of the novelist in the prefaces to *The House of the Seven Gables*, *The Blithedale Romance*, and *The Marble Faun*, in which he not only draws a sharp line between the Romantic novel and the realistic, but emphasizes the superiority of the first. When a writer calls his work a "romance," he writes in the preface to *House of the Seven Gables*,

> it need hardly be observed that he wishes to claim a certain latitude, both as to its fashion and material, which he would not have felt himself entitled to assume had he professed to be writing a Novel. The latter form of composition is presumed to aim at a very minute fidelity, not merely to the possible, but to the probable and ordinary course of man's experience. The former—while, as a work of art, it must rigidly subject itself to laws, and while it sins unpardonably so far as it may swerve aside from the truth of the human heart—has fairly a right to present that truth under circumstances, to a great extent, of the writer's own choosing or creation.[2]

Developing this thought in the preface to *The Blithedale Romance*, Hawthorne rejects comparison with daily reality as a valid criterion for evaluating Romantic works, basing his choice of subject on the need for distance between the surrounding world and the world of creative fantasy. "At a distance everything becomes poetry: distant mountains, distant people, distant circumstances. Everything becomes romantic,"[3] wrote Novalis, defining one of the basic positions of Romanticism.

Hawthorne also postulates a "suitable remoteness" as the condition for the very existence of literature.[4] In the sketch "The Custom House," which prefaces *The Scarlet Letter*, the "strangeness and remoteness" of things from their usual appearances in a room filled with moonlight allow reality and fantasy to "meet, and each imbue itself with the nature of the other."[5]

For Hawthorne, the main means of separating the world of artistic work from surrounding life was not geographical distance but time. Preferring historical narrative, he joined an already established tradition which, for obvious reasons, attracted Romanticists.

One of Hawthorne's main themes was the history of New England, which served, in a certain sense, as a point of departure for all his literary activity. Since his first compositions, Hawthorne immerses himself in an atmosphere of history, resurrecting times long past. What is more, his imagination is nourished less by images created by fantasy than by real episodes from the history of New England. Facts recorded in various chronicles and other historical sources serve as the basis for many of the stories making up his first collection, *Twice-Told Tales* (1837, 1842). "The Gray Champion," "Endicott and the Red Cross," "The May-Pole of Merry Mount," "The Gentle Boy," "Legends of the Province House," and others are based on documented evidence. However, Hawthorne's task did not end with the reconstruction of facts, and their use in no way leads to his full dependence on them.

Hawthorne refused to write the apologia of the Puritan past demanded by official historiography. The world of the first settlements in New England appears in his works not only, and not so much, in an aura of solemn grandeur and heroic deeds worthy of the admiration of future generations. "Glory bought with blood" does not inspire him to paint an idealized version of history on his canvasses. It's true that among the stories one does find an element of legend ("Gray Champion" and "Endicott," for example). But even in such cases, Hawthorne's attitude to the events he depicts is never one-sided. The heroism of his forebears does not obscure from his view their cruelty, savage fanaticism, extreme intolerance, and despotism.

The beginning of "Endicott" (1838) is characteristic in this regard. The story concerns a heroic page in American history, when the young community defended its dignity: John Endicott, the leader of the Salem band and subsequent governor of the Massachusetts Colony, tears the English banner from its pole, challenging the power of the hated king and of Archbishop Laud, who enjoyed Endicott's special protection. It would seem that everything should lead the writer to relate this important event in purely heroic-patriotic tones, but he chooses otherwise.

Without diminishing the heroism of the act itself, which has a central place in the story, Hawthorne removes the gloss that obscures the true face of the past. He widens the picture by means of the background, which is not stipulated by the development of the plot but which is necessary for a full reconstruction of the past in its incompatible combinations of good and evil, existing side by side in one society and in the same people. This allows us to see the event not in isolation but in the context of the reality of its time. As a result, the heroic episode is shown to be not raised above but, on the contrary, immersed in reality in which, side by side with firmness of character and unbending will and fortitude, are revealed qualities far from praiseworthy. The writer achieves not only a three-dimensional effect, a depth of image; more important, he complicates the relationship to the past, which becomes ambivalent and enlivened by a unity of heroism and virtue, on the one hand, and evil and shame, on the other.

> At one corner of the meeting-house was the pillory, and at the other the stocks; and, by a singular good fortune for our sketch, the head of an Episcopalian and suspected Catholic was grotesquely encased in the former machine; while a fellow-criminal, who had boisterously quaffed a health to the King, was confined by the legs in the latter. . . . But among the crowd were several, whose punishment would be life-long; some, whose ears had been cropped, like those of puppy-dogs; others, whose cheeks had been branded with the initials of their misdemeanors; one, with his nostrils slit and seared; and another, with a halter about his neck, which he was forbidden ever to take off, or to conceal beneath his garments.[6]

This impartial-sounding description seems only to relate objectively what falls within the observer's field of vision, as if the speaker were used to all manifestations of human cruelty and nothing can any longer surprise or upset him. But this sense of an imperturbably smooth description is deceptive. The author suddenly destroys its calm, somewhat unhurried flow with his own commentary—coming from another historical time, from a different morality, intentionally or unintentionally pronouncing judgment on what has occurred: "Methinks he must have been grievously tempted to affix the other end of the rope to some convenient beam or bough."[7]

Thus the author does not leave the reader in the dark as to his own view of the picture he has drawn. Even more important to this is the contrast he painstakingly creates between heroic deeds worthy of the admiration and grateful memory of later generations, and cruel earthly reality, which, a century and a half later, inspires rage, horror, and shame. Although it is preferable to see the past in a golden haze of glory, Hawthorne feels himself heir to both of its traditions; he knows that as a writer he must not, dare not, consign either one to oblivion.

The severity Hawthorne grasps and conveys so superbly, which is the trait noted and vividly drawn by everyone who has ever written about New England, is presented in his works not only as the result of severe conditions, of the confrontations with untamed nature and the many deprivations that became the lot of the first settlers. Hawthorne stands wholly on the side of the victims persecuted by the Puritans: the child of Quakers whom they poison with their hatred, remaining convinced that they are living in full accord with the word of God; the young people, making merry at the May-pole, celebrating spring and the joy of life that was killed in the end by adherents to Puritan morality.

These stories lack altogether any heroic-patriotic element. Puritan mores do not receive the many-sided light that balances positive and negative judgments in "Endicott"; they are shown in a purely negative one. But in these stories, Hawthorne does not yet examine the Puritan consciousness as a thing in itself; he does not open it up to reveal it from the inside. It is shown in conflict with different ethics and world-views, to which Hawthorne unconditionally gives all his sympathy.

A number of stories—from "The Minister's Black Veil" and "Young Goodman Brown," to the gloomy masterpiece "Ethan Brand"—are devoted to revelation of the inner essence of the Puritan consciousness. Thanks to a fantastical nighttime adventure, the hero of "Young Goodman Brown" (1835) comes to understand that piety, which his countrymen so fervently uphold, is no more than a mask concealing the horrible face of vice, and that their seemingly beloved service to God is limited to words, while in their hearts they revere the Devil. This discovery causes Brown to doubt the higher and ultimate goodness of the world and of existence, to doubt love and himself. But he still fears to look in that abyss which, he suspects, is open in his soul.

If, in "Young Goodman Brown," the object of description is, above all, the external world, the *ways* of Puritan society, the true meaning of which accidentally reaches the innocent consciousness, the subject of "Ethan Brand" (1851) is the *soul*, gnawed by an ulcerous awareness of *one's own sinfulness*. In Hawthorne's portrayal this becomes a curse which robs the person of the very possibility of existing. Burdened beyond his strength with sin, Brand throws himself into the glowing kiln. Fire, which consumed him in life, becomes the only means of bringing peace to his suffering soul.

The doctrine of Original Sin, the cornerstone of Puritan ideology, is shown by Hawthorne in an entirely negative light. But its reconsideration is not carried out "point by point." It embraces all of Hawthorne's world-outlook experience, as he contrasts iron Puritan orthodoxy with views more relevant to the new century. It would be difficult to present those views in the form of an elaborate doctrine or theory, but a deep internal conflict with established ideas permeates Hawthorne's works on all levels, in every component of artistic structure—from plot, character description, and author's digressions to concrete images and intonation.

Let's take, for example, one of Hawthorne's early stories, "Sunday at Home" (1837). Hawthorne has many similar sketches; there is no doubt that he had a particular fondness for this form, with its loose plot, in which the main interest lies in the movement of the author's mind. The story clearly reveals autobiographical traits; however, its value is, least of all, in its possible use as a source of information about the writer's life, but, above all, in its lyrical content. Rather than facts, something nearly intangible is presented: spiritual impulses, a play of moods, persistent intellectual work. Remaining, in this miniature lyric chronicle, grounded in the genre of discourse on moral themes, a genre fully within the tradition of Puritan literature, Hawthorne, in essence, enters into debate with orthodox Puritan thought.

As an object of reflection he chooses one of the commandments but gives it a meaning that differs deeply from the stern teachings of piety and repudiation of this world. At first, nothing foreshadows any disagreement; in the early-morning picture, Hawthorne seems to be setting the stage for the usual mood of a piece of this sort. Through the exultant ringing of the lines, however, we catch a different strain. The narrator, remaining at home, prefers to observe events from a distance, satisfied that his "inner man" is attending the service. He bases his reasoning on the idea of removing faith from the domain of the church, of its transformation from a "social" affair to a personal and "inner" matter:

> . . . a devout heart may consecrate a den of thieves, as an evil one may convert a temple to the same. My heart, perhaps, has not such holy, nor, I would fain trust, such impious potency. It must suffice that, though my form be absent, my inner man goes constantly to church, while many, whose bodily presence fills the accustomed seats, have left their souls at home.[8]

What is far more essential is that Hawthorne reconsiders in this story the very idea of holiness, proposing categories that do not fit the framework of traditional Puritan morality, with its emphasis on the sinfulness of the flesh and everything worldly. He watches a group of girls with genuine admiration, emphasizing in every way their earthly beauty:

> Were I the minister himself, I must needs look. One girl is white muslin from the waist upwards, and black silk downwards to her slippers; a second blushes from topknot to shoetie, one universal scarlet; another shines of a pervading yellow, as if she had made a garment of the sunshine. . . . Nearly all—though it is very strange that I should know it—wear white stockings, white as snow, and neat slippers, laced crosswise with black ribbon, pretty high above the ankles. A white stocking is infinitely more effective than a black one.[9]

Hawthorne includes such a picturesque scene, shining with the whole rainbow, not merely for colorful description; it unambiguously speaks of the coming into existence of a new world-view, of new ideals which, in counterbalance to Calvinist doctrine, proclaim the beauty of the earthly world. Of course, Hawthorne still believes in, and actively maintains, the primacy of the spirit over flesh, the transcendental over the worldly, the heavenly over the earthly, the universal over the individual. In this, he is a direct descendant of his Puritan past.

Nonetheless, the opposition of spirit and matter (one of Hawthorne's basic contradictions) is related not only to the traditions of Puritanism, but to the aesthetics of Romanticism as well. This opposition runs through all his work, establishing itself even in his language with constantly repeating pairs—on the one side, spirit/spiritual, ideal/airy, and so forth; and on the other, world/worldly, earthly/material, and so on. Despite the constant opposition—and the unconditional ruling in favor of the ideal, the transcendental, and the universal—the earthly (to the Puritans, transitory and decaying) takes on a lively reality for Hawthorne.

In the short story "Sunday at Home," the "lifting of the heart," opening itself up to supreme good and beauty, turns out to be beyond the power of the preacher with his weekly sermon. The listener's thoughts wander uncontrollably. When the service has ended, the singing of the "sons and daughters of music" lingering in the church, and the "careless note" on the organ, remind the narrator of angels who "came down from Heaven, this blessed morn, to blend themselves with the worship of the truly good."[10]

The internal polemic that breathes through Hawthorne's works does not, however, mean a complete break with Puritanism. In subjecting his heritage to reconsideration, Hawthorne proceeds from its basic categories, which preserve their primary significance for him. It was Hawthorne's sense of his own inner connection with Puritanism that allowed him to create a masterpiece such as *The Scarlet Letter* (1850), a novel noted not only for its precise grasp of life in Puritan society but for the depth of its penetration into the consciousness of the individual and society and the peculiar Puritan cast of mind—with its emblematic, symbolic, providential leanings. All of this is laid in the foundation of the novel's structure. The duality of vision suggested by such an approach is announced on the first pages of *The Scarlet Letter*, with the juxtaposition of two symbols, but also of two concrete objects defining human existence: the flower and the prison.

Duality of vision defines the artistic system of the novel, which is constructed according to the norms of Romantic aesthetics, perceiving the world as forever divided into the ideal and the material. The harmonious mingling of these two aspects—the duality of the world in Puritan ideology, on the one hand, and the Romantic aesthetic, on the other—accounts for the artistic perfection of the novel, about which Henry James wrote (many scholars after James consider it to be among the highest manifestations of Hawthorne's genius):

> It is simpler and more complete than his other novels; it achieves more perfectly what it attempts, and it has about it that charm, very hard to express, which we find in an artist's work the first time he has touched his highest mark—a sort of straightness and naturalness of execution, an unconsciousness of his public, and freshness of interest in his theme.

It is well known that the story which forms the basis of the novel occupied Hawthorne long before he began its writing. The woman with the scarlet letter on her chest first appears in the story "Endicott and the Red Cross" as a background character. She figures in his notebooks as well. An entry from 1844 is directly related to the plan for the novel: "The life of a woman, who, by the old colony law, was condemned always to wear the letter A, sewed on her garment, in token of her having committed adultery."[12] That woman became the heroine of the novel, Hester Prynne.

Gradually other participants in the drama took shape in the writer's mind. On October 27, 1841, Hawthorne entered in his journal: "To symbolize moral or spiritual disease by disease of the body; —thus, when a person committed any sin, it might cause a sore to appear on the body; — this to be wrought out."[13] This note clearly contains the kernel of the future Arthur Dimmesdale. In part, it can also be related to Roger Chillingworth, who, under the influence of consuming desire for revenge, becomes more and more misshapen. And directly about him: "A story of the effects of revenge, in diabolizing him who indulges in it."[14]

The haze of time dividing the events of *The Scarlet Letter* from Hawthorne's day in no way inclined the author to depict the events in idyllic tones. Hawthorne's penetration into the nature of the Puritan mind does not indicate an acceptance of the tenets of Puritanism. "Respect for them," as Perry Miller has truly observed, "is not the same thing as believing in them—as Nathaniel Hawthorne preeminently demonstrated."[15] In his approach to historical material, Hawthorne went essentially against Romanticism's traditional interpretation of history, something that in many ways determined the significance of his artistic achievements in this genre. Romanticism saw the past as the antithesis to a present unacceptable to both the hero and the author. In a certain sense, the Romantic writer, turning to history, escaped in somewhat the same way as did the traditional Romantic hero. Imbued with positive qualities that have been lost by contemporary society, the past often became the embodiment of the social, ethical, and aesthetic ideals of the author. The Romantic idealization of the past could be expressed through its portrayal as the golden age of a new Arcadia, a medieval brotherhood of outlaws. The same thing was achieved by means of aestheticization, when past eras were pictured as the reign of beauty and harmony.

Against the background of the traditional historical romance, *The Scarlet Letter* is distinguished precisely by the complete absence of any idealization of the past, as are Hawthorne's stories. It is, rather, the opposite—in his attitude to the past a note of judgment dominates. This strengthens the impression of objectivity in the author's approach to the description of events, counterbalancing the prevailing, emphasized subjectivity of narrative in Romanticism. Especially important is the fact that this impression is not formed by accident but is the result of a conscious effort on the part of the author, who uses to this end a series of artistic devices that enrich his palette.

Among these devices are the insistent references to the novel's "primary source," which allegedly is simply a collection of authentic accounts left by a certain customs surveyor, a Mr. Pue. In its time, this was a common literary device: If we are to believe the authors, the majority of works of the period were composed of "manuscripts found in bottles," old chests, attics, or, at the very least, inherited from relatives who had passed on. Not satisfied with this general indication, Hawthorne, to be more convincing, brings in "material evidence"—a piece of scarlet cloth, which turns out to be the very same "scarlet letter." Its appearance, which has such an inspiring effect on the author, is called upon to confirm the reader's sense that what follows is not a fiction but a true story.

The context in which these facts are presented plays an essential role. *The Scarlet Letter* does not open with the usual preface, informing the reader of the author's intentions and describing the strange circumstances surrounding the discovery of the manuscript. It is prefaced by an extensive autobiographical sketch telling of Hawthorne's service in the custom-house during the years preceding the novel's creation. The portraits of his co-workers, "drawn from life," the unquestionable veracity of the biographical information, the very tone of the narrative—at times confidential, at times colored with a light self-irony—all strengthen the objective sound of the work, disposing the reader to perceive the events that follow as true. This striving for objectivity of narrative, breaking with the subjective tendency in the genres of Romantic prose which Hawthorne used, in many ways determined the originality of his artistic vision. He was not always able to resolve this contradiction with equal success, but his double tendency is so strongly revealed that to this day the debates have not died down over whether he should be numbered among the Romanticists or—if unsuccessful—the Realists. Nowhere in Hawthorne's work is this dual unity expressed in such a perfect—and, at the same time, natural—form as in *The Scarlet Letter*.

From the first moment, when Hester appears on the scaffold with her baby, and the eyes of the crowd gathered to stare at her public punishment are fastened upon her, the Puritan community is presented as an extraordinarily severe and limited world—a world of merciless cruelty, lack of freedom, suppression of the individual. "[H]ow like an iron cage was that which they called Liberty," writes Hawthorne in the story "Main Street."[16] These words are fully applicable to Puritan society as it is shown in *The Scarlet Letter*.

The writer does give the first settlers their due, noting their admirable strength of spirit, sincerity of faith, strength of conviction, and unbending will. But he clearly sees other sides of the Puritans as well—their religious intolerance, emotional constraint, dogmatic thinking, unshakable belief in their own infallibility—which arouse in him, as an heir to the Puritan legacy, open hostility. Reflecting on the fate of New England since the time of the first settlements, Hawthorne reaches the conclusion that those changes which have secured the break with the Puritan past—Puritan ways, ideology, thought, and morality—have been beneficial.

The specific nature of the Puritans' cruelty is clearly revealed upon comparison of the scene of Hester's punishment with the analogous episode in Victor Hugo's *Notre-Dame de Paris*. Quasimodo, at the pillory, also meets the open hostility of a crowd with no compassion. A hail of stones falls on the unhappy victim, accompanied by whoops, swearing, and ridicule. The sight of his suffering arouses only frenzied merriment, his requests for help, laughter. In this scene, however, there is something simplehearted, instinctive, and natural, ritualistic and festive, as if an ancient sacrificial rite is being carried out, one that promises the participants purification and salvation. Hugo links the crowd's behavior with " . . . cet état d'ignorance première, de minorité morale et intellectuelle. . . ."[17]

This is the root of the difference between the pictures created by Hawthorne and Hugo. In place of *ignorance première*, the American Romanticist has sober, calculated, *conscious* cruelty, a consciousness not primitive, not underdeveloped, but haughtily pretending to inner knowledge of the higher secrets of human and divine law and to indisputable moral rightness. The underlying conviction of its own infallibility that united all Puritan society greatly increases the gravity of its accusations, and is, to Hester, the most unbearable part of the punishment. In the face of monolithic judgment, which is presented as something sanctioned from above, the laughter that causes Quasimodo's pain seems to her more desirable.

The care with which Hawthorne reconstructs the life of Puritan society in the novel, paying attention both to its structure and its government, and to its generally gloomy atmosphere—the inescapable consequence of Puritanism's curse on human nature—and the diligence with which he studied the social-historical background, in turn, strengthen the effect of authenticity for which the author strives. This is aided by a reinterpretation of Romantic literature's traditional historical perspective, which has already been discussed. As a rule, the Romantic writer saw the movement of history as a descent leading to the decline of the individual and society. In *The Scarlet Letter*, precisely the opposite sense dominates, resting, without a doubt, on national experience: the conviction that a spiritual rebirth awaits the country, of which the novel's heroine was, for the author, a far-off precursor. Hawthorne, the skeptic, was not inclined to regard the present in a rosy light—on the contrary, it inspired gloomy thoughts, which took on an openly tragic hue. Nevertheless, the imperfection of the surrounding world did not depreciate that which allowed Americans to move "one step further" from the past.[18]

The Puritan consciousness was of particular interest to Hawthorne. He not only presented it as a whole, an aggregate of ideological and ethical components formed under the influence of Calvinism, he set its mechanism in motion. Hawthorne made the symbolism characteristic of the Puritan consciousness a most important component of the structure of *The Scarlet Letter*. Just as the real Puritans saw in every event the embodiment of divine will, just as their thinking maintained the dualism of the world in which, behind the endless variation of forms of earthly existence is revealed a world of immutable divine laws, so, for Hawthorne's characters, the visible always has a hidden meaning. What is concealed must always make itself known in the end through some sign. Along with this predetermined emblematic system, which was independent of their will and which revealed the essence of divine Providence, the Puritans created their own secondary system of signs, serving as a set of signals of the first. One of the latter is the scarlet letter, called upon to serve as a symbol of Hester's sin. In symbolic meaning, her daughter, little Pearl, is close to that emblem, and a direct analogy is created between the two: the little elf-girl's gold-embroidered scarlet dress makes her look just like a living scarlet letter. Her whole appearance, her uncontrollable ways and "wild" behavior, are seen by the community as indications of her sinful origin.

In this way, the system of signs multiplies in the course of the plot's development. The scarlet letter appears on Dimmesdale's breast—a sign of his complicity in sin and at the same time of the torments of his conscience, which invisibly consume his soul. Then, in the scene of his repentance, a heavenly sign is introduced. It is significant that the sign's meaning can be unclear both to the hero and to the whole community: No one knows whether the radiance in the sky signifies approval or judgment. Hawthorne again conveys with great precision the nature of Puritan thought. As Winthrop's journal shows, the Puritans often left open the question of a sign's meaning, satisfied with the fact that a sign, the meaning of which must be guessed at, was sent. Furthermore, in the course of time, its meaning might change, as does the meaning of the scarlet letter on Hester's breast.

As a result, the structure of *The Scarlet Letter* resembles an extremely complex system of mirrors in which the reflection of an object is doubled infinitely, appearing each time in a new, symbolic aspect. This extensive branching system of emblematic meanings is not limited to the central action of the main characters; the wood, the square, the jail, sin—everything has its sign and is a sign.

Along with this, the peculiarity of the Puritan consciousness is represented in *The Scarlet Letter* through a combination of various narrative layers. Arranged in a complicated, hierarchical relationship, these layers, or levels, serve as reflections of each other and, at the same time, as expressions on a different level of the meaning of the events presented. They include concrete events—allegory, symbol, the fantastical, and, partly, irony. The last refers not to the ironic coloring of the narrative, which informs us of the author's attitude, but to that irony which separates the image from reality. This emphasizes the conventionality of the narrative, which is not the result of particular conventional methods but is characteristic of literature, as of any art form compared to the true reality of life, reminding us that what is before the reader is not a "lump of the earth" placed "under a glass case," but an artistic design.

The episode of Dimmesdale's public confession can serve as an example. Admitting to his sin, Dimmesdale tears the ministerial band from his breast, so that everyone can see the fateful letter blazing there. Here, it becomes part of the allegory, embodying his moral sufferings, which find concrete, physical form in this bodily curse, before which the art of medicine is powerless. The unhealing wound is said to resemble in form and color the scarlet letter his beloved has been sentenced to wear until her death. Fairly frequently, Hawthorne uses such methods for expressing the inner world of a character. The closest example is in the story "Egotism; or, the Bosom Serpent," in which the ulcer of egotism materializes in the form of a snake that settles in the hero's body, gnawing day and night at his insides. However, in the above-mentioned episode, as in many other cases throughout the novel, Hawthorne avoids a direct description of what was actually revealed on the preacher's bared breast to the view of those present. The reader knows that it horrifies not only the crowd of witnesses but the author himself.

Hawthorne does not limit himself to a simple bringing together of various types of narrative, but goes on to offer several interpretations of events. Some of the witnesses see a scarlet letter; others, following matters no less attentively, do not. As in the episode of Dimmesdale's night vigil, when the sky is split by a gigantic flash of lightning, Hawthorne leaves the final choice to the reader, emphasizing the conventionality of events, characters, and fates described. Intentionally retreating from solving the dilemma—preserving in its telling an element of incomplete information, of uncertainty—he again strengthens the effect of authenticity in the narrative. Perception of events plays a key role. It is obvious that should the perceiving consciousness be within the framework of Puritanism, the symbolism characteristic of it would be alive. Where this connection is shaky, the result would be different. Hawthorne could not but keep in mind the nature of his contemporaries' consciousness, colored by skepticism about any kind of miracle or sign. The combination of narrative layers allowed his readers to perceive the events depicted in the novel from a distance, ascribing allegory to the historical consciousness he describes.

But it only appeared to allow this, as allegory in *The Scarlet Letter* is in fact the main means of embodying the novel's Romantic vision. If on the primary level of depiction of events, a duality is preserved (see/don't see)—which is necessary, as has been said, to strengthen the effect of "objectivity," on the level of plot development, character portrayal, and so on—there is no trace of this; everything is directed at the single goal of supporting the allegory. This construction leads to the significant genre complexity attained in *The Scarlet Letter*.

Richard Brodhead considers the presence of narrative levels, which differ according to the principles of artistic organization of material, a characteristic of the works of Hawthorne and Melville, for both of whom multiplicity of meaning is "a function not of the reality," as it is depicted in their works, but "of the ways in which it brings that reality into existence."[19] Neither writer, Brodhead stresses, strives to conceal the basic differences between narrative layers in order to give his novels the appearance of a single narrative structure. They " . . . are fundamentally unwilling to delegate to any one style of vision or organization the exclusive right to represent their world. As a result, they generate in their works a conflict of fictions, and the reality of their imagined world, rather than lying in any one of these fictions, comes into existence in their interaction."[20] Brodhead examines the types of narrative in the structure of Hawthorne's and Melville's novels, proceeding from the idea that they are, in principle and fact, independent of each other and that the one uniting factor in the systems of both writers' novels is, in his opinion, their interaction.

This approach leaves out the most essential element of these structures—the Romantic vision lying at the foundation of the works of these American writers. This is the organizing and defining source which, in the final account, regulates the interaction of the various types of narrative found side by side in the prose of Hawthorne and Melville, and which allows for the integrity of their artistic world despite the heterogeneity of the elements that constitute it. The combination of these elements might vary with every case; one or another of them might take a dominating position among the rest or, on the contrary, fall out altogether from a work's artistic system. What is more, this system allows for the presence of elements opposed to it by nature—the Romantic in realism, the realistic in Romanticism—without changing the essence of the system itself. An example of the first case is the work of Dickens, of the second, Hawthorne.

Of greatest interest is the way in which Hawthorne correlates various types of narrative, remaining within the framework of Romantic prose, not allowing the work to become an arbitrary, chaotic pile of isolated components.

Conflict is the category that allows us to examine these questions. The nature of Romantic conflict has been thoroughly studied by Y. V. Mann in his book *Poetika russkogo romantisma* (The Poetics of Russian Romanticism), many theses of which have general theoretical significance and are applicable to literature of other nations. Mann (correctly) points out that conflict is "a structural category in the full sense (that is, in meaning and form), which leads us into the depth of the artistic order of a work or system of a work"; it *"correlates and coordinates diverse elements in various planes of the artistic structure."*[21]

I have already examined Hawthorne's treatment of Romantic conflict in the historical romance. Let us turn to other levels of the structure.

One of the basic and most characteristic features of Romantic conflict is the particular position of the main character, the Romantic hero. In *The Scarlet Letter*, Hawthorne rigorously follows this requirement. Hester is cast out of the community by Puritan law. Although she continues to live in her former house on the outskirts of Boston, she can fully be called an exile. Nevertheless, the basis for, and form of, ostracism chosen for her by Hawthorne, in fact, strengthen the non-Romantic aspects of the narrative. The "sin" that has set her outside the law is the very category that embraces in itself the essence of the Puritan consciousness. Thus the concretization of one of the elements of the conflict becomes an additional means of describing the society that had formed in New England and enhances the novel's historical authenticity.

In this light, the truly remarkable description of the heroine's appearance is interesting. Hester's stunning beauty comes alive in her portrait: her black eyes, luxurious dark hair tossed over the shoulders, majestic bearing, tall, handsome figure, noble and dignified, yet at the same time, filled with life and passionate ardor, like one of the "prophetic pictures" in Hawthorne's story. The individualization of Hester's portrait shows that Hawthorne strove to transform Romanticism, weakening its most typical features. For this reason, the general typological features in Hester's portrait are replaced in part by individual features.

Hawthorne does not go this far with all of the characters in *The Scarlet Letter*, however. In descriptions of other characters, unlike that of Hester, he stresses those traits which follow the general features of Romantic heroes, as, for example, in the description of Roger Chillingworth. Beginning with his appearance, in which Hawthorne particularly points out his eyes, which gleam with a red fire, and ending with the actions through which Chillingworth carries out his revenge against Hester's beloved, subordinating the latter's consciousness and intensifying with relentless torments the suffering of his sick conscience—everything in this character's makeup reveals him as a villain. And through this, Romanticism's characteristic parallelism between the external and the internal is established.

Like the hero, the villain in a Romantic work is an exceptional, extraordinary figure; therefore, his character and actions must be on a scale larger than life. In this system, and in conformity with these requirements, Chillingworth, the Romantic villain personified, takes on the face of the Devil. Such a description serves all the more to secure Chillingworth a place in the drama of *The Scarlet Letter*, in which the Devil is a reality of the Puritan consciousness. In addition, the description points to the link between this image and the folkloric tradition derived from medieval Christianity.

A sort of transfer occurs in this description, however. Resorting in his sketch of Chillingworth to images from the folk consciousness, Hawthorne, from the beginning, presents the images as his own evaluation—

later supported by references to the opinion of the Puritan community. On the other hand, in the image of Hester—whom Hawthorne immediately allows us to see, both through his description and through the eyes of the people around Hester—there are no elements suggesting any such link with folk tradition; her individual traits shine through. Because of this, the conflict between the protagonists takes on a special coloring. Although Chillingworth acts out of extremely personal motives, doing so entirely independently of the Puritan community, in his revenge he is virtually united with that community. This all the more vividly sets off Hester's position as the Romantic heroine estranged from her surroundings and the bearer of a different kind of consciousness which rejects the Puritans' conservatism and cruelty.

Hawthorne's main method of describing Hester (and Dimmesdale, as well) is psychological analysis, in which he attains extraordinary subtlety and depth, capturing not only the general shape of her thoughts and shifts of her moods but even the fleeting impulsive fits that shake her passionate nature. An example is the already mentioned scene at the pillory. Alternating, with great artistry, the general view of the crowded square with the heroine's inner world, Hawthorne convincingly demonstrates Hester's superiority over her surroundings and vividly conveys her indomitable spirit, oppressed not only by the narrow morality of the Puritans but by all their gloomy, repressed thought, their false understanding of spirituality. In this almost static scene, the meeting of the crowd's gaze and Hester's embodies a dramatically intense battle between two kinds of consciousness, in which each defends its particular understanding of the world. Their duel is not expressed in the external action—there is not even a verbal exchange between the adversaries, not to mention any of the armed battles, duels, and tournaments that Romantic literature so loved to depict (a comparison with Walter Scott's "Old Mortality" strikingly demonstrates the unique nature of Hawthorne's approach to the description of conflict). Shifting the confrontation between Hester and the Puritan community to the plane of consciousness, and turning it into a psychological confrontation allows us to make the analogy between Hawthorne's treatment of Romantic conflict and later realistic literature.

Hawthorne's psychologism, however, has inherent features that distinguish it from the psychologism of the realistic novel. Compared to the latter, it is limited, first of all, by its sphere of application: psychologism in *The Scarlet Letter* is the property of the central character or characters, while the rest remain very conventional figures in whom the "paint and pasteboard" are clearly felt. Even in the characterization of the protagonists, however, psychologism is used exclusively in regard to that which reveals their relationship to the central conflict. This makes for extraordinary intensity in the communication of their emotional state, but does not mean a portrayal of rich, fully developed personalities. All the reader knows about them is limited to the sphere defined by their "sin," which virtually stands in for their entire character. Henry James noted this peculiarity. "The people," he wrote of *The Scarlet Letter*, "strike me not as characters but as representatives, very picturesquely arranged, of a single state of mind."[22]

Ivor Winters spoke about essentially the same thing: "And Hawthorne had small gift for the creation of human beings, a defect allied to his other defects and virtues: even the figures in *The Scarlet Letter* are unsatisfactory if one comes to the book expecting to find a novel. . . ."[23]

The measure of fairness of both judgments is contained in the last word. Correctly noting traits inherent in Hawthorne's psychologism, both James and Winters approach *The Scarlet Letter* as a realistic novel, and on that basis reach their final evaluation. Forewarning the reader, Hawthorne, in the prefaces to his books, intentionally calls attention to the difference between the romance and the realistic novel, the first of which always attracted him. What is more, psychologism in Hawthorne's works is built almost entirely upon description, which, in its turn, rests on an analysis of inner impulses and the motives for characters' actions and behavior, and which appears of its own accord extremely rarely in dramatic situations. Nor, essentially, is the speech of the characters themselves used to delineate them.

It is worth noting that dependence on description for representation of the characters' inner world is typical not only of Hawthorne but of all Romantic prose; characters' psychology is an area in which Hawthorne's achievements are especially significant. Not in vain did Hawthorne himself, speaking of his works, use the term *psychological romance*.[24] No doubt, *The Scarlet Letter* comes under this definition. Infinitely widening the possibilities of psychological portrayal, in comparison with Romanticism, by revealing it through action, realism did not do away with its earlier forms, based on description.

For Hawthorne as an artist, the road to comprehension of the essence of things lay in the psychology of the individual. This is eloquently spoken about in the sketch, "The Old Manse." Reflecting on the field on which one of the first battles of the American Revolution took place, Hawthorne recalls a local legend about one of its participants:

> Oftentimes, as an intellectual and moral exercise, I have sought to follow that poor youth through his subsequent career, and observe how his soul was tortured by the blood-stain, contracted, as it had been, before the long custom of war had robbed human life of its sanctity, and while it still seemed murderous to slay a brother man. *This one circumstance has borne more fruit for me, than all that history tells us of the fight.*[25]

Individual psychology was of greater value to Hawthorne than history—his artistic quests moved in this direction as well. His direct successor in this sense was Henry James, who shared with Hawthorne a particular interest in moral questions. It must be said that, with James, this sometimes takes on forms with a fantastical coloring, which clearly reveals a link with Romantic traditions. A vivid example of this is *The Turn of the Screw*, in which James gives his Romantic influence its due.

Of course, the method of psychological analysis in James's work had increased immeasurably in complexity since Hawthorne's time; but the structure of the narrative gained complexity even with Hawthorne, transforming the genre of the romance. This did not always lead to creative successes: Most scholars believe that in no other major work did Hawthorne achieve such perfection as in *The Scarlet Letter*, although F. O. Matthiessen, for example, rates *The House of the Seven Gables* higher than Hawthorne's recognized masterpiece. In *The House of the Seven Gables* the increased complexity of narrative structure can be seen clearly. Allegory, which played a major role in *The Scarlet Letter* as a means of embodying the Romantic vision, here stays in the background. It does not disappear altogether: the dilapidated house, the neglected garden, the sickly, pure-bred chickens—all of these expressive details serve as an allegory for the degeneration of the mighty Pyncheon family, whose fate is the center of the novel; on the whole, however, its role is significantly diminished. A much greater emphasis is placed on other elements of Romantic narrative. The first of these is the theme of the family curse. The fantastical and mysterious also play an important role in the novel's structure, although James finds an abundance of the fantastical even in *The Scarlet Letter*.

Romanticism's traditional theme of escape receives a deeply original treatment in *The House of the Seven Gables*, through which the novel's action reaches its culmination. Barely hinted at in *The Scarlet Letter*, this theme, most probably as a result of the specifics of the nation's formation, did not play an essential role in the work of American Romanticists, though it appears in unique interpretations in Cooper's *Leatherstocking* series, in *Moby Dick*, and in *Walden*. The development of this motif in *The House of the Seven Gables* is remarkable, not only for its exceptional dramatic tension, the equal of which can probably not be found in Hawthorne's other works. Concluding the episode, so important for an understanding of the novel's ideological scheme, with the heroes' return, the author gives the episode a meaning that is entirely new to the tradition of Romanticism. The escape motif itself sounds in a new way: There is nowhere to run. In the foggy distance to which Clifford and Hepzibah flee, escaping a cruel and vicious world, neither happiness nor peace awaits them. Such an interpretation of the theme gives the reality reflected in the novel a shade of tragic hopelessness.

Finally, Hawthorne introduces to the novel a second narrative structure—the story of Holgrave, the action of which forms a parallel to the main plot. Its function, however, is not simply to open up the novel's framework; Holgrave's story makes it possible to develop the action on two planes, giving clear form to the author's thoughts about the power of the past over human fate. Present and past form an indissoluble whole, impossible to step out of. The approach to time, though, is far more complex in the structure of the novel: The plot develops, along with the present and the historical past, in time as well, acquiring an all-significant, universal meaning.

Structural change in *The House of the Seven Gables* is not limited simply to a greater variety of Romantic narrative elements. As if to balance out this "listing," Hawthorne undertakes an essential step, from the point of view of the narrative system. He moves non-Romantic characters to the center (there is no Romantic hero in this novel); it was this move that set the stage for the different critical evaluations.

In *The Blithedale Romance*, the narrative structure is again reorganized. The author's attention is focused on a group of characters among whom the true Romantic heroine particularly stands out—the beautiful Zenobia. The degree of conventionality in her depiction and that of the novel's second heroine, Priscilla, is much higher than in *The Scarlet Letter*: Both figures also function allegorically, each personifying a social position. One, Zenobia—with her stunning beauty, brilliance of mind, and breeding, and surrounded by luxury—is a "daughter of wealth"; the other—pale, fragile, and timid Priscilla—is a "daughter of poverty." They are bonded in sisterhood not so much by the demands of the plot as by their allegorical roles. The fateful mystery surrounding Westervelt is balanced out in the novel's structure by the introduction of realistically drawn characters, the farmer Silas Foster and old Moodie, in whose depiction the grotesque plays an important role.

The social background is significantly widened in this novel. Unlike *The Scarlet Letter*, in which the action embraces the essentially monolithic world of the Puritan community, *The Blithedale Romance* is typified by an alternation of episodes that convey heterogeneity of social being. Scenes in the cozy home of the gentleman-writer Coverdale are followed by depiction of the ascetic lodgings of the colony of idealists who aim at transforming the world by their own labor and example, by an idyllic picture of revels in the woods, by the prosaic details of daily life on the farm, by the mysterious atmosphere of the "veiled lady's" seances, in which the sensitive Coverdale perceives profanation and common humbug playing on the instincts of the crowd, and by what is probably the most unexpected scene in a Romantic work: the squalid inn where, it seems, the very air is poisoned with hopelessness and the despair of the regular patrons.

The form of romance did not stay unchanged with Hawthorne. He saw Romantic narrative structures not as something frozen but as dynamic forms capable of development, open to the perception of new phenomena not yet mastered by literature. The attempt to embody these phenomena leads to modification of forms and narrative structures themselves, which are harmonized in Hawthorne's works within the framework of Romantic poetics. This inner transformation, which answers indirectly the dynamics of the nation's development, can at least partly explain the special "tenacity" of the Romantic tradition in American literature.

YURI KOVALEV

The Limits

of Herman Melville's Universe

The works of Herman Melville are a unique and outstanding phenomenon in the literary history of the United States. Melville has long
been numbered among America's classic writers, and his remarkable *Moby-
Dick, or, the Whale* is considered, with good reason, a masterpiece of world
literature. Melville's life, works, correspondence, and journals have been
thoroughly studied. There exist tens of biographies and monographs and
hundreds of articles and publications, thematic collections, and collective
works dedicated to various aspects of his writings. Yet, Melville, the man
and the artist, as well as his books, both during and after his lifetime,
remains a riddle that has never been entirely solved.

Melville's life and work are filled with paradoxes, contradictions, and
hard-to-explain peculiarities. An example is his complete lack of serious
formal education. He never studied at any university. Necessity forced
him to leave school at the age of twelve. And yet Melville's books tell us
that he was one of the best-educated people of his time, well versed in
many sciences and especially in philosophy. The deep insight into the
fields of gnosiology, sociology, psychology, and economics that the reader

encounters in his works suggest not only sharp intuition but a solid store of scientific information as well. Where, when, how did he acquire this? It can only be supposed that Melville was capable of extraordinary concentration, allowing him, in a short time, to assimilate and consider critically an enormous amount of information.

Or we might look at the nature of Melville's evolution through the genres. We have become accustomed to a more or less traditional picture: The young writer begins with poetic attempts, then tries his hand at shorter prose forms (sketches, essays, stories), turns to novellas, and finally, having achieved a certain maturity, undertakes large "canvasses." With Melville the process was reversed: He began with novellas and novels, then turned to short stories, finally ending his creative journey as a poet.

There was no immature period in Melville's artistic life. He broke into literature—"burst" into it. His first book, *Typee*, brought him widespread recognition, first in America, then in England, France, and Germany. In following years his skill increased and his subject matter became deeper; but inexplicably his popularity fell. *Omoo*, *Redburn*, and *White-Jacket* were received by the critical and reading public without great enthusiasm; *Moby Dick* aroused only cold bewilderment; and his last novels, *Pierre* and *The Confidence-Man*, were met with displeasure and incomprehension. How is this not a paradox?

By the beginning of the 1860s Melville was "mortally" forgotten by his contemporaries. In the seventies, an English admirer of his talent searched unsuccessfully for Melville in New York. To all his queries he received the indifferent response: "Yes, there was a writer by that name. Nobody knows what happened to him. Probably died." But Melville, who "probably died," was living in New York at the time, where he worked as a freight inspector for the customs department. Here we have yet another enigmatic phenomenon, which could be called "Melville's silence." In fact, the writer "fell silent" in the prime of his strength and talent (he was not yet forty years old) and remained silent for three decades. If he wrote anything during those years, it was not discovered until thirty years after his death, when his biographers turned their attention to his archives. The only exceptions are two collections of poetry, which were published in tiny editions at the author's expense and went entirely unnoticed by critics.

Equally unusual was the posthumous fate of Melville's legacy; until 1919, it might not have existed. The writer was so completely forgotten that when he did in fact die, his name was misspelled in the short obituary notice. The year 1919 was the hundredth anniversary of his birth, but the occasion was greeted neither with ceremonies nor with commemorative articles. Only one person noted the date: Raymond Weaver, who had just begun work on Melville's first biography. That book, titled *Herman Melville: Mariner and Mystic*, came out two years later. Weaver's efforts were supported by the English writer D. H. Lawrence, who enjoyed enormous popularity in America at that time. Lawrence wrote two articles on Melville, which were included in his sensational collection of psychoanalytic essays, *Studies in Classic American Literature* (1923).

America remembered Melville. And how! His books began to be reprinted in massive editions; unpublished manuscripts were drawn from his archives; films were made, plays written, and operas composed based on his subject matter; artists were inspired by his images; Rockwell Kent did a series of brilliant drawings on the theme of the "white whale."

Naturally, the Melville boom extended to literary criticism as well. Literary historians, biographers, critics, and even people in fields unrelated to literature (historians, psychologists, and sociologists) got down to work. The tiny stream of Melville scholarship became a raging torrent. Today, that torrent has quieted down somewhat, but it has by no means dried up. The most recent splash occurred in 1983, when, in an abandoned barn in upstate New York, two suitcases and a wooden chest were found containing manuscripts by Melville and letters from his family members. Some 150 Melville scholars are now engaged in studying the new materials with an eye to making the necessary corrections in existing biographical work.

It must be noted, however, that the Melville "renaissance" had only a remote connection to his hundredth anniversary. Its source must be looked for not in the writer's personal fate but in the general frame of mind that characterized American spiritual life at the end of the teens and the beginning of the twenties. The overall sociohistorical development of the United States at the turn of the century, and especially during the First World War, had raised in the minds of many Americans doubt of, even protest against the pragmatic values, ideals, and criteria that had guided the nation throughout its first one and a half centuries. This protest was realized on many levels (social, political, and ideological), including the literary. It found voice as the ideological-philosophical basis of works by O'Neill, Fitzgerald, Hemingway, Anderson, Faulkner, and

Wolfe—writers who traditionally are numbered among the so-called Lost Generation, but whom it would be more correct to refer to as the "protesting generation." It was precisely at this time that America recalled those Romantic rebels who had asserted the supreme value of human individuality, protesting everything that suppresses, oppresses, and deforms that individuality to fit bourgeois morality. Americans rediscovered the works of Poe, Hawthorne, Dickinson—and, at the same time, the forgotten Melville.

Today, it would occur to no one to doubt Melville's claim to a place on the American literary Olympus. In the pantheon of American writers in New York he holds a place of honor alongside Irving, Cooper, Poe, Hawthorne, and Whitman. He is read and revered. An enviable fate, a great glory, which the writer could not have contemplated during his life!

2

Melville once wrote to Hawthorne:

> My development has been all within a few years past. I am like one of those seeds taken out of the Egyptian Pyramids, which after being three thousand years a seed and nothing but a seed, being planted in English soil, it developed itself, grew to greenness, and then fell to mould. So I. Until I was twenty-five, I had no development at all. From my twenty-fifth year I date my life.

Translating this into biographical dates, it is easy to see that Melville associated the beginning of his development with his work on *Typee*, his move to New York, and his introduction to American literary life.

The many critics who have attempted to present Melville as a solitary genius—standing apart from the hopes and aspirations of his time and from the social, political, and literary struggle of his era—are either honestly misguided or have knowingly distorted the facts in favor of their preconceived ideas. It is simply impossible to understand Melville's personality and the direction of his inner development separately from American life in the 1840s, a life filled with contradictions, paradoxes, and incomprehensible strangeness.

By the time Melville entered the literary profession, American Romanticism was already completing the first phase of its history. The older generation (Irving, Cooper, Neal, Paulding, Kennedy, Simms, Bryant,

Whittier) had not yet left the stage, but new names had already appeared to replace them: Emerson, Thoreau, Longfellow, Poe, Hawthorne, Richard Henry Dana, and others. The main task of the early Romantics had been to "discover America." They were all drawn into the powerful current of nativism—a cultural movement, the main objective of which was the creation of an artistic-philosophical understanding of America, its ways, nature, history, social and political institutions. The literature of the 1820s and 30s opened for readers a world of boundless prairies and virgin forests, powerful rivers and waterfalls; shared with them the lives and ways of old Dutch settlements; unfurled before them the heroic pages of the War for Independence; described events from America's colonial history; pictured life on Southern tobacco plantations. Nativism promoted the formation of a general conception of America in the minds of Americans. Without it, a national identity—and, consequently, a national literature—could never have come to be.

In the process of their artistic assimilation of American reality, however, the Romantics of the first generation discovered with alarm that the historical development of their young government was moving dangerously away from the enlightened dreams of the Founding Fathers; their optimistic predictions were not coming true; their wonderful, enlightened slogans were being distorted; their democratic ideals had been emasculated. Economic progress was accompanied by crises; "the sovereignty of the people" thrived side by side with slavery; the pioneers' heroic conquering of new territories involved the rampant plundering of natural riches, those very new lands becoming objects of speculation; the individual's right to "life, liberty, and the pursuit of happiness" guaranteed by the Declaration of Independence, did not prevent the government from exterminating the Indians with unprecedented cruelty; corruption penetrated every level of authority, including the highest; lies, slander, and demagogy became "normal" methods of political struggle; the obsession with wealth attained fantastic heights.

The early Romantics (Irving, Bryant, Cooper, Paulding, and so on) doubted neither the basic principles of democracy, nor the benefits of capitalist progress, nor the political institutions of the United States. They felt that Americans' moral illness ("Moral Eclipse," as Cooper put it) came from without and was fully curable. Their task was to reveal defects, expose imperfections and deviations from the healthy norm, and thus contribute to their elimination. It was this that inspired the rise of the

Romantic utopias that became an almost indispensable component of American literature right up until the Civil War. What is referred to in this case is not the description of utopian experiments, but a purely literary phenomenon.[1] Writers would create some (purely theoretical) social and human ideal as a background against which the defects of American reality showed up with particular clarity. Such were the worlds of Irving's old settlements of New Netherlands or Cooper's *Leatherstocking Tales*, in which noble Indians live in perfect harmony with wise nature.

In the 1840s, the above-mentioned trends in American economic and sociopolitical life had not only not abated but, on the contrary, had intensified significantly. The crisis of 1837 shook the nation's economy and called into existence numerous radical-democratic movements. Disputes between North and South became seriously aggravated. The expansionist mood intensified. The seizing of new lands occurred to many as a constructive escape from a bad situation. In 1846, America began its first—and, alas, not its last—expansionist war.

Under these circumstances, the Romantic utopia lost none of its effectiveness as a weapon for criticism of the day's morals and norms. We can easily understand why Melville entered into a literary tradition that had existed for more than two decades: it had far from exhausted itself.

At first glance, *Typee* is an honest, somewhat naive description of the adventures of an American seaman-whaler taken prisoner by cannibals. The book is largely given over to the author's unsophisticated observations of the customs and ways of the Polynesian savages. But on closer examination, it becomes clear that the narrator-sailor is not as artless as he might wish to appear. The greater part of what he says is the truth, but it is far from the whole truth. The picture of Typee life as presented by him is idealized and incomplete; it is drawn in opposition to the defects of American civilization. The contrast between the ideal of the cannibals and the depravity of bourgeois society runs like a red thread through the entire narration, turning it into a classic example of a Romantic utopia.

3

It has already been stated that Melville belonged to the second, younger generation of American Romantics. This generation had its own life, ideas, and understanding of the goals and tasks of its art. Within the Romantic movement, groups and associations formed (Knickerbockers,

Young America, Transcendentalists, among others) and began to carry on
bitter polemics with each other. The literary struggle converged with the
political struggle, and partisan aims became an integral part of aesthetic
principles and programs.

Perhaps the most essential feature of the views and work of the younger
generation of Romantics was its suspicion of the validity of the principles
of American democracy and of the effectiveness of its sociopolitical institutions. This suspicion was responsible for the shift in the general
"mode" of literature in the 1840s and 50s, as it became more and more
imbued with a spirit of pessimism. The works of Edgar Allan Poe,
Nathaniel Hawthorne, and Herman Melville confirm this shift.

Here, it would be in order to describe some aspects of Melville's philosophy, although the task involves nearly insurmountable difficulties. This
is due not only to the fact that Melville left no theoretical writings (his art
must therefore be our only source), it is, most of all, because the author's
world-view was never a complete and stable system but an ongoing process of thought without end. On the one hand, Melville, by studying and
observing concrete reality, searched for revelations of general laws; this
explains his irrepressible bent for symbolic generalization. Often, the laws
he "discovered" turned out to contradict each other, leading again to
complicated, contradictory symbols. On the other hand, Melville attempted to comprehend reality by imposing on its chaotic movement the
established ideas and philosophical categories developed by human
thought over many centuries. He could even be considered a Kantian
idealist were it not for one essential point: Melville dimly suspected that
human ideas themselves were a peculiar reflection of real existence. This
thought informs many of his works, but it comes through with particular
force in *Moby Dick*.

Like certain of his contemporaries—Emerson, Poe, Hawthorne, and
Whitman—Melville was a Romantic humanist who saw human consciousness as a trinity of intellect, moral sense, and psyche. Yet he was
unlike the others. Emerson saw in human consciousness a fragment of the
"super-soul" and on that basis created his optimistic theory of self-reliance, with the aid of which, he proposed, all the world's conflicts and
contradictions could be resolved. Hawthorne believe that the soul was an
inseparable union of Good and Evil, that any attempt to destroy Evil
would lead inevitably to the destruction of Good. His world-view contained minute amounts of optimism. Poe, despite his admiration for the

power of intellect, was a pessimist: he considered psychological instability to be the main feature of consciousness, thwarting and distorting the functioning of reason and moral sense. Melville was a pessimist as well but in an entirely different sense; he did not believe in the existence of Emerson's "super-soul," nor did he accept the metaphysical ideas of eternal evil in the soul of man or innate psychic instability. Melville's values included, above all, uncompromising democratism, the idea of the universal equality of races and peoples, belief in the virtue of labor, and boundless respect for the laborer. In this sense, Melville was close to the young Whitman, author of *Leaves of Grass*. For all his inclination toward universal generalization and symbolic abstraction, Melville's consciousness was more historical than that of the others. While recognizing the healthy foundation of the "soul of the people," Melville spoke of the destructive influence on that soul of civilization's progress, particularly of bourgeois ethics. He saw no way to halt the destructive process. This is the root of his unique, "fundamental," so to speak, pessimism.

In the mid-1840s, Melville linked his artistic fate (though not for long) to the activities of "Young America," a literary and political group affiliated with the left wing of the Democratic party. The Young Americans stood for thorough democratization of all aspects of national life, including literature. They saw the future of the American word as the product of the combined creative efforts of the "Homers of the Masses"—poets of the people, for the people, writing about the people. Their aspirations were dear to Melville, although there was in his relations with his colleagues a shade of skepticism and light irony. Most of the group were writers, commentators, and critics for whom the word *people* had a fairly abstract meaning. They thought of the people and labored for the good of the people, but they themselves stood apart from the people. The needs and interests of the people were a subject that required explanation. From the beginning, Melville shared Whitman's sense of unity with the people. The people's needs were no riddle for him. He stepped onto the deck of literature from the sailor's quarters; he himself was the people. He had perfect grounds for calling himself a "ruthless democrat."

Melville's introduction to the activities of Young America was important for a different reason: He entered into the literary life and struggle of the era; he began to recognize the responsibility of the writer, to develop his own point of view on the general nature of the sociohistorical development of America and on the role of art in that development. The young

Melville became a regular participant in discussions at the home of the group's leader, Evert Duyckinck. He began to speak out, as critic and commentator, in the pages of Young America's publications; he took part in disputes with the Knickerbockers, came to the defense of national literature, and probed the questions of Romantic aesthetics, of which he was at first most attracted to the problems of the imagination, its limits and role in artistic creation. Insufficient experience and immaturity were more than compensated for by youth and spirit. Melville, a steadfast soldier, remained true to some of Young America's ideas even after others in the group had laid down their arms and retreated.

Melville shared completely his contemporaries' doubts and concerns about the true nature and future of American democracy. The rift between the ideal and the real, between the "moral model" and the actual social behavior of his countrymen, of which Melville had become aware fairly early, gave his intellect a clear direction. He took the course of artistic exploration of universal laws and powers regulated and directed by human activity. This was the road to *Moby Dick*.

The first step along that road was the novel *Mardi*, a work in which Melville suffered crippling defeat as an artist. The book ended up over-loaded with reports from the fields of history, philosophy, sociology, politics, and aesthetics. Information was abundant but badly digested and unsystematic. Melville was unable to find an adequate form for its artistic exploration. *Mardi* presented a strange impression. Even today, it is hard to believe that it is the work of a great master. It has neither unity of subject nor integrity of form: Its characters are abstract and, for the most part, conventional. Equally conventional is the reality surrounding them. The illogical development of the plot is accompanied by at least three complete transformations of the book's main hero, all of them entirely ungrounded. At the beginning, the hero is a runaway sailor from a whaling ship who finds himself in a frail, tiny boat a thousand miles from the nearest shore. Next, he is a romantic "deliverer," madly in love with a beautiful girl he rescued. Later, he is a seeker of truth, an inquisitive traveler, an observer of life, hoping to gain wisdom through philosophical discussion with the Historian, Philosopher, Poet, and King. Naturally, the narrative style is not consistent. At times, it gravitates toward Melville's own early writings, at others toward the poetic styles of Byron, Shelley, and La Motte-Fouque, at still others toward Rabelais, Swift, and Voltaire. It is not surprising that many contemporary scholars find in *Mardi* four separate books under one cover. Each has its own style, subject, aims, and artistic structure.[2]

Mardi's failure can be partly explained by Melville's inexperience as a writer. But its main cause, apparently, was Melville's overly straightforward interpretation of one of the main principles of Romantic aesthetics, according to which the imagination is seen as the shortest path to knowledge of higher truth. The young Melville stumbled against that which two decades earlier had tripped up the young Poe when he ruined his wonderful vision for the poem "Al Aaraaf," attempting to create a "purely imaginative world" by removing from it "everything earthly." It turned out that the imagination cannot work in isolation from earthly stuff, cannot create something from nothing; and Poe left his poem unfinished. Approximately the same thing occurred with Melville. He completed his work, it is true, but was forced to transport it into a theoretical-allegorical plane which did not save the situation; the aesthetic damage was irreparable.

It is worth adding that in the mid-1940s a polemic flared up with new strength in American criticism concerning the types of large-scale prose works: The "romance" clashed with the "novel." Melville was attracted by the arguments of the defenders of the romance, who maintained that the writer's task is to penetrate, by means of the imagination, the essence of things rather than to skim the surface of facts, as is done in the novel. In letters to publishers and friends, Melville, already at work on *Mardi*, complained more than once of being "constrained by facts," of his wish to "soar," to free himself from the empirical. He finally resolved to do it; he soared and discovered that it was impossible to fly in a vacuum of pure imagination.

Like Poe, Melville drew a lesson from his failure. He realized that higher powers and laws could be approached by human consciousness only through their revelation in concrete reality. Therefore, his task was to learn to comprehend the general in the personal, to present the concrete movement of life in such a way that the effects of universal laws are revealed, made clearly visible in all their complexity and inconsistency.

4

Mardi's failure disappointed Melville; but he was neither surprised nor discouraged. Most likely, he foresaw the catastrophe and despaired of the

book even before it saw the light of day. Barely had he completed the
manuscript and sent it to the publisher when he returned to his writing
desk and began, with alarming energy, to work out the ideas that had
begun to take shape in his mind even as he was working on the earlier,
unsuccessful novel. The result was two books of an entirely different
sort—*Redburn* and *White-Jacket*. They are not equal; *White-Jacket* is the
epitome of the American sea tale of the 1840s, a book filled with the
relentless, uncompromising spirit of democratism, focused on the important social problems of the time, permeated with fierce invectives against
the established order of things, at sea and in the government. *Redburn* is,
so to speak, the stepping stone to *White-Jacket*. In it we find in embryonic
form much that will come through in full force in Melville's subsequent
works.

Both *White-Jacket* and *Redburn* give witness to the fact that Melville
had turned away from the idea of "pure imagination," recognizing its
fruitlessness and no longer attempting to soar. He turned again to his
own life experience, to books from which, with a generous hand, he began
to draw "facts." Imagination was given a different role: to tie those facts
into a system, penetrate below their surface and glimpse their regularity
and deepest sense. The numerous meanings of facts and the possibility of
interpreting reality at many levels now became evident to Melville. From
this comes the general shift in the poetic style of Melville's prose, the
weakening and nearly complete disappearance of its allegorical base and
the swift growth of Romantic symbolism. All of this may be found in
Redburn and *White-Jacket* and then, in full flower, in *Moby Dick*.

5

At the end of 1849—having completed work on *White-Jacket*, the last
chapters of which had nearly exhausted his strength—Melville escaped to
Europe, ostensibly to make arrangements with London publishers regarding the printing of his books in England. The journey lasted seven weeks.
Melville spent time in Paris, Brussels, Cologne, the Rhineland, and London. On February 1, 1850, he returned to New York and began work on
Moby Dick, the general plan for which had already formed in his mind.
Half a year passed, agonizing and oppressive, before he reached the conclusion that it was impossible to work under existing circumstances. With
money borrowed from his father-in-law, he bought the farm "Arrowhead"

(not far from the small town of Pittsfield) and in September moved there with his family.

What prompted Melville to leave New York—with its active literary life, its proximity to libraries, journals, and presses, along with the possibility of constant contact with his literary friends and companions from Young America—and withdraw to a desolate farm? The answer is simple: He couldn't work. In Melville's New York residence a population had occurred. Besides Melville, his wife, and their newborn son, his mother and sister had moved in, as well as his younger brother, Allan, with his wife and their children. In a letter, Melville noted that there is nothing in the world more terrible than a teething baby. Melville could only dream of that special creative state in which "one can hear the grass grow." He could hear nothing over the screaming of babies.

With the move to the farm, however, Melville's involvement in the literary and social life of the nation did not end. Melville maintained ties with Young America, often traveling to New York and receiving visits by Young Americans in Pittsfield. He continued to contribute to journals and to speak out in defense of national literature. It is also significant that at just about the same time, Nathaniel Hawthorne settled in Lenox, Massachusetts, only five miles from Melville's farm. Melville met Hawthorne, and their acquaintance soon grew to close friendship. Their regular meetings and correspondence, their long conversations about literature; exchanges of opinions about various pressing questions concerning American social, political, and spiritual life; discussions of purely professional writers' problems—all had great meaning for the creative evolution of both men, especially Melville, who was fifteen years younger.

For a time, Pittsfield became a center of American Romantic art. Here, in 1850–51, the authors in constant communication, two outstanding works of Romantic literature were published: *The House of the Seven Gables* and the novel about the White Whale.

Moby Dick, Melville's masterpiece, has a complicated and unclear creative history. Attempts to reconstruct it, using Melville's correspondence, give us an approximate, incomplete, but generally trustworthy picture. To all appearances, the author had planned to write one more seafaring novel, this one about a whaling fleet. It was meant to complete his marine trilogy (*Redburn, White-Jacket, Moby Dick*), which would embrace all the forms of navigation in 19th-century America. Apparently Melville wished to write an adventure tale about the whaling industry but at the same time a book that would investigate the widest economic, social, political, and philosophical questions affecting the life of the United States and, perhaps, all of humankind. This original idea already made inevitable a strengthening of the symbolic nature of Melvillian Romanticism which, as we know, was realized in the final text of the novel.

The road to that final text was not easy, however. Financial necessity held the author in its grip. Debts grew like snowballs. Melville was plagued by the thought of commercial success. Recalling the lessons of *Mardi*, he restrained his inclination toward abstract construction and built strong dams against his raging torrent of philosophical thoughts. He had to write a popular adventure novel about whalers, although everything in him—including his inherent sense of a writer's responsibility before time, history, and society—protested this necessity. In his letters to Hawthorne, Melville complained that he had no right to write as he wanted to; "yet, altogether, write the other way I cannot." This continued for quite a long time. The writer struggled not so much with the White Whale as with himself, and, it seems, was even victorious over himself. In any event, in August 1850, he wrote to his publisher that the book was nearly finished, and he hoped to send the manuscript shortly.

                                6

Now begins the "dark" period in the novel's history. Melville did not, as he had promised, provide the manuscript "shortly." He continued to work on it for nearly a year, and the result was not at all a "popular adventure novel" but something entirely different: a vast structure embodying, in its complex system of symbols, America—present, past, and future.

What had happened? What had inspired Melville to "open the floodgates" and unloose the thoughts, ideas, and images that had been straining to burst free? Literary historians have any number of hypotheses on this matter; they can be found even today, with various modifications, in works on Melville. Some critics search for the explanation in Hawthorne's influence; others speak of the influence of Shakespeare's tragedies, which Melville read avidly during his work on *Moby Dick*. Still others find the clue in the general nature of America's social and historical development and in the political atmosphere at the end of the 1840s and the beginning of the 1850s. This author is inclined to believe that it is these last who are correct, despite the fact that one finds clear evidence of Hawthorne's and Shakespeare's influence in the text.

We must recall that, by the middle of the century, the socioeconomic, political, and ideological contradictions in American life had become acute. In September 1850, Congress, under pressure from the South, passed its inhuman law concerning runaway slaves, essentially turning the entire country into a slave-owning society. The nation was aroused. The Abolitionist movement became massive. People held mass meetings protesting the "barbaric" acts of the government. The antislavery theme made its way into literature, taking dominion there. Beecher Stowe began *Uncle Tom's Cabin*, Hildreth adapted *The Slave; or, Memoirs of Archy Moore*, John Whittier denounced slavery in impassioned verse, Lowell published *Biglow Papers*. Brochures, pamphlets, and leaflets were printed by the thousands. Thoreau made (and later published) his celebrated speech, "Slavery in Massachusetts," in which he renounced his homeland. The list could be continued, including well-known and lesser-known writers, commentators, and philosophers. What more can be said, if even the "Sage of Concord," Ralph Waldo Emerson, joined the Abolitionists? America resembled a steam boiler in which the pressure far exceeded safety levels. The arrow on the gauge had passed the red mark, heralding an imminent explosion. The country was hurtling toward war, crossing, without noticing it, the point of no return. Melville, we presume, did not know this, but his instinct was true: He predicted catastrophe in the near future. From such a point of view, it was most important to determine the reason for all reasons, to understand which laws, strengths, or, perhaps, Higher Will was guiding the deeds of people, peoples, and governments. On what could Americans count in a moment of crisis?

In light of these circumstances, all considerations regarding popularity and commercial success withered before the social responsibility of the writer. Melville abandoned them and began to restructure the book. He had an enormous amount of ideological material. No existing artistic form could contain it. A new, as yet unknown type of narration was needed, which is conventionally referred to as the synthetic novel. Certainly *Moby Dick* is an adventure novel, but it is also a "nautical," "social," "philosophical," and, if you like, "coming-of-age" novel. All of these aspects do not appear side by side in *Moby Dick*, but grow into each other, forming an indissoluble whole permeated by a complex system of polysemantic symbols. To this must be added that the narrative is tied together by a single style (in which, indeed, are felt the influences of Hawthorne and Shakespeare) and by Melville's unique language, which critics are fond of likening to an ocean wave.

Moby Dick is generally recognized as one of the great works of Romantic symbolism in American—and, probably, world—literature. Its complicated system of symbols forms, so to speak, the aesthetic foundation of the novel. Everything in it—events, facts, the author's descriptions and reflections, its human characters—has, besides its direct meaning, another, more important symbolic one. There is also complete agreement among critics with regard to the claim that Melville's symbols are both universal and highly abstract. Lost from the field of vision, though, is the fact that, for all its abstractness, *Moby Dick*'s symbolism grows directly from the writer's contemporary sociopolitical reality.

Let us turn to the group of symbols linked with the sailing of the *Pequod*. The *Pequod* itself, in its symbolic meaning, requires no great effort to interpret. The ship is government—a traditional symbol known to literature since the Middle Ages. But in *Moby Dick*, it doesn't exist by itself. The success or failure of the ship's sailing depends on many factors but most of all on three characters: the ship's owner, Bildad, Captain Ahab, and his chief mate, Starbuck. Bildad is old. He's a pious money-grubber and a hypocrite—the classic image of an old Puritan. He has almost no energy left, and what does remain is spent in a miserly fashion. Starbuck, too, is pious and devout; but he is not hypocritical. He is an experienced seaman and a skillful whaler, but he has neither initiative nor scope. He has little confidence in himself or in his life goals. Finally, there is Ahab, a complex character, contradictory, with many meanings. In him are combined Romantic mystery, unpredictable behavior, a fanatical hatred of evil and a limitless ability to create it, maniacal stubbornness in striving for a determined goal, and the ability to sacrifice for that goal his ship, the lives of his crew, and even his own life. No obstacles exist for Ahab.

The differences between these characters are evident; but, in order to understand their true sense and meaning in the narrative, one must look at that which unites them. They are all New England Quakers, descendants of the first settlers, successors to the "pioneers." This is significant. Melville always had a particular interest in New England, and not only because he himself was a descendant of the Puritans. He saw New England, correctly, as the leader of America's socioeconomic progress. New

England set the tone in many spheres of national life, particularly economics. It was this group of states that first set out on the path of industrial-capitalist development. In many ways the fate of the country depended upon the thoughts and actions of the residents of Massachusetts, New Hampshire, and Connecticut. From this comes the author's heightened interest in the foundations, morals, and people of New England.

In light of this concern with New England, the characters of the three New England Quakers in the novel take on additional symbolic meaning. Bildad, with his piety, shameless greed, reluctance to risk, and old man's weakness and pettiness, symbolizes the New England of yesterday, its past. Risk, long sailing on the stormy sea, is not for him. The *Pequod* leaves on a voyage, and Bildad remains on shore. Starbuck represents today and, like all todays, is somewhat obscure. He can take the ship out to sea, but he is unfamiliar with the feeling of pursuing a great goal. He is unenterprising, unable to shake free of the power of yesterday. He would unquestionably have brought the *Pequod* home to Bildad.

Ahab is another matter. He might be associated with the activists of the new era taking shape in the middle of the 19th century, when the new pioneers were no longer clearing the forests for crops or defending themselves against Indians and wild animals. They were building factories and plants, ships, and railroads. They were trading with the entire world and opening banks in American cities. They were the leaders of Progress; they furthered the economic prosperity of their land (whatever that prosperity may have cost the people) and considered themselves the salt of the earth. In their world, business was sovereign, enrichment the supreme goal for which everything could be sacrificed, including human life. Ahab, of course, is not a businessman, nor is he a captain of industry; those are the heroes of Norris, Dreiser, Sinclair, Lewis, and others. His determination, ability to overcome all impediments, not to be held back by his understanding of justice; his lack of fear, pity, or compassion; his bravery and enterprise; and, most important, his scope and his iron grip—all this makes us see in Ahab a prophetic image of the future empire builders of the second half of the century, each of whom pursued his White Whale, overstepping legal, human, and divine laws.

The other group of symbolic meanings is associated with Captain Ahab's fanatical madness, which destroys the ship entrusted to him and the lives of its entire crew (with the exception of Ishmael). Of course, fanaticism and madness are not new subjects in world literature. Indeed, in American literature we find no few works treating them, beginning with the novels of Brockden Brown and ending with the stories of Poe. What is noteworthy is the following: In the work of American Romanticists in the 1840s and 50s, the problem of Evil, brought about by fanatics in the name of Good, and the problem of fanaticism in general, held an extremely important place. In those years, many writers turned to the history of the Puritan settlements of New England, to those episodes in which religious fanatics, attempting to exterminate imagined evil, created, in the process, real and irreparable evil. It was no coincidence that the Salem witch trials became a fashionable subject in literature. Longfellow, Mathews, Hawthorne, and other writers made it a subject of their works.

It is not difficult to explain this interest in fanaticism; during this time, it was a problem with not only moral-psychological but sociopolitical implications. The main conflict of the era was between North and South. By the end of the 1840s, political passions had reached an extraordinary pitch. Southerners fought bitterly for new territories, forcing Congress to pass legislative measures serving the slave interests. They were ready to resort to anything, including a governmental split and secession from the Union. In Melville's eyes, they were fanatics who in their blindness could destroy America. Melville was no less frightened by the New England Abolitionists who put all their Puritan zeal into freeing the slaves. In the autumn of 1851, he was able to observe an outburst of activity by Abolitionists in Massachusetts, where New England's traditional Puritan fanaticism began to take on an explosive character. The Abolitionists could not be stopped by reprisals, massacres, or laws; they were prepared to do anything and already felt the warm glow of the martyr's halo above their heads.

It is well known that Melville was on the side of the Abolitionists, although he was not one of them. The idea of eliminating slavery and racial discrimination was dear to him. (It also received symbolic reflection in his novel.) He understood that social evil, embodied concretely in the slave-owning system, was entirely real and not at all imaginary. But he also felt that fanaticism in battle, even in a just cause, could lead to even greater evil, to horrible catastrophe. From this arises the symbol of fanatical madness. Ahab is a strong and noble spirit. He has taken a stand against worldly evil. But he is a fanatic; therefore, his attempt to attain his shining goal is fatal.

So we see that, however complicated, abstract, and universal *Moby Dick*'s system of symbols may be, it has as its basis the living reality of national life.

Melville's artistic study led him to a not-at-all-comforting conclusion. An attempt to formulate in one sentence the philosophical message of *Moby Dick* would produce something like this: In the world (even in the universe), there is no higher power or providential law governing the lives of people and society and bearing responsibility for them. In the fight against evil, man has no mentor or helper. He has nothing but himself to lay his hopes on. This conclusion was monstrous in its boldness: Melville had abolished God. It was not without reason that, in a letter to Hawthorne which he wrote upon finishing *Moby Dick*, he announced, "I have written a wicked book."

Melville's contemporaries did not accept Melville's creation. They preferred not to understand it, alluding to the "strange" and "cloudy" philosophy that permeates the narrative. They were not accustomed to such reading. Only a handful of people—among them, Hawthorne—understood and accepted the novel. So it happened that the White Whale lay down in the depths, only to rise to the surface and show its strength three quarters of a century later.

7

Moby Dick was the high point of Melville's artistic evolution. After it, the descent began. Melville did not begin to write less. In the next five years he created a number of stories and novellas (most of them are included in the collection *Piazza Tales*) and three novels; but none had his former range and depth. Some biographers are inclined to explain this prolific period by the fact that "the devil, with creditors' notes in his pocket," once again "looked in through the open door." It is hard to believe that they are correct. Melville had not exhausted his creative impulse, nor had he lost his taste for literary activity. But this activity now took a different direction.

Of the diverse factors affecting Melville's life after 1851, we will examine two—solitude and the "failure syndrome." Solitude came about as a result of various objective circumstances. Hawthorne left Lenox, moving first to West Newton, then to Concord. Young America disbanded. Quarrels at home estranged Melville somewhat from family life. Melville had never been an introvert; social intercourse was an important part of his existence as a writer. He was now forced to withdraw into himself, and this depressed him. Solitude among people became the latent theme of many of his writings, showing up especially strong in *Bartleby*.

When we speak of the failure syndrome, we are dealing with a fairly complex concept. This refers, of course, to the failure of *Moby Dick*. Melville in no way felt that the novel had been unsuccessful, that he had been unable to accomplish his determined goal; rather, he was quite satisfied with the results of his labor. The failure was of another sort: America had not heard Melville's prophesy. He had been unable to break through to his countrymen's consciousnesses. They were unable, or did not wish, to understand him. The form of the novel itself was unusual, but what prevented the American reader from grasping novelty of form or untraditional ideas? This question led the writer to ponder two important questions. One of these concerned the tastes of the reading public. How do they arise? What forms them? Melville was forced to look at popular fiction, at the vulgar romantic clichés and cheap devices that enthralled the buyers of books. The other question concerned the validity of that system of artistic principles to which Melville adhered and to which we refer today as the "Romantic school." These problems were the basis of several of Melville's stories ("Piazza" and "The Fiddler"), as well as the novel *Pierre, or the Ambiguities*.

Pierre was entirely unlike anything else that had come from Melville's pen. In it, the reader found a full set of Romantic, even "Gothic" clichés: a horribly involved plot, fateful passions, murder, suicide, strains of incestuous love. All of this was accompanied by ironic commentary from the author, who on one hand appeared entirely in earnest, but on the other was in no way able to take seriously the behavior and thoughts of his heroes. We have every reason to consider *Pierre* a malicious parody of the popular fiction of the mid–18th century. But the matter does not end there. *Pierre* is also a novel about literature. Its hero is a young writer trying to make a name for himself by writing novels and stories. Melville guides him through literary circles and salons, through newspapers and publishers, only to bring him to utter defeat. The "literary" part of the novel is written no less maliciously than the Romantic. If we can call the latter a parody, the former fits quite well the definition of satire. Melville spared no one, not even Young America, to whose satirization an entire chapter is dedicated. It must be added that the novel is permeated with self-mockery. Any attempt to define the author's views in *Pierre* inevitably leads to the conclusion that Melville took the position of "ironic romantic," that is, the artist who, according to Schlegel, "looks from above at all things, rising always above all earthly creation, including his own art, virtue, and genius."

As a work of art, *Pierre* does not deserve a high rating, nor does it add to Melville's glory as a writer. But that is not the issue. No writer is insured against failure. What *is* the issue is this: Given the circumstances of America in the mid-1850s, the skepticism of Romantic irony led to the conclusion that the artist is powerless, that any attempts to speak the bitter truth are pointless, since people, guided by their own interests, would not wish to understand it. It is no coincidence that the idea of the uselessness of all books is present in the novel. Apparently this idea had some connection with Melville's own fate as a writer, when he fell silent five years after the publication of *Pierre*.

8

In his novels and stories written during the mid-1850s, Melville constantly turned to those problems which most troubled his contemporaries: war and slavery. It must be stressed, however, that Melville's treatment of these problems was unique. Unlike many of his colleagues, Melville did not choose to examine the problems in a social, political, or religious light. The lessons of *Moby Dick* were not lost on him. He arrived at the same thought as many other Romantics (each by his own path)—specifically, that the future of America depends on the social behavior of Americans and that that behavior is determined by individual morality and social custom. Two generations of Romantics had, over the years, doggedly studied American customs. For better or worse, they had answered the question, "Why are we the way we are?" An answer was essential; without it, no changes for the better were possible. The Romantics of the younger generation, following the example of their elders, again turned to the past, to history. They revived the historical novel but gave it entirely new qualities. They were attracted not to the heroic pages of the glorious past, not to the splendid victories in the War of Independence, but to something else: the historical roots of contemporary customs, the origin of that system of ethical values that was about to destroy their country. The standard of the genre became Hawthorne's *The Scarlet Letter*.

Melville's one historical novel, *Israel Potter: His Fifty Years of Exile*, for all its originality, is entirely characteristic. It is a novel about war and the fate of a soldier, as well as something of a discourse on the idea that "the victor gets nothing." Its hero is a private soldier, a "creator of independent America," one of the tens of thousands of volunteers who gave all for their homeland but received no reward. All his life, the soldier spent in exhausting battle for a piece of bread, yet he died destitute.

What makes *Israel Potter* unique as a historical novel is the fact that historic events, though plenty are included, play only a secondary role. The author's thoughts are expressed mainly through the interactions and relations of the characters. There are four such characters in the novel, all of them real historical figures: the unknown soldier, Israel Potter; the scholar and diplomat, Benjamin Franklin; the adventurer and naval commander, John Paul Jones; and the "hero of the Ticonderoga" and commander of the Green Mountain Boys of Vermont, Ethan Allen.

Melville proceeded from the idea that any morality, individual or social, is formed on the basis of the natural ethical feelings of a person or a people, subject to the influence of defined moral conceptions. The bearer of natural moral feeling in this novel is the hero of the title, a man of the people—farmer, trapper, sailor. He is honest and hard-working. He loves his homeland and is prepared to give up his freedom and life for it. He does not ask himself why he loves it. His involvement in the War of Independence he sees not as duty or responsibility but as natural and necessary. He has a certain inner independence, a spiritual freedom, which determines his actions and words. On the other hand, Israel Potter is a character with almost no individuality. He is sketchy and, to some degree, stereotypical. So he must be. In the author's conception, Israel is less a person than the *possibility* of a person. He is a sort of foundation on which the ideal national character could be formed. His morality is natural, and as such is not suited to social use, as is shown by his bitter fate.

Melville believed that the natural moral foundation of Americans had disappeared under many layers, which stifled the inner freedom and independence of the individual. Too many doubtful rules, too many false representations of the idea of human work, had been hurled at the foundation of that healthy people. What rules and ideas are here referred to? Those we now call the ethics of bourgeois society (or of the business world), which were first formulated for his countrymen by Benjamin Franklin. Not in vain did Melville ignore Franklin's varied activities as scholar, philosopher, enlightener, and diplomat, retaining only one role for him: moralist.

Melville saw Franklin's system of ethics, the alpha and omega of 19th-century bourgeois morality, as a huge web entangling the minds of his countrymen and suppressing the free manifestation of natural moral feeling. Melville was not alone in his belief. We may at least cite Emerson and Thoreau, who were also concerned with this problem. They linked its theoretical solution with the concepts of self-reliance (Emerson) and passive resistance (Thoreau). Melville was acquainted with these ideas and put them to an artistic test in one of his best novellas (*Bartleby*), which is frequently compared to the works of Gogol and Dostoyevsky. The test result was negative. The hero, "relying on himself" and braving "passive resistance," perishes. His opposite (the narrator), who represents Franklin's morality and silences the voice of natural conscience with philanthropic acts, prospers and flourishes. In other words, Melville did not share transcendental optimism. The only spectral hope he could see was in the cloudy image of the New Man, who would appear from the far legendary West in the form of Ethan Allen.

9

These very problems—the problems of correlating morals and customs with social practice, looked at in a psychological and philosophical light—are the subject of Melville's last and most ironic, bitter, and pessimistic novel, *The Confidence-Man*. True, it is difficult to find any work of Melville's from the 1850s in which these problems are not present. Whatever the themes of his stories and novellas—war (*Israel Potter*), slavery ("Benito Cereno," "Encantadas"), the role of art and fate of the artist ("Piazza," "The Fiddler," "The Bell Tower")—they are always treated primarily in a moral-psychological light.

After completing *The Confidence-Man*, Melville felt that he had reached the end of his journey. This was a complicated feeling. He was overwhelmed by exhaustion. That is understandable; in ten years, Melville had written nine novels and a book of stories, not to mention journal articles and essays. His strength had come to an end. But there was something else. Life moved swiftly forward; the Romantic method could no longer grapple effectively with material reality. Melville, the Romantic, felt this acutely. He tried to overcome the crisis of Romantic ideology while remaining within the framework of Romantic thought. Nothing, of course, came of this. He felt that there was nowhere left to go. Melville had run up against a wall. From this came the feeling that his life had been lived out, although he was only thirty-seven years old. From this, too, came a state of depression laid on top of general exhaustion.

In an inexplicable tide of family feeling, Melville's wife, brothers, and many relatives—on his father's (Melville), mother's (Gansevoort), and wife's (Shaw) sides—came to a unanimous conclusion: "Herman must not write any more." The great rebel did not resist this sentence, from which we conclude that he thought the same. Everyone believed that Melville needed rest and travel. His father-in-law even gave him money (on loan, presumably). In the autumn of 1856, a long journey began that lasted a year and a half and remained in Melville's memory for the rest of his life. Among numerous other places, he visited Scotland, London, Liverpool (where he saw his old friend Hawthorne), Malta, Salonika, Constantinople, Alexandria, Cairo, Naples, Rome, Venice, Milan, Turin, Genoa, the Netherlands, England again. Melville's store of impressions was enormous, but he didn't quite know what to do with them; he didn't even take notes.

In the meanwhile, Melville's relatives and friends were engaged in feverish activity, in the hopes of securing for him some sort of governmental appointment, preferably along diplomatic lines. Why not? Irving was ambassador to Madrid, Cooper a consul in Leon, Hawthorne in Liverpool. But their efforts proved in vain. Then a new idea was born: Melville should lecture, particularly as, at that time, writers' lecture tours were widespread. Melville lectured for three years, traveling to the far cities and villages of provincial America. His route stretched from Pittsfield to Tennessee and Ohio, from New York to Baltimore and Milwaukee.

Melville later made several more attempts to enter government service, all unsuccessful. Only in 1866 did he receive the duties of assistant to the inspector of New York customs. A new, unfamiliar life began. He left home in the early morning and worked until evening inspecting freight. In the evenings he worked in his garden, where he cultivated roses. His family was happy: He was not sitting at his desk writing papers. At any hour of the day and in any weather, he could be found in the New York harbor or in the customs office. The work was not easy, but this did not appear to bother him. Melville was a strong man.

The customs job lasted nineteen years. Melville retired in 1885, six years before his death. At first glance, it might seem that American life and literature had passed him by, touching him little. But that is only at a superficial glance. Melville was acutely troubled by the tragic turns in American history. The Civil War and Reconstruction left painful traces in his heart. He refused the status of a professional man of letters but did not cease to be a writer. Only, he now no longer depended on publishers and royalties; he did not need to consider public tastes. He wrote less—only in his free time, of which he had little.

Even at the end of the 1850s, Melville had begun to write poetry, and he continued to write it until his death. His poetic legacy consists of several collections: *Battle Pieces and Aspects of the War* (1866), *John Marr and Other Sailors* (1888), *Timoleon* (1891), the long philosophical poem "Clarel" (1876), and many odd poems, most of which came to light only after his death. As a poet, Melville did not look for popularity. He printed, at his own expense, only twenty-five copies of some of his collections (*John Marr* and *Timoleon*).

On the whole, Melville's poetry has a lyrical-philosophical flavor. In this way, it recalls Emerson's poetic legacy. We must note, however, that it is based not only on abstract reflection but on the real life of America in Melville's time. This is confirmed by his poems about the Civil War (*Battle Pieces*) and the collection *John Marr and Other Sailors*. His contemporaries noted the originality of Melville's poetic form, which differs significantly from that of traditional Romantic poetry and in its structure is often close to prosaic speech. Scholars of our time, with the advantage of perspective, have without difficulty established its connection with Whitman's "free" poetic style. It has become clear that Melville spoke a new word in poetry. Not in vain are his collections now reprinted in editions of many thousands.

After his retirement in 1885, Melville returned once more to literary activity. He had by this time accumulated numerous sketches, notes, and uncompleted poems. He began to systemize them, "put them in order." He was able to publish two more collections during his life; the rest remained in his archive for more than thirty years before coming to light.

The swan song of Melville's late work was the novella *Billy Budd*, which he began working on in 1888 and completed shortly before his death. *Billy Budd* in many ways resembles such works of the 1850s as "Benito Cereno" and *Bartleby*, but, in the interim, much had occurred in America, including the Civil War, all of which had vitally influenced Melville's ideas and his understanding of social ethics. It is not surprising that the resolution of the central conflict between humanity and law in *Billy Budd*, if it is looked at next to Melville's early works, shocks one with its unexpected-

ness and even elicits a feeling of protest in the reader. This was a different
Melville.

   Billy Budd shared the fate of many of Melville's late works. First printed
in 1924, it was immediately recognized as one of the highest achievements
of American short prose. Nobody was surprised by such a rating. By that
time, Melville had occupied his proper place on the American Olympus.

PAVEL BALDITZIN

Mark Twain's *Autobiography*

as an Aesthetic Problem

Mark Twain's *Autobiography* poses serious questions for the scholar. First, the textual ones: In what form should his work be presented? What should be included? How is the author's last will to be determined? Should one observe the chronology of written and oral recollections?[1] Should the material be presented in thematic blocks, as in Bernard DeVoto's *Mark Twain in Eruption* (1940), which served as a kind of supplement to the former? Or should one draw from the enormous mass of Twain's late recollections and reflections only that which provides a "history of his life," as did Charles Neider in his *Autobiography of Mark Twain* (1959)? Each of these approaches has its merits and its failings. Eighty years after Twain's death, there is still no complete scholarly edition of his autobiography.[2]

It is essential, as well, to consider the place of Twain's autobiography in the history of literature and of the genre. It is revealing that in works on the history and theory of autobiography in general, Twain's *Autobiography* barely receives notice; its innovative nature is not fully recognized. Like all of Twain's late works, his autobiography must be analyzed if one is to gain a deeper understanding of the significant break that occurred in American literature at the beginning of the 20th century.

In my opinion, the main question is an aesthetic one: What constitutes the originality of Twain's autobiography, which openly breaks so many accepted rules and taboos in an already free genre of European literature? Wherein lies its innovation? Is it merely an expression of Twain's creative temperament and gift, or did it break new ground in the development of the genre?

A certain traditional perception of this work has gained general acceptance. Most see it as one of the author's late masterpieces, citing the remarkable pages of childhood recollections which unquestionably are among the best of American prose, or the examples of political commentary directed against American plutocracy and imperialism. On the other hand, in reviews, articles, and books, one continues to find criticism of the autobiography's compositional incongruity and inappropriateness to its chosen genre. The explanation for this is generally found in the peculiarities of the author's gift. Mark Twain is usually seen as an intuitive artist, "unconscious and dramatic" (Howells). Twain himself more than once encouraged this view, proclaiming, in his *Autobiography*, the main principle of narrative to be absolute freedom: "the law of the narrative, which has no law" (MTA, I 237). His work, however, always relied on a fully professional approach and a deeply conscious choice of genre-related principles, compositional methods and proportions, and narrative forms and structures. Twain's works are distinguished by free form and a combination of heterogeneous, even conflicting, genre formulas.

Mark Twain based his *Autobiography* on an unexpected, contradictory, but very informative, mix of journal and reminiscence:

> Finally in Florence, in 1904, I hit upon the right way to do an Autobiography: Start it at no particular time of your life; wander at your free will all over your life; talk only about the thing which interests you for the moment. . . . Also, make the narrative a combined Diary and Autobiography. (MTA, I 193)

Citing this, Paine reaches the following conclusion: "I often thought it the best plan for his kind of autobiography, which was really not autobiography at all, in the meaning generally conveyed by that term, but a series of entertaining stories and opinions—dinner table talks, in fact . . ." (MTA, I vii).

In essence, everything is a matter of one's understanding of the genre—either as a canon or a prepared structural model, though it may have several varieties, or as a *genre in development*, which is not defined by strict requirements and prohibitions. In the latter case, the genre serves not only as the body, the form, but as a kind of wave, or energy, embodying the life and individuality of the artist and always destroying petrified literary forms, as has been occurring in all new literature since the end of the 18th century. This is the only possible approach to Mark Twain's work as a whole, and to his autobiography in particular. He wrote: "Within the last eight or ten years I have made several attempts to do the autobiography in one way or another with a pen, but the result was not satisfactory; it was too literary" (MTA, I 237). Twain yearns to break the "too literary" canon of the genre while preserving almost all of its prescriptions, even deliberately parodying them and, breaking its prohibitions, to introduce new forms and methods. Mark Twain is a writer of that era which advanced the slogan "reality and personality" (Zola), the era of experimentation and passion for all things modern. He is a writer who, above all, valued sincerity and directness in the presentation of the creative "I" in any work. In place of objective criteria for the identification of genre, which presume determined thematic or formal boundaries, appear different values: openness, the variability of any genre, flexibility and adaptability for concrete goals—more subjective ideas, which depend upon the aims of the artist himself and the approach of the scholar or critic.

It is worth emphasizing that autobiography developed as a genre with particular intensity during the era of the destruction of aesthetic traditionalism, and did so upon the wreckage of accepted genres—as did, in fact, the novel, which developed under the influence of autobiography—establishing itself outside the system of genres, as a non-genre.

Mark Twain, who highly valued factual literature, was well acquainted with the autobiographical works of his forerunners. He knew the *Confessions* of St. Augustine and *The History of Abelard's Misfortunes* (at least in Lamartine's retelling). He frequently referred to *The Autobiography of Benvenuto Cellini*, Rousseau's *Confessions*, and *The Autobiography of Benjamin Franklin*, which he often parodied. Twain had also read various memoirs, including those of Kazanova and Saint Simon. He had a good understanding of the structural principles of these genres; however, he chose for himself the *law of creative free play, literary clownery, combining a serious and a humorous view of the world*, embodied in the form of lively improvised conversation. An analytical and rational approach—an explanation of his own personality and fate—is only an element of this play; its main features are the spontaneous emergence of the character of Samuel Clemens/Mark Twain, the affirmation of the relativity of any limitations to character, including those of genre, and the conscious aestheticization of the plasticity and limitlessness of human nature.

The task of autobiography is postulated by its name. Contemporary literary scholarship has revealed within it the following structural contradictions: The human self is simultaneously the subject and object of the description; the internal and external aspects of the self; "I" and "others"—the individual and history, that is, the facts and meaning of life, its sum, or, as a theorist of the genre, G. Gusdorf, has expressed it, the "diagram of fate": the unity and contrast of chance and natural order in a life, of its integrity and incompleteness, of the striving for objectivity as opposed to self protection or self-glorification, and of honesty and invention, "poetry and truth," as Goethe expressed it in the title of one of his autobiographical books. What's more, the writer's autobiography, like the painter's self-portrait, is a mirror not only of his life but of his creative manner, the embodiment of his artistic world, method, and style. In any autobiography, as in memoirs, there exists a contradiction between past and present, between the former, younger self and the present, wiser one.

Scholars generally consider the best-defined and most adequate form of autobiography to be the "history of the soul"—the confession, the search for self-knowledge—although another variety stands out as well: the external, in which "the public sector of existence" dominates.[3] Twain's autobiography is seen as an example of the external type. Indeed, many people and events are described in it, both celebrated and unknown: General Grant and President Theodore Roosevelt, the author's parents and family, Bret Harte, American humorists, the inventor Paige and the storyteller Gillis—so that some have reached the conclusion that it is not an autobiography at all but ordinary reminiscences. Nonetheless, Samuel Clemens' history of the soul is presented in the autobiography, although, naturally, in Mark Twain's familiar key—via the external embodiment of inner states and troubles, more dramatically than introspectively, and more in comic play than in analysis.

The fundamental contradiction of the *Autobiography* lies in the fact that both object and subject are contained in one person. A person—in his or her own perception—is never complete, cannot be limited physically or qualitatively. Self-knowledge merely imitates an external approach, as we perceive ourselves not analytically but synthetically and intuitively, not formally but *in process*. Even the limitations of space and time in our lives are seen only relatively, through others.

We can observe neither of the natural boundaries of life: birth and death. Even so, death is implied in autobiography, and many works in this genre have been intended for posthumous publication, as the title of Chateaubriand's *Memoirs from the Grave* suggests. This is present in Twain's *Autobiography*, which begins with the preface, "As From The Grave." In it, the author points to the love letter: "the frankest and freest and privatest product of the human mind and heart" (MTA, I xi). Here, already, is a paradox: a "love letter from the grave." However, an appeal to the future is emphasized here, along with a striving for sincerity and freedom of speech.

Freedom, to Mark Twain, does not at all signify self-exposure, as in the *Confessions* of Rousseau, but first and foremost a rejection of the fetters, of the formulas and literariness of autobiography. Freedom and sincerity of self-expression are a rejection of volition, a subordination to general and higher strengths, to one's own talent and temperament, reflections and recollections, which form, as if by themselves, the stream of life and consciousness that carry and form a person, simultaneously revealing that person; a subordination, finally, to future, posthumous, fate and judgment. The goal of autobiography is truth, not only in the everyday and the psychological sense but as a reflection of the author's deepest thoughts on man and religion, on society and government. Twain's *Autobiography* destroyed the illusions of American consciousness, which its author himself shared—destroyed them directly, in chapters of commentary, as well as by means of its entire structure, its incompleteness, its many layers and voices. Yet, unfortunately, it is a work that remained nearly unknown in its entirety to the succeeding generation of Americans. It reflects epoch-making shifts in human consciousness and in the structure of European culture at the turn of the century.

The limits of human individuality are not felt from within; we feel, rather, our own limitlessness. Mark Twain frequently describes himself as one of the heroes of a narrative. Here, the artistic doubling of his character comes to his aid. The persona of the comic hero-narrator Mark Twain is conceived and realized in literary play in the guise of Clemens.

Mr. Clemens' character traits are described in the spirit of Mark Twain. A revealing example is "A Corn Pone Prayer" (dict. 15.08.1906—MTE, 107–109), which presents a psychological analysis of the clash between interests and ideals, in the form of a humorous anecdote, based on the well-known scriptural phrase, "Ask and ye shall receive," which recalls one of the fabliaux by Jean Bodel, *De Brunain la vache au prestre*. The comic presentation takes away none of the depth of the psychological trauma of the child who has discovered the following: "I had found out that I was a Christian for revenue only and I could not bear the thought of that, it was so ignoble." But, after confessing this to his mother, "I gathered from what she said that if I would continue in that condition I would never be lonesome."

Mark Twain recognizes and reveals the peculiarity of his character, his paradoxes. Recalling the difficult days when, in the first year of their life together, the Clemens home in Buffalo was transformed into an infirmary—Olivia fell ill during her pregnancy with their first child, while her best friend was dying—the author notes: "The resulting periodical and sudden changes of mood in me, from deep melancholy to half-insane tempests and cyclones of humor, are among the curiosities of my life. During one of these spasms of humorous possession I sent down to my newspaper office . . . [an] absurd map of Paris. . . ." (MTE, 250). So the humorous story, "The Fortifications of Paris," is explained and unexpectedly continued while, simultaneously, the other side of laughter is revealed: It is born of suffering and pain.

Twain's character not only is revealed, it is shown in the making, in its development. Moreover, the author proceeds in the 19th-century tradition, beginning his life story with family history, describing the two lines of his descent: His mother's side is traced back to the earls of Durham; his father's line included the judge who sent King Charles I of England to the scaffold. It was from him that Twain inherited his anti-monarchist and revolutionary inclinations, which manifested themselves both in his character and in his work until the last years of his life. Citing his own joke, that of his ancestry, he chose not the aristocratic line but this very Clemens, "who did something; something which was very creditable to him and satisfactory to me," Mark Twain emphasizes: "Ostensibly this was chaff, but at the bottom it was not. I had a very real respect for that ancestor, and this respect has increased with the years, not diminished" (MTA, I 121). Not only his family roots are considered but also his upbringing, surroundings, soil—the plot of land in Tennessee, for instance, which had such a powerful influence on the life of the Clemens family, on the formation of their characters over several generations. "It kept us hoping and hoping during forty years, and forsook us at last. It put our energies to sleep and made visionaries of us—dreamers and indolent. We were always going to be rich next year—no occasion to work" (MTA, I 94). Reading this confession and the stories about his brother, Orion, and his Uncle James, who was the prototype for Colonel Sellers, one begins to understand much about the character and fate of the author.

The analysis of Twain's own personality rests on the concepts of heredity and environment, although they too become the object of humor. The discussion of hereditary character traits leads to an unexpected conclusion:

> Whenever we have a strong and persistent and irradicable instinct, we may be sure that it is not original with us, but inherited—inherited from away back, and hardened and perfected by the petrifying influence of time. Now I have been always and unchangingly bitter against Charles, and I am quite certain that this feeling trickled down to me through the veins of my forebears. . . . And I have always felt friendly toward Satan. Of course, that is ancestral; it must be in the blood, for I could not have originated it. (MTA, I 83)

Mark Twain explains this, too—quite realistically—as the spiritual legacy of his mother, of her capacity for suffering. "Her interest in people and other animals was warm, personal, friendly," he writes:

> She was the natural ally and friend of the friendless. It was believed that, Presbyterian as she was, she could be beguiled into saying a soft word for the devil himself. . . . This friend of Satan was a most gentle spirit, and an unstudied and unconscious pathos was her native speech. (MTA, I 116–17)

The serious and the comic, the concrete and the abstract, the external and the internal—all are inseparable in Twain's recollections. This synthesis is directly realized in many characters and events.

Characters in the recollections become, in essence, embodiments of Twain's internal life, stages in its development. Mark Twain tells of a Scotsman named MacFarlane whom he met in Cincinnati around 1856, when he, the future writer, was twenty years old and MacFarlane, an expert on the English dictionary and the Bible, was forty. The portrait of the homespun philosopher, which is itself based on the contrast with Clemens, both in MacFarlane's age and in his humorless character, brings out, first of all, the peculiarities of Clemens himself, who is self-taught; more interested in historical, scientific, and philosophical books than in fiction; and attempting to understand what exactly man is.

What are the limits of our "I"? How is it shaped? These are questions that every autobiography attempts to answer. The events of life, people, in one way or another influencing the formation of character, consciously or unconsciously chosen as examples for emulation—all of this necessarily enters the makeup and structure of our self. Twain's *Autobiography* issues from this premise, showing how the external becomes internal, how circumstances form character; the process of recollection provides an image and its explanation.

Usually in autobiography, one voice prevails—that of the author—although a polemic is felt as well. Mark Twain strives to surmount this necessity of the genre by including in his work, as he often did in his pamphlets, various documents, other people's words and letters, other voices. His unexpected, and truly brilliant, discovery is a *polyphonic form of autobiography* in which various points of view interact around the main subject. Twain does this best in his reminiscences of family life, which were supplemented by his biography written by his daughter, Susy. She helps us to see Twain from the outside, from, in fact, an unusual side. The daughter's text interweaves with the general flow of Twain's narrative, providing the autobiography with a sense of dialogue, making it stereoscopic. Other autobiographies have similar inclusions; but it is only with Twain that this becomes a conscious and regular artistic method.

The humorous play organizes various points of view. For example, Clemens' physical appearance is described through the juxtaposition of two portraits: one false, based on the ready formula of a comparison with another person, taken from a Philadelphia newspaper of 1864, which caused bitterness in its object. The other—as Twain says, the "impartial opinion" of his daughter, a naive and touching text—provides something more than a portrait, revealing a sense of love and joy in family relations free from sugar-coated sentimentality, of which the humorist Twain was an enemy. In this way also, certain, difficult problems for the writer are dodged, such as the conflict between his goals and the literary tastes of the time, as presented through the eyes and pen of his beloved wife, Livy. This is expressed in the *Autobiography* by means of the family game of censorship, in which Livy crosses out the parts Twain's daughters particularly like. Twain does not avoid discussion of his artistic compromises but presents them via conflicting views and comic play.

The polyphony and stereoscopic quality do not disappear in those places where it seems that Twain's view prevails, such as the descriptions of American humorists or of Bret Harte. The literary portrait of this writer, who has outlived his glory, is magnificent. His behavior and psychology are presented in interaction with the author and other people. The key episode is the story of Clemens' quarrel with Harte, who had personally attacked Clemens' wife. This episode explains much about Twain's character as well, showing his love, faithfulness, and chivalry toward his wife. Twain does not conceal his biases; he emphasizes his hostility toward Harte but, at the same time, continuously notes his positive qualities. Twain's explanations of Harte's personality reveal his own; his recollections of another man supplement his self-portrait, revealing the author's self.

Any autobiography, like any memoir, is built on the meeting of two times, two "I's": present and past. Facts, the author's feelings and thoughts, are all presented in the most recent interpretation and light. Their truth is relative, as is the idea of the natural order of fate. From this come the contradictions of the genre. Mark Twain reveals this conflict, expressing it through transitions from memoir to diary, and vice versa. In his recollections of childhood he revives the feelings of a little boy with nostalgia and love, creating, as in *The Adventures of Tom Sawyer*, "the psalm in prose." The author doesn't conceal his position: "I know how a boy looks behind a yard-long slice of that melon, and I know how he feels; for I have been there" (MTA, I iii). The idyllic scene concludes, fully to Twain's taste, with a comic judgment: "I know the taste of the watermelon which has been honestly come by, and I know the taste of the watermelon which has been acquired by art. Both taste good, but the experienced know which tastes best." Sincerity acted upon by humor. In other places, the author, turning to current affairs, emphasizes his interest, which makes way for discussion of topical events, as in the beginning of the sketch about the killing of 600 Moros (MTA, II 187). The description of his daughter Susy's death is wedged between two political lampoons, as events in public life intrude on family affairs.

Twain's *Autobiography* is extraordinarily expressive in its presentation of the author's personality via the very shift of his interests and the subjects of his judgments or recollections. The uneven rhythm of his character and fate are tangible in these shifts. In its pacing and style, this work conveys Twain's biological rhythm, the sociorhythm of his life. Its improvisational form is remarkably appropriate to its task. As at a jazz concert, the reader feels the heat of his soul, hears the sounds of Twain's living voice.

Autobiography is a special genre, belonging at once to different spheres and existing on the border between life and art. First and foremost, it is a document with historical, social, or didactic meaning; it doesn't exist "in itself" and "for itself," like the novel or story. The *Autobiography* is an appendix to life, an attempt to explain or express it. A piece of art is teleological; that is, it has a super-objective, to use Stanislavsky's word. It is built with an understanding of its end; therefore, in any turn of events, in any character, there is a certain finiteness—the author's position. Mark Twain was beautifully able to structure the plots of his works and draw characters, but he understood all the impossibility—the literariness and artificiality—of such an approach to himself. In such a case, the living, incomplete person becomes the hero of a novel, a defined character or model, as in Benjamin Franklin's *Autobiography* or *The Education of Henry Adams*.

Twain's personality in his autobiography is defined only in the given situation, in specific stories or episodes. In general, it is inherently un-finished; one image or state is incongruous with another, subsequent, image or state. Unexpectedly, the hero appears, emerges as if by chance, doing so most strongly through spontaneous utterances, gestures, and actions, in various planes—from without and within and, most of all, in the very process of creation, of telling. The teleology is externalized. The completeness of separate episodes, passages, and arguments only high-lights the incompleteness and flow of the composition, the personal open-ness, the many meanings of fate. The entire sum of methods in Twain's *Autobiography*—its improvisational nature, the lack of chronology in the recounting of his life, the associative approach, the emphatic use of in-vention, the changeability of the person of the author/hero—opens it to any reading and opinion, even to any principle of presentation. It ad-dresses not the past but the future, as its conclusion can be found only in history through the eyes of descendants, readers, scholars, and publishers. This looking to the future in Twain's *Autobiography* is not a formula but the whole form of the work.

In life and history, any fate has no single meaning. There are no closed endings, as values change. Mark Twain was aware of this cardinal element in the understanding of any person. He chose not to draw a "diagram of his fate"; he wrote a cardiogram that must still be interpreted. A novel portrays the incompleteness of the person only in the development of its plot. Completion comes with the ending. That is the freezing point where Tom Sawyer ends up one and unchangeable, like Oliver Twist or Julien Sorel, although perceptions of literary characters are also subject to change.

One more factor: Which occurrences, events, and meetings are important in a person's life, and which are not? What is worth inclusion in an autobiography, and what may be left out? Twain's position is that not only famous people but even the most unnoticed may be present in an autobiography—for instance, not only important thoughts but sometimes chance ones "about tautology and grammar" or about the German language. He affirms the significance of the private and the apparently unimportant; it is through this that the person is revealed.

The inclusion of pamphlets and commentary is integral to Twain's *Autobiography*, although such sections are found in other examples of the genre as well. Not only "life" but "opinions" are the subject of autobiography. Many pages of the book are given over to political satire and to discussion of man and history, religion and morality. In this way, the personality of the writer is revealed from yet another side; the reader learns directly the author's world-view, his opinions on various eternal and topical problems. And again, the explanation is externalized, opened to future interpretation.

Not surprisingly, the position of the author of an autobiography is usually extremely biased, since every person is forced to assert himself in struggle and conflict with others. The author of his own life can go nowhere outside himself; he cannot escape the confines of his own personality. He cannot objectively judge his life, does not want to blacken it—others generally do that—and so it ends up that many works of this genre become apologies for the authors' lives, self-glorification or self-justification. Here is yet another paradox of autobiography: When describing a character, even one close to himself, the author maintains his distance; when describing himself, he is, in principle, unable to do this, as at any given moment he is, as a character, incomplete, not fixed. As he becomes aware of himself, he changes. Because of this, autobiographies do not usually embrace life's entire journey but only certain parts of it—as a rule, childhood, youth, and perhaps other important stages. Twain endeavors to overcome these limitations of the genre, to present himself even in his later years, only not descriptively, in recollection, but directly, through opinions and spontaneous comments on various events.

The form, or—as one scholar has expressed it, the "anti-form" of Twain's *Autobiography*—entails the inclusion of whole works, fictional and philosophical. For instance, the inclusion of "Captain Stormfield" is not one more of Twain's jokes, although there is a measure of humor in it, but the revelation of an important principle, as the *Autobiography* is constructed on continuous reference to the writer's work. *Tom Sawyer* and *Huck Finn*, as well as the circumstances surrounding the creation of many of his works, are all present. Just as Villon included most of his poetry in his *Lais* and *Testament*, so does almost all of Twain's work appear in his *Autobiography*—in references, commentary, and even directly. That is, the *Autobiography* is conceived not as a separate and complete work but as a kind of supplement and afterword to other books, such as *The Innocents Abroad* and *Roughing It*. Its super-objective is to embrace all of Twain's writing. The autobiography is thus both a part of Twain's work and the whole, a reflection of the writer's entire life. This is an unusual and extraordinarily fruitful aesthetic system, open, inherently, to all genres and forms, able to take in even material formerly unthinkable in such a genre, and to transmit it.

Mark Twain's *Autobiography* is a play on genre in which all standards and clichés of the form are used, while, at the same time, new possibilities are searched for, both through parody and through the use of principles of other genres. The traditional idea of autobiography is burst, as the late Mark Twain burst in eruption of his humor many stable views of the time.

Mark Twain constructs his *Autobiography* not as a confession or a *bildungsroman* but as a collection of books of various forms and genres. It is an encyclopedia of one man, a testament, an endeavor to collect everything lived and thought, written and told. From this comes its structure, more reminiscent of "sacred writings," of the Bible. A person is an entire universe; the history of his life could be equal to the history of a people—such was the general belief in the 19th century. Twain creates a form adequate to this task, capturing his life in the most varied perspectives and genres.

The main object of all Twain's late work is the reconsideration of values, the destruction of the myths of American and European culture, including: the Christian religion and the belief, since the Enlightenment, in the goodness of human nature, bourgeois democracy and individualism, and the position of the Anglo-Saxon race and the United States in the world. This is manifested in several sarcastic parodies, from the short *A Salutation-Speech from the XIXth Century to the XXth* to the extensive *Soliloquys* of the Belgian king and Russian czar, in his *parodia sacra*—in *Letters from the Earth*, in which he parodies the Old Testament, and in *The Mysterious Stranger*, in which he parodies the Gospels. In both of these last, the main role is played by Satan, who holds an unfavorable opinion of man and civilization. The *Autobiography* also strives to reevaluate philosophical and religious, social and political foundations of Western culture, not for the sake of destruction or of humor but in the hope of discovering new cultural forces and of preserving true values: the independently thinking person who does not yield to the pressure of the crowd; a society based on the principles of justice and cooperation; friendship and respect between peoples, between all people; equality and peace. At the same time, the harsh criticism of all European culture in Twain's late work is an affirmation of the best of that culture. The crisis in it is reflected in Twain's writings, particularly in his *Autobiography*. It is a turning point toward a new perception of man and the world—from a closed perception of one's own country, people, and continent to a global vision, from an isolated idea of human personality to a universal one.

In the last years of his life, Mark Twain leaned toward the idea of cyclical history and the "triumph over man"—a most incomplete being, slave to events and circumstances. This is felt in his *Autobiography*. Yet, even so, he was unable to draw pessimistic conclusions from these views. Such thoughts, on his lips, are tempered by laughter, filled with irony. They are built on paradoxical combinations of mutually exclusive theories and subordinated to the general spirit of free artistic play, in quasiphilosophical works such as *What Is Man?*, in satires such as *In Defense of General Funston*, and in autobiography.

Twain's creative individuality is revealed not only internally and externally but in a third dimension as well: *in the process of his artistic mastery of the world around him*. In his *Autobiography*, a politician describes his plans and actions, a religious man his approach to God, the artist his fantasies and creations. But the writer has the unique ability to more fully embody himself in words, realizing his own self in the text on the levels of genre, form, and style. This is the core of autobiography: the person writing, creating. The book's aesthetic sense of integrity is in its style, in the image of the Mark Twain remarkably familiar to us by his works, yet always revealing new sides and traits in his *Autobiography*. The artist is a harmonizing whole, not in the sense of formal completion or genre definition but as the genius, permeating everything, to the last comma, making even the words and views of others his own.

The main hero of the *Autobiography*, as in many of Twain's stories and comic sketches, is a peculiar clown portrayal, both of the author, Samuel Clemens, and of the ordinary American, a man of his time and people, in whom are embodied certain traits of national character. The principles of his construction are a creative game Twain plays with himself—with his life, the surrounding world, the reader, finally, at its heart, *transition and swing of opposites*—from naiveté to experience, from limitation and foolishness to wisdom and depth, from sincerity to deceit, from truth to invention. These jumps, crossings, and changes reflect the essence of Twain's vision, which is based on humorous *l'envers universe*, on a comic turned-over-world. Coupling—a characteristic feature of the laughter tradition, as of all comic literature—is the essence of Mark Twain, the comic "twin" of Samuel Clemens, as is emphasized by the pseudonym. The *Autobiography* exposes the dialectics of the life and work of the character and image of Twain—person and persona.

The untraditional, paradoxical nature of Twain's autobiography, built on the foundation of aesthetic freedom and openness, reflects one of the major directions of the new era in literature, the essence of which is the highest possible development of creative individuality and the emergence of talent, free of the constraints of tradition in genre or in literature as a whole.

DMITRY URNOV

The Russian Man
at Russell Square

Reflections on the Critical Conception

of T. S. Eliot

> T. S. Eliot used No. 24, where
> he worked in the editorial office
> of Faber and Faber, as his
> London address.
> —*The Oxford Literary Guide to
> the British Isles*

Upon finding myself in Russell Square, I went up to No. 24, and saw a sign reading: "Entrance around the corner." It looked like a footnote in the spirit of Eliot. One heads for a primary source, and is told to "look somewhere else," but "somewhere else" the question is not particularly cleared up either.

"Eliot is difficult" is the persistent categorization of him, the persistent general opinion, extending not only to his poetry but to his articles as well. Have we, however, met no other theoreticians whose thought was complicated and expressed in a complicated way? Is he really more diffi-cult than Kant? The difficulty in Eliot is specific, lying, above all, in the fact that we often cannot find, either in the text or in the subtext, those

theses which have proved so influential. The difficulty is in the elu-
siveness.

Turning to Eliot's articles, we indeed find ourselves in a difficult position. The dictionary fails us. "He never makes it very clear what he means
by analysis," if, by *analysis*, we are to understand at least a selective critique
of literary phenomena.[1] Much else remains equally unclear in Eliot's positions, from specific ideas to entire conceptions, although in works on him
we often meet the familiar formulations: "Eliot developed," "Eliot
showed." In fact, if we focus on the available main works, Eliot developed
nothing and showed nothing. He has, in fact, not one scholarly paper. If
he did write one, then it was something fundamentally different from the
traditional ideas of literary-critical activity. Reading Eliot, we find ourselves not in the world of particular ideas, but in the world of a particular
relationship to ideas. Eliot puts forward not at all what he thinks, but
what—or, rather, how—things seem to him. He offers the play of ideas as
fundamental, substantially proven, mandatory positions. By whom and
where "proven"? On this point, Eliot follows with provisos and excuses,
which generally boil down to the idea that this could all be proven and
shown, but that, for lack of time, with one thing and another, somehow
never comes around. "He implies a re-reading of the entire course of
English literature, but he leaves it to others to fill in the details."[2] When
"others," rolling up their sleeves, attempt to construct such a system to
support Eliot's generalizing, sketchy ideas, nothing comes of it; concrete-
historical details don't fit into the scheme.

We have already come across a similar situation—in the Romantic
period, when a fragment, called a "fragment," was created as a finished
work; when the interpretation of a work was actually another work, a
creation about a creation; when a thought broken off was, in fact, complete in its "incompletion." But, we must recall, such a "fragment" cannot
be completed; such an "interpretation" itself demands critical interpretation. The "broken-off" thought cannot be thought through to its end.
Irony came into the Romantics' world-view just as the distance between
idea and fact underlay their special observation. They lived in search of
possibility, seeing possibility as possibility, making ends meet, if necessary,
at the cost of their own lives. This is why Eliot's method—or, rather, his
manner of reasoning, which he defined himself as thinking on the order of
"metaphorical fantasizing"—merely resembles the Romantics' freedom of
thought. For the Romantics, *possibility* is the search for an organic natural

law, revealed or not in whichever direction one gropes (or revealed only to a certain degree, in "pieces"). For Eliot, who spoke constantly of possibility—or, to be more precise, of the effort to "make possible"—it was merely a search for a practical solution, one not meant to have universal-fundamental significance.

Why did all this take root so firmly in English soil? One fact is beyond doubt: All of Eliot's opponents—even the most extraordinary and qualified, who tried to show how he "mythologized" or, simply speaking, constantly cheated—turned out to be weaker than he was. There was some strength on his side—above all, the strength of opinion—which supported him in the face of any argument.

It is sometimes said that Eliot's critical articles made a strong impression with their specialized nature, that he judged poetry like a poet and, thanks to this, revealed a new path. It is enough to recall how widespread "literature on literature" was at the turn of the century, to establish that, in and of itself, the "philosophy of composition" could not give Eliot an exclusive place in the literary field of his time. A service record for the introduction of new ideas and methods was issued retroactively by Eliot scholars; today, not one of these ideas is credited to Eliot. Rejection of the "biographical method"—the principle of "close reading," and so forth—drew attention, in its day, as an idea specifically Eliot's. But none of those ideas was his own. Combining the ideas of others into some new fusion—that is Eliot.

It is necessary to examine the core that united the ideas. This core is found between Eliot's poetry and his criticism. The two sides of his activity contrast with each other: chaos/strict organization, rebellion/orthodoxy, nihilism/establishment. Even the intonation of Eliot's poetry and articles gives the impression that behind the poetic and prosaic lines, two different voices are heard. One voice belongs to a despairing, over-strained decadent, the other to a "dictator." Decadent weakness and dictatorial strictness, but none of the normal, intermediate steps. The ruined, obsolete losers at whom the poet now laughs, now cries, make up an audience whom the critic-theoretician addresses with ideas of "order" and "tradition." What can be the real content of those ideas, if "hollow men" are called upon somehow to realize them—"shape without form, shade without colour"? The answer is clear: opinions put into circulation one at a time, playing the role of "ideas." Playing the role, indeed; in his way, Eliot was right when he shrugged his shoulders, perplexed as to why his utterances were quoted so stubbornly. They are not *utterances* in the traditional sense of the word, when a person says what he means (with Eliot, utterances are a representation of the process of speaking, possible under the given circumstances); if there are no such possibilities, that person must search for others.

If, for the Romantics, incompleteness and fragmentariness were elevated to genre and method, this was done with the awareness of inadequacy before truth, with enormous effort and thought. Outwardly, Eliot argued with the Romantics; but he used their ideas, and he raised imprecision to a method—not, however, in the form of whimsy (we find that with the decadents—Remy de Gourmont, for instance). On the contrary, Eliot has an apparently strict construction of historical-literary schemes, which, without exception, are just as loose as they appear strict. This is not the traditional pursuit of the market, but a position that is normal in its way, accessible to one aware of his own inner emptiness. Such emptiness is not a vice, against which the mind in crisis can somehow struggle. It is the historical lot of "hollow" men, historically, socially, even individually empty. With precise psychological calculation, Eliot appealed to them. "Paralysed force, gesture without motion," he wrote of them in poetry. In articles, the same paralysis becomes the building material of Eliot's conceptions. Paradoxically, he "rebelled." In no way did he try to remove fetters; instead, he laid on new ones. In the words of one critic, that "enslavement"—within the framework of Eliot's ideas of "order," "tradition," the "classics" and "culture"—was called upon not to eliminate emptiness but to protect it from outside, critical infringement.

If Paul Valery, who, like Remy de Gourmont, suggested a great deal to Eliot, needed disclaimers to justify creative sterility and forcedness (in "Letter on Mallarme," for instance), Eliot boldly proceeded from the idea of creative crisis. He and his position represent the Hegelian idea of the secularization of art—only not in the early stage, when various forms of spiritual activity break free from the power of religion and gain independence, but in the last stage, when there is liberation from any halo of "holiness" (understood, of course, as a certain inspired mystery). That is the essence of it. Its power—that is, the reason it became widespread and had such influence on people's minds—lay in its indication of a way out of the crisis situation, a way convenient and accessible to many: the declaration of our century as "critical"—in other words, not creative. Thus, literature is moved to a secondary position as "raw material for the critical industry."

Eliot elevated "failure" to the status of a rule—a theory of creative failure without such provisos as "even if only" and "despite." Eliot had his own disclaimers, of another nature:

> Eliot has created and imposed a taste—a set of habits in reading and writing—of very high standards; [he] has set going a serious criticism with respect to these standards; and [he] has set abroad a current of ideas which [have] vitalized the profession of literature by reducing the claims made for it and then eloquently affirming the claim that was left.[3]

This is an authoritative opinion. It was not enough to evaluate that opinion as expressed; it has been suffered through and tested by the author on himself. Having agreed to the well-foundedness of the opinion, however, we must decipher it. After all, the claims of "the profession of literature" have undergone a long evolution, from the ideas of the independence of art—maintained by romanticism, with Kant at the head (more precisely, *in* the head)—to various degrees and sorts of doubt in the power of art or, at least, in the ability of people to master that power. Even with the Romantics, the need arose for "creative behavior" to supplement creativity itself. At the end of the Romantic era, the same idea, in an entirely contemporary form, was developed by Kierkegaard. Reflecting on the nature of art, Baudelaire, following Coleridge and Poe, introduces the epoch-making proviso: "not only a poet, but a philosopher as well." Thus, because of a lack of strength on the part of the "poet," the "philosopher," or the "scholar" to stand alone, the surge of creativity is shored up with calculation and philosophy, on the principle not of abundance but of insufficiency. Finally, at the end of the century, various ideas were developed about the mutual fulfillment of the arts, the unification of science and art, and so forth. Which claims for literature were thrown off and which maintained under the influence of Eliot's authority?

How, for instance, did Eliot change and virtually solve the debate over *Ulysses* in the 1920s? When his opponents were engaged with the usual critical issues—was it a good or a bad, was it readable or not, was the author successful—Eliot, not even touching on any of those matters, stated the question in a completely different way. He did not ask, "Can this book be read?" but, "Can it be used as a literary standard?" He answered in the affirmative.

In her diary, Virginia Woolf—who was close to the epicenter of that whole literary earthquake and who had read *Ulysses* with an extreme, special interest, sincerely did not know what to think of the book, whether or not it was literature. But then, as if by military decree, a tactical decision was made concerning how one must view the book. Eliot wrote:

> I hold this book to be the most important expression which the present age has found; it is a book to which we are all indebted, and from which none of us can escape. These are the postulates for anything that I have to say about it, and I have no wish to waste the reader's time by elaborating my eulogies; it has given me all the surprise, delight, and terror that I can require, and I will leave it at that.[4]

That is what Eliot said of *Ulysses*.

Eliot says "surprise, delight, and terror"; he does not say whether he read the book. Nit-picking? Oh, no. This is Eliot; his text is a system of signals; painstakingly and with difficulty, he places the words on paper as if offering an intellectual game to the reader. With each turn, Eliot glances up significantly and asks: Does the reader understand where this is leading? All the while, he avoids the question of whether the book can be read.

The same thing is evident in light of other opinions of *Ulysses*, expressed at the same time, such as that of Arnold Bennett, who admitted having difficulty getting through Joyce. Making this admission in the spirit of Eliot—who, as he did in the case of *Ulysses*, always chose his words with great care—Bennett said: "We can understand the author," and, "He must be appreciated." For Eliot, who grew up on philosophy and who elevated a way of reasoning to the level of basic gnosiological method, there was nothing accidental in the choice of certain words and the omission of others. This should not be understood literally, as if Eliot advised judging a book without having read it. If he says that *Ulysses* surprised and delighted him, then he must have read the novel. But that has no significance for its evaluation! This is the essence of the matter. What is important is the book's impression, as a basis for judgment; the intermediate process, for the sake of which literature exists, is not considered.

In *Ulysses*, Eliot saw a fact that would become typical, that would grow into a phenomenon and give birth to an entire "population" of producers and consumers of similar literary-critical production. Similarly, it was not the psychologically remarkable episodes from *Ulysses* that Eliot defended; they needed no defense. Other critics did not deny Joyce's merits, though they did doubt the mechanical construction and therefore the sterility of his effort to create a contemporary epos or, at least, an anti-epos. But that was what Eliot did not doubt; after all, he was never interested in any realistic, or even feasible, solution to the literary-critical problem. "All that only gets in the way," he once said of the formulation of various critical questions; and he put forth completely different ones, beyond the sphere of creative organics.

Noticing a problem, Eliot searched not for a way to solve it, but for a way to use the "promising" problem that arose. Holding to this position, it is natural to seek the most malleable sides in any question; often, those are found far from any fruitful path one might find in trying to solve the problem. I repeat: Eliot was a pragmatist; he understood the solution of any problem only in the form of organized "possibilities." The question of how artistic a work *Ulysses* truly is did not interest him. Eliot saw in Joyce's book a possible and needed center for the unification of distinct literary opinions.

To a certain extent, critical misses and blunders can be explained by the polemics. Problems whose solutions demanded new methods and new designations were, in their time, held in typical Victorian disregard. Descriptive investigation of literature as an object was hindered by confusion between ethical and aesthetic ideas. "What value is and which experiences are most valuable will never be understood so long as we think in terms of those large abstractions, the virtues and the vices," wrote I. A. Richards.[5] The main vice of old criticism, which was called "romantic and impressionistic," was thought to be, "to know when we are not talking about poetry but about something else suggested by it."[6] In other words, preconception, an arbitrariness of sorts, laxness. For this reason, the founders of the new criticism, with few exceptions, rejected rapture and censure, which had been lavished by 19th-century criticism, as a serious evaluative system. Striving to answer the most essential critical questions, the progenitors of the new schools measured art and the history of literature not by "fits of inspiration" but as a process that slowly and gradually produces a genuine and significant result, accumulated through general, shared effort. From this, we may assume, comes Eliot's subordination of individual talent to tradition, his sadly famous phrase "Great poets steal." For this reason, F. R. Leavis drew up a "great tradition" of second-rate writers. This is the beginning of a subsequent lowering of the critical language—in essence, a restructuring of critical values, a restructuring caused by the fact that a writer is now seen not as a creator and artist, but as a craftsman. Instead of saying "a work of art is created," the question of "how the book is made" is addressed.[7] Critical evaluation, accordingly, becomes "not a mystic rapture but a process."[8]

However, enough time has passed since that system was advanced for both its polemics and its real principles to become clear. Why did a distortion that was temporary and polemical take hold and become a position, a method? Is there no organic property here, due to which we hear over and over, like an old clock with moving figurines, always the same minuet? Not only is Henry James judged according to his merits, but *Hamlet* must, to be consistent, be admitted an "unsuccessful play" (Eliot's opinion). Defoe is not considered true art; Dickens is not included in the "great tradition" (Leavis's opinion)? Why, then, all these gears and screws, fit together with much difficulty, if we know they tell the wrong time?

Ben Jonson, for instance, drew the attention of scholars as a writer who theorized.[9] Eliot swept aside scholarly efforts: "It only fails to remodel the image of Jonson which is settled in our minds."[10] The remodeling undertaken by Eliot consisted of proof of the unprovable or, in any case, unproved in the course of the centuries since "rare Ben" came to be recognized as a classic. Eliot's remodeling began with the wish not to recognize that Ben Jonson is not entirely solid as an artist. Eliot stated the question thus: "Jonson has suffered in public opinion, as anyone must suffer who is forced to talk about his art."[11] "Forced" by whom? Why "forced"? Forced by the nature of his talent, which was significant, verging on brilliance, on Shakespeare, but which, all the same, was creatively insufficient—this would seem clear. But Eliot proposes that we make an effort, just one effort! According to Eliot, we have to accept a certain "if," a condition, having met which we will receive "satisfaction"; that is, the reader's perception of the plays of Ben Jonson will be formed if. . . . But "if" leads to the rehabilitation of creative failure which, as a sort of agreed-upon condition, we are supposed not to notice.

Eliot approached Ben Jonson's plays just as he looked at *Ulysses*—eliminating the question of whether the book was readable and replacing it with the question of what could be drawn from the text. We get an "important" book, but one that does not serve the purpose intended.

"It is a world like Lobachevsky's," wrote Eliot. "The worlds created by artists like Jonson are like systems of non-Euclidean geometry. They are not fancy, because they have a logic of their own; and this logic illuminates the actual world, because it gives us a new point of view from which to inspect it."[12]

"A logic of their own," a "new point of view," a "world." Who will deny that Jonson has his own logic? With the aid of various "ifs," however, Eliot is not trying to prove the existence of Jonson's logic, but to do something else: justify a creative failure, which, in fact, did not prevent posterity from valuing Jonson according to his due without betraying literary-critical sense. It is on this critically unprovable subject that Eliot says "if" and sets conditions which, for the moment, he seems to be asking us to accept and which he goes on to use in such a way, reasoning in such a tone, that it is as if he had actually proven his thesis, which boils down to the claim that a creative failure, given certain assumptions, can pass for art.

"Certain assumptions," perhaps; having convinced the reader to make these assumptions, Eliot reasons as though no assumptions had been made. He uses vivid comparisons: Euclidean geometry and non-Euclidean geometry; its own laws. *Is* such a parallel possible when we are discussing, not various types of art but art versus nonart? (Eliot did not dispute that Jonson was unable to implement his own laws.) Euclidean and non-Euclidean—it's all geometry, various forms of the same kind of thinking, mathematical by nature. Ben Jonson, his world, and, say, the world of Shakespeare—these are not various laws of "world-building," but, above all, are different abilities to carry out one's laws.

Euclidean and non-Euclidean geometry have the same source. That is, there is only one way of thinking—axiomatic and logical; the two geometries simply have different axioms. On the other hand, fantasy and logic really are not one and the same thing, but are different worlds, different forms of activity. Ben Jonson—for all his merits and achievements, which have raised him nearly to the level of Shakespeare, at a certain point, suffering creative failure—began to engage in something else. At a certain moment, "rare Ben" ceased to be an artist. If we hold to the geometric analogy, we must say: He is not engaged in any kind of geometry, Euclidean or non-Euclidean.

Eliot, however, needs to stretch his points; he does so, again, according to the nature of that philosophical tradition which rests on "pronouncements" and "gesture," rather than on known information. If we compare Eliot's opinions on one and the same subject, opinions that contradict each other and are not provided with disclaimers on that point, one characteristic of his system—or, rather, of his way of thinking—becomes clear: He doesn't really believe what he says; he merely wants to think it.

All criticism, the more so when it is focused, uses the work criticized, examining not only what the author has said, but what is said in the work itself, as well as what the critic can say in connection with this. The critic may be stronger than the author; he may use the work to advantage. What we are discussing, however, isn't the freedom and scope of interpretation, but sterile arbitrariness, when the interpreter is not stronger than the author, but, on the contrary, is unable to handle the latter, to respond to the author on the author's ground. A specialist who perpetually comes across such an interpretation writes: "Envying the artist's creative freedom, the critic tries to enslave it with the help of interpretation, or to steal the work. The unnaturalness of interpretation is a sort of declaration of possession, a sign that the work has become the property of the critic, a property with which he can do what he chooses."[13] Also, every such "declaration" must have a stamp—"T.S.E."

It has been said, correctly, that, under Eliot's influence, certain claims in the literary profession were thrown off and others affirmed. But what was thrown off and what affirmed? Eliot's adversary was the entire, established literary world, a world that existed on both sides of the Atlantic, not without internal ties but with a fair amount of division. Eliot invaded this world not only as one more avant-gardist, though a major one (this is what distinguishes him from any other visible and influential figure of the literary movement of the time). Poetic avant-gardism was only one side of Eliot's activity, which, in the eyes of many, did not accord with the other sides. The impression of Eliot as contradictory came about through a one-sided look. His inner, consistent position aimed at reconstruction of the literary world. Contemporary literary historians state that Eliot succeeded in bringing this about.

If, earlier, it could be said that someone was "not a poet" (Keats, for instance, was "killed" by this verdict), it was said at that time in an entirely different sense than it is today, with no longer any ill will, of people who occupy canonical status. Traditionally, "not a poet" meant "stands at zero on the scale of poetic merit." Today, the evaluation is made on a scale of different merits.

In his time, when Eliot and his followers were only beginning to defend their position, the attractiveness of their program lay in the maximum specificity of their approach to literature. I. A. Richards wrote at that time: "It is strange that the speculations upon the arts should so rarely have begun from the most obvious fact about them."[14] Let us grant that. But from what did they begin, and with what did they conclude, their system of judgment? Richards considered himself one of Eliot's "creations," though he argued with Eliot. (See the speech by Richards delivered at a symposium dedicated to Eliot in 1965 in the Institute of Arts.)

Richards is considered to have revealed the sociosymbolic nature of art. At least, he focused his own interest on it and encouraged others in the same direction. From the start, Richards proceeded from the ideas of Tolstoy, who saw the deciding feature of art in its ability to "infect," in what is called in contemporary critical language, art's "communicative function."

Richards, of course, displayed critical acuity in turning to Tolstoy's ideas on art at a time when, to put it mildly, these ideas were viewed as an old man's fancy, a sort of "whim of genius." Richards did not focus on the sermonic message of "What is art?" Instead, reasoning with critical correctness that a great artist could have nothing of substance to say about the nature of his trade, he closely examined Tolstoy's opinions on the "infectious capability" of art.

In his own way, Richards interpreted this capability. He disputed Tolstoy, in doing so, bringing about an inaccuracy in his reasoning. At first glance, this is so small, so barely noticeable, that it might seem to be a result of translation. But no—with the further development of Richards's thought, it is clear that this is a system. "The more unusually a feeling is conveyed, the more strongly it affects the perceiver. The perceiver experiences more pleasure the more unique that state of mind in which it is communicated, and merges with it that much more eagerly and strongly." So reasoned Tolstoy, his "What Is Art?"

Richards interpreted Tolstoy's unusual feeling as follows: "Some special experiences are interesting and owe their attraction partly to their strangeness, their unusual character."[15] He disputed Tolstoy's claim, though he was, in fact, no longer addressing Tolstoy. "But many unusual and special experiences are unattractive and repellent," Richards said, as if contradicting Tolstoy; but Tolstoy never claimed the opposite. Tolstoy was discussing one of the necessary conditions for the "infectious" power of art, which he did not see as the experience of something special and unusual. "Dyspeptics, amateurs of psycho-analysis, fishermen and golfers,

have most remarkable things to recount"—that is how Richards understood the word *special*.[16] No, an unusual experience itself, whatever it may
be, is only as remarkable as the artist's ability. That is what Tolstoy had in
mind.[17]

Richards, on the other hand, concentrated his attention more and more
on perception—to such a degree that it might have been a question not of
the ability to "infect" but to be "infected." As he put it: "Thus people of
very different capacities for discrimination and with different attitudes
developed in very different degrees can join in admitting it. The possibility of being enjoyed at many levels is a recognized characteristic of
Elizabethan drama." Not the *ability* to give pleasure, but the *possibility* of
being enjoyed. Richards wished to put the work of art in a passive position, moving the problem of evaluation to the sphere of perception rather
than creation and virtually abolishing consideration of the specifics of
creation.

"The more unusually a feeling is conveyed"—with this phrase, Tolstoy
began his analysis of artistic ability; with experience increased and renewed, with the power of life, worthy and sufficient to be conveyed. "If
you are able not to write, don't write"—so, after all, he also said. Tolstoy's
second, equally necessary condition, is the ability to convey that feeling
"more or less clearly." And his third: to "infect" others.

Such is Tolstoy's answer to the question, "What is art?" An answer
normative in its way, as Tolstoy found it necessary to explain it fairly
strictly under the onslaught of various imitations of "art," when, as he put
it, "We have lost the very idea of what art is." This was at the beginning of
modernism, the time of the extraordinary growth and dissemination of
the trade, the first wave of mass "use of art" and its corresponding mass
production, when, in Tolstoy's words, "Most things passing for objects of
art are just those things which only resemble art, but which basically lack
art's main property" (XI).[18] Tolstoy reasons systematically: "Every false
work praised by critics is a door through which the hypocrites of art will
immediately burst" (XII).

Tolstoy took up the fight against the new art during the period of its
triumph, when it was difficult to doubt the rights and importance of this
novelty. Let us grant that he did not see the merits of the new, but he
certainly did not think up the dangers it concealed. Indeed, even
Baudelaire and Kipling had this nonart, noncreation—something they
knew for themselves, and which Tolstoy, an artist to the marrow of his

bones, felt. In this regard, his critical sense did not betray him in the least, just as the critic who said of Wordsworth, the great Wordsworth, that at a certain point he simply ceased to be a poet, was correct. To recall this, of course, does not mean to undervalue, overthrow, or (as is sometimes still said, pressuring our sentiments) "to not love" Baudelaire and Wordsworth. Great gift is in need of neither our love nor our appreciation. Their greatness is objective, independent of whether you and I display our "love." Investigating the nature of this greatness and talent, however, is important to the matter at hand, to an evaluation of current literature, in which, after all, not only the best sides of this gift are developed. On the contrary, the same proviso—"not only a poet, but also," say, "a philosopher," which, with Baudelaire, was a symptom of crisis, a conflict between organic and mechanistic principles—today has been turned into a programmatic justification of all kinds of nonpoetry. Thus, judging by certain new material, Tolstoy was not mistaken in the essence of the matter, in the formulation of the question, "What is art?" when he sounded the alarm on the multifaceted but basically unified tendency of nonart, aided by many factors, to pass for creation, for art.

Having lived a long life and been witness to radical changes, Tolstoy could conjecture a great deal. As a man of his century, however, he barely foresaw that a theoretical, open, conscious, and serious—very serious, as serious as the formulating of the question of life and death can be— justification would develop for militant nonart, the same formulation that was "basically lacking the main property of art." And we arrive at the highest degree of antiactivity, that is, altogether the wrong activity. Thus, all along the chain of "literary business," from the producer to the consumer of literary production, changes are made, serious changes: art as a product, with an integral influence on the reader, gives way to demonstration and explanation of the process of writing, the creative effect of which is by no means guaranteed.

This is the consequence of symbolism's invasion of art—not symbolism, the literary current from Baudelaire to Blok, but symbolism—the method of thinking, of logical operation, which by its very nature is not artistic. "Symbolism" and symbolism are connected, but "literary symbolism" redesigned the logistics of art. With regard to art, it was centripetal; whereas, modernism cultivates actual symbolism, that centrifugal force pointing to something outside, which, in the hands of the modernists, quickly carries us out to the periphery, then altogether beyond the boundaries of art. Confusion of these two symbolisms—which are linked, of course, but which nonetheless are different—is one more basic, widespread blunder. Like any "oversimplification in modeling," it eliminates the difference between the object and its artistic image, the "well-drawn object." Logical-positivist symbolism and poetic "symbolism" correspond to each other, just as do "midnight tasks" ("mental exercise") and "Alice's Adventures," just as do the lectures of Charles Lutwidge Dodgson and the creative world of Lewis Carroll. The point is not that students hated Dodgson (while there was no objection to Lewis Carroll from young audiences), but that one and the same person carried on absolutely different forms of activity. Are they connected? Of course, like the world and the "world" of every writer, if we are dealing with a writer, a real writer.

Eliot forgot none of this, but his evaluation of the contemporary situation was precisely that the time had come to act, rearranging and substituting certain key evaluative concepts in art. This, judging by everything, is what constituted the "Eliot revolution," so widely felt in the West, and yet so difficult to define: the elimination of certain distinctions, which Eliot brought about, combining in himself the symbolist and the "symbolist." The quotation marks were removed, and that was that. Eliot's position was a literary variant on pragmatism, neopositivism, and conventionalism—that is, of a spiritual tradition raised on the subjective-idealist principle: "Let us agree. . . ."

Unlike any other theoretician seeking ways to study literature, Eliot formulated the question more fully and widely; concerned with the creation of literature itself, he created a whole literary world, populating it, as is expected of a deity, with his image.

As in any art, everything is held together in Eliot's work by the unity of the author's person. The system of critical constructions, his apparently precise formulas, neutralized, however, by refined provisos, covered, like a protective cocoon, the figure of a man, who has said at the very beginning of his journey: "No, I am not Hamlet, I'm an extra in a passing scene." However, creative impotence, admitted from the start, was then treated, in stipulative, roundabout ways, as a normal condition, the only way possible for a contemporary artist to treat it. Seeing around him only extras and no actors, Eliot decided to put on the show anyway. His "critical" system teaches us how to play the leading role with the skills of an extra, and we end up with a show, a ritual, a game, which resembles the game in Antonioni's film, *Blow Up*—tennis without a ball. Note, this is not some other tennis, say, anti-tennis, in which the object is to lose rather than to win. No, the point is that the given activity, on the contrary, resembles tennis in every way, with the exception that the ball is eliminated from the game, the nerve is taken out, the life is removed. Who plays such tennis? Not necessarily tennis players. A skilled, wonderful actor—a chance person, chance, at least, with regard to tennis—having, perhaps, many various talents, only not those demanded by tennis: a quick eye, strong swing, and good reactions—that is, the qualities without which one is no tennis player, however much style one may have. A new champion will come along, who hits and receives differently, but who hits the ball and receives the ball.

And I turned the corner, and went into the rooms once occupied by the publisher Faber and Faber, now by London University. I turned to the doorman and asked:

"Tell me, was this where Eliot worked?"

The first response was a glance simultaneously indifferent and indignant. Then he said:

"Yes, yes, all sorts of people come here. They bother me for nothing. What do they come here for? Why do they ask? It's been twelve years since then. The press itself moved a long time ago. Go ask there."

He took a scrap of paper, wrote down a new address, and underneath, in large letters, wrote: "It's been twelve years." As if to underline his words, the doorman gave me a glance which clearly said: "And you really want to stir up this book dust?"

Suddenly I felt that glance send me, too, across the line he had so expressively traced.

And Eliot's shadow beckoned to me.

MAYA KORENEVA

Eugene O'Neill
and the Ways of American Drama

Eugene O'Neill came to the American theater at a critical moment in its history, the result of which was that drama took shape as a national art form. His work is significant not only in being generally recognized as the highest achievement of his country's drama, but because O'Neill laid the foundation for the literary form in the United States. For the first time in U.S. history, drama stood beside poetry and prose, forms whose genealogies can be traced to the first settlements in the New World. Thanks to O'Neill's work, American drama stepped over national borders and became an important part of world theater. Such plays as *The Emperor Jones*, *The Hairy Ape*, *Anna Christie*, *All God's Chillun Got Wings*, *Desire Under the Elms*, *Strange Interlude*, *Mourning Becomes Electra*, *The Iceman Cometh*, and *Long Day's Journey Into Night* have been produced in theaters around the world; many have entered the treasury of 20th-century literature.

The years during which O'Neill's talent came into being were marked in the American theater by the extreme domination of commercialism. From the first, O'Neill rejected the temptation of easy success on the "Great White Way," tying his creative fate to one of the barely-heard-of "little theaters" that began to appear in the teens of this century. Who would have guessed at the time that the foundation was being laid for a national drama? Rebelling against the deadly omnipotence of Broadway, O'Neill undermined the dominion of commercialism on the American stage. Drama's orientation, which on Broadway remained mass entertainment geared to the tastes of the undiscriminating public, became, for the first time, artistic value. O'Neill's victory was far from final, as is attested to in part by the fact that, in the 1930s, he was forced to cut all his ties with the theater and retreat, to the end of his days, into his "great silence," broken only once by an unsuccessful production of his masterpiece, *The Iceman Cometh*. But all the same, however great the difficulties before American drama to this day, O'Neill created the preconditions for its development, which did not exist in his time.

The main radical change which O'Neill brought about in American drama was the reconsideration of its relationship to reality, which became the foundation of the playwright's future success. Life, which defies all formulas, became for him as an artist a source of creativity, the final goal of creativity, and the measure of artistic truth. At the same time, he fully realized that "truth, in the theatre as in life, is eternally difficult, just as the easy is the everlasting lie."[1] Not deluded by the tinselly splendor of the "age of jazz," during which he had his first successes, O'Neill revealed in *The Emperor Jones*, *The Hairy Ape*, *Desire Under the Elms*, *All God's Chillun Got Wings*, *The Great God Brown*, and other plays, the deep tragedy of modern man, alienated from his true essence, the person whose dignity is trampled by various forms of legalized inequality and lack of freedom, whose spiritual aspirations are sacrificed by society to material success.

Painful meditation over the nature of the life surrounding him led O'Neill deep into the heart of things, to grasp the sense and direction of national existence. The world of his drama is not a chaos of absolutely independent, self-sufficient, chance events. As in all great drama of the past and present, the life conflicts and personal tragedies of his characters are the echo of powerful processes, taking place in the depths of society, created by that abyss that has opened in the course of history between once-proclaimed ideals and the cruel reality of facts. The artistic study of life that O'Neill undertook in his works led him to realize the social nature of events. Interpreting the social and spiritual past of the United States in historical perspective, he discovered for America dramatic themes and conflicts that reflect the basic contradictions in the nation's social development. The artistic world that O'Neill created is astonishing in the range and fullness of its grasp of reality—astonishing largely because American drama before him knew no such way of examining and interpreting material.

The birth of drama as a national art form coincided in America with the era of world cataclysms which revealed to the utmost the antihumanism of bourgeois society. Its hostility to the individual determined O'Neill's hostility to it, the sharp critical cast that marks all of his work, about which Arthur Miller eloquently wrote in his autobiographical book, *Timebends*. Not denying that he, like many, found O'Neill's plays to be archaic in the 1930s, Miller goes on to relate how he later came to understand their true meaning. "One approaches writers from one's own historical moment," he correctly and accurately observes. For Miller, who in his time had not heard the voice of his great predecessor, the "historical moment" that allowed him to penetrate O'Neill's dramatic world came with the failed production of *The Iceman Cometh* in 1946. ". . . I was nevertheless struck," Miller confesses, "by O'Neill's radical hostility to bourgeois civilization, far greater than anything Odets had expressed. Odets' characters were alienated because—when you come down to it—they couldn't get into the system, O'Neill's because they so desperately needed to get out of it, to junk it with all its boastful self-congratulation, its pious pretension to spiritual values, when in fact it produced emptied and visionless men choking with unnameable despair. If content had been the gauge of radicalism rather than certain automatic journalistic tags . . . it would have been O'Neill who was branded an anticapitalist writer first and foremost. Odets, after all, would have reformed capitalism with a dose of socialism; O'Neill saw no hope in it whatsoever. . . . It was O'Neill who wrote about working-class men, about whores and the social discards and even black men in a world of whites, but since there was no longer a connection with Marxism in the man himself, his plays were never seen as critiques of capitalism that objectively they were."[2]

Examining circumstances, O'Neill strove to comprehend the consistencies concealed within the infinite variety of phenomena. The social conflicts presented in his plays receive philosophical interpretation through the problem, central to all of his work, of the individual, which, for him, becomes a measure of the inhumanity of bourgeois society. Presented in all its magnitude in *The Hairy Ape*, the problem of the individual later took various artistic forms. But, for all the variety of concrete forms of the basic conflict in O'Neill's work, regarded in this perspective, it grows into a confrontation between proprietary society, possessed by the thirst for ownership, and life itself. Awareness of the fatal outcome of this confrontation lies at the base of O'Neill's celebrated pessimism, which has more than once been written of with disapproval by critics—and not only in the United States. Only our times have made it possible to comprehend the catastrophic scale of this immense conflict, confirming the truth of the most dismal visions and prophesies of this playwright, who raised American drama to a level of philosophical generalization formerly unattainable.

In opposition to inhuman society, O'Neill made the individual his higher value, and the human soul, irreparably deformed in the course of the historical process, his main object of study. "Apart from his concern with the complexities of personal psychology," wrote Harold Clurman,

O'Neill brooded on the drama of man's soul in America. Something has gone astray. The poet who yearns to explore realms beyond the narrow confines of his job fails to follow his bent and as a result wastes his being. The simple laborer, proud of the strength which turns the wheels of our magnificent civilization, finds himself scorned and adrift in a mechanism in which he is merely a cog. The artist wishes to attain the effectiveness of the man of affairs; the businessman envies the artist's imagination. . . . The would-be aristocrat from the Old World, with his dream of grandeur, is rendered absurd in the factory of a materialistic democracy. But without that strain of grandeur the dignity of a true manhood is somehow damaged. The son has little of his [father's pioneering] grit; the father, in his struggle to master the soil of his farm (America?), impairs his capacity to love.

O'Neill dramatizes himself and us as people cut off from but still seeking some principle of coherence. For want of it, everyone feels isolated and frustrated. O'Neill's strength lies in the persistence of his quest for a wholeness which has been shattered in the New World.[3]

In O'Neill's dramatic world, the social context of which is revealed with unquestionable clarity, the dilemma of modern man takes on a cosmic dimension: He comes up against reality not only on the level of circumstances, social situation, or system. He is a part of Life, which opens up for the playwright enormous possibilities for universalization. The protagonists of O'Neill's major works are marked by a high level of generalization, be they:

a former Pullman porter, the self-named Emperor Jones, for whom retribution awaits for crimes committed;

the stoker Yank (*The Hairy Ape*), who has discovered injustice in the social
order, in which labor, which creates all things of value, is devalued and
degraded by the power of capital;

the talented architect Dion Anthony, zealously trying to shatter the god
of commerce, Billy Brown (*The Great God Brown*);

Eben and Abbie, whose true love is born in renunciation of mercenary
desire, for which they pay with the life of their child and their own lives
(*Desire Under the Elms*);

the young Chinese princess Kukachin, who sends, from the kingdom of
death, not vengeance but blessings to her beloved, and love (*Marco
Millions*);

the descendant of the Puritan Mannon family, Lavinia, willingly accepting
death to atone for her ancestral curse (*Mourning Becomes Electra*); or

that motley company of social outcasts for whom Harry Hope's saloon
serves as a last refuge (*The Iceman Cometh*).

The conflicts developed in O'Neill's drama have the individual as their
second pole. He studied the individual with the same passion and obsession with which he tried to grasp the reasons for social ailments. Fearlessly
plunging into the depths of his characters' suffering, penetrating the secrets of the human heart, he discovered the indissoluble link between
consciousness, the whole inner world of a person, and the external world,
under the ruinous influence of which the human psyche, which seems so
absolutely independent of it, is irrevocably deformed. The human soul
becomes the main arena for the struggle between the individual and
society, and simultaneously, its main object. It is at the individual that the
aggressive forces of society are aimed, trying to crush, to destroy everything individual and personal in it, to thrust upon the individual the
standards of bourgeois practicalism and conformity, leading, in the final
account, to spiritual petrification.

Seeing in this intrusion the reasons for the inevitable defeat of the
individual, O'Neill in no way gives the latter the role of passive victim.
His protagonists desperately, obsessively, literally to the point of frenzy,
resist the pressure of society, the intentions of the world to fully subdue
them. In so arranging the forces in conflict, O'Neill substantially differs
from modern European drama at the turn of the century while preserving
an unbroken link with it in the definition of the nature of conflict and
life's tragedy, and in his treatment of action. Like the protagonists of

modern drama, his heroes are unable to establish, or even reveal, themselves by means of actions or deeds. This is because the sphere of action is the sphere of bourgeois society, the sphere of the dominion of vulgar mercantile interests, subordination and force, where the existence of a whole and free individual is impossible. Thus, their resistance is sharply delimited, excluding action, and is wholly confined to the sphere of consciousness, which, however, does not prevent the characters and their struggles from taking on, in a certain sense, heroic proportions.

As is usual in modern drama, with which O'Neill's work is genetically linked, the conflict between the character and society does not take the shape of direct confrontation, but is dissipated in daily life, eroded by its current. At the center of O'Neill's artistic transformation of the conflict is the drama of consciousness, itself comprehending its own inadequacy, its estrangement from the sources of existence, its loss of the fullness of life and integrity, which alone give an individual self-worth. It is this self-worth, indefinable by any measures or social regulations, that the heroes of O'Neill's plays defend.

Even doomed to perish, they resist to the last, affirming their dignity with faithfulness to themselves. Resistance demands of them extreme concentration of will and spiritual effort. But their strength is already ebbing, undermined by the unequal fight and, particularly, by the fact that the destruction has penetrated inside, causing the fatal process of disintegration. Yet the protagonists' resistance continues despite the obvious inevitability of defeat. While they can, they, like Jones, Yank, or Dion, struggle. If they are overcome, it is not because they betray themselves or those higher values which, consciously or not, they were defending, but only because their strength is exhausted. Their furious struggle contains a certain paradox: In the affirmation of the self-worth of the individual, the protagonists come to *self*-denial, *self*-negation, as, to attain their goal, they sacrifice and reject themselves. This furious—to the point of selflessness, to the point of self-destruction—resistance to circumstances gives the protagonists of many of O'Neill's plays, unlike those of modern drama, the right to be called heroes in the traditional sense of the word.

Running a bit ahead, it can be noted that obsession knowing no bounds in the assertion of the self-worth of the individual is typical not of O'Neill's characters alone. If we turn to the work of American playwrights of the subsequent period, we see that it is unquestionably a characteristic of certain protagonists of Arthur Miller and Tennessee Williams, such as Willy Loman (*Death of a Salesman*), John Proctor (*The Crucible*), Eddie Carbone (*A View From the Bridge*), Quentin (*After the Fall*), Blanche (*A Streetcar Named Desire*), Chance Wayne (*Sweet Bird of Youth*), Val and Lady (*Orpheus Descending*), and Shannon (*The Night of the Iguana*). The same can be said of Edward Albee's characters: Jerry (*The Zoo Story*), George and Martha (*Who's Afraid of Virginia Woolf?*), Julian (*Tiny Alice*), Agnes and Tobias (*A Delicate Balance*), as well as the plays of Sam Shepard: *Red Cross, The Tooth of Crime*, and *True West*.

In their nature, cast of mind, position in life, and view of the world, these characters are completely different; but they all share a readiness to sacrifice everything, including their lives, to prove the truth of their conception of individuality. Defending their convictions, their essence, they all end up destroying themselves, either physically or spiritually. This characteristic of O'Neill's heroes was thus established in the further development of American drama, becoming, in its way, an inherited trait. It is noteworthy that the characteristic is bestowed on characters who were the true discovery of American theater. This is only natural—they were marked with the essential aspects of the national character, the national consciousness, which proclaimed the self-worth of the individual and made it the measure of social progress, although, as O'Neill—and, after him, other American playwrights—showed, the proclamation differed substantially from reality.

Upon comparison with European drama of the turn of the century, one other important trait of O'Neill's protagonists stands out distinctly. To a certain degree, the old hierarchy of characters is preserved in European drama: with extremely rare exceptions (for instance, *The Weavers* by Hauptmann), the heroes represent the privileged layer of society, which unquestionably guarantees them a position of greater independence and, accordingly, greater spiritual freedom. But it is here, too, that danger awaits them. The temptation is for conscious or unconscious self-glorification; it is the temptation to consider themselves above the crowd and the "trivial" concerns of life that absorb it, to see in their superiority a sign of favor. This danger was revealed clearly enough in *Brand*, where it receives an unambiguous interpretation. Ibsen takes the side of the hero, whose ideals are trampled by the crowd, the moment it heard of a cod run that promises a rich catch.

In O'Neill's work such an attitude to the prose of life, such arrogant disregard for reality on the part of the protagonist and its "primitive," "everyday" concerns, is impossible. Beginning with his early "sea plays," his protagonists are the flesh and blood of the lower classes, passed over by social justice, for whom the heavy burden of daily life, be it in its very lowest form, is the only reality of existence. In many of his plays the "cod run" is not evidence of the baseness of the characters' interests and needs, but a vital necessity. As such, it is not like the calculation of "vegetable oil" and "buckwheat" that concludes *Uncle Vanya,* or the prospect of sitting at the desk of a hotel, with which Jean tempts Miss Julie in the play by Strindberg. It is, of course, a matter not of the particular details of one or another plot, but of that conception of reality and the aesthetic principles connected to it, which stand behind it.

In admitting, like the characters of modern drama, the weight of necessity, which grows to fateful proportions, O'Neill's protagonists, unlike them, do not experience degradation. For them, this is an organic, natural element of existence, although they strive to sever the ties connecting them to it. They perceive daily life, with its annoying, oppressive "trivial affairs" not as something that exists apart from them, threatening to finally overwhelm them with its insignificance, and therefore to be loftily rejected—pulled into the swift current of daily existence, they, located on the lowest rung of the social ladder, are virtually deprived of the possibility, even in their dreams, of breaking free from the cruel fetters of daily life. It is not given to them to cast off its weight either by plunging into the sweet world of reverie, like the Student in *The Ghost Sonata,* nor through hope of atoning for the past, like Mrs. Alving, nor with the dream of moving to Moscow, like Chekhov's three sisters, nor with lofty love for a beautiful girl, like Matthias Clausen in *Vor Sonnenuntergang* by Hauptmann.

Even in those cases where O'Neill's characters represent the milieu typical of modern drama (Dion Anthony in *The Great God Brown*; the protagonists of *Mourning Becomes Electra* and *Long Day's Journey Into Night*; James Tyrone in *A Moon for the Misbegotten*), it is not characteristic of them to look down on daily life. If one is shown to have such an attitude, it is evidence of his moral decline (Jones, *The Emperor Jones*; Con Melody, *A Touch of the Poet*).

As in all literature, drama's interest in the lot of the unfortunate grew in the course of its development. A great deal was accomplished in that area by modern drama, which, with its original aims, its conception of reality, and its very structure, hastened the appearance on the stage of the hero from the lower classes. For modern drama, however, this remained a matter of the future. However great the tragedy of Firs in *The Cherry Orchard*, it nonetheless is on the periphery of the play.

O'Neill made a decisive turn in this direction, from the start placing the person from society's lower strata at the center of his playwriting system. In this sense, his dramatic world is closer to Irish drama, particularly to the plays of Synge and O'Casey, which O'Neill echoes in other ways as well. It is enough to recall such plays as *Bound East for Cardiff*, *The Moon of the Caribbees*, *The Rope*, *The Emperor Jones*, *Beyond the Horizon*, *The Hairy Ape*, *Anna Christie*, and *The Iceman Cometh*. We see a long procession of people rejected by society: sailors, farmers, dockworkers, prostitutes, vagabonds, blacks, frequenters of saloons.

The merit of the picture O'Neill draws does not lie only in the accuracy with which he re-creates layers of reality that did not fall into the field of vision of his predecessors on the American stage. The picture is inspired by an understanding of the world portrayed so as to arouse compassion. O'Neill ventures more, however. Depicting the tragic fate of his "low" characters, he advances the social questions most important for his time and poses the fundamental question of existence. This is one of the cardinal differences between his work and the above-mentioned *The Weavers*, Gorky's *Enemies*, and similar plays (in which the basis of the conflict is the class antagonism tearing society apart and in which the characters are depicted as the victims of social injustice) and Ibsen's *A Doll's House* (with its clearly marked "thesis"). In both cases, the solution to the conflict is envisioned by the playwrights in a change in the social structure, although ways of implementing this task vary widely in the plays mentioned. O'Neill is not enthused by the idea of social transformation. He does not propose any program for the restructuring of society; but the field of sociophilosophical problems in his work is significantly wider.

In O'Neill's artistic world, no less socially determined than Gorky's or Hauptmann's, in which, by his own admission, the determining factor was "the relation between man and God," the dilemma of the modern man (which, it is worth emphasizing again, O'Neill often embodied in the figures of representatives of the lower strata of society) takes on cosmic proportions.[4] Man is seen as being enmeshed not only in certain circumstances, a certain social situation or system, but in the paradigm of life, the orbit of the world order. Although they are an important element, O'Neill's drama does not end with the questions of social injustice, with the basic flaws of the social structure and the false ideals leading to the spiritual impoverishment of American civilization. Behind these questions there remains a vast, clearly perceptible expanse in which is raised the problem of man's place in a universe in which God has died.

The focus on reality, which was the cornerstone of O'Neill's aesthetic, radically transformed American drama. Following O'Neill, playwrights widened the range of drama's possibilities, investigating layers of American life formerly untouched. Reality in the living variety of experience more and more decisively won its place on the stage.

It was by no means easy for this young art form to explore reality. A rapid broadening of drama's horizons concerning theme and subject matter was but seldom combined with a deep penetration to the essence of things, of situations and conflicts. While certainly achieving a high degree of verisimilitude in their presentation of modern man's dilemma, playwrights of the 1920s were, as a rule, unable to comprehend how the dramatic situations they chose to depict were related to the nation's overall life. Nor could they portray characters and circumstances on a large scale or give them universal significance. Even when playwrights managed to touch upon specific weaknesses and painful spots of contemporary society, and when the problems embodying major contradictions of their time appeared to be outlined clearly, it was as though something had intervened to prevent these playwrights from realizing the possibilities inherent in the material.

Then the grotesque, an indication of the repudiation of society that causes the alienation of the individual, gives way to sentimentality to a great extent neutralizing the play's message, taking off its edge, as happens in Elmer Rice's play *The Adding Machine*. In *What Price Glory?*, a play by Maxwell Anderson and Laurence Stallings, the action aimed at an earnest, truthful presentation of the horrors of the Great War suddenly degenerates to a trivial, gross comedy dominated in its latter part by the rivalry between American officers and soldiers for the tender mercies of French *filles de joie*. The entire play comes to be oriented to the standards of entertainment established by the commercial theater. The characters in John Howard Lawson's *Processional*—so excitingly fresh and fascinating at the beginning because of the author's original, even brave, approach to characterization—fade into stereotypes, turning into embodiments of ready-made sociological formulas, while at the same time losing both the interest and the trust they aroused in the reader or the audience. The happy end crowning Sidney Howard's play *They Knew What They Wanted*

smooths the conflict at the heart of the situation presented by the dramatist, giving the impression that he had chosen an easier solution.

With the distance of time, imperfections are clearly visible in these
works, created at the initial stage of the formation of American drama. In
many ways they explain the plays' extremely fast "aging"—written in the
1920s, today they are of mainly historical interest—although, strange as it
sounds, at the time the above-mentioned flaws in a certain sense eased the
way for these plays to reach the viewer, and insured their success.

The audience by no means always craves the new or perfect. The American viewer is no exception to the general rule. Schooled by the commercial theater to like works in which superficial content is packaged in
strictly designed and easily mastered formulae, he is often satisfied with a
moderate amount of novelty. Conservatism of traditional taste is a phenomenon common to all art forms. The unique position of drama is
determined by the fact that theater—as the sphere of its existence—is a
public art, in which the confrontation of artistic innovation and traditional taste often takes the form of sharply dramatic conflict.

The situation that took shape in American drama in the 1920s clearly
confirms this. The awarding of the Pulitzer Prize in 1924 serves as one
example. Without a doubt, conservative taste was one of the factors that
inclined the choice in favor of Sydney Howard's *They Knew What They
Wanted*, with its easy solution, rather than *Desire Under the Elms*, which
linked the fates of its protagonists to the fate of American civilization.

This orientation of traditional taste is felt not only in the fate of specific
works, but it influences the general development of the art, spurring the
artist to seek stronger and stronger means of influencing the social consciousness. The American audience, with its historically small aesthetic
experience, is not always a "suitable" partner for American art, which,
coming up against uniformity of perception, did not fail to recognize the
normative character of its demands. Not wanting to submit to the dictatorship of established norms, in which the danger of the commercializa-
tion of art is obvious, the artist often saw as his alternative flinging a
challenge to the reigning taste. For O'Neill, the content of the creative act
was never exhausted with that challenge; but this factor was a constant
part of his aesthetic program, showing up in various ways during different
stages of his work.

The situation in the United States had a deciding influence on the
development of American drama in the 1930s. The depression of 1929,
which paralyzed production, gave a powerful spur to the social protest

movement, in which literature, too, participated. Drama's rapprochement with the radical leftist movement led to the intensification in it of moods reflecting the widespread craving for social justice, the striving to rebuild society on a new basis. Thus, the idea of "drama of the 30s," in reference to the United States, is defined less by the boundaries of time or aesthetic categories than by its ideological orientation.

The impulses to investigate the social problems that arose in the preceding decade received further development in the 1930s. Converted to Marxism or sharing convictions close to those of Marxism, many playwrights came to realize the class nature of society, which, in its turn, led to an accentuation of conflict as a specifically social conflict. This circle of writers—among whom Clifford Odets, Lillian Hellman, and Albert Maltz took the lead—was fairly wide. Along with criticism of conditions, their plays more and more distinctly expressed a social ideal which, in many cases, took on characteristics of the socialist ideal—plays such as *Black Pit* (1935) and *Private Hicks* by Maltz, *Days to Come* (1936) by Hellman, *Stevedore* (1933) by G. Sklar and P. Peters, *Mulatto* (1936) and *Haiti* (1937) by Langston Hughes, and *Waiting for Lefty* (1935) and *Till the Day I Die* (1935) by Odets.

In no other period was so much grief and suffering presented on the American stage, but the picture on the whole was not at all marked by gloom. Even tragic situations looked undeniably optimistic, although faith in the future was by no means always combined with a realization of ways and means to attain these goals. The heroes of William Saroyan's plays *My Heart's in the Highlands* and *The Time of Your Life* (both 1939) would not be called fighters, but their opposition to life's adversities bears the stamp of heroism, and the hope expressed in the plays for the victory of good allowed them to join the main current of drama of the 1930s.

Belief in the victory of justice is often combined with the theme of the new world, which entered drama during this decade. It probably appeared first in the play *The House of Connelly* (1931) by Paul Green. Written at the turn of the decade, it bears the stamp of a transitional time. The conflict receives a tragic solution: The dying world—if only temporarily—celebrates a victory over the new one. The sense of irreparableness in the author's position, however, no longer reflected the atmosphere in which the production was staged and changes were made in the ending eliminating the tragic outcome, although the new ending, certainly, destroyed the play's gloomy integrity.

The elucidation of social conflict in the drama of the 1930s, compared to that of the preceding decade, is attested to as well by the sharpness of the social criticism in the plays lacking a direct contrast between the old and new worlds. The most outstanding work of this type was Lillian Hellman's *The Little Foxes* (1939), which concentrates within itself all the energy of a rejection of relations permeated by the insatiable craving for profit, an energy that permeated the atmosphere of the thirties. In this sharply critical view of conditions, above all, the continuity between O'Neill's theater and the drama of the thirties is expressed. It is in this sense that we should understand the words of John Gassner, who, reflecting on American drama's "leftism," wrote: "It started with the Depression or it started long before. It ended with the end of the Depression and the start of World War II, or it never died."[5]

However, continuity by no means boils down to simple repetition, to the use of predecessors' discoveries, like a banner passed to whomever continues on. Connections between separate periods in the development of American drama are immeasurably more complex than that. Study of past experience reveals not only "continuation and development," but debate in many areas, in which rejection and repudiation, return, and resurrection of rejected ideas are no less essential.

The relationship between O'Neill and the drama of the 1930s, which involved fundamental differences of ideological and aesthetic views, was not easy. The divergence was not only in the fact that, as A. S. Romm writes, "The individualist and anarchist O'Neill remained on the sidelines of the liberation movement of the 'red decade,' and did not absorb its advanced ideas."[6]

In the very stating of the problem, Romm a priori proceeds from only one factor, the playwright's consciousness ("not having absorbed advanced ideas"), thus predetermining his final conclusion. In the same way, he postulates the unconditional rightness of the drama of the thirties—it did not "remain on the sidelines"—in its relations with the founder of the national dramatic tradition, the outcome of which was decided by a complicated ideological-aesthetic struggle. An evaluation of that struggle cannot be onesidedly negative toward O'Neill and positive toward the drama of the thirties, as in the quotation cited, if only because, in the following period, American drama faced an urgent need for a deeper consideration and understanding of O'Neill's bequest.

It has already been said that the 1930s were marked in drama by a clarification of the social conflict, which can justifiably be numbered among its most important achievements. But the picture will be far from complete, and the evaluation unobjective, if we speak only of achievements. Along with them came serious losses, at times quite outweighing the merits. The clarification of conflict by means of the reflection of class contradictions in dramatic clashes led to a noticeable simplification, a straightening out. The polarized juxtaposition, presented in many variations, between the disenfranchisement and poverty of the masses and the omnipotence and cruelty of the rulers of the world who have become wealthy by unjust means, though reflecting the real contradictions of the time, tended toward oversimplification and led to a petrification of dramatic structure, which was in itself incompatible with the original aims of O'Neill's theater. Despite the author's enviable inventiveness in plot construction, the action becomes predictable, losing the spontaneity that embodies the flow of life, destroying the very life O'Neill had managed to breathe into American drama. Although to different degrees, this is felt in the work of virtually all the major playwrights of the 1930s.

In a certain sense, the consequence of the elucidation of the social conflict was the loss of the high level of generalization contributed by O'Neill. Absorbed in the urgent concerns of the day and the demands of the political moment, confined to the revealed interests of and contradictions between classes and social groups, drama in the thirties remained deaf to the philosophical questions that grew out of O'Neill's analysis of social conflict. It was not troubled by ontological problems, the posing of which more clearly than anything indicated the innovation of the forefather of American drama. Choosing, like him, a hero from the lower classes, the playwrights of the thirties confined the situation represented to certain circumstances, tying the resolution of conflict to the resolution of class antagonisms, to change in the social structure. The answer to the questions posed appeared clear and unambiguous. The consequence of such an approach, however, was that just beyond the border of their consideration rose, probably, those most difficult questions which O'Neill had fearlessly rushed to meet.

There were other reasons, as well, for the narrowing of the scope of American drama in the 1930s. The focus on social aspects led to a substantially lower intensity of the search for an ethical ideal in those years. It lost its independent significance in the system of values on which drama's attention was focused; therefore the moral quest of the characters was virtually ignored by the majority of playwrights. Most often, the moral conflict was included in the social conflict, appearing only as one of its supplementary characteristics. A character's moral aspect was most often predetermined by his or her place in the social conflict, which inevitably led to a patness and oversimplification, both in the depiction of characters and in the development of the action, which the writers were rarely able to avoid.

At the same time, drama in the 1930s preserved its closeness to the theater of O'Neill—apart from what is mentioned above—in one other respect: It most often addressed social and political problems in the genre of family drama, examining the sphere of social existence through the prism of private life. Unlike the situation in Europe, the theater of social action in the United States was on the whole not deeply influenced by agitprop. Most works thus influenced are openly geared to their precise moment, designed for one-time use. At the same time, the most outstanding of these works—such as, for instance, the celebrated "Living Newspapers"—owed their existence not only to agitprop, but to such homespun varieties of theater as the revue, music hall, and burlesque. Where this influence more deeply penetrated American drama—for example, in the Odets play *Waiting for Lefty*—it is presented through traditional dramatic forms.

In his work, Odets did not limit himself to criticism of contemporary society. He proclaimed a new world, reflecting even in the titles of his plays—*Awake and Sing!* and *Paradise Lost*—the central conflict in drama of the thirties, affirming the existence of a paradise which his characters must regain, as well as faith in a victory over gloomy reality. However, Odets' radicalism, born of a particularly emotional perception of the ideas that were in the air, was not deep. More than any other major American playwright, Odets was a product of his time. The waning of the democratic movement was accompanied in Odets' work by a waning of themes brought to life by the rise of popular discontent. At the same time, there was a change in tone. The joyous anticipation of the downfall of the old world, which colored the whole decade, and the ringing in of the new, gave way to a minor chord of doubt, a premonition of catastrophe, of the tragic ordeals to be borne by humankind during the Second World War.

When compared with the plays of the 1930s, this change of tone is striking in the works of playwrights of the postwar period—especially Arthur Miller, Tennessee Williams, and Edward Albee—reflecting substantial inner shifts. Conflict, which formerly was based on the opposition of classes and social groups, has now clearly moved inside. This, by itself, indicates a return to O'Neill. Like their great predecessor, they strive in their study of reality to go from the personal to the general, while the drama of the 1930s moved, as a rule, in the opposite direction, from the general to the personal, from social processes to the fate of a single human being.

While continuing to base their work on social conflicts, Miller, Williams, and Albee brought back to American drama the philosophical, universal meaning it had gained under O'Neill's pen but had lost in the thirties, when nearly the only exception to the rule was the work of Thornton Wilder. Addressing the problem of the complete alienation of the individual allowed it to rise once more to that level. Entailing such traditional themes for American literature as that of the individual under the open sky, the pioneer's theme of taming the wild continent, which involves the reunification of man not only with nature but with the most universal forces of existence, and the theme of the sanctity of nature in all its forms, this problem is distinctly present in the characters of the protagonists of the most significant plays of the postwar period. The interpretation of alienation as the manifestation of the inevitable depravity of contemporary society, of its hostility to the human being, unexpectedly brings together Willy Loman (*Death of a Salesman*) and Shannon (*The Night of the Iguana*), Eddie Carbone (*A View from the Bridge*) and Jerry (*The Zoo Story*), and Julian (*Tiny Alice*) and Quentin (*After the Fall*).

O'Neill, however, not only defined the issues of American drama for many decades to come, he gave it an artistic language. With O'Neill, thanks to O'Neill, it gained its aesthetic form, its unique appearance. Idiosyncratic in its very nature, his work is marked by traits that vividly embody the national peculiarity of American drama. It is to O'Neill's artistic experiments that the latter owes the variety and richness of form it has today.

One of the most important (from the point of view of drama's further development) aspects of O'Neill's creative search was the system he created of recurrent images, which were to become an integral part of the language of American playwriting.

The system of images in O'Neill's plays is extraordinarily branching. They appear as leitmotifs in separate works, defining the ideological-aesthetic system as well as uniting them—with all their differences—into a single, whole world. Among the most significant of these leitmotifs are the symbols of fog, closely linked with the image of the "ole davil sea" which personifies, in O'Neill's theater, the power of the vital and cosmic element, independent of, and incomprehensible to, humanity; the image of "belonging," having profound philosophical and social meaning which, reflecting the sense of historical rootlessness characteristic of Americans as a nation, implies in O'Neill's work an extremely wide range of the search for "one's place," be it a place in the social system or in the universe, and is also a measure of truth, both of social ideals and values, and of the individual; the image, presented in many versions, of the deadening of life ("death in life," "life in death," etc.), embodying the world's fundamental hostility to man; the image of the jungle, and that of the "angry God," which are firmly rooted in American drama.

First appearing in O'Neill's work as the immediate reflection of personal experience, the image of the jungle was one of his happy discoveries. The situation reproduced in one of his early works, *The Emperor Jones*—the single combat between man and nature—resurrected the nation's historical past. This appeal to national experience not only extended the scope of events, it removed any trace of exoticism, which would have been unavoidable if such a play were to appear in Europe, where that conflict was experienced in prehistoric time. In America, where the confrontation between man and nature was a key factor in the young nation's formation, it secured itself among the leading themes of all of American art.

Gradually the image of the jungle in O'Neill's work draws close to the image of the modern city. With this, its indifference and cruelty toward man take on an emphasized "mechanical" character. At the same time, the image of the jungle somehow becomes stratified, appearing in various elements of the plot. So, for instance, in the play *All God's Chillun Got Wings*, it is clearly carried into the depiction of the environment, hostile to the protagonists of the neighboring blocks, in which whites and blacks live in eternal hatred toward each other. In their description, "brutality and some mechanical quality"—an obvious echo [of] *The Emperor Jones*—is often particularly stressed. At the same time, the theme of the jungle is introduced by means of the African mask, in which the heroine sees a threat to her own "self" and which, at the climax of the play, she attacks with a knife, as a symbol of her hostile surroundings.

All the elements of a work's artistic structure are connected with each other; thus, a certain accentuation or coloration of one inevitably entails a corresponding transformation of the others. For example, the highlighting of the struggle between man and nature in his conflict with the world intensifies a kind of animalism in the delineation of the hero. This "animalism," however, is understood not as limitedness or spiritual poverty brought about by the deforming influence of social relations but as the "primitiveness" of nature, knowing neither the fetters nor the corrupting influence of civilization, as something primordial. Such animalism serves as a means of describing both the characters and the action and is expressed in the likening of human nature and behavior to the habits of an animal and/or in the exposure of human relations through the relations between human and animal.

Such animalism can be seen (and often is) as the result of the penetration of American drama by the aesthetic of naturalism with its fatalism of biological determinism. Although it would be pointless to deny the influence of naturalism on drama, as on American literature in general, such an explanation is nevertheless unsatisfactory. In that case, we lose sight entirely of the appeal, so essential to the system of American ideology and culture, to historical experience, an experience which, given the circumstances of the New time, with its inherent social relations, demanded the resurrection of primitive, "pre-social" forms.

Furthermore, in O'Neill's work, "animalisticness" of characters and action often serves as a means of affirming the aesthetic of realism. The layer of animalistic images, which permeates, say, the fabric of a play such as *Desire Under the Elms*, directly contributes to the solution of the main artistic task: to re-create the specifics of rural life, the perception and thinking of a man whose existence is defined by closeness to the natural sources of life. In Russian literature we meet an approach which, in many ways, is analogous to the depiction of rural life and the embodiment of the peasant's perceptions of the world in the poetry of Nekrasov.

Essentially, such a portrayal of the world and experience of a person living in the country—in the United States, on a farm—is a fairly traditional device; at least, it was well established in literature by the time O'Neill wrote his plays. What is of principal importance is that, thanks to O'Neill, such "naturalness," or "primitivism," became securely rooted in American drama as an element of the consciousness of characters who were in no way connected to the farmer's world and life. This is both a paradox and an artistic discovery: Yank, Jones, and other of O'Neill's protagonists represent the most urbanized country in the world. Their embodiment of nature allows various phases in the nation's experience to be combined in a single image: the past and the present. The image of the jungle resurrects the conflict between man and primordial nature as one of the factors of the nation's formation and at the same time embodies the basic conflict of modern times—the tragedy of the alienation of the individual, doomed to defeat in the confrontation with society, the casualty of which becomes human nature, desecrated nature.

At the intersection of natural and social existence, the image arises of the cage, the pen, the zoo—all intended to subdue ungovernable nature. The obvious continuation of these images is the prison. The mutual connection between these images, their transformation one into the other, appeared first—and extraordinarily vividly—in *The Hairy Ape*. The analogy, declared from the start, is supported on various levels of the play's structure by means of further plot development, the animalistic description of the stokers—particularly the play's protagonist, Yank, the hairy ape—who resemble powerful beasts, and by the image of the city-jungle, which becomes one of the most stable images in American playwriting.

The innumerable variations of this many-layered, polysemantic image attest to its particular meaningfulness and its significance in the system of artistic devices used to reveal American circumstances. Playwrights have addressed it in various ways; its use not only has not fettered individuality of the artist but, on the contrary, thanks to the flexibility of the image, has led to its more active manifestation. At times, it makes itself known only by a light hint, some lone signal. Fairly rare in the drama of the thirties, for instance, it crops up in Ralph's comment in Odets' *Awake and Sing!*: "Jake's right—everybody's crazy. It's like a zoo in this house."[7] In other cases, it is found in the foreground, defining the whole ideological-artistic structure of a work. The solid chain of associations built up in the course of American drama creates a constantly widening context in which the representation of reality through the prism of this image is painted in ever new colors.

The image of the city-jungle with all its components plays an important role in the dramatic world of Tennessee Williams. Although in the poetic *The Glass Menagerie* (1945), the hostile universe threatening the Wingfields' tiny world never intrudes on stage, its voice—the voice of a big city—carries in, according to the author's remarks, just like the voice of a jungle, emphasizing its aggressiveness toward the individual, its incompatability with the higher aspirations of the spirit.

In *A Streetcar Named Desire* (1947), this image is more accentuated and developed on several levels. The first appearance of the play's hero, Stanley Kowalski, with a piece of bloody meat, underlines the animalistic traits of his character, which receive a killing rebuke in Blanche's monologue, which lowers Stanley to the image of an ape. This episode unquestionably calls to mind the protagonist of *The Hairy Ape*.

As with O'Neill, animalism in this and other plays preserves ambivalence, simultaneously representing both the destructive forces of society directed against the individual and nature, the life-creating source, trampled by ruthless society. The destructiveness of Stanley's animalism is conveyed by his rape of Blanche and is crowned by her incarceration in the psychiatric hospital, where the image of bars is associatively linked both to a cage in a zoo and to a prison (again, clear echoes of *The Hairy Ape*). At the same time, Stanley's animalism contains a certain positive charge, making him the bearer of the living element of nature—not by chance is he compared to a handsome rooster. Of course, Stanley's perfection is merely physical and is accompanied by moral and spiritual weakness; however, even in this form it opposes society's alienating infringements on human nature.

The image of the jungle as a symbol of the hostile world is also created in *Suddenly Last Summer* (1958). Here, it appears in the primary sense of the word. It is a tropical forest whose aggressiveness toward man is excessive; in the description even of the plant world (trees, flowers), its carnivorousness is emphasized. The play's main idea is expressed in concentrated form in the symbol developed in the description of the desert Galapagos Islands, where insatiable birds of prey, falling from the sky on barely hatched, helpless turtles, tear their undefended flesh. The author compares these birds to children, the hungry pack pursuing the hero and then, in the literal sense, tearing him to pieces and eating his body while the hero himself appears as the powerless victim of a cruel world.

Like Williams, realizing the tragic fate of contemporary man, Arthur Miller illuminates a different aspect of the jungle image. Animalistic motifs so essential to Williams' dramatic world in character description and plot structure, and linked from the start to the development of the jungle image, are nearly nonexistent in Miller's work—a fairly rare case in American drama and therefore deserving of particular attention. Most significant for Miller is the layer of associations generalizing the laws of social existence. In his work the jungle appears, above all, as a metaphor for the big city or for society as a whole, where human relationships are based upon the law of dog-eat-dog, justifying the merciless fight of everyone against everyone in the pursuit of material success.

The events of *Death of a Salesman* (1949) unfold in just such a city-jungle, where giant houses have surrounded Willy Loman's tiny house. In the stone prison they create—which, like the arches of a jungle, the sun never penetrates—life suffocates. The death of Willy's plants symbolizes his own fate: The city pitilessly discards the hero in life's backyard, where there is neither light nor air, then kills him.

Describing the protagonist's tragic lot, Miller stresses the mechanical nature, the heartlessness, of the world celebrating its victory over him: the scene with the tape recorder, when Willy's complaints and protests to the owner of the company are drowned out by the child's recorded—that is, not "alive"—voice, thoughtlessly enumerating the names of the states and their capitals. In this way, O'Neill's theme of the mechanical environment, hostile to man, which appears as early as *The Emperor Jones* and which since then echoed many times in his other plays, is revived and further developed.

As one would expect, next to the image of the jungle in *Death of a Salesman*, the theme of the nation's origins arises. That period is conceived of in the play as a striking contrast to the contemporary world. For this reason, interpretation of the theme of man's struggle with nature is replaced by the somewhat idyllically treated, Rousseauesque theme of unification with nature, which puts the actions of the pioneers in the legendary light of a golden age, an earthly paradise, before the fall, marked by the beginning of the age of the jungle.

Developing the theme of success central to *Death of a Salesman*, Miller carries the image of the jungle into its sphere. He carries this out mainly by means of Willy's brother, Ben. If the protagonist is a complete failure, Ben is his complete opposite. He is the embodiment of success. In the description of this character, however, many factors are pointed out which make it impossible to maintain that the reason for Willy's failure in life is rooted in himself. First, over the course of the play, it remains unclear how Ben has attained his goal: despite his brother's endless questioning, he stubbornly preserves silence about this attainment. The only things he constantly repeats are that, at the age of seventeen, he entered the jungle; at twenty-one, he came out of the jungle a rich man; and that he is in a great hurry (a clear reference to Ben Franklin's dictum, which has become a national motto, "Time is money").

In the given context, the "jungle" could signify both the plunder of the African continent and actions at home according to the "law of the jungle." Whatever concretely stands behind the image, intentionally left unclear by the playwright, "the way to wealth" appears an unjust one for Miller.

Second, Ben is the only character who exists alone in Willy's imagination (the play is constructed as a combination of planes of subjective and objective reality). This unquestionably emphasizes the transparency and illusory nature of success against the background of the tragedies brought about by American conditions. The nearly word-for-word repetition of the same lines inevitably calls to mind the sense, already familiar from O'Neill, of "mechanicalness," revealing the inhumane nature of the pursuit of success, which supplants high social ideals.

The image of the cage or prison takes on particular significance in Miller's work. In the plays *After the Fall* and *Incident at Vichy*, which are linked, in that they address the same questions, the final expression of human cruelty, embodied in the philosophy and deeds of fascism, is the concentration camp. The playwright, however, is not inclined to close the circle of questions raised with only one historical phenomenon, although that question may have global significance. Reflecting on the course of history, Miller comes to the conclusion that the fates of humanity are interconnected. With such an approach, the concentration camp is seen as the result, not only of fascism but of all of history. The accusing glance turns from the other—Germany—to the self—America. A similar process takes place in the soul of Quentin, the protagonist of *After the Fall*. Miller does not allow the individual to take cover in the niche of his own infallibility, instead putting the entire burden of guilt on social institutions. He sees the possibility of victory over evil in the overcoming of the universal isolation of people, fatal for humanity, in a society of total alienation. As a gloomy warning, the towers of the concentration camp hover over Quentin's "private" world—a symbol of human estrangement and the victory of evil.

The image of the jungle has many meanings in the work of Edward Albee as well. *The Zoo Story* (1959)—which appeared just when American social consciousness was freeing itself from the yoke of McCarthyism and which became, in its turn, an expression of and factor in that process— contains a direct association—with the zoo cage, and an indirect one— with the prison. Appropriately the action reaches its climax in the hero's monologue, "the story of Jerry and the dog," which symbolically portrays the collapse of all human relations and values in a society in which alienation reigns. Tobias's monologue about the cat in *A Delicate Balance* is analogous in meaning.

Animalism plays an important role in the depiction of characters in *Who's Afraid of Virginia Woolf?* (1962). Martha's father is several times compared to a red-eyed white mouse. Honey's father is also compared to that animal, but in accordance with his profession as a "man of God," his representative is a "church mouse." Contrary to the allegorical meaning of the image, however, he has noticeably prospered at the expense of his parishioners: church money is found to be depleted, while his own not only remains intact but has increased. And Honey herself, dim, a faceless creature, resembles a gray mouse. Her husband, Nick, on the other hand, is endowed with a vivid, attractive exterior, although he turns out to be merely a stallion, subordinating his nature to low goals—the attainment of success.

The characters in *Tiny Alice*, representing surroundings hostile to the hero—the perverted, mercenary, predatory world, trampling all spiritual values—are depicted in a similar way. The ugliness of the relations that dominate in that world is represented by the images of the hyena, the beast feeding on carrion, and the snake, a "vermin" whose touch arouses revulsion, making spiritual contact impossible.

The use of animal images is typical of the work of Sam Shepard, less in character description or plot structure, although Shepard does not reject such a method altogether, than on the level of allegory and symbolism (*The Tooth of Crime* [1972], *Angel City* [1976], and others). This capacious image-symbol, reflecting the essence of the surrounding world, is presented, for instance, in *The Curse of the Starving Class* (1976) in the monologue about the eagle and the cat. As is usual with Shepard, the most ideologically and aesthetically significant elements of the structure are carried beyond the level of the plot. The carrion bird circles in the air, looking for prey and falling upon it like a stone. But a second claimant quickly appears—a cat. The rivals lock into each other with their claws. The eagle shoots up into the sky, intending to drop his enemy from on high, but is unable to free itself from the cat's paws. So, locked in a death grip, they fall together to the earth. The monologue recalled at the end is the climax of the play. The image of the cat and the eagle, which prefer mutual destruction to giving up their prey, metaphorically embodies the irreconcilable antagonisms tearing apart contemporary American society, the cruel world, in which the relentless struggle for prey supplants all other thoughts, feelings, and interests.

Also, the result of historical circumstances is the establishment in American drama of the image of the "angry God," first introduced by O'Neill. The stern Calvinist God reigned alone over the American consciousness for the first century and a half, and even later, despite attempts from the time of the first settlements to soften the Almighty's fury at mortals, to replace God's wrath with mercy, He remained in most people's imaginations the embodiment of omnipotence, mercilessly chastising the sinful human race.

An equally essential part of the American tradition was the struggle, carried on both within and without the church, against Puritanical dogma. Conceptions of God also underwent change. American drama—in which both the canonical view and the effort to overcome it were important features of the reality represented—did not remain on the sidelines.

O'Neill was interested not only in the re-creation of the particulars of American life, past and present, however essential it might have been by itself; in his eyes, the features of reality took on significance on the basis of the possibilities they provided for examining, through their prism, the philosophical, metaphysical aspects of existence. The focus on philosophical aspects, which grew from the soil of earthly reality, became, thanks to O'Neill, a distinctive characteristic of all American playwriting. For this reason, O'Neill is concerned neither with the doctrines of any one faith nor with the various postulates corresponding to the numerous currents of Christianity, but with the problem of faith—in other words, of the supreme values and ideals in a world in which, in the words of Nietzsche, "God is dead," as well as the problem of an unjust world order, sanctified over the centuries by the authority of God.

The image of the angry God first appears in *Thirst* (1914), in which O'Neill twice compares the sun to "a great angry eye of God."[8] Reflecting the peculiarities of the author's subjective interpretation of events, this lyrical image is an unmistakable reference to the Puritan perception of existence; it also embodies the idea of a world hostile to man. From that point on, this image takes a central place in O'Neill's drama. Among the most important works in this sense is *Desire Under the Elms*, in which one of the sources of the tragedy is shown as the severe God of the Puritans, the God of stones, darkness, and loneliness. The domination of Puritan morality lies at the base of the tragedy of the heroine of *Strange Interlude* (1927), and the tragedy of the Mannon family in the monumental trilogy *Mourning Becomes Electra* (1931). It is in this, and not only in racial inequality, that O'Neill sees the causes for the protagonists' tragedy in *All God's Chillun Got Wings*. When, in one of the concluding scenes, Ella requests Jim's forgiveness, and asks whether God will forgive her, Jim answers: "Maybe He can forgive you for what you've done to me; and maybe He can forgive what I've done to you; but I don't see how He's going to forgive Himself."[9] With this, the merciful God of the preachers and the spirituals, on whom the heroes formerly placed their hopes for salvation, disappears in an instant. The delusion dissipates. For the first time, He appears to them in His true light: as the creator of universal injustice, the source of all earthly sufferings. It is also important that such a way of thinking corresponds to the characters' inner condition; it does not come across as words laid on their lips by the author, propping up his dramatic construction from the outside.

That began American drama's still ongoing quarrel with God, on whom playwrights place the responsibility for evil in the world. From the embodiment of good, from stronghold and defender—even if He be, according to the Puritan view, severe or even cruel—He is transformed in O'Neill's work into an immoral force senselessly playing with the fate of the universe entrusted to Him (*Marco Millions*).

Tennessee Williams took the next step. In *The Night of the Iguana* (1961), God unconditionally appears as the bearer of evil. True, this interpretation is suggested by the play's protagonist, Shannon. He himself is torn between the need (or habit?) to believe in a merciful God and his own insight, the result of observations of shameful and cruel, *untrue* life. It is evident in the context of the play, however, that his conception of God as the bearer of evil, more than anything, reflects the views and attitudes of contemporary man. There is a direct echo of this image in the image of the birds of prey in *Suddenly Last Summer*, which are like a hypostasis of the highest all-destroying force.

Recalling the story of his conversion, which occurred as he was reading a sermon in church, Shannon exclaims: "'Look here,' I said, I shouted, 'I'm tired of conducting services in praise and worship of a senile delinquent. . . . all your Western theologies, the whole mythology of them, are based on the concept of God as a senile delinquent and, by God, I will not and cannot continue to conduct services in praise and worship of this,

this . . . this. . . . Yeah, this angry, petulant old man. . . . a cruel senile delinquent, blaming the world and brutally punishing all he created for his own faults in construction.'"[10]

This image is developed in the same key in the work of Albee. In *The Zoo Story*, mentioned above in another context, two ideas of God come up against each other. One embodies the concept of a divine being, spread throughout the world, making sacred the most insignificant creature, the most insignificant thing; the other is of a God who has "turned his back on the whole thing some time ago."[11]

The problem of the search for God as the finding of higher spiritual values is at the center of *Tiny Alice*. Albee, however, intentionally removes from the hero's inner struggles any trace of God-seeking. Julian craves service and devotion; he cannot be satisfied with contemporary existence, locked into the narrow sphere of earthly concerns and interests. Dreaming of breaking the chains of solitude, burdensome to him, he prays to an unknown power, traditionally called God, to appear to him in any form so that he can join it, dissolving in it both his life and his very being; but in the end he is mercilessly destroyed by it. As Albee shows, the very idea of God is completely eroded for modern man, who, lost as in a dark forest, among His many incompatible images, reaches the conclusion that God has turned into an absolutely abstract idea, void of life, unable to slake the thirst of a suffering spirit.

As has been shown, the images of the jungle, cage-prison, and "angry God" are indeed widespread in American 20th-century drama. Deeply woven into its fabric, they are passed on as if in a chain from one playwright to the next. Accumulating new meanings in each new context, they create, by means of association, a dense force field. The use of one element in a work calls up echoes of numerous associations. Their transformation into recurrent images, the basis for which was laid by the work of O'Neill, was possible thanks to their high level of content. This makes these images into a subtle means of assimilating existence, making it possible to reveal the national experience in its most essential manifestations. As a result, it is possible to speak of a formed system of aesthetic components in American drama which derive from the work of its founder and reformer and which are nothing other than elements of a code of national culture.

V. M. TOLMATCHOFF

The Metaphor of History

in the Work

of F. Scott Fitzgerald

Reading the books of F. Scott Fitzgerald, one has a nagging sense that in each of his major works the author consciously or unconsciously is attempting to give a new interpretation to something he already knows—to continue and broaden some metaphor which, though very personal, is in many ways unclear even to him. Before the reader is evidence not only of the enlargement of a powerful literary idea, gradually embracing more and more of life's reality, but of the circular paths of an artistic, nearly poetic, thought, struggling with a sort of riddle of time, and therefore involuntarily turned to the past, to its sources. This informs Fitzgerald's prose with a measure of both the old and the new. It is both turn-of-the-century—alive with a sharp sense of what has passed, of the change of eras—and, at the same time, fascinated by the way time takes shape in history and myth. In Fitzgerald's opinion, Mark Twain's epoch-making novel *Huckleberry Finn* is marked by a similar dual unity: "Huckleberry Finn took the first journey back. He was the first to look back at the republic from the perspective of the west. . . . And because he turned back, we have him forever."[1] In its turn, *The Crack-Up*—autobiographical observations de profundis of the 1930s, which nostalgically reconstructs the forever bygone era of the 1920s—was a formulation of Fitzgerald's hitherto chaotic, unactualized, basically lyrical and Romantic historicism. Fitzgerald's historicism is unique, perhaps at times naive and melodramatic. Nonetheless, it is just about the most important aspect of his world-view, favorably distinguishing him from the majority of his contemporaries. One way or another, all scholars note Fitzgerald's sharp sense of time. A typical example is the opinion of Matthew Bruccoli: "Fitzgerald had a keen awareness of history—and of himself as the product of history. He understood that he was an exemplary figure (serving as a pattern, serving as a warning, serving as a type)."[2] At the same time, it seems that a full description of Fitzgerald's historical method has not yet been undertaken. That defines the goal of this essay: to show the unity of Fitzgerald's historical understanding of the world, which is realized on the most varied levels—biography, world-view, image, composition.

Fitzgerald's conception of time is not abstract but primarily biographical. Fitzgerald creates history out of his own biography; like Oscar Wilde, he confirms historical fact with his life-in-art. The Jazz Age becomes a metaphor connected with most of Fitzgerald's characters. The author's own idea of creative success and his reputation in the eyes of his readers are nearly the physical boundary of his life, the tragic Wildism of his work. The most important thing in this "life" is visual observation followed by psychological interpretation. This has its own lyrical-biographical matrix, unlike, for instance, Dos Passos with his epic attempts to re-create the widest possible stream of life. What formed this matrix and later became a symbol of Fitzgerald's writings were his interconnected relationships to wealth and women. What he said about the rich (Hemingway's reaction to them) and about Zelda's influence on his work is well known: Very important factually, at the same time it must not obscure the aesthetic side of Fitzgerald's "biographical" historical method (at times more obscured, as in *The Great Gatsby*, at others more sharply outlined, as in *Tender Is the Night*).

Carlos Baker has noted the general side of this aesthetic regarding the work of Hemingway: "It was . . . an age of indirect 'transcription,' when the perfectly sound aesthetic theory was that the author must invent out of his experience or run the risk of making hollow men of his characters."[3] In other words, closeness to reality betokens a certain "un-made up" quality, or picturesque concreteness, which the imagists consider the best

symbol, the nondescriptive-descriptive image. In his "biography of selection," Fitzgerald is close to the general aesthetic goal of the post-Flauber-
tian generation of American writers of the 1920s: ". . . to recapture the
exact feel of a moment in time and space, exemplified by people rather
than things . . . an attempt at a mature memory of a deep experience."[4]
The depth of sensual experience in this context is the measure of "super-
knowledge," the measure of skillful selection. The desire to be both outside of reality and in it is a kind of Romantic irony that makes it possible
for the author to confirm in a world known to be unconfirmable, unyielding to words, and, most important, to distance from himself the events of
his own life, making them not "Romantic." *Consciously*, Fitzgerald would
have liked to become a positivist Flaubertian. However, unlike Hemingway—with the latter's well-known inclination for "not-I": for exem-
plariness, the unsaid word, Cezannesque "museum-like" formulated-
ness—Fitzgerald is too lyrical, too fascinated by the poetry of the world's
material abundance and its sometimes deceptive, corresponding emotions. For this reason, the character closest to Fitzgerald's heart is "I"—
Fitzgerald himself; the world of the rich is very much his own.[5] From this
comes the philosophical meaning of his statement: "We were products of
prosperity. The best art is produced in times of riches."[6] From this comes
the physical-Romantic affinity that Dick Diver establishes between
Gerald Murphy and the author of *Tender Is the Night*.

This, of course, distressed Hemingway, with his motto "to write truly."
Hemingway felt that Murphy would never have behaved like Fitzgerald
and therefore accused his friend even earlier, in correspondence with M.
Perkins, of cheap Irish love of failure and "damned, bloody romanticism."[7] In his attempts in prose to be "not himself," Fitzgerald always
suffered defeat.

Particular interest in the atmosphere of well-being—ragtime, auto-
mobiles gleaming with nickel, the affluence of a country tennis club, the
fashionable bar—inevitably is present in Fitzgerald's work; nevertheless,
it does not make him a real historical writer. Here, the question again
arises of a general comparison of Hemingway and Fitzgerald. If the problem of the aesthetic ideal interests Hemingway as a problem of a somewhat abstract, model Style, it interests Fitzgerald as the experience of a
fragile, too earthly, and therefore magnetic beauty. Fitzgerald is interested
in the beauty of the material world, embodied in wealth, for its muta-
bility, fragility, and ambiguity. In the style of a Romantic, he pays it too

much attention not to notice its duality: its outer brilliance and mystery, its "secret fissure," fate, and curse. Thus, for Fitzgerald, wealth is a characterization that changes its meaning with time: a symbol of youth, with its optimism, thirst for success and recognition, its magical possibility of the impossible, and, at the same time, a symbol of aging—of life as retribution, as the defeat of what is individual and active by that which is impersonal, idle, all-equalizing.

In this way, wealth (the rich and the "new rich") is the embodiment of the Verharne-Kiplingesque "thing" (the banker, lighthouse, submarine cable, Kapshdadt), a metaphor for the newest creative energy, a heroism of sorts: It is the Nietzsche/Schopenhauer concept of the powerful illusion; it is a national myth; it is the other side of downfall. But most fundamentally, it is the model of contemporary tragedy.

Wealth, with Fitzgerald, is subject to the tragic law of Spencerian equalization—a form of contemporary fate to which all of Fitzgerald's characters, for all their remarkable individuality, are subject. Dick Diver and Nicole change places as inexorably as do Dreiser's Carrie and Hurstwood. The striving forward, the illusion of free will, are Fitzgerald's law of unhappy happiness.[8]

Fitzgerald is as much a historicist as he is a Romanticist. From this comes the main *historical* conflict in his prose—the irony of beauty, revealed in the unsolvable contradiction between illusion and reality, between potential and fulfillment. Keats's odes inescapably touch the deepest strings of Fitzgerald's soul.

The Romantic experience of the illusory nature of "material" beauty makes Fitzgerald's work complete. Writing at the time of the publication of *The Great Gatsby*, Fitzgerald said: "I am so anxious for people to see my new novel which is a new thinking out of the idea of illusion (an idea which I suppose will dominate my more serious stuff) much more mature and much more romantic than 'This Side of Paradise'."[9] It is precisely this stated measure of Romanticism, however, that brings about Fitzgerald's conscious or unconscious psychological shift, his distortion of beauty as perceived by the idealist (or "Priest," as he calls Dick Diver in his plan for *Tender Is the Night*), which is transformed from a guiding star into a fatal, nihilistic phantom. Fitzgerald, it's true, is attracted less by the fact of the downfall of a strong individual, in and of itself (the ironic hero in Fitzgerald's prose is always a bit "femininely" passive and particularly undefended against the vulgarity of the world), than by his fascination with the enigma of the individual taking in, against his will, something larger than himself, and so growing into the image of his age or generation. For Fitzgerald, the downfall of such a hero is a biographical and historical downfall, a symptom of the interruptedness of history and the age of the writer. His typical hero always carries a burden of guilt for his historical period and age of unrealized possibilities, of a certain numbness before the grip of the "beast of the age." From this comes an incongruity between the character's real age and that imagined by the reader: Daisy is *only* about twenty-two; Gatsby, like Nick, is thirty. The work of the mature Fitzgerald gives the sense of an end long approaching. It is as if Fitzgerald's "strongly weak" individual were late in being born.

There is a certain paradox here. Fitzgerald, author of the ultracontemporary (for the 1920s), "Menckenesque" novel, *This Side of Paradise*, and stories about flappers, is, at the same time, an artist who sums up his time, an artist of the American fin de siecle—in essence, a last splash of the American Gilded Age in the 20th century.[10]

I would say that Fitzgerald has a dual attitude to his character as a historical figure—authorly programmatic and inescapably human. At the level of conscious artistic conception, his attitude is fully typical of the positivist (Spencerian) treatment of existence, which, in its way, was close to both Hardy and Conrad and, after them, to Fitzgerald.[11] Behind it, the illusion of human will—the thirst, whatever happens, for self-determination (in love, career, success)—comes up against the all-equalizing, indifferent force of the universal mechanism. Strictly speaking, this conception is mechanistic and ahistorical to the degree that it lacks the theme of self-knowledge, the desire to conceive of time in ethical terms, which is alien to the idea of the amoral cycle.

Schopenhauer/Spencerian pessimism—so familiar, in particular, to Hemingway—is native to Fitzgerald in many ways, as it is to the entire post-Victorian generation.[12] "Our skepticism or cynicism . . . is due to the way H. G. Wells and other intellectual leaders have been thinking and reflecting life. Our generation has grown up upon their work."[13] Equally native is the Nietzschean idea of "victory in defeat" (". . . life is essentially a cheat and its conditions are those of defeat, and the redeeming things are not 'happiness and pleasure' but the deeper satisfactions that come out of struggle"[14]). These moods are echoed, as well, by the idea, in Fitzgerald's prose, that idealistic impulses are doomed to failure by the image of Dr. Eckleburg's empty eyes on the billboard among the mountains of ash in *The Great Gatsby*, and by the recurring motif of the "long autumn" in *Tender Is the Night*. For this reason, the surrounding world is for Fitzgerald—as it is for Mencken, whom he always admired—the "circus" of American life, a "comedy," a "marketplace," basically tawdry and unheroic. But together with this, the "fool's dance" ("In the Middle West there was wealth without background, tradition, or manners in the broad sense of the word"[15]), the special illusory nature of the age of jazz, acts as the other side both of real tragedy and of high poetry, possible in *Gatsby*, where everything is out of place (the heaps of ash and millionaire's villa do not so much contrast as complete each other), where everything, including tragedy, is unreal.

Wealth and the Jazz Age are Fitzgerald's Romantic equivalent of Hemingway's idea of the codex. Fitzgerald's "rich" are a paradoxical analogy to Hemingway's "poor" (matadors, gangsters, jockeys, barmen, and so on), an aesthetic version of the "search for the grail," the "search for the Father" in a vulgar and nonidealistic era when even the vaguest individual aspiration to something higher (given its *general* glaring absence) echoes tragedy.

Tragedy gilds everything it touches—that is Fitzgerald's "Wildean" conclusion, which he reaches not by means of Socratic arguments on the nature of beauty, but by observation of the contemporary, *American* "vanity fair," where now and then American Julien Sorels appear.

It is quite natural that, for instance, Mencken saw in *The Great Gatsby* only an action novel, melodrama, anecdote. *Fiesta*, however, was perceived in somewhat the same way. Hemingway's indignation at this extends to Fitzgerald's novel: "It's funny to write a book that seems as tragic as that and have them take it for a superficial jazz story."[16] At the same time, for Hemingway, this is a barred exit, an *experience* of tragedy, a romanticization of it. In this sense, both Dick Diver and Fitzgerald are, for him, uncontemporary heroes. Perhaps for this reason Robert Con is not simply a projection of Harold Leb but a generalization aimed at Fitzgerald. One way or another, Hemingway's very desire to see a Romantic in his "friend/enemy" is natural and penetrating. It is precisely the elemental, lyrical-biographical experience of tragedy that takes Fitzgerald's writing beyond the limits of positivist conceptions and makes him into a historian.

The author, it's true, in many ways strives to describe an ahistorical tragic situation—the eternal conflict between the lively, creative consciousness and inert existence which so attracted the writers of the turn of the century: Maupassant or Proust. On the other hand, it is enough to compare the fellow novels *Sister Carrie* and *The Great Gatsby* and *Tender Is the Night* to see the clear inconsistency in Fitzgerald's "positivism."

He is too much the student (the Princeton set of 1913) in his reading, too unserious, and sometimes uneven as a writer, too fascinated by life and his writing career. His "image" against the background of the trendsetters of the 1920s (Joyce, Eliot) is not terribly contemporary. What's more, Fitzgerald is almost old-fashioned in his fascination with the person as such, with the Balsacian riddles of "splendor and poverty," with being lost as a special measure of lyrical sensitivity to existence. In this sense, the person, we will risk saying, does not interest Hemingway; everything there is too clear to him. Another matter is the person as a measure of application. Hemingway was, of course, quite right in his refusal to make his heroes "lost," which he programmatically announced in two debating epigraphs to *The Sun Also Rises*. However, even if we assume that they are lost, it is somehow apart from that lostness—outside their generation, without age, children, or past.

Fitzgerald's biographical "card" is nearly always on the table. This allowed Malcolm Cowley to say of Fitzgerald that he created in a roomful of clocks and calendars. It is natural to assume that an intense interest in the passage of time, stated "Bergsen fashion" in the textbook-famous concluding lines of *The Great Gatsby*, is personal to Fitzgerald as a writer; he never tried to conceal this. We may turn to two statements about the way the image of Gatsby was formed. "He was perhaps created on the image of some forgotten farm type in Minnesota that I have known and forgotten, and associated at the same moment with some sense of romance"; "I never at any one time saw him clear myself—for he started as one man I knew and then changed into myself—the amalgam was never complete in my mind."[17]

Thus Gatsby was a sort of metaphor for the author's historically dynamic, Romantic feeling, a look at "himself," his own "novelistic" face. The novel is, for Fitzgerald, nearly the strongest type of self-description, the other side of biography, the "safe conduct" of his creative "alter ego." "In the true novel you have to stay with the character all the time, and you acquire a sort of second wind about him, a depth of realization."[18]

In other words, *The Great Gatsby* is the author's first mature reflection about himself, an attempt in prose to consider the field of his literary activity from two perspectives, the dramatic—involving events, calculated, directed from the past to the future—and the lyrical, looking backward, not considering dramatic effect but revealing the inadequacy of the past, the one-sidedness of overly strict evaluations. *The Great Gatsby* is the first landmark and, as it happened, a truly fateful one, both in the history of the Fitzgerald character and in the history of the author. (Fitzgerald, having put too much that was personal into the book, was emotionally unprepared for its lack of success.) This, in essence, was the first real step toward recognition of himself as not new at all but as the last novelist of the old world.

Indeed, the year 1925 was fated to be a critical one for Fitzgerald. For this reason, *The Great Gatsby* is an overburdened novel—a personal novel, a novel of its decade, and of its generation—the book and its image as a historical occurrence seemed to become interchangeable with the name of their creator. Too much points to this overburdening: the upsetting result of the "sweet life" with Zelda from October 1922 to April 1924, on Long Island; Zelda's infatuation with Edouard Jozan in June 1924, on the Riviera; and, of course, the stubborn recognition by Fitzgerald of his lack of a place in "*real* history," of his creative fatigue. "I feel old too . . . the whole burden of this novel—the loss of those illusions that give such coda to the world so that you don't care whether things are true or false as long as they partake of the magical glory."[19] "That September 1924, I knew something had happened that could never be repaired."[20] "America's greatest promise is that something is going to happen, and after awhile you get tired of waiting because nothing happens to people except that they grow old, and nothing happens to American art because America is the story of the moon that never rose."[21] In the last statement the personal tragedy is brought "outside," romanticized, as the past immediately preceding it is unintentionally romanticized—the historical setting of the novel. Then the Fisk-Gouldian past, projecting Gatsby into the unheroic present, becomes, without any irony, "gilded." "Here were figures more romantic, men of great dreams, of high faith in their work. . . ."[22]

The "gildedness" of Fitzgerald's characters comes of their mythological status, their right to be a "generation within a generation." As I have said, fascination with the calendar was typical of Fitzgerald's thinking—who is not a graduate of Princeton is already of the "flapper" or "pre-flapper" generation. There is something childlike but at the same time inflexible in this hard division—the psychological illness of age, "captive to time"

(Pasternak). It is interesting that Fitzgerald considers himself part of the post-Victorian but prewar generation—"pre-Hemingway." We "belonged to the period before the newspaperman and American war hero on the Italian front."[23] He probably bases his reckoning not on real age. Tom Buchanan, Gatsby, and Nick Carraway are approximately of the same age; but they belong to different eras, Tom and Gatsby—in fact, to contrasting ones, the "new" and the "old." The disappearance of "old" America during Prohibition was the "biographical" downfall of the author himself. Resurrecting what has gone, experiencing himself anew, is, naturally, dear to Fitzgerald; but somehow, due to a fateful Romantic demonism, it shortens his real age. His journals point to his creative "complete death in earnest": "Drunk at 20, wrecked at 30, dead at 40."[24]

Nonetheless, however Fitzgerald may have mythologized the era of the 1920s, lyrically extending it into a biography of tragedy, into a history of a life "blazing like a rocket" but unrealized, his historicism is not only individual in outlook, it leans on literary tradition.

His literary generation was for Fitzgerald a general intellectual store of knowledge, a sphere of reading and a creative community. Upon the advice of Edmund Wilson, he drew up a list of necessary reading; he discussed his innermost plans with Hemingway, who previously had acquainted him with Maxwell Perkins; he advised Thomas Wolfe. He was learning to write. It is as if Fitzgerald wished to place his periods wherever the artists of *his* tradition did not place them. If Hemingway, who learned to write in the same way, wished in his "classics" to go beyond the confines of literature, to create a literature "outside" literature, an anticultural literature, Fitzgerald, on the contrary, as a Romantic, lived by the idea of communal creation, of the "voice" of the era. His lyricism recreates literary material close to him, which in its own way follows the recommendation of T. S. Eliot in his essay "Tradition and the Individual Talent": "A good style . . . doesn't form unless you absorb half a dozen top-flight authors every year. Or rather it *forms* but, instead of being a subconscious amalgam of all that you have admired it is simply a reflection of the last writer you have read, a watered-down journalese."[25]

Fitzgerald never concealed the importance of his sphere of reading, nor the degree of influence on him that his favorites had: Keats, McKenzie, Wells, Conrad, Dreiser, Spengler. In *The Beautiful and the Damned*, the literariness is, so to speak, external, on the level of various epigraphs, ironically allowing the author, again comparing himself with his friend and rival, to refer to the novel thus: "T.S.P. A Romance and a Reading List Sun Also Rises. A Romance and A Guide Book."[26] In *The Great Gatsby*, the accord between the author's intentions and tradition is internal. This novel, seemingly completely personal, is literary in many ways. I point to at least four series of parallels:

1. The series of "sound" parallels (I refer to the names of some characters: with "The Story of the *Gadsbys*" (1888) by Kipling; and also the poetic echo of two other titles: "Tono-Bungay" (1909) and "Babbitt" (1922); and the theme of ruined love between Dick Heldar and *Maisie* in Kipling's "The Light that Failed" (1890).

2. The series of plot, "descriptive" parallels: the ending of "Nostromo" (1904): the "accidental" murder; the "poetry" of shoes, jackets, and wallets in *Sister Carrie* (1900).

3. The series of compositional parallels with *Heart of Darkness* (1902): the narrator (who both participates in events and later recounts them) who is captivated by the "magic" of a powerful individual.

4. The series of textual parallels: with *Tono-Bungay*—especially the last chapter of the novel (Book 4, Chapter 3), with its concluding lines: "We all do our business then disappear, striving for some unknown goal, forward, onto the open sea," echoed in the final chord of *The Great Gatsby*.[27]

The degree of literary borrowing is always a delicate question. For us, within the framework of our stated subject, what is important is the establishment of the fact that there are literary echoes, and its *historical* aspect: the indisputable creative turning to various texts points to a mature sense of literary continuity. At the same time, the historical-literary background of Fitzgerald's prose allows us to point also to the original traits of the artistic historicism of *The Great Gatsby*, to the conception of "point of view" in the novel. In this context, let us look at the seemingly well-studied echo between Fitzgerald and Conrad.[28]

For Fitzgerald, Conrad was a great authority on the art of writing. Admission of his unpaid debt to the English writer is a leitmotif in Fitzgerald's correspondence over many years. In a letter to Mencken (May or June 1925), he notes: "By the way you mention in your review of *Sea Horses* that Conrad has only two imitators. How about . . . Me in *Gatsby* (God! I've learned a lot from him)."[29]

The compositional structure of *Heart of Darkness* and *The Great Gatsby* are marked by an indisputable similarity. The figure of Marlow fills the same compositional role as does Nick Carraway. Both are narrators, recounting in the first person events of the past. We must note, it's true, that in Conrad's work, the narrator is not, in fact, Marlow but the author's "I." Marlow tells of events which have had a profound influence on him, and he gives them, to the best of his abilities, modern philosophical commentary. But the second "I," present on deck, also has a definite relationship to Marlow's story. It now and again makes itself known, bringing certain correctives to the description of the situation. Correspondingly, the story has a double opening—one from the author's "I" (informing us who is telling, where, how, and about what), the other from Marlow, who, gazing at the water, begins to speak of his respect for people, "of ideas," and recalls in connection with this an event from his own youth.

What are the correctives mentioned above? The most important lies in the fact that the author's "I" considers Marlow's entire tale unconvincing. And that is understandable. Marlow speaks of the past not as of some anecdote, taken as such—" . . . to him the meaning of the episode was not inside like a kernel but outside, enveloping the tale which brought it out only as a glow brings out a haze . . ."[30] In other words, Marlow speaks not for the sake of the past (anecdote), but for the very process of telling in the present; he is interested in today's reaction to what has been. As a result, he does not so much recall the past as try to convey the feelings aroused in him by those recollections. For this reason, Marlow's story does not really captivate readers; almost all of them fall asleep by the end of the narrative. He himself admits that to communicate how one experiences life in a certain period of time is impossible. Marlow lacks a sense of history; his memory is associative, his method of reconstructing the past, impressionistic.

Fitzgerald has a different sort of narrator—as do Faulkner, in *Absalom, Absalom!* and Robert Penn Warren, in *All the King's Men.* For American writers, Conrad's type of narrator is a recognizable figure (in Henry James, point of view is, as a rule, not personified), a biographer and historian. Perhaps in the final account he gives a subjective picture of reality (of the "enigmatic" past), but his striving to present this picture in as many-sided a way as possible is clear. For this reason many versions of the reconstruction of the past are juxtaposed (*Absalom, Absalom!*), or the teller makes additional investigations in archives and libraries (*All the*

King's Men). That is, the lapse of time between the occurrence of events and the time at which their story is concluded is, without a doubt, filled for the narrator with moral (creative) meaning. Such an event in the past (and the thoughts connected with it, most often, involving the problem of choice, overcoming, trial) becomes a turning point in the teller's biography. Through it are measured the inevitable questions that arise about the meaning of life, the connection of times, and so forth. In this way, this type of narrator becomes, if we recall the words of August Schlegel, a "historian-prophet, turned to the past," a witness to the particular redemptive fullness of time. Ishmael, if we are to speak of Melville, can again return to the story of Ahab, which he has reconstructed *many times*, and Warren's Jack Burden can continue writing the book about Cass Mastern. For some, this length of time, this psychological vacuum between past and present is comforting; it gives a new direction to their activity. For others, it is unbearable, resulting in a sort of historical neurosis which threatens insanity and death (Quentin Compson).

Nick Carraway, too, discovers himself in reflection about the past. In the autumn of 1923, he tells of events of one year before. In fact, he does not *tell* but *writes*. Nick is a writer. For this reason, two kinds of interpretation of the past touch in the novel. The first is connected with the image of the "historian-biographer," the second with the shape of the "novel within a novel," which, following the work of Proust, had by 1925 become the intellectual fashion. *The Great Gatsby* is one of the first, rather imperfect, "novels within novels" in American literature of the 1920s, a lyrical discussion "in images."

After the tragedy of the summer of 1922, Nick returns home, to the Midwest. Nearly a year goes by before he picks up the pen. Before us is the process of creating a book, followed through to completion by its creator. The author's doubts about what he has written are conveyed by these comments: "He told me all this very much later, but I've put it down here . . .";[31] "only Gatsby, the man who gives his name to this book . . ." (page 126). Apparently Carraway has an idea of the book; but at the same time, his personal attitude toward the material being arranged has been formed gradually. He solves compositional difficulties as he goes along, comparing various—verified and unverified—facts and accompanying them with commentary.

It was not by chance that Nick began to write: ". . . I was rather literary in college . . ." (page 128), he says of himself. After college, Carraway

probably keeps, from time to time, something like a journal, entering
there (in fragments) various observations. He made some notes during
the first half of the summer of 1922, that is, when he had only just met
Gatsby. But during *that summer* Nick did not give him the same significance *as later*. "Reading over what I have written so far, I see I have given
the impression that the events of three nights several weeks apart were all
that absorbed me. On the contrary, they were merely casual events in a
crowded summer, and, until much later, they absorbed me infinitely less
than my personal affairs" (page 169). All the more surprising is it that
Nick, who at first was not particularly interested in the circumstances of
Gatsby's life, nevertheless makes many notes about them. What kind of
notes? And how?

To answer these questions we will try to determine when Nick and
Gatsby made each other's acquaintance. We have two facts from which to
reckon: (1) Nick and Tom Buchanan's visit to Myrtle's apartment; (2)
Gatsby receives on Saturdays. About the first fact: Nick and Tom appear
in Wilson's garage on Sunday ("The supercilious assumption was that on
Sunday afternoon I had nothing better to do" [page 143]). When they
leave, Nick notices that an Italian boy is placing torpedoes along the
railroad track—in a few days it will be Independence Day. If we look at a
calendar from 1922, we will discover that July 4 came on a Tuesday. Therefore, Sunday's events took place on *July 2*.

About the second fact: Gatsby's calling hours are on Saturdays. In
June, Nick was not yet acquainted with his neighbor; he meets him on a
Saturday during the first half of the month (July 8 or 15), after receiving
an official invitation to visit. This occurs on July 8. About *two weeks* after
meeting Gatsby, Nick meets Jordan Baker in New York. In his words, the
meeting took place at the "height of summer," in other words, in the
middle of July. Therefore, the second date proposed, July 15, is eliminated.
In July, Carraway sees Gatsby only two or three times and is only mildly
interested in him. Nevertheless, during the *first half* of July, Nick notes in
the margin of the train schedule (July 5, judging by the heading) the
names of those who visit Gatsby. And what a list! It takes up a good three
pages. It is hard to believe that Nick did this just by chance. The only
thing we can suggest is that he makes such notes *regularly*.

A year later, Nick writes the story of Gatsby, and these notes—now on
a schedule yellowed by time—help him reconstruct a faithful picture of
the historical background of events. However, Carraway puts this list into

his novel with changes; this is of no little importance—the novel's historical field loses its static quality and gains duration. Listing the colorful
names of the guests, Nick also notes what happened to them *later*. There
are four such figures: the doctor Webster Civet, Ripley Snell, Henry L.
Palmetto, and the young Quinn. And what do we learn? The doctor
drowned, Snell was put in prison, Palmetto threw himself under a subway
train, and the Quinns divorced. But how did Nick learn the fate of people
he barely knew? After all, since October 1922 he has lived in the country,
somewhere in Minnesota or Illinois; the doctor died in Maine, and Palmetto killed himself in New York. One thing unites these facts: All of
them could have been found in newspapers, especially in those sections
where items of a sensational or scandalous nature are printed. Nick is
interested in such information; it was from the newspaper that he learned
of Jordan Baker's supposed fraud and of Meyer Wolfsheim's dark past.
When the narrator mentions the notice of Gatsby's end, it becomes clear
that Carraway makes use of various sources to create the story of the past,
including the newspaper, all of which he compares, doubting the truth of
his own version, which has gradually become not only the compositional
pivot of *The Great Gatsby* but its main moral-historical component.

If we try to distinguish as much as possible an independent line in the
novel connected with Nick, we discover that although it is frequently not
clearly expressed, it is even so the complete story of a person for whom the
events of the summer and fall of 1922 were a turning point, a serious test of
his views on life. Carraway's line develops parallel to Gatsby's, doubling it
in many ways. Only here does it become clear that Nick is the only
character in the novel whose personality and views change in the course of
events—rather, not in the course of events, but in the course of his own
gradual thinking out of them. A change of places has occurred. Gatsby's
story is over; but, in being over, it opens up the novel. Now Gatsby is no
longer "revealed" through Nick, but the reverse—Carraway unwittingly
writes his own biography, in which Gatsby is the most noticeable historical reference point.

It is clear to readers that Nick the narrator differs from Nick the participant in events; he is more mature and insightful. But what is the deeper
meaning of his age? Could it really be that his return home in the fall of
1922 can be explained by the fact that he was able to see several faces in the
wealthy Gatsby (the "outer," vulgar and striving vulgarly whatever happens, even in the name of a high goal, to express himself, but also the

"inner," full of an integrity which can only come from high and pure feelings), and now intends to reflect upon this more or less soberly, "far from the madding crowd"? Nick unintentionally answers this question; frequently the information that he reports by the by is of greater interest than that which he discusses according to his plan. Such information tells us that even in the incident involving him, there are grounds for moral conflict, allowing him to doubt *himself* (in the case of Gatsby, this does not occur, which, in fact, cannot but lead to his "death"—a metaphor for the final incompatability of high goals and low means), to doubt his ability to judge others quickly and impartially, to doubt his critical (writer's) gift.

In two similar situations in the past—the relationship with the girl from his hometown, about which even Daisy, who has not seen Nick for a long time, knows; and the little affair with the girl from Jersey City (1:169)—Nick leaves the solution to difficult circumstances to chance. It is natural to suppose that a situation resembling those first two is again arising, growing into a genuine tragedy. This time, too, it is resolved by events that apparently do not depend on Nick (the explanation in the Plaza Hotel, Gatsby's death) but which he can no longer dismiss. The development of his relationship with Gatsby, on the one hand, and with Jordan Baker, on the other, helps him to understand the vulnerability of his too-wise position; it is impossible to take part, even "carelessly," in events, in the circle-dance of "careless" (page 267) deception (every one of the novel's heroes deceives somebody), and at the same time to stand above them, although the "alibi" of participating in a "lost" battle, to some degree, gives him grounds for this. Carraway finds the strength to admit (during his last conversation with Jordan Baker) that he, too, is one of the "counterfeiters". This leads him—like Charlie, the hero of *Babylon Revisited*—to *return*, to gain a special tragic soberness, to become closer to the mysteries of life and death. It is possible that there is another reason behind his departure for the Midwest. It could be that Carraway, having taken the important step of learning his own place in life, and having rejected any further moral compromise, now considers it absolutely necessary to fully clarify his relationship with the girl from his hometown and, perhaps, to marry her. The lesson of the summer of 1922 could not fail to have left a mark on Nick. In his thoughts he returns over and over to the past—reliving it, giving it new meaning. This makes it clear why he takes up his novel—intensive moral reconsideration of the past makes possible the birth of a writer.

In the same way for Fitzgerald himself, the novel is a symbol of what he has won back from the past (the all-cleansing river of life), a history of his critical thought, confirming, despite the limited time he is given, his place in existence. Nowhere does he express this more strongly than in certain fragments of *The Great Gatsby*. The most important thing in Fitzgerald's attitude toward history (where that attitude is emphasized, it is vitally important for him) is the tradition of critical (historical) understanding as a moral principle. The investing of historical understanding with moral strength (poetry), the tragic experience of history, of "Dantesque" spirals of creative self-knowledge, at times reveal in Fitzgerald a writer who, like Dostoevsky, and by virtue of his "love-hate" relationship to the Catholic chapters of his biography, is close to the ideal of the Christian theodicy: the possibility of creative redemption for suffering. For this reason, the symbolic theme of the search for life's higher meaning is embodied in *Gatsby*, albeit inconsistently. Maxwell Perkins, in particular, who knew better than any the weaknesses and strengths of his friend, the author, noticed this level of the book.[32]

Thus Fitzgerald's relationship to history, whatever side we look at—the biographical, psychological, historical-literary, or compositional—was Romantically strained. The sense of a decisive historical step, and at the same time of an imperceptible shift in time, when "what has been ideally conceived . . . has turned vulgar, material" is the main, deeper, both materially and poetically, event of Fitzgerald's artistic world.[33] This lyrical tone, this particular *Americanism* of his, compensates for much—a certain naiveté, unevenness in his writing, "commercial" elements.

Fitzgerald's relationship to history is double-edged, the desire to say as well as possible what only he knows seems to have devoured him, to have shortened his life. For this reason, Fitzgerald's creative fate contains a kind of irrevocability, which was somehow cultivated by him. Thomas Wolfe, for instance, saw in this "romance with himself" the beginning of his decline, a menacing warning to the writer's talent. One way or another, it was precisely this "fateful" trait of Fitzgerald's which, for following generations of readers, became a metaphor for the tragic enigma of the *contemporary* writer in America.

NATALIA YAKIMENKO

Ernest Hemingway

The Road to Literary Craft

Ernest Hemingway was decidedly set against the idea of critics studying his early journalistic period. Louis Henry Cohn's attempt, in 1931, to collect and analyze for the first time the newspaper articles written in the early 1920s ran up against the author's fierce resistance.[1] Hemingway felt he was being deprived of one of his main rights as an artist: to select and publish the best of his work and to conceal and reject what was unsuccessful, incidental, or simply written as a journalistic opus, "hurriedly, for money, on the topic of the day." Hemingway sincerely felt that his early journalism "had nothing in common with his other writing, which was absolutely distinctive beginning with his first book, *In Our Time*." From 1951 to 1953, Charles Fenton's desire to release research on "the apprenticeship of Ernest Hemingway," using materials from various newspapers for which Hemingway had worked, again raised harsh protests from the writer. Hemingway even·considered copyrighting his articles in the *Toronto Star* in order to prevent Fenton from using them in his book.[2] In letters, he was openly indignant: "I know few things worse than for another writer to collect a fellow writer's journalism which his fellow writer has elected not to preserve because it is worthless and publish it."[3]

Gradually, following the course of America's literary development, the question of the relationship of Hemingway's experience in journalism to his artistic work moved to the forefront, placing his reputation in doubt. Donald Barthelme, a contemporary American writer of "meta-literature," recently mentioned Hemingway's name in a typical context: "It seemed clear that the way to become a writer was to go to work for a newspaper, as Hemingway had done—then, if you were lucky, you might write fiction. I don't think anybody believes that anymore."[4] In a paradoxical way, Hemingway became a new symbol of an old literary tradition that appeared in America after the Civil War. It extolled the role of direct life experience—the "universities" of life (to use the association, inescapable, in the Russian context, with Maxim Gorky's book)—in the formation of the artist and affirmed the idea that the newspaper is the best school for the writer. The majority of American writers at the turn of the century— Hemingway's direct forebears—had journalistic training: Norris, Twain, London, Crane, Dreiser, Lardner.

Sherwood Anderson took a decisive step toward breaking with this tradition. It was from Anderson that Hemingway first heard of the inevitably ruinous influence on the writer of such work. Gertrude Stein held the same opinion.[5] In 1924, following the advice of his literary mentors, Hemingway left newspaper work. In 1933, he renewed his journalistic activity, this time not to abandon it until shortly before his death. But he nonetheless continued to hold a disdainful attitude toward the trade. Hemingway many times repeated modified versions of Anderson and Stein's old claim: journalism traumatizes the writer; "he will always have the scars from it."[6]

But all the same, Hemingway himself, to a certain degree, roused critics' interest in his early journalism. In a series of sketches written for *Esquire* between 1933 and 1936, he avidly made use of the role of "veteran newspaperman," sharing gripping recollections from his youth as a reporter—about the Lausanne Conference, his acquaintance and friendship with William Bolitho, and so forth. Hemingway was somehow impressed with the image of the omnipresent reporter who, from the scene of events, sends anonymous reports to his paper by telegraph. His revulsion, it seemed, was at another sort of journalist: the columnist, who everywhere unabashedly writes "I, me, my pieces," and in general "projects his personality rather than [going] for the facts."[7]

Furthermore, Hemingway had serious reasons for not allowing critics to study his early journalism. Fenton's first research revealed that Hemingway the journalist definitively represented his detested category, the columnist. Nonetheless, Fenton tried to prove that journalism formed Hemingway's creative individuality, that the celebrated "reporter's" style characteristic of his early prose was the product of this experience. As a result, he attached particular meaning to the one purely journalistic period in Hemingway's life, his six-month employment at the *Kansas City Star* in 1918. Hemingway himself praised that paper's collection of stylistic rules, calling them, in an interview in 1940, "the best rules for writing I've ever learned." But later, in correspondence with Fenton, Hemingway's constant position was one of battle against exaggeration. He could not agree with the idea that he had been "taught to write" by his colleagues at the *Kansas City Star*, Pete Wellington, the assistant editor, "who was brilliant at training reporters" but no more than that, or the leading columnist, Lionel Moise, whose "style . . . was flamboyant and rhetorical," and whose talent was "undisciplined."[8] And, of course, Hemingway would never have agreed with the idea that "the most rudimentary extension would alter" some typical *Kansas City Star* paragraph "into the fragmentary sketches [he] was producing five years later in such work as 'A Very Short Story' and 'The Revolutionist.' "[9] Now, when it is known exactly which passages in the *Kansas City Star* came from Hemingway's pen, one can see a considerable mythology in the idea of a particular "journalistic source," or of the lessons of objective and economic writing. Hemingway's most interesting and successful writings of 1918 have a clear shade of "literariness."

Describing a night shift at the city hospital, Hemingway—simply an anonymous author for his readers at the time—was not content with a dry listing of events. His ambitious intentions are given away by his lofty comment about "the wider range life and death tragedy—and even comedy," in the hospital.[10] This material, which is considered to have "evident similarities" with the prose miniatures in *In Our Time*, contains historical reminiscences that demonstrate the young writer's erudition: about the sufferings of the old typesetter threatened with the loss of a finger, he says, "the French artist who vowed to commit suicide if he lost his right hand in battle, might have understood."[11] A paraphrase of the well-known dictum "to know yet to dare" adorned his passage about tank-driving recruits as a possible motto for the bold fighters.[12] The ethnic color of his passages on Leo Kobreen, an acquaintance of Hemingway's and a Russian emigré who outwardly resembled Kerensky, is maintained by the exotic comparison of American office boys to "Cossacks of the business world."[13]

It was to be expected that the journalistic experience provided by the *Kansas City Star* would reveal itself in 1920, when Hemingway first began to publish under his own name in the *Toronto Star Weekly* and had the freedom to choose his subject matter and the way of presenting it. However, Hemingway's articles demonstrate clear contempt for the Kansan City rules. Not only are they full of stylistic excesses, they are "literary" through and through.

The history of Hemingway's literary apprenticeship is thrown into a different light altogether if we pay due attention to his earliest credited journalism from 1920. Articles and sketches written before his acquaintance with Sherwood Anderson, before he traveled to Paris and met Gertrude Stein and Ezra Pound, can give an idea of the initial orientation of Hemingway's talent. By them, one can judge just how "bookish" the young Hemingway's perception of reality was, how comfortable he felt in that cultural element and, on the contrary, how alien to his inner nature were the principles of journalism, with its fixation on facts. In this, Hemingway's early journalism resembles his first artistic work.[14]

In his articles, Hemingway reveals an inclination toward the burlesque, parody, and satire in which he can operate with prepared formulas and devices and make use of material already mastered, which has been made sense of by the surrounding culture. He needs additional support and a clearly designated context to express his position, his attitude to the object of description; therefore, he uses many historical and literary allusions, open and concealed quotations and paraphrases. Polemic acts as a purely journalistic method of creating context in his articles. Linguistic reality has independent meaning. Wordplay rather than facts lies at the base of many of his descriptions.

Here is the beginning of his second article published in the *Toronto Star*: "The land of the free and home of the brave is the modest phrase used by certain citizens of the republic to the south of us to designate the country they live in. They may be brave—but there is nothing free." Hemingway further plays upon the many meanings of the word *free*, recalling that it costs $75 to join the order of "Freemasons." He crowns this combination with the flashy and empty phrase: "The true home of the free and the brave is the barber college."[15]

The young Hemingway was irresistibly drawn to verbal effect. In his early articles it is easy to find examples of wordplay. He eagerly used hackneyed quotations, aphorisms, and allusions in comical, "lowering" contexts. "When Prohibition came into effect, the St. Louis brewers believed that the end had come to the brewery business. . . . Chicago saw the handwriting on the brewery wall, but didn't believe it for a moment" (p. 75). But Hemingway could be surprisingly serious in his treatment of commonly used poetic images and metaphors: "Canada is a closed book to the average Yank, a book with a highly colored jacket by Robert W. Service" (p. 54). "Even if you escape all the various brands of criminal homicide that Chicago offers, the nightgowny person with the scythe has another sickle up his wide-flowing sleeve. There have been to date four hundred and twenty people killed this year in Chicago by motor cars" (p. 59). It is hard to suppose that the writer of such a sentence would ever wish or be able to describe death "scientifically."

Hemingway's discussion of the changing American Wild West turns into a rather empty and forced play on words, drawing on a quote from Tennyson's "Morte d'Arthur": "In place of the Redskins biting the dust it is now the commercial traveler that bites the dust. Where the elk once roamed, the Elk now roams, but with him are the Mason and Odd Fellow. Thus, to coin a phrase, the old order passeth, giving way to the new" (p. 58).

But the central structure of this 1920 article about life in Chicago during Prohibition—the heyday of bootlegging, gambling, and crime—is the colorful formula Hemingway has found: the American West has moved to Chicago. This formula is nourished by, and based on, the image of Chicago rooted in mass consciousness: "It was as good as the movies portray. It had faro, dice, wide-open towns, bad Injuns, red eye, gamblers in frock coats, Bill Hart bad men, discriminate and indiscriminate killings, and all the jolly features" (p. 58). It remains for Hemingway to put his observations of Chicago into a stable structure. The conclusion is ready: "So there is murder, drink and gambling in the new Wild West just as in the old" (p. 59).

An equally clear-cut formula serves as the core of another satirical article from 1920, "Car Prestige." It is that contemporary American society is a new feudal system in which people are divided into classes according to their automobile. Making use of varied comic effects and devices, altering the names of cars in an Alice in Wonderland way, Hemingway convinces his readers that to become the owner of a "Pierced-Sparrow" is in no way inferior to receiving knighthood.

Robert O. Stephens noted in his research that, as a journalist, Hemingway worked largely as "an interpreter of events, not as a reporter."[16] On many occasions, as we see, it was not even events or phenomena themselves that were the main objects of his interpretation; in his early articles, the road to reality often passes through plays on linguistic and cultural formulas. Interpretation itself might consist of the insertion of an occurrence into an already familiar model.

This tendency makes itself felt even in those of Hemingway's articles in which the author's orientation to his own life observation, experience, and knowledge dominates. Dominates, but not singly.

The opening of the article (very important for Hemingway in its subject matter), about those who refused to serve in the army during war but were taken for heroes after it ended ("Popular in Peace—Slacker in War," March 13, 1920), was built on an ironic play on bombastic militaristic-patriotic rhetoric: "During the late friction with Germany a certain number of Torontonians of military age showed their desire to assist in the conduct of the war by emigrating to the States to give their all to laboring in munition plants. Having amassed large quantities of sheckels through their patriotic labor, they now desire to return to Canada and gain fifteen percent on their United States money" (p. 10). The overblown-enthusiastic stylization provided a necessary, contrasting background for the main part of the article—sarcastic and deliberately practical advice for everyone who wished to be mistaken for a war veteran.

Equally straightforward, in this 1920 article, Hemingway used elements of parody and preaching. The article ends with an angry address to shameless frauds: "Go to your room alone some night. Take your bankbook out of your desk and read it through. Put it back in your desk. . . . Stand in front of your mirror and look yourself in the eye and remember that there are fifty-six thousand Canadians dead in France and Flanders. Then turn out the light and go to bed" (p. 11).

Critics have justly noted the distant thematic dialogue between this early article and the story "Soldier's Home."[17] Nonetheless, in the most important sense, there is an abyss between the two. The differences here are of an entirely different sort from those revealed by a comparison, such as has been made more than once, of, for instance, Hemingway's reporting on the Greek refugees in 1922 and the prose piece based on it, which became the second chapter of *In Our Time*.[18] There we find a divergence of details, clearly illustrating the ways in which prose will always differ from journalism, even if the author, material, and time of writing are the same. Here, there is a difference in the very type of perception and thought.

In another article as well, Hemingway seeks support in other texts and in the words of others: "Lieutenants' Mustaches" (April 10, 1920), which is devoted to the same problem, significant for him, of genuine and sham veterans. This article is his first well-known attempt at describing the inner state of a soldier returning from the front. Through a dialogue between two veterans, Billy and Jack, Hemingway immediately distinguishes and illustrates the sore spots of this subject; but he does not pass up the opportunity to play upon them in a comic key and draw a straightforward conclusion. In the article, two Canadian lieutenant-veterans observe an old building being destroyed. The conversation revolves around various sorts of explosions. Veterans of the front, they would like to feel themselves experts in this area. Inner honesty, however, forces them to admit that they "ain't efficient ourselves" and that, in general, they "didn't get nothing permanent good out of the war except the lieutenants' mustaches" (p. 19). The constant source of comedy in the article is the veterans' unwillingness to listen to each other's war reminiscences. The lively, situationally grounded dialogue concludes with Billy's story of a different sort of veteran, a "young fellow . . . had kind of a sentimental turn," whom he met at his sister's: "He looked kind of familiar but I couldn't quite place him. I was in the other room readin' the paper and he was talkin' with my sister's friend. 'Betty,' says he mournful like, 'this is the way I feel,' and he recited that thing by this Kipling bloke. 'Me that has been what I've been. Me that 'as seen what I've seen—' you know how it goes. Well, when he come to the place where it goes 'Me that stuck out to the last—' I recognized him. . . . Used to be batman to the R.T.O. at Boulogne . . ." (pp. 19–20).

Hemingway directly quotes three lines from Kipling's poem, "Chant-Pagan," which consists of the monologue of an English soldier returning home from service in an irregular army. Knowledge of the poem unites all the characters in the article, although it is none other than the false veteran who recites it to the girl. It is possible that Hemingway thought to use the situation as a means of discussing not only that character but also Kipling's text. This is fairly surprising, if we recall that Kipling was Hemingway's favorite writer during his school years and that he openly imitated Kipling's novellas in the prose pieces he attempted to write in 1919–20.[19] This article contains an attempt, albeit timid, at "estrangement" of the Kipling text, and polemic with it.

To a much larger degree but in an entirely different way, Hemingway made use of the opportunity for dialogue with Kipling's "Chant-Pagan" as a complete work in the story "Soldier's Home" (1924), which is devoted to the same theme—return from war. Here, Hemingway productively assimilates Kipling's artistic experience on both the methodic and the conceptual level. Economically and expressively, Hemingway characterizes his hero, Krebs, as a real soldier simply by naming the places where he fought: "At first Krebs, who had been at Belleau Wood, Soissons, the Champagne, St. Mihiel and in the Argonne did not want to talk about the war at all."[20] It would seem that Hemingway was simply generalizing his own artistic practice when he placed on the lips of Lieutenant Henry in *A Farewell to Arms* the celebrated argument that "abstract words like 'glory, feat, valor' . . . were obscene next to the concrete names of towns, numbers of roads, names of rivers . . .", that "in the end, only the names of places retained dignity."[21] But, judging by "Chant-Pagan," Hemingway must share the honor of that discovery with Kipling, whose hero also spoke of himself as him "that was through Di'mond 'Ill,/An' Pieters an' Springs an' Belfast—/From Dundee to Vereeniging all."[22]

It is interesting to compare other characteristics of Kipling's and Hemingway's heroes as well. Kipling's soldier "stuck out to the last" in war; Krebs, on the front, "had done the one thing, the only thing for a man to do, easily and naturally."[23] Krebs "did not want to come home."[24] Kipling's hero is simply enraged that he must "take on/With awful old England again." For an old soldier, living according to the rules of society is torture, but, suppressing his indignation, he is forced to submit:

> I am doin' my Sunday-school best,
> By the 'elp of the Squire an' 'is wife . . .
> To come in an' 'ands up an' be still,
> 'An honestly work for my bread . . .

Krebs's parents vainly try to incline him to fulfill the same elementary, Sunday-school obligations to society—to believe that "We are all of us in [God's] Kingdom," and to "look for a job."[25]

> Oh! it's 'ard to behave as they wish
> (Too 'ard, and a little too soon),
> I'll 'ave to think over it first—
>
> ME!

Krebs could have said just the same of himself.

The initial condition of the heroes of "Soldier's Home" and "Chant-

Pagan" is superfluousness and alienation. The image of the former soldier in both Kipling's and Hemingway's treatment is the image of the "outsider," the man who has lost his connection to the world in which he belongs, both by birth and by upbringing. Both writers present return-from-war as a process of giving new meaning to universally recognized institutions, values, and rules. Moreover, Kipling and Hemingway stress the same thing: The experience of war places in doubt, above all, the imperatives of Christian morality.

Not by chance did Kipling title his poem "Chant-Pagan", and build it on a series of contrasts. The indignant hero opposes his "Me!" to "awful old England"; real, free, camp life to regulated, decorous existence; the military trade to all other occupations; and, finally, the elemental pagan frame of mind to church Christianity. Such a hero can realize himself, in the author's thinking, only through return to the past, not only in the literal, but in the symbolic sense as well: from peace to war, from Christianity to Paganism. And at the end of the poem, the hero decides to search for his former life:

> And I think it will kill me or cure,
> So I think I will go and see.
>
> ME!

Amazingly, "Soldier's Home" ends with the hero's decision to "go and see" his sister Ellen playing baseball. (An interesting article by Robert W. Lewis, Jr., analyzes the role of sports as ritual and metaphor in the story.[26]) Hemingway the artist is not constrained to think in contrasting pairs; the image he creates of the veteran is complex and many-sided. Krebs does not search for a return to the past; war, for him (as for Hemingway) is devoid of any attraction. Also alien to him are the laws to which peaceful society submits. Hemingway's hero is ruled by apathy; he wants only one thing: for "life to go smoothly."[27]

We can only guess to what degree Hemingway was conscious of the intertextual correlation of his story to Kipling's poem. Did he, for instance, intend the direct echo in the ending of his work? In prose, especially of his early period, Hemingway carefully concealed his literary sources; literary allusions were elusive elements of the context. But the 1920 sketch "Lieutenants' Mustaches" leaves no doubt that Hemingway knew Kipling's poem and focused on it.

In his mature years, too, Hemingway tended to view the saturation of contemporary work with literary and historical reminiscence as an artistic flaw, a sign of a writer's weakness, an attempt to find the easy road in literature. In this way, his attack on William Saroyan in 1935 is typical:

> Soon the world will echo to it like Roland's horn at Roncevaux. You can use that some time in a piece. It's in Spain but that's the French spelling. I give it to you, Mr. Saroyan. For nothing, kid. It's a literary reference. You like them I know. They're easy to find. There's a book full of them. *Putnam's Dictionary of Thoughts* they call it. Hell, I'll give you mine, pal.[28]

Hemingway's biased judgments could be partly the result of projection of his own journalistic experience onto literature. As a young newspaper writer, he did not miss opportunities to shine with erudition, openly demonstrating his knowledge of mythology, ancient and recent history, literature, art, architecture, and music. Perhaps it was precisely this super-ficially intellectual style that came most easily to Hemingway. It was natural for him to think of life in cultural categories: in sketches, when he gave in to free association, Shere Mohamet Khan, the Afghan prince, resembled "a man out of the Renaissance" (p. 241); the figure of his friend Bill Bird reminded him of "the lean and graceful lines of an early Italian primitive" (p. 201); the view of the earth from an airplane explained cubist art (p. 202); the sound of the *muezzin* recalled Russian opera (p. 239); squabbles in the French parliament were like "the free fight in the ciga-rette factory when Geraldine Farrar first began to play Carmen" (p. 266). The man "with the Eugene O'Brien 'Chase me I won't run' look" (37), and the brave Belgian lady with "a face like a composite Rodin's group of the Burghers of Calais waiting to be hanged" (p. 275) fleet across the pages of his articles. The omnipotent king of the American press, William Ran-dolph Hearst, is a complicated combination of "the Emperor Nero, the worst phases of the Corsican, George the Third . . ." (p. 54).

After he began to write prose, Hemingway rejected such comparisons and they disappeared. In his first book, *In Our Time* (1925), the only remaining trace of them is found in the story "Out of Season," in the entirely unimportant sentence: "'. . . Thank you,' said Peduzzi, in the tone of one member of the Carleton Club accepting the *Morning Post* from another."[29] Such indirect descriptions answer the question, What does it resemble from what is known, imprinted, already assimilated by culture? They therefore do not further that increase in the "general fund of knowledge," that collecting of "grains of the new," which Hemingway referred to as the artist's higher task in *Death in the Afternoon*.[30]

For fully understandable reasons, it was natural for a young journalist such as Hemingway in 1918–22, still only dreaming of a writer's career, to draw more from that enormous "fund of knowledge" than he added to it. This all the more, as the "knowledge" added by the artist is not at all identical to the journalist's "information." Some of Hemingway's early articles devoted to fishing were full of concrete, practical information and recommendations ("Camping Out," June 26, 1920; "Trout-Fishing Hints," April 24, 1920). With the meticulousness of an enthusiast, Hemingway enumerates all possible kinds of worms, bait, lines, hooks, and habits of fish. Constantly polemicizing with "sports journalists," he creates his own textbook on fishing. The polemic provides a sense of context: "Sporting magazines have fostered a popular fiction to the effect that no gentleman would catch a trout in any manner but on a fly . . . sporting writers . . . take every opportunity to stigmatize the bait fisherman. . . . The oldtimer, firmly implanted in the seat of the scornful, reads the twaddle of the American trout-fishing critics and smiles" (p. 22); "nearly all outdoor writers rhapsodize over the browse bed. It is all right for the man who knows how to make one and has plenty of time" (p. 45); "magazine writers and magazine covers to the contrary, the brook, or speckled, trout does not leap out of water after he has been hooked" (p. 52). The context was local and insignificant; but only against that background could all the originality and novelty of everything Hemingway wrote about fishing as a journalist be perceived. Polemical attacks were the only way to give interest to characterless information, useful to few.

What qualities he was able to give to such information are classically illustrated by the story "Big Two-Hearted River," which contains two incidents of direct textual dialogue with the early articles. These incidents are well known. In the story, Nick Adams catches grasshoppers and makes pancakes using the methods recommended to readers in "Camping Out" and "Trout-Fishing Hints." The only thing that has not been noted is that Hemingway's hero makes one single deviation from the recipe for pancake preparation, and this turns out to be a strikingly capacious method of describing his inner state. The rule ran: "Drop the batter in and as soon as it is done on one side loosen it in the skillet and flip it over" (p. 46). In the story, Nick chooses a more dependable, safer method of turning the pancakes, and it becomes clear that he is striving to avoid the smallest risk to his fragile inner balance: "Nick pushed under the browned under surface with a fresh pine chip. I won't try and flip it, he thought. He slid the chip of clean wood all the way under the cake, and flipped it over onto its face."[31]

In this story Hemingway shows himself master of the method of communicating the shades of a person's inner state through the description of a series of external actions which, according to T. S. Eliot, define through "objective correlative." The characterless rule of fishing in the story is not made merely concrete in the individual actions of the hero, it becomes a fact of high art, which, as M. M. Bakhtin wrote, "first of all creates a concrete intuitive unity . . . of two worlds—places the person in nature, represented by his aesthetic surroundings—humanizes nature and naturalizes man."[32]

The most Hemingway strove for in 1920—but which he did not entirely achieve even in such semi-artistic sketches as "Trout-Fishing" (April 10, 1920), "Indoor Fishing" (April 20, 1920), and "The Best Rainbow Trout Fishing" (August 28, 1920)—was a clear and emotional illustration of fishing as such. As soon as the young Hemingway tried to cast off the limitations of simple advice and "information," he quickly fell into superficial aestheticization, though of a very curious nature. He attempted to achieve clarity through cinemagraphic analogies. The beginning of the sketch "The Best Rainbow Trout Fishing" is stylized like a scene from a film. The reader is told to imagine three fade-ins "in rapid succession": a tall precipice, covered with pines, a short sandy descent to a river, and a pool. "There is the setting," summarizes the author. "The action is supplied by two figures that slog into the picture up the trail along the riverbank with loads on their backs. . . . These loads are pitched over the heads onto the patch of ferns by the edge of the deep pool. That is incorrect." He sharply interrupts his "cinematic tale" to comment ironically on the stereotypical picture. "Really the figures lurch a little forward and . . . the pack slumps onto the ground. Men don't pitch loads at the end of an eight-mile hike" (pp. 50–51). What follows is a short continuation in the same spirit: "one of the figures, the other . . . ," after which the story turns to a normal "literary" vein. Slightly less obviously, Hemingway imitates cinematic technique in "Trout Fishing." "If you are . . . [an] angler you have a vision of a deep, dark hole where the waters of the creek disappear. . . . Someone is crouching out of sight on the bank and looping worms onto a hook. That is you. Then you gently swing the gob of worms out onto the water . . ." (p. 14).

These early experiments, based on an attempt to reconstruct through words the effect of a "moving picture," provide interesting additional material for study of the complex and, in general, little-addressed question of "Hemingway and film." The influence on Hemingway's prose of the cinematic principles of montage and segmentation, partly via the work of Gertrude Stein who experimented with techniques of dividing up and presenting material "step-by-step," is fairly indisputable. It is easy to find an example from, for instance, "Soldier's Home." But, importantly, what is broken up there is not external but psychological reality: "[Krebs] liked to watch [girls] walking under the shade of the trees. He liked the round Dutch collars above their sweaters. He liked their silk stockings and flat shoes. He liked their bobbed hair and the way they walked."[33] In Hemingway's prose, the new structure is not applied from above to material foreign to it, as it is in his journalism; it participates in the inner transformation of that material.

In his early articles, Hemingway made use of the most varied, limiting constructions. In his first article on boxing ("Prizefight Women," May 15, 1920), the historical parallel wholly controls the thematic development. Hemingway's proclaimed objective was to describe what the first women in Toronto allowed to attend a boxing match "saw" and "how they acted": "They came ostensibly to see Georges Carpentier give a sparring exhibition. In reality they saw a series of gladiatorial combats and they smiled and applauded through it all." Hemingway places this summary at the beginning of the article, going on to develop and illustrate it for the benefit of his audience, "those Toronto women who do not attend prizefights." (This choice of audience, of course, immediately reveals the author's moralistic inclination.)

Michael Reynolds proposes that Hemingway pays a great deal of attention to the reaction of the spectators in order to conceal his own still very limited knowledge of boxing.[34] But this explanation, at first glance logical, does not take into consideration the nature of the historical sources Hemingway uses here. The young Hemingway was sensitive to the historical connotations of the word *arena*, which first referred to the site of gladiatorial fights. The possible parallel between boxing and gladiator combat is outlined at the beginning of the article; the conclusion is wholly devoted to its development. Hemingway notes how restrained is the reaction of true boxing experts at the match and how out of place is the female laughter. In the development of his thoughts he gives a colorful description of ancient gladiatorial duels, ornamenting it with such uncommon words as *cestus* and *Cisalpine*, and commenting with a quotation from *Romeo and Juliet*: "In the old days at the colosseum in Rome the ex-gladiators and their pals who sat at the side of the arena applauded the deadly thrusts. They clapped when a swing of the cestus bashed in a Cisalpine gladiator's face. They may have cheered when the man with the fishnet and the trident entangled his opponent with the short sword and they clapped when he finished him with a few well-placed thrusts of the spear. But they didn't laugh. They knew what it meant. . . . 'He jests at scars who never felt a wound.' And as on last Saturday night the laughter was reserved for the nobility. . . . Lecky, the historian, says that the majority of the old gladiatorial crowds were women" (pp. 31–32).

The young Hemingway did not try to conceal the source of his disturbing information about the customs of the Roman colosseum. In the book mentioned—*History of European Morals, From Augustus to Charlemagne*, by the Irish historian and philosopher W. E. H. Lecky—the chapter entitled "The Pagan Empire" contains a small section: "The gladiatorial shows—their origin and history; their effects upon the theatre; nature of their attraction; horrible excesses they attained . . . the passion for them not inconsistent with humanity in other spheres."[35] Lecky shows the genetic link between gladiatorial battles and religious ceremonies accompanying human sacrifice. He maintains that the enthusiasm for gladiatorial combat hampered the development of the art of dramatic tragedy in Rome, as no stage effects could compare in their emotional impact with the spectacle of genuine death in the arena to which the Roman was accustomed. He proves that, although the sight of human or animal suffering normally evokes loathing and horror among civilized people, much depends on habit and custom. The Spaniard who first attends bullfights as a young child loves this spectacle just as the Roman loved the gladiator fight, and all people, generally, are complacent about the cruel punishment of criminals. The way that boys show themselves in fights, and adults in sports, forces us to suppose that there was nothing in gladiatorial combat that was contrary to human nature. The section on it is included in Lecky's book in the context of a general analysis of the philosophy of stoicism, which, in his opinion, lies at the root of Roman ways. Lecky writes of the attitude that sees death as "a law and not a punishment," about belief not in "immortality," but in "posthumous reputation," of the cult of self-control and the conviction that one is master of one's feelings, and also of the fact that the most important thing for the Roman was the preservation of his own pride.[36]

There is no other way to explain many interesting correlations with Lecky's book, except to say that Hemingway was solidly acquainted with it and essentially influenced by it. For instance, in the journalistic formula of his 1923 piece "Bullfighting a Tragedy," the echo of Lecky's comparison of dramatic tragedy with the Colosseum ritual is clearly heard. In *Death in the Afternoon*, explaining the philosophy of the bullfight, Hemingway follows Lecky in telling of Spaniards' peculiar attitude toward death. Lecky went to the very source and discovered that "the Spanish Celts raised temples, and sang hymns of praise to death."[37] The essence of Hemingway's general principle is the same: "For a country to love bullfights, its people must be interested in death."[38] It is entirely possible it was from Lecky's book that Hemingway drew his first information about the general stoical system of values that would be embodied in the pages of his books by "Heroes of the Code"—which, in his early works, are exclusively matadors, representatives of the Latin world.[39]

When, in 1923, Hemingway the journalist began to write about bullfighting, his historical perspective was entirely revealed: "I am not going to apologize for bullfighting. It is a survival of the days of the Roman Colosseum. But it does need some explanation" (p. 344). His slightly earlier prose miniatures on the subject contain no such direct comparisons. But even there, buried entirely in subtext, the steady association with the Roman custom colored Hemingway's vision.

In the miniatures that were to become chapters 9–12 and 14 of *In Our Time*, Hemingway constantly keeps in sight not only events in the arena but the reaction of the crowd. He does not use the word *spectator* to refer to those attending the bullfight; the fight is directed by a monolithic mob, which "whistles," "roars," "yells," "shouts," and throws objects into the arena. It judges, extols, or punishes the matador. It can "hoot" him out of the arena (Chap. 9), it can throw itself over the barrier and cut off his pigtail (Chap. 11), or it can greet an idol such as Villalta, roaring with delight (Chap. 12). In Hemingway's miniatures the crowd ruthlessly demands a complete spectacle and has no sympathy for the young matador who, after killing five bulls in a row, becomes ill in the arena (Chap. 9). The dying Maera also hears the demanding "shouting going on in the grandstand" and makes an effort to speak, but is unable to do so.

In his illustration of the bullfight in the miniatures, Hemingway achieves the highest degree of universalization of experience. Discarding everything incidental or temporary, he attains such concentration and simplification that the phenomenon is reduced to its archetypal essence. In the end, "the true generalization," as T. S. Eliot once observed, "is not something superposed upon an accumulation of perceptions; the perceptions do not, in a really appreciative mind, accumulate as a mass, but form themselves as a structure."[40]

In Hemingway's journalism of 1919–20, an entirely different model is realized. In these articles, too, he felt an insistent need to generalize but satisfied the need with a multitude of quotations, allusions, historical parallels, and extensive commentaries, as well as by inventing his own or by echoing or parodying the "formulas" of others. This method demanded minimal effort from Hemingway himself and was maximally accessible to his audience. After all, it assumed a fixing and a grounding by the author of the thoughts and associations of his own which arose in connection with the object of description. To convince ourselves that it is not journalism's particular orientation to the audience that plays the main role here, we need only turn to Hemingway's prose of the same period: All of these traits characterize it as well.

Faulkner was not mistaken when he numbered Hemingway among a rare type of "conscious creators."[41] Proposing that there lies at the base of Hemingway's prose a consciously mastered method, Faulkner seems to guess at its source: "Thanks to his creative instinct, or to the advice of wise mentors, [Hemingway] realized that he could achieve the most flexible style, at the same time consistent in its principles. Hemingway learned not to be a stylist, but to write so that his teachers said: 'This is a true method,' and always remained true to himself."[42]

Hemingway's first mentors are well known: Sherwood Anderson, Gertrude Stein, Ezra Pound. Before he met them, Hemingway merely demonstrated in his journalism of 1920 what he himself, with great contempt, referred to as "undisciplined talent." His early journalistic activities and newspaper work were, in the final account for Hemingway the writer, little more than a fact of his external biography. His "creative instinct" was awakened later. After an analysis of his articles of 1920, one may assert that his style and method were not the result of newspaper experience but of purely literary factors. It stands to reason that this does not mean that Anderson, Stein, and Pound taught Hemingway to write. But under their influence his idea of the essence of writing was formed, and for a "conscious creator," that is a great deal.

Not Hemingway but Faulkner, wishing to restore justice, untiringly spoke of Anderson as the "father" of an entire generation of American writers. Hemingway unwittingly paid tribute to Anderson's lessons when, for instance, he discussed literary craft, saying that "good writing is true writing," that "knowledge of life" is the basis for imagination, and when he spoke of the superficiality of literary "tricks."[43] Anderson's credo in *Winesburg, Ohio* is formed in the same terms: "If you are to become a writer you'll have to stop fooling with words. . . . It would be better to give up the notion of writing until you are better prepared. . . . you will have to know life."[44]

What Hemingway did as a journalist before he met Anderson in January 1921, fell, for the most part, under the definition of "fooling with words." Four articles out of seven written in 1921, before his departure for Paris, were examples of pure parody or comic narrative ("Trading Celebrities," "Our Confidential Vacation Guide," "Condensing the Classics," "On Weddynge Gyftes"). But by 1924, in a passage from "On Writing," the following discussion appears: "It was perfectly easy to use tricks. . . . But being new didn't make them better."[45]

"Knowledge of life," of which Anderson spoke and in which young Hemingway believed, was of a particular sort. It could not be attained and realized through that superficial contact with people and events which, for Anderson and later for Hemingway, was synonymous with journalism. The most disparaging way Anderson could describe his literary rival Sinclair Lewis was to call him a man with a "sharp journalistic nose for news of the outer surface of our lives."[46] Genuine knowledge of life required that one "get below the surface," reproduce "the lower rhythm,"[47] or what Hemingway, in a letter to Malcolm Cowley, called "the inner true thing."[48]

At the same time, Anderson gradually came to represent, for Hemingway, the writer-liar.[49] Anderson's persona—the "absentminded" "bard of life," "unsophisticated" in both general and literary matters and relying on intuition—may have played no small role in this. Sentimentality was a natural side of this image.

The pretentiousness of this pose irritated Hemingway; but when he presented himself as the fisher and hunter—refusing to admit to obvious literary allusions in his work, or mentioned with concealed annoyance attempts by Pound and Cohn to trace the literary origins of the titles of *In Our Time* and *A Farewell to Arms*—he unwittingly paid tribute to Anderson's tradition.[50] Just as did another of Anderson's pupils, William Faulkner, with the persona of the unsophisticated Mississippi farmer to which he so eagerly resorted in public.

In speaking of literature, the Paris intellectuals among whom Hemingway found himself in 1922 took an entirely different approach. The ideal was proclaimed to be "diagnostic,"[51] "critical" art,[52] which would give precise witness to "the inner nature and conditions of man."[53] The "analytical, scientific" mind was declared the highest merit of an artist; its aim was the persistent observation of its object. In an article on Swinburne, Eliot wrote: "His language . . . is very much alive, with this singular life of its own. But the language which is more important to us is that which is struggling to digest and express new objects, new groups of objects, new feelings, new aspects, as, for instance, the prose of Mr. James Joyce or the earlier Conrad."[54] Thus, the lessons Hemingway received in Paris did not, in the most important way, contradict Anderson's—to see language not as an end in itself but as a means of gaining knowledge of the world. Pound's letter of 1926, written about "An Alpine Idyll," gives a clear idea of the direction in which he was urging Hemingway to develop his talent: "I wish you wd. keep your eye on the object MORE, and be less licherary. . . . Bein licherary means that the reader . . . has to work to keep his eye on the page during the introductory pages. . . . ANYTHING put on top of the subject is BAD. Licherachure is mostly blanketing up a subject. Too much MAKINGS. The subject is always interesting enough without the blankets."[55] Two months later, again writing about "An Alpine Idyll," Pound told Hemingway: "These short repeating sentences TOO DAMN IMPRESSIVE. You'd git the sak for telegraphing in that manner."[56] Reporting remained the aesthetic norm, comparison with which determined the quality of prose. But, we assume, it is not the realistic sort of reporting found in journalism, including Hemingway's, that is referred to here, but reporting as a symbol of objective observation of life.

The quality and style of Hemingway's journalism in Paris changed substantially. He most likely could no longer write in his former manner. But all the same, it remained at base the same "subjective" journalism, the author's instrument of direct self expression. With prose, it was another matter. As Jackson J. Benson originally notes, Hemingway became an artist with his own unique voice wearing the mask of a reporter.[57] It was the aesthetic theories of Anderson, Pound, Stein, and Eliot, however, that caused him to do so, to a significantly greater degree than it was his own life experience—so that, in the final account, the real inner history of Hemingway's literary apprenticeship barely corresponds with the legend of the newspaperman who became a writer, which, as Benson recalls, once inspired American journalists and students dreaming of a writer's career.[58]

SERGEI CHAKOVSKY

"The Whole History
of the Human Heart
on the Head of a Pin"

Toward Faulkner's Philosophy of Composition

It would be patently unjust to claim that William Faulkner's literary opinions have not been accorded proper critical airing. His succinct, expressive, often refreshingly straightforward statements (however vague or ambiguous on certain points) have become indispensable for a variety of scholarly ends. They have been called up to support divergent, even conflicting, critical conceptions (Walter Slatoff's *Quest for Failure* and Warren Beck's *Man in Motion* readily come to mind as the most telling examples).

One can never be excessively mindful of Faulkner's notice: "I am a fiction writer and I am not responsible for any construction made on any interview I have ever given."[1] Could he have scared us to the extent that wearing his words thin with use (they are a gold mine of lively footnotes and imposing titles) we have also been judiciously observing a tacit pledge of not taking them seriously enough? It wouldn't be wise at this point to press such a possibility too hard, for reasons more than social self-preservation.

Faulkner was not just being shy, he was, to use the lingo he would have undoubtedly appreciated, methodologically correct, insisting that the writer "is of no importance. Only what he creates is important . . ." [LIG, p. 238]. Unlike his more "literary" predecessors and contemporaries— Henry James or T. S. Eliot—Faulkner was no theorist. Crowded or lured to "talk shop," he often would seem impulsively incoherent, obscure, if not intentionally misleading or self-defeating. I think he genuinely loved silence (his best writing is, in a way, masterfully simulated silence, a sort of "extrasensory" medium[2]), yet his spoken literary opinions are not the most amply and authentically documented of all American authors. One needn't be a great psychologist to assume that it is precisely due to their temperamental authenticity that those remarks afford us a rare insight into the writer's creative mind.

An obvious implication of Faulkner's stern warning is that aside from his tax statement (presumably), anything he said or wrote would be more or less fiction.[3] Whether it actually means a lie is, of course, a further problem. What is relevant now is that, "literary" or not by his own lights, Faulkner obviously considered writing his main line of trade. He was vastly competent at it and sufficiently self-conscious to instill the problems of composition as a "shadow" theme into his novels, to say nothing of working as a "script-doctor" in Hollywood or giving penetrating if capsular critiques of writers from Shakespeare to Hemingway. Given the pervasive nature of the simile of the writer as a carpenter or a bricklayer, one would rightly assume that his approach to art was also fairly technical; even as a young man he "would scoff at the word *inspiration*" [LIG, p. 11].

There are many flowery ways to call someone of Fielding's or Melville's stature one's literary progenitor. Faulkner alluded to these writers humbly yet with reserve as "masters from whom we learned our craft."[4] After all, it wasn't just from them that he "got quite a lot" but

> from a man that probably you . . . never heard of . . . Thomas Beer . . . was to me a good tool, a good method, a good usage of words, [a good] approach to incident [FU, p. 20]. Like any professional he would admire a book "for its craftsmanship" although there might be "nothing in it" that [he] would ever read again [FU, p. 202].

Yet on other occasions, Faulkner would recommend that a writer "take up surgery or bricklaying if he is interested in technique" [LIG, p. 244]; or, retreating into his "nonliterary, old-veteran-sixth-grader shell," he would say: "I didn't have enough mathematics to have a disciplined mind." "I read because what I read was about people . . ." [LIG, p. 108].

Faulkner would reiterate time after time that he was "not enough of a conscious craftsman," being too "busy writing about people" [FU, p. 56], "just try[ing] to tell the truth of man" [LIG, p. 54]. A concomitant idea of the writer's social function emerged in his later years: "Everybody's aim is to help people, turn them to Heaven. You write to help people" [LIG, p. 56]. But, then, "the writer's only responsibility is to his art. He will be completely ruthless if he is a good one. Everything goes by the board: honor, pride, decency, security, happiness, all to get the book written" [LIG, p. 239].

Faulkner disclaimed any interest in ideas; yet, he was a match for a sophisticated interviewer such as Loïc Bouvard on purely intellectual and literary grounds. Then, on a later occasion, he would discard the suggested "literary classification" of his work in favor of what is predominantly an ideological one: ". . . the only school I belong to . . . want to belong to, is the humanist school" [LIG, p. 141].

To measure up to the conception of art as "salvation" for humanity, the author should be "demon-run," possessed with the vision of "man's history in its mutations, in the instances in which it becomes apparent, his triumph, his failures, the whole passion of breathing" [FU, p. 145].

We may pause here, for what this sampling amounts to is hardly news to anyone: Literature for Faulkner was much more than "tricks of the trade"; it was also much more than "telling about people." It was what it presumably should be first and foremost—verbal art. There is also a characteristic touch as regards the relationship between "craft," artistry, and what we may loosely term the "ideology" or "philosophy" of composition.

In a curt letter of reply to an obviously puzzled reader, he would insist on his "prerogative of using these people when and where he saw fit," "to pick and choose the facet of the character, which would "move the story" most effectively, not to "tell all of the truth" about him [FU, p. 24]. To do that, the author has to cast off the "demon's" attire and get back into his carpenter's or bricklayer's overalls. He would then have to become ruthless enough to summon as tools not just the articles of what semioticians call the "language of fiction"—a more or less patent set of instruments like "point of view," "symbolism," "handling of incident," or "violence"—but also "Christianity," "the South" itself, if not "the whole passion of breathing."

What we are left with is either a totally unscrupulous, opportunistic raconteur who would "rob his mother"—or, as the Russian saying goes, "wouldn't spare his own father for a smart word"—or an unusually broad, syncretic conception of literary craft. Given the scale of Faulkner's artistic and moral achievement, the first option, whatever water it might hold, needs hardly more than acknowledgment here. As for the second, it obviously presents us with a critical problem and thus calls for a closer look.

In the first of his class sessions, Faulkner gave this piece of advice to an aspiring author: "Read, read, read. Read everything—trash, classics, good and bad, and see how they do it. Just like a carpenter who works as an apprentice and studies the master" [LIG, p. 55]. "The young writer would be a fool to follow a theory" [LIG, p. 244]. This may well be so, and yet. . . . Pressed for an answer, Faulkner would grant that a student may "come to the teacher and say, 'Why did this writer write this scene in this particular way?' which becomes a matter of craftsmanship then" [LIG, pp. 181–82]. What he most likely meant to say was "empty craftsmanship," i.e., what remains when the "fire" and the "force" are gone.[5] Hence, the problem with the critical function: "It is not directed toward the artist himself. . . . The critic is writing something which will move everybody but the artist" [LIG, p. 252].

Moving the artist can hardly stand as a measure of validity of critical work. Thus, it is amply documented how profoundly Faulkner was touched by Malcolm Cowley's historic and in many ways heroic project of rendering him "portable," despite the somewhat distorted perspective on his work that it suggested. Getting back to the key question of "how they do it": Wasn't criticism earnestly trying to cope with it from Aristotle to the Russian formalists, Anglo-American New Critics, and French structuralists?

In 1927, Victor Shklovsky anticipated Faulkner's recommendation almost to the word:

> If you want to become a writer, you should examine a book no less attentively than a watchmaker examines a watch or a driver—a car. . . . Discarding the ignorant pressing the ball of the horn or the half-knowledged shifting of the gear handle as respective degrees of stupidity. . . .
>
> The man who understands regards a car without haste, making out "the how and the why," why it has many cylinders, and why the wheels are big, and how the transmission is placed and why the rear of the car is sharp, and [the] radiator unpolished.
>
> This is the way to read . . . to understand how things are made.[6]

As history has shown, the problem with such "million-dollar" pieces of advice is that, should one follow them literally, he will find himself computing the squaring of the circle or dealing with "empty craftsmanship": the tail, not the body of the "comet"; bumpers, grills, windshield wipers—not the power unit, not the "car" itself. Hence, the resurging feeling in the scholarly community that we are more and more becoming "drivers" who have learned how to put the "car" to various uses, with sometimes only a minimum of functional knowledge as to how it actually operates.

What, presumably, should constitute the center of our field of knowledge—the study of literature as an artistic activity—is quietly being pushed out to the liminal position of a beloved, yet illegitimate, child—to be played with, even spoiled, but not really counted on for the continuation of the "family" trade.

If there is so much as a grain of truth in what Faulkner says about our line of trade (and I assume there is), there seems to be no other way but to retrace one's steps in search of the initial "mistake"—like Sutpen did, although utterly fatal results are undesirable. Or rather, like Faulkner did in his literary dialogues, trying if not to atone, then to account for what he saw as his "failure."

This leads to the proposition I would like to submit: In their cumulative content, Faulkner's assorted statements of opinion amount to a viable, if embryonic, philosophy of composition; that it is worth the effort of our "constitutive consciousness," to borrow Arthur Kinney's expression,[7] to bridge the "poles" of his judgments since they address some of the central problems at issue today; also that, in their dialectically integrated form, they may help us deal with Faulkner's achievement as an artist in a more concentrated and consistent fashion.

That a work of art is neither an automobile, let alone a fence, hardly qualifies for the initial misjudgment—for, according to an old German saying favored by philosophers, any simile is "lame." What it points to is that you cannot figure out the *how* unless the decision has more or less been made as to the *what*. Also, on where the existential "problematic center" of the thing-to-be is to be looked for. Thus, we can hardly speak of craft in any sort of meaningful way outside of reference to artistic value.

At the peak of the controversy between the structuralists and the anti-structuralists, which became quite public in the Soviet Union in the mid-1970s, I once witnessed a characteristic exchange. "The structure is jolly good," said the older scholar, "but the poem is bad." "Tastes will differ," countered his younger opponent. "This is also beside the point. All I was interested in is how it is put together." Heated as the debate was, the opponents had a characteristic error in common. Can the structure be "good" if the poem is "bad"? Can we say anything worthwhile about "how it is put together" if its being good or bad is "beside the point"? Wouldn't our version of the structure, then, also miss the point, the way it would if we conceive of a car as of a place of permanent dwelling or of a violin as an instrument, say, for driving nails into the wall?

"Poetry," said Faulkner, "must be first-rate—there are no degrees of it."[8] As we know from everyday experience, there are "degrees"; moreover, they are becoming more and more flexible, to accommodate such refined notions as "the second-best nature poet on the campus." Yet the paradox is more than a sign of Faulkner's notorious maximalism. What it piercingly points to is that, in relation to art, value is part of definition; that value ceases to be adjectival, more or less optional (as in a general philosophic case), but tends to become substantive, to supplant the very notion of the qualitative identity of an object. That is why any formal definition of what is a "work of art" is likely to be apprehended as inadequate unless it proceeds from what it is not.

True enough, "it is neither real (physical, like a statue) nor mental (psychological, like the experience of light or pain) nor ideal (like a triangle)." Yet, isn't it also more than a sort of language or, in Wellek's positive formulation, "a system of norms of ideal concepts which are intersubjective"?[9] But is it really? The element of artistic value seems to fit in here rather smoothly: "In a successful work of art," elaborates the authoritative theory, "the materials are completely assimilated: What was "world" has become "language.""[10] Since most misreadings occur as a result of failure to grasp the *fictional* side of literature, one can never overstress the specific "sovereignty" of a work of art in regard to everyday reality, the fact that "the nature of literature emerges most clearly under the referential aspects."[11] It wasn't for nothing that Faulkner called himself "the sole owner and proprietor" of the mythical kingdom of Yoknapatawpha, thus trying to guard the integrity of his imaginative world against all vulgar notions of literary representation.

What's become of the "loud world"? one may ask. Has it really dissolved, "fled" in fear of poetic license? Had it been so, if I may continue this paraphrase, there would have been "no grief or sorrow" on the part of the artist—or of the artist's ultimate triumph either. Could it be the other way around? What was more or less "language"—on the "phatic," signal-coordinating stage of artistic communication—becomes "world" in its own right—"fictional" or "bizarre," as it is, yet so true and inevitable as to be accepted by the real one, "of necessity"?

However paradoxical it may sound, what we broadly call the *language* of a work of art is essentially nothing but a strategic means of overcoming the language, the semiotic status of a verbal representation assigned to it by convention. In other words, a work of art is a semiotic object that strives to become semantic, to acquire full meaning, to turn from a model or a complex sign of reality into its natural, immutable phenomenon. All of this calls for some elaboration, for it is the controversial yet inescapable sphere of the relationship between art and reality where the problems of meaning, value, and craft seem to take their root.

In a letter to Malcolm Cowley, Faulkner made an important confession. The first part of it is proverbially well known: "As regards any specific book I am trying primarily to tell a story, in the most effective way I can think of, the most moving, the most exhaustive." Of no less importance in the present context is what follows: "But I think even that is incidental to what I am trying to do, taking my output (the course of it) as a whole. I am telling the same story over and over which is *myself and the world*."[12] Obviously intended as a kind of selfless revelation (coming from a writer about to be inaugurated as the Balzac of the South), this phrase is important in at least two additional respects. Projected upon the character, the opposition manifests its centrality in the first paragraph of the first Faulkner novel: "Lowe, Julian, number—, late a Flying Cadet, Umptieth Squadron, Air Service, known as 'One Wing' by the other embryonic aces of his flight, regarded the world with a Yellow and disgruntled eye . . . they had stopped a war on him."[13]

Thus, the nonexistent ("number—") member of an equally nonexistent ("Umptieth") squadron regards nothing less than the *world* with "a Yellow and disgruntled eye," since "*they* had stopped a war on *him*." This is the first paradoxical introduction of the theme of the novel which soon "dawns upon" Lowe and his boisterous though also "nonexistent" fellow traveler—"Number no thousand no hundred and naughty naught Private (very private)" Joe Gilligan: "They stood feeling the spring in the cold air, as if they had but recently come into a new world, feeling their littleness and believing too that lying in wait for them was something new and strange" [SP, p. 19].

The reason I keep adducing this quote now under circumstances as different as Faulkner's attitude to women and the craft of fiction is, I think, obvious. The conflict between man and the world—or, rather, between the world's view of individual man as a simple link in the immutable chain of causes and events, a "sum of what have you," a "shadow," a second-hand doll filled with historic "dust"—and the perception of man as a sovereign world manifests itself at every level of Faulkner's artistic creation. This conflict is rendered dramatically vivid in the character Judith Sutpen's implicit likening of life to the "rug" into which man is trying "to weave his own pattern," unaware of "a lot of other people"[14] who are doing the same. Beyond the immediate ideological implications in regard to, for example, the story of Sutpen's grand "design," this antithesis is also at the core of Faulkner's style. What stands behind his inner monologue, or the long sentence, is the desperate attempt of a fictional narrator to embrace, or digest, and, ultimately, to overpower the heterogeneous "facts" of reality that obstruct the fulfillment of his dream of the world.

On another plane, this, of course, is also a poignant metaphor of the artistic creative process; for, if "any writer, to begin with, is writing his own biography" [FU, p. 103], his books are of necessity about how the books were written, or rather, how they were given birth to (since what seems to have driven Faulkner from the outset of his career was the idea that "words brought into a happy conjunction produce something that lives"[15]). This early fictional remark brings into a challenging focus the problems of literary craft and those of the "life" of a work of art. In order to bridge the conceptual gap between them so as not to have to deal in empty craftsmanship, on the one hand, or half-mystical generalities, on the other, some theoretical preparation of the ground is necessary.

Whatever the intended meaning of Faulkner's confession to Cowley, there is nothing reprehensible or even very original in writing about "myself and the world" while ostensibly "telling about people"—for one thing, because fictional people who become characters *are* part of the writer's self; and, for another, because, with all the clairvoyance of an undisciplined mind, Faulkner was thus laying bare what we would call the axiological basis of literature.

What I mean is that, just as linguistically verbal art builds itself upon what R. Jacobson calls the "poetic" function of the language, so, in general philosophic terms, it is a continuation—or, rather, a creative application—of the value-judgment capacity of the social man who not only learns about things as they are but, in the words of the philosopher O. G.

Drobnizky, "*endows* the surrounding world with meaning in order to be able to orient oneself and act there."[16]

This, of course, is a crucial juncture, for "endowing" old "things" with new meaning, "writ[ing] a book on the back of a postage stamp or a prayer on the head of a pin" [LIG, p. 175] is essentially what literature is about. Why should the author attempt to put "the whole history of the human heart on the head of a pin"? Faulkner's explanations of the metaphor are most expressive as lyrical pieces. They are also quite plausible psychologically ("We tried to crowd and cram everything into each paragraph, to get the whole complete nuance of the moment's experience . . ." [LIG, p. 107]; yet, they seem to be rather wide of the point, as it manifests itself in the broader context of his literary comments and artistic practices.

Man's "tragedy," he said to Loïc Bouvard, "is the impossibility—or at least the tremendous difficulty—of communication. But man keeps on trying endlessly to express himself and to make contact with other human beings. . . . The artist is the one who is able to communicate his message" [LIG, p. 71]. I hardly have to remind you that the "impossibility" of communication is what Benjy is moaning about and "trying to tell Caddy," what Judith Sutpen is actually saying and living through, the idea of the tragically disjointed nature of human worlds informing the composition of all of Faulkner's major novels. It still takes a reminder, then— exclusively for the purpose of bringing out the indivisibility of what seems to be purely philosophical and purely "technical" in what I see as Faulkner's key metaphor of literary craft.

Wherefrom the "impossibility" of artistic communication and, hence, the author's "agony and sweat"?

More than any person, perhaps, the artist is "free," yet is "responsible, terribly responsible" [LIG, p. 70], even if the "only responsibility" of the artist is "to his art." The artist's freedom certainly lies in the right to "create his own language" [LIG, p. 71].

Yet, undertaking the demiurgic task of re-creating the world according to what he feels and knows it to be, the artist doesn't have a free hand at assigning meanings to objects of reality. Neither they nor the human language that represents or tries to represent them are exclusively the artist's to tamper with; for composition is not just freedom of imagination, but also "an obligation that [a writer] assumes with his vocation, that he's going to write in a way that people can understand it. He doesn't have to write it in the way that every idiot can understand it—every imbecile in the third grade can understand it, but he's got to use a language which is accepted and in which the words have specific meanings that everybody agrees on" [FU, pp. 52–53]. That is why "it takes two to make the book, the poem" [LIG, p. 116]—or, should one say, to *negotiate* the book, the poem, since, like politics, art is the craft of the possible?

The task the author must accomplish is twofold. First is the dialectical: to fill the old form—a "pin," a "stamp"—of a familiar life object or situation with the new human content, the artistic effect stemming from the interplay between the "habitual" and the "acquired" identities of something being depicted, the eventual collision they are brought into causing the "explosion" of meaning. Since at least the outer form of the real-life object has to remain credibly intact at all times, one may call artistic work a classic instance of trying to have your cake and eat it too; yet the tonality would be somewhat inappropriate. For, given the scope of Faulkner's imagination and the urgency of his poetic feeling, the task is not just intricate, it is heartbreaking: to put the whole universe of the human soul on the pinhead of the space allotted to the anonymous link in the chain of being, of the historical split second of man's individual existence. When accomplished, as it is in his best works, it brings about the aesthetic effect of eruptive intensity, since it it highly cathartic—i.e., it is philosophically and morally meaningful.

The other task the author must accomplish is more "technical," yet it is no less an important aspect of the meaning of the metaphor. Thus, the "long sentence," with all its psychological significance, is primarily a means of infusing vast background information into the "pinhead" of the event described (which otherwise might have seemed trivial or incredible). The fact that Faulkner's novels tend to choose for themselves such a convoluted style is due primarily to the characteristic disparity between the potentially accepted and the artistically intended meaning of their basic plot sequence. To fulfill this meaning, the author has to put three hundred-plus pages of narrative on the factual pinhead of that one-page "Chronology" appended to *Absalom, Absalom!*—ostensibly for the sake of clarity, but also, I tend to think, as a gesture of triumph.

The triumph is much more than jubilation of a crafty liar who managed to engage our attention for a week or more with, say, a minute's worth of hard facts. Yet the "lie" he gives us is not the one Charles Bon gives Henry Sutpen, causing him to remark: "You give me two and two and you tell me it makes five and it does make five" [AA, p. 146]. Well, it doesn't, and eventually it cannot but cost both the deceiver and the deceived. As Faulkner remarked in a letter to Saxe Commins: "[Estelle] can have you believing in ten minutes that black is white. Of course, in eleven minutes you know better, but sometimes it is too late by then."[17] With Faulkner's major works, we do not—and, I think, will not—know "better"; for, however fictitious or downright "incredible," they are also true. What is the mechanism of their truth? This is a challenging question, almost untouched by contemporary criticism. It has everything to do with craft, yet it is much more than "narrative technique," since it redirects us to the existential basis of a work of art. Although I cannot pursue the question in any detail here, the following consideration hopefully will clarify the point.

What we often seem to stop short of is recognition of the intergeneric nature of a work of art, of its transitivity in regard to the established modes of existence. Elaborating on the above-quoted, basically sound and fine and hence more or less standard definition, one might say that, at its conception *ideal* becomes *psychological* for the reader ("like the experience of light or pain") in order eventually to transgress its "mental" status, to become if not actually "physical like a statue," then no less "real."

Faulkner seems to have grasped this dual—incipiently subjective, yet designedly objective—nature of art with astonishing insight. In the famous description of his "life's work in the agony and sweat of the human spirit," he defined it as an attempt "to create out of the materials of the human spirit something which did not exist before,"[18] yet something objective, real enough to serve as a "kind of keystone in the Universe; that . . . if it were ever taken away, the universe itself would collapse" [LIG, p. 255]. What Faulkner succeeds in achieving in his output as a whole is turning the esoteric language of human imagination into a solid world of his (i.e., individual yet godlike man) "sole ownership," thus "helping nature," in the phrase of a character, "make a good job out of a poor one" [SP, p. 253].

At the core of what we cumulatively call "artistic value" would then be some sort of social appreciation of the human cognitive-creative effort potentially needed to bring about such qualitative transition. What we loosely term *craft* would appear to be essentially the way to handle that more or less alchemical and hence (as Faulkner's "theory of success" points out) never fully accomplishable task. Pending the charge of excessive broadness of such syncretic definition, let me point out that neither

NIKOLAI ANASTASIEV

The Tower and Around

A View of Vladimir Nabokov

Half-knowledge, not to mention complete ignorance, is the most fertile ground for the creation of myth. In the darkness it is easy to create idols and easier yet to shatter them, to cause them to rise or be reviled, and, in either case, to create an image, with impunity and inspiration and with no concern for its veracity. But in the light, proportion is restored, praise and abuse must be put to the test by reality, now accessible to all.

Not long ago, only some three or four years ago, Vladimir Nabokov was an underground figure for us. Many had heard of him and few had read him; so it is not surprising that in the mass consciousness he grew into a mysterious being, a collection of incompatible elements. To some he seemed, by rumor, a genius, a prophet; to others, also trusting to hearsay, he was an aesthete-charlatan. Some spoke of his high spirituality, others thought him a purveyor of literary obscenity.

Now Nabokov is emerging from the thick shadows of legend. The hero of the novel *The Gift*, the writer Godunov-Cherdyntsev, clearly an autobiographical figure, finding himself in a foreign land (Germany), reasons as follows:

Of course, it is easier for me to live outside of Russia than for others, because I know for certain that I will return—in the first place, because I carried out the keys with me, and the second because some day, it doesn't matter when, in a hundred or two hundred years, I will live there in my books, or at least in some scholarly footnote.

His mistake is in the length of time involved (*The Gift* was written in 1937), as well as in his foreknowledge of the critical genres and of his own popularity.

Of course, far from all of Nabokov's works have been published; that will be a matter of long years. His legacy—as novelist, short-story writer, poet, playwright, scholar, critic, pedagogue, and translator—is truly enormous. Nabokov's bibliography alone forms an 800-page volume.

But much has seen the light; as more appears, publishers turn ever more eagerly to his work. Open any journal, of city or countryside, and you will certainly find Nabokov. Occasionally, the same works are printed at the same time by different publishers. The story "Tyrants Destroyed," for instance, appeared almost simultaneously in the weekly *Knizhnoe obozrenie* (Book Review) and the Riga journal *Daugava*.

All of this involves a certain sense of hoopla, particularly as, with rare exceptions, the publications are accompanied by ecstatic forewords and afterwords; hardly "scholarly footnotes." On the other hand, this is easy to understand psychologically. Although it wasn't for 100 years, this world-class writer was banned long enough. We now hurry to settle accounts and let the busy protectors of pure aesthetic and, especially, ideological mores, not frighten us with threats of the spread of "Nabokovism" (though such voices are heard as well).

Let us leave the marginal, however, and agree that familiarity with Nabokov is essential and inspiring. We have read *The Defense*, *Mary*, *Camera Obscura*, *Invitation to a Beheading*, *The Exploit*, and *The Gift*, as well as many stories, poems, translations, and *The Waltz Invention* (play). We have been somewhat exposed to the English-language Nabokov: *Pnin* and *Lolita*, which vicariously so horrified us (and, in the beginning, not only us).

So now we may judge not by hearsay. True, our judgment is doomed to be inconclusive—and not because, in fact, any critical judgment of literature must be so. Even less because of a lack of material: Even if one knows all of Nabokov, one has the sense that he cleverly and stubbornly slips from hard evaluations. He's that kind of writer.

Nabokov has likened literary composition to chess composition, another field in which he has had his share of success:

> . . . competition in chess problems is not between black and white, but between the creator and an imaginary second-guesser (just as, in literature, the true struggle is not between the novel's heroes, but between writer and reader), and therefore a significant part of the problem's value depends on . . . the quality of "illusory decisions"—deceptively aggressive first moves, false trails and other dirty tricks, craftily and lovingly prepared by the author, to ensnare whoever enters the labyrinth with a false Ariadne's false threads.

So it is. Lured by the obviousness of what we have read, we confidently move out into the text, of which we have already constructed an orderly outline; but here, by chance it appears, is a turn of subject, a sudden change of tone and style, a sentence, flying in from God knows where; and our whole imagined structure shatters with a crash. We have to begin all over.

That is why every reading of Nabokov is merely one version. But a version must have a corresponding form. In my view, this is a fragment, a link in a chain of observations.

Nabokov shared the fate of many members of the Russian intelligentsia of his own and older generations. The October Revolution suddenly disrupted the life that people had been living and had planned on living, the life they assumed would continue for decades. The Petersburg mansion on Morskaya Street (now Gertsen Street), the ancestral estate in Rozhdestveno, and the privileged Tenishesvoe School all turned into a mirage. In the summer of 1919, the 20-year-old Nabokov, after a circuitous journey around Europe, ended up in London, where he entered Cambridge University. Three years later, his father, a prominent politician, scholar, man of letters, and publisher, was killed in Berlin. He had been a leader of the centrist faction of the Constitutional Democrats and a member of the first Duma, after the dispersal of which he had gone to Finland, where he issued a declaration protesting tsarist rule. His punishment, however, was light: three months in prison and a ban on further participation in the Duma. In the Wrangel government he had been minister of justice; in Berlin he was publisher of the emigré journal *Rul'* (the Helm). He was hit by a bullet not intended for him as he shielded his longtime and like-minded friend Miliukov, shot at by a Russian monarchist fanatic.

Vladimir Dmitrievich Nabokov was, according to those who knew him (and to his son's recollections), a cold man who did not allow familiarity even with those close to him. His children always called him "sir." Nevertheless, although he differed from him in many ways, Nabokov was extremely influenced by his father and always preserved respect for him, as well as a secret, undemonstrated love. This is easy to sense, reading *The Gift*, *Drugie berega*, and other works.

After his father's death, Nabokov moved to Berlin, where he stayed for a long time. There he began to publish under the pseudonym "V. Sirin." Strictly speaking, his first literary attempts had been undertaken while he was still in Petersburg; but the two volumes of poetry he published there had gone unnoticed, and today they are of only bibliographic interest. Soon after, the novice writer entered the wide circle of Russian literary emigration.

But he immediately took a place there all his own. His compatriots' evaluations were diametrically opposed. After reading *The Defense*, Ivan Bunin exclaimed: "This little boy has drawn a pistol, and in one shot put away all the old men, including me."

Even earlier, Iuly Aikhenvald, the first critical pen of Russian emigré literature, having just heard the novel *Mary* (1926) read by the author, named Nabokov "our new Turgenev."

Vladislav Khodasevich, whose character is easy to discern in the poet Koncheyev, of *The Gift*, always held Nabokov in high esteem.

Nina Berberova carried the impression made on her by *The Defense* all her life. In her book (now published in the Soviet Union), we find: "An enormous, mature, complex writer, like the Phoenix, born in the fire and ash of revolution and exile. From now on, our existence has gained meaning. My whole generation has been vindicated."

On the other side were writers grouped around the Paris journal *Chislo*—Georgii Adamovich, Georgii Ivanov, and Zinaida Gippius—who wrote of Nabokov skeptically and sometimes with open malice. Adamovich saw him merely as an excellent imitator of the French; Ivanov wrote that his stories contained "vulgarity, though with a shade of virtuosity," while his poetry was "simply vulgar." Finally, he called him "an imposter, a cook's son, a renegade, a sorry scoundrel."

It's never good to call names, but in this case the critics' sense of reality clearly deserted them.

"A cook's son"? The name *Nabokov* first appears in 17-century chronicles and remains ubiquitous—Nabokovs were military and civil officials,
university professors and extremely successful landowners. The writer's
grandfather held a prominent position in the government of Alexander II,
was a retainer of great Prince Constantin, and took part in the coronation
of Nicholas II. His grandmother came from the landowning Shishkov
family. His father has already been described. His mother was heir to the
wealthy Siberian gold-mining Rukavishnikov family.

What kind of a "cook's son" is that?

Nabokov, however, did not remain in debt. Using his recently made-up
pseudonym (one of many), "Vivian Kalambrud," he published a translation of the mythical English poem, "Night Journey," in which he incidentally portrayed a decadent poet absorbed with the mystery of death:
Seated on the edge of the bath, with a rose in one hand and a razor in the
other, the poet prepares to commit suicide. His prototype is easy to
identify.

All of this, however, is bickering in a noble family. What is really interesting and essential is this: Neither his detractors, nor even his admirers, ever considered Nabokov fully their own. Why? Nina Berberova
recalls an evening in Paris, when Bunin, Khodasevich, Mark Aldanov, and
Nabokov began to discuss Tolstoy. "Nabokov announced that he had
never read *Sebastopol Sketches* and so had no opinion about them. 'Alas,' he
said, 'it has never been my lot to look at those "sins of youth".' Aldanov
concealed his indignation with difficulty; Bunin, turning green in moments of rage, swore foully under his breath. Khodasevich laughed skeptically, knowing that *Sebastopol Sketches* had been required reading in Russian grammar schools."

Is it that Nabokov liked to demonstrate independent judgment and
views, not stopping at shock value? This is plausible, especially as "independent" is perhaps the softest of possible words. He was a writer of
downright inhuman arrogance. He recognized no authorities; he would
either become enraged by, or reject with contempt, the smallest critical
observation; to praise—at least, externally—he remained indifferent. In
his well-known book, *Russian Literature in Exile*, Gleb Struve, whose
father was a political confederate and close acquaintance of Nabokov's
father, devoted a fair amount of attention to Sirin, praising him highly.
But he did so in the context of emigré prose, and Nabokov did not like

this. He wished to see nobody next to him; he was insulted by any neighbor; indeed, after his move to America, Nabokov would always react painfully when he was referred to as an emigré writer. In short, he responded with a haughty letter, and a long friendship came to an end.

The surest way to earn Nabokov's dislike was to try to talk with him about traditions or, God forbid, influences. He once said with complete candor that he couldn't stand it when a banner was raised over his head with other names on it. He was still far from world renown but, responding to a questionnaire concerning Proust for *Chislo*, Nabokov drily observed that one cannot speak of influence based on chance echoes (incidentally, this response appeared in the same issue as Ivanov's attack). And later, when interviews with the maitre became the norm, he waved away such questions altogether. When clear reflections of Kafkaesque horror are detected in *Invitation to a Beheading*, Nabokov discredits them. When he wrote the novel (1938), he had not read Kafka. This is hard to believe; it was precisely in the mid-1930s that enlightened Europe discovered *The Trial*, *The Castle*, and many formerly unknown stories. Asked about Joyce, he says: "My real meeting with *Ulysses*, if you don't count a fleeting acquaintance at the beginning of the 20s, took place in the 30s, when I was completely formed as a writer and had developed an immunity to literary influences." Among the classics, Nabokov valued Gogol extraordinarily; but just try to find in his extensive essay even the shadow of a hint that he is in any way indebted to his predecessor.

Nabokov's contemporaries, particularly those who had won favor with the reading world, he simply disparaged. Thomas Mann he found uninteresting; Hemingway was merely a "contemporary replacement for Mayne Reid," Sartre and Faulkner were "insignificant pets of the Western bourgeoisie." Edmund Wilson, a well-known American critic and long-time friend of Nabokov, let it slip in a letter to him that he considered André Malraux to be the best contemporary writer. Nabokov spared no pains in answering, and in four pages tore the French writer to pieces as a stylist.

Nabokov regarded the successes of his living compatriots with particular envy. Solzhenitsyn, also not the picture of humility, upon receiving the Nobel Prize, sent Nabokov a letter, in which he said that the latter was even more deserving than he of that award. There was no response, but Nabokov told his biographer, Andrew Field, that Solzhenitsyn's letter contained many grammatical errors. He compared *Doctor Zhivago* to the

sentimental prose of Madame Charskaya and in general took every opportunity to denigrate Pasternak as a novelist. The attacks became stronger as
signs increased that *Doctor Zhivago* was supplanting *Lolita* as number one
on the bestseller list. Yes, this writer, who appeared so free from worldly
concerns, possessed ordinary human envy. Bunin once foretold complete
solitude for his young colleague, and he was not mistaken. But can this be
explained by his character alone?

Here is one other suggestion. Emigré writers, even those who at home
avoided involving themselves in political affairs, once abroad began to
take part in animated discussion of political problems. They entered into
polemics, wrote articles, and constantly looked to the East, toward the
home they had left. Circles, salons, clubs, foundations, and journals were
formed. Nabokov took no part in any of this, seeing in such activities a
fuss unworthy of an artist. The reader of *The Gift* can see this.

It cannot, of course, be said that Nabokov remained entirely indifferent
to events in the world, particularly in Russia. He had a position, a fully
defined one.

> In these days, when the putrid scent of an anniversary wafts out from
> there, why should we not celebrate an anniversary as well? Ten years of
> contempt, ten years of loyalty, ten years of freedom—is that not enough
> to merit one anniversary speech? One must know how to despise; we
> have learned the science to perfection. We are so saturated with it, that
> at times we are too lazy to mock its object. A light trembling of the
> nostrils, momentarily narrowed eyes—and silence. But today, let's
> speak. . . . I despise not the person, not the worker Sidorov, but that
> ugly, witless little idea that transforms simple Russians into communist
> fools, which makes people into ants.

So wrote the twenty-eight-year-old Nabokov when events which had
estranged him forever from his homeland were still fresh in his memory.

"My longtime dispute with the Soviet dictatorship has nothing to do
with matters of property. I despise the old, solid Russian who hates the
communists because they stole his money and land." Nabokov wrote this a
quarter of a century later. He had the moral right to do so; he'd had plenty
to lose, both position and land, but he did not object to the Soviet system
on the grounds of property.

In one of his last interviews, Nabokov recalls a meeting in Berlin at the
beginning of the 1920s, with Aleksei Tolstoy and Andrei Bely. The latter
was, in his eyes, one of the best novelists of the century, the former a man

who chanced to be in the field of literature. But that was of no significance. What matters is this: "Both writers at that time held openly pro-Soviet positions (and both were about to return to Russia), so it stands to reason that a Russian of the white camp, which I was at the time and which, in the specific sense of the word, I remain today, would not have wished to speak with 'bolshevisans' (fellow travellers)."

Nabokov was absolutely unable to find a common language with Prince D. P. Sviatopolk-Mirsky, who also hastened back to Russia, later to vanish in the Stalinist camps. With Edmund Wilson—a friend and, it might be said, benefactor, who did a great deal to help Nabokov and his family settle on American soil—he parted not least over opinions. Although, like many members of the Western intelligentsia, greatly distressed by the Soviet–German Pact of 1939, to the end, Wilson was faithful to the ideal of socialism. This was unacceptable to Nabokov. (Incidentally, Nabokov also objected to the fact that, in *Doctor Zhivago*, Pasternak sees the October Revolution as historically inevitable.) According to Field, Nabokov even proposed a fantastical theory: the fact that the novel was published by a leftist press in Italy meant the Kremlin was craftily spreading its ideological influence around the world.

Such matters, such a position. It need not cause holy horror, but things must be looked at soberly. And, of course, there is no need—as is sometimes done—to represent Nabokov as nearly a socialist sympathizer. This, of course, is a new mythology.

It is another matter that Nabokov publicly stated his sociopolitical views extremely rarely. In *Drugie berega* he recalls that, after entering Cambridge, he at first engaged in many agonizing arguments about Russia, the revolution, Lenin, and Kerensky. But "I very soon abandoned politics, and gave myself entirely to literature." So it was, and indeed such estrangement transformed Nabokov (it's true despite all the nastiness of Ivanov's tone) into a renegade among those who shared with him the fate of exile.

Yet, all the same, it would be naive and frivolous to define Nabokov's spiritual and literary status merely according to his character or social behavior.

It is time, finally, to turn to his work.

If you want to understand a poet, advised the wise Goethe, go to his homeland. But where is Vladimir Nabokov's home? For many, there is no question: Russia, of course. Of course, he's a Russian writer. What's more, we sometimes hear that when he turned to the English language, giving up his Antaios connection to his native soil, the Russian language, Nabokov diminished as an artist ("The Ruin of a Gift" is the title of an article prefacing *The Defense*, in which this idea is particularly distinct). We will leave the extremes, however, and return to the essence of the matter.

At first glance, everything indeed appears crystal clear. We can even begin with his pseudonym: Sirin is the bird of paradise of old Russian woodprints. In *Drugie berega*, a confessional book, the author writes:

> The real history of my time at the English university is the history of my efforts to hold on to Russia. . . . I would sit for hours by the fire, and tears would come to my eyes from the pressure of emotions, from the banality of the smoldering coals, the solitude, the distant bells, and I would be tormented by the thought of how much I had missed in Russia, how much I would have managed to stuff into all my soul's pockets and carry out with me if I had foreseen the parting.

Nabokov's autobiography appeared in three forms: *Conclusive Evidence* (English, 1951), *Drugie berega* (Russian, 1954), and *Speak, Memory* (English, 1966). The three differ in many ways, but the subject of Russia, as Blok would have said, always remains at the fore. And this despite the fact that the author spent fifty-eight of his seventy-eight years far from the land of his birth.

And his poetry? Read almost any poem, and you'll hear the aching note of longing, see the Russian countryside, feel the pain of an incurably homesick heart:

> There are many like me. We
> roam the world sleeplessly
> and know: the buried city
> will rise again; everything in it will be
> wonderful, joyous, and new—
> and only the former one, our home
> we will never find.

("Petersburg," 1921)

> Our Immortal happiness
> will always be called Russia
> We have never seen a more beautiful land,
> and we've been in many lands

Our chance home in a foreign place,
where the exile's dream is peaceful,
as if by a wind, by a sea, by a secret,
is always surrounded by Russia

("Homeland," 1927)

I will thank you, homeland
I will thank you for my evil fate!
Full of you, unrecognized by you,
It is with myself I speak

(from the novel *The Gift*, 1937)

And so on, right up to the last works. Nabokov has nearly ceased to write in Russian, but we heard the same melody, the same theme of loss. In his first mature English poetry, the author also turned to Russia, only then the symbol was language—the last connecting thread, breaking.

Poetry and memoirs are revealing of the heart; in them everything is said directly. In prose, especially in the more conventional novels, there is a mediator/character between the author and the reader—not merely a mediator, in fact, but one who craves, and receives, independence. But even here, Russia and Russians create a constant background, sometimes even a direct theme. *Mary*'s Lev Ganin appears, with a changed name, in *The Defense*, then is transformed into Fedor Godunov-Cherdyntsev. Even as an English-language writer, Nabokov remains with Russians: We are acquainted with Professor Pnin of the novel that bears his name, and with the writer and scholar-psychologist Van, from the novel *Ada*. The name is different, but the hero traces his genealogy to an 18th-century Russian noble family.

It is another matter that, in Nabokov's prose, Russia is not only the object of pure lyrical emotion but of biting satire. Of course, this is the new Russia, in which the future writer could not find a place for himself. Indeed, this is no longer, strictly speaking, Russia—even the name did not remain. In the novel *The Exploit* (1931), the Cambridge student Martin Edelweiss (also an autobiographical figure) undertakes a desperate journey home but finds only ashes—Zurlandia, a symbol of night and death. Five years later, Nabokov would write the story "Tyrants Destroyed," a picture of the same enormous torture chamber—this time without a made-up name—ruled by an all-powerful dictator: "Everything is filled with him, everything I love is disgraced, everything has become his likeness, his mirror, and in the eyes of passers-by, in the eyes of my poor schoolchildren, his image shows more and more clearly and hopelessly." The monster can be escaped only through suicide or laughter. The hero chooses laughter: "Rereading my notes I see that, trying to portray him as terrible, I have only made him funny—and have executed him with that old tried and true method."

Much later, in 1962, *Pale Fire* appeared, a terrifying book, a book-centaur (the title is taken from Timon of Athens). The 999-line poem by its hero, John Shade, is accompanied by an enormous body of commentary in which dark passages of the text are explained. Here, there is no Zurlandia, but there is Zembla—an even more terrible picture of a home left behind, where robot-people, fanatics, and murderers such as Gradus, an agent of Zemblan counterespionage, appear.

But behind the hostility, insult, disappointment, and even malice, there still remains unforgotten, unshed love.

And what of Nabokov the critic, literary historian, and translator? Russia may have disappeared, but her literature remains: "Pushkin and Tolstoy, Tiutchev and Gogol, stood at the four corners of my world" (*Drugie berega*). Nabokov opens the American page of his autobiography reading lectures on the Russian classics. In 1944, a small book, *Three Russian Poets*, was published, containing translations of Pushkin, Lermontov, and Tiutchev. In 1960, his *Song of Igor's Campaign* appeared, and soon after, he began the Herculean work of translating *Eugene Onegin*. That translation—accompanied by a detailed, 1,000-page, linguistic and historical commentary—saw the light in 1964, immediately giving rise to a heated and protracted debate: in an effort to convey its meaning with absolute accuracy, Nabokov had presented Pushkin's novel in prose.

In short, to the end of his days, Nabokov preserved his inner ties to Russia and Russian literature. But was he a Russian writer in the sense meant when we refer to those who became the four corners of Nabokov's world, or to those who were with him in emigration—Bunin and Shmelev, Aldanov and Zaitsev?

That is not so obvious; indeed, it is questionable.

It is not important that the action of Nabokov's books rarely takes place in Russia, that it is more often in Germany, France, America, or Switzerland. After all, unlike those who found themselves far from home as mature adults, having already established themselves as writers in their homeland, the author of *Mary*; *King, Queen, Knave*; *Despair*; and *The Gift* never had a chance to really know Russia.

Nor does it matter that Nabokov's homeland really is, simply, his child-hood, that in his dreams he longs for the smooth granite of Petersburg monuments, the summer emerald of birch trees, and the fallen leaves of country woods—the scenes of city and country where he grew up. Nabokov's image of his homeland has a peculiar trait:

> It has fastened itself, this longing, to one small corner of the world, and it can be torn away only with my life. Today, if I imagine the grass of, or the ravines of the Urals, or the salt fields of the Aral Sea, I remain as cold in the patriotic or nostalgic sense as I would be, say, towards the wormwood of Nevada, or the rhododendrons of the Blue Mountains; but give me, on any continent, woods, fields, or air that remind me of Petersburg Province, and my soul turns upside down.

All of this, too, can be understood and explained biographically.

Aside from memory, however, with its individual coloring; aside from subjects, themes, characters; aside from language, in the end there exists some elusive remainder, substance, foundation. There exists a tradition, a legend, a national artistic ideal which, while not isolating one literature among others and, of course, not raising it above them, gives it a sharply defined character.

The artistic ideal of the Russian classic literature was not close to Sirin's heart; it could even be said that he was in constant conflict with it.

In his preface to *Eugene Onegin*, Nabokov wrote, clearly aiming his remarks at Belinsky:

> This is not a "picture of Russian life," it is at best a picture of a small group of Russians living in the second decade of the last century, a picture which is thickly populated with characters quite clearly bor-rowed from European Romantic prose, and which depicts a stylized Russia; a picture which quickly falls to pieces if we take it from its French frame and remove its French actors, playing English and Ger-man roles and prompting the Russian-speaking heroes and heroines. The paradox for the translator is that the single important Russian element in *Onegin* is Pushkin's language, flowing and glimmering in poetic rhythms formerly unknown to Russia.

The Gift is, by rights, considered the best of Nabokov's Russian-language novels. It is also the book that had the most dramatic fate (with the possible exception of *Lolita*). In 1937, it was printed in *Sovremennye zapiski*, only in a shortened form. The entire fourth chapter—Godunov-Cherdyntsev's biography of Chernyshevsky, or rather, his free, extremely biased fantasies about the latter's life—was omitted. The complete novel saw publication only in 1952.

The author explains the essence of the conflict through one of the novel's characters, the publisher Vasiliev: "There are traditions of Russian society which an honest writer would not dare to make fun of. I don't care whether you're talented or not, I only know that to write a parody of a man whose sufferings and works have nourished millions of educated Russians is unworthy of any talent."

We can understand this. Chernyshevsky, in *The Gift*, is not an ideological leader but a third-rate writer, a crude philosopher-materialist. His life is, in fact, described in an openly parodying, contemptuous tone. The tragedy of thought and struggle is transformed into an obscene farce, the vulgar details of family life are recorded with rapacious observation.

Of course, I do not mean to force anything on anyone. The reader will decide who is right in this dispute between a fictitious publisher and a fictitious writer. I imagine that many will accept the views of the first, which were voiced, incidentally, in a relatively recent speech at an event celebrating the 150th anniversary of Chernyshevsky's birth. I myself, I must confess, when I first read *The Gift* as a student, was prepared to take this position. But I now think otherwise.

It was not the urge to write satire that moved the author's hand, it was an ideal.

Nabokov expressed its essence indirectly when he said that Dostoevsky dishonored his talent with "journalism," and that Blok should never have imagined himself a thinker, as this caused irreparable damage to his poetry. He formulated the same ideal directly in a lecture in 1958, which later formed the preface of *Vladimir Nabokov—Lectures on Russian Literature* (1981). It is titled "Russian Writers, Censors, Readers," and in it Nabokov says the following. In Russia there have always been two forces standing in the way of the freedom of the culture's creative spirit. One is the government and its censors, and the other: "anti-government, socially conscious critics, utilitarians, the political and civil radical thinkers of the time." These were honest people, Nabokov continues, who sincerely wished their compatriots well. But they too despotically suppressed literature—they merely did so from the other side. "For all their merits, these radical critics (Belinsky, Chernyshevsky, Dobroliubov, Pisarev, Zaitsev, Blagosvetlov, and certain others became as much an obstacle on the road to art as did the government. The government and the revolution, the tsar and the radicals, took equally philistine positions in art," as both demanded that the artist fulfill "a social demand, with no imagination." The nature of the social demand does not matter; what is important is that, in all cases, it limits the artist's freedom.

But perhaps the lines drawn by Nabokov the critic and pedagogue are limiting to Nabokov the writer?

It cannot, of course, be maintained—I will speak about this later—that his books contain no events at all or, to put it more broadly, no atmosphere of the time. They do; it can be felt in *The Defense* and especially in *Invitation to a Beheading* and *Lolita*. But on the whole, the task the hero of *The Gift*, Nabokov's double, has set himself in writing his book about Chernyshevsky is close to Nabokov's heart and extremely important to him. That is to "construct a biography in the form of a circle, circling its apocryphal subject so that it takes on the form less of a book—which, with its finiteness, is opposed to the circular nature of all existence—than of one cyclical, that is infinite, sentence."

In other words, Nabokov is inspired by the goal of creating a balanced masterpiece complete in itself. What's more, he must also show the methods of its creation. This is felt and understood even by those who are especially partial. "The subject of Sirin's creative work," wrote Khodasevich, "is creative work itself." Much later, Field expressed the same thought: Nabokov writes as if "a painter said: 'I'm not going to show you a landscape, I want to depict various ways of depicting a landscape.'" In short, he is a master, a Daedalus-creator, a virtuoso. It is for this reason that Nabokov is unable to settle into any genuine, sincere relationship with Russian classic literature. Yes, he admires and loves it but in his own way, above all, in terms of form, detail, craft. What did Nabokov's American students hear about the Russian classics? That Gogol was one of the first to employ the technique of painting in the art of prose. That Tolstoy presented an absolutely original concentration of time. That Chekhov, with inimitable skill, combined seemingly incidental and insignificant details. About the ideal of service, deeply ingrained in Russian literature, about that which compels the writer to sacrifice style and proportion, Nabokov never said a word.

This was because he himself valued something entirely different in literature. "For me," he says in the afterword to *Lolita*, "a story or novel exists only insofar as it provides what I will simply call aesthetic pleasure, and that, in its turn, I understand as a special state, in which one feels oneself somehow, somewhere, in some way connected to other forms of existence, where art . . . is the norm. Everything else is journalistic garbage or, so to speak, the Literature of Great Ideas, which, in fact, is frequently identical to ordinary garbage but which is presented in the form of huge plaster fragments and carried down with great care from century to century."

In *Speak, Memory*, Nabokov writes that the years he spent at Cambridge were "the history of my attempts to become a Russian writer."

I believe he never became one.

Where, then, is the home of the writer Vladimir Nabokov? Not, of course, in Germany, although he lived there for a long time, although it is there that he earned a name for himself as a writer and there that became the setting of many of his books. From beginning to end, however, Nabokov felt himself a stranger in Germany. Perhaps this was in part because Germany took his father from him; but, above all, it was due to some deep inner incompatibility with the German cultural tradition, even more with that burgher self-satisfaction which in his rich imagination assumed extraordinary dimensions. Gifted with a rare linguistic ability, he did not even make a serious attempt to master the German language. In the preface to the English edition of the novel *King, Queen, Knave*, we read: "I didn't speak German, I didn't have German friends, and I didn't read one German novel, either in the original or in translation." We assume he is being coy here; scholars have shown fairly convincingly that the novel *Brother and Sister*, by the German expressionist Leonhard Frank, which was published shortly before that statement, did not escape the attention of the author of *The Defense*. There is indeed an echo, but it is only an echo; there is no sense of any inner similarity.

Nabokov spent the last eighteen years of his life, from 1960 to 1977, in Switzerland. This country, too, is reflected in his work. Together with the heroes of *Ada* (1969) and especially *Transparent Things* (1972), the reader is transported to a white expanse of alpine resorts, descends to cities, changes hotels, wanders through publishing offices, and so on. But the hidden dramas of Swiss life, as they are reflected in the works of, say, Frank and Duhrenmatt, didn't trouble Nabokov the writer in the least. Switzerland is simply a location, a fictional stage-set.

America is another matter. In 1936, Nabokov left Berlin for France and a few days before the occupation of Paris crossed the Atlantic, to spend the next twenty years in the United States.

"A spiral," we read in *Drugie berega*,

> is the inspiration for a circle. In it, disconnected and freed from the plane, the circle ceases to be flawed . . . a colored spiral in a glass mosaic—that is the model of my life. The thesis is my twenty-year Russian period (1899–1919). The antithesis is my time of emigration (1919–1940), spent in Western Europe. The fourteen years (1940–1954), which I spent in my new homeland, mark the beginning of a synthesis.

In a certain sense, that was probably the case. His Russian childhood and European experience nourished each other, so that, across the ocean, a new form arose which preserved, of course, a genetic memory of all that had been lived and written.

Let's begin by noting "my new *homeland*." Nabokov never said, never could have said, anything of the sort about the European countries.

Further: language. In 1941, Nabokov's first English-language novel appeared, *The Real Life of Sebastian Knight*. Sirin was left in the past; Nabokov had appeared, a writer who became in time, in the opinion of many, a key figure in the literature of the United States.

In a review of *Ada*, the *New York Times* called the author "the greatest living American novelist." "A Postscript to Tradition and Dream," written by the prominent English critic W. Allen at the request of *Inostrannaia literatura* (Foreign Literature), says that "in contemporary American literature the name Vladimir Nabokov reigns" (I. L., 1977, no. 12). The leaders of the school of "black humor," John Barth and Thomas Pynchon, speak of Nabokov with great enthusiasm. Pynchon has stated: "The writer who really and reliably supports us all is Vladimir Nabokov."

Nabokov is often compared to Conrad, but it is a very weak comparison. There is no such writer as Jozef Teodor Konrad Nalecz Korzeniowsky (the real name of the author of *Lord Jim* and *Nostromo*); there is only the writer Joseph Conrad. A Pole by birth, he never wrote in Polish. So the "case of Nabokov" is unique; there are no analogues, at least not on Nabokov's artistic level.

The preconditions for Nabokov's bilingualism appeared during his childhood: his first words were spoken and read in English. In *Drugie berega*, Nabokov recalls how his father, a passionate Anglophile, suddenly noticed with embarrassment that his five-year-old boy, surrounded by English tutors, had trouble expressing himself and could not read at all in Russian. Necessary correctives were made in his education, but English had already irreversibly entered the blood of the future writer.

From which, of course, it does not follow that the name-change from Sirin to Nabokov was painless. It says in the preface to that same book: "When I decided in 1940 to switch to the English language, my misfortune was in the fact that for more than fifteen years previously I had been writing in Russian, and in that time I had laid down my own stamp on that tool, on my mediator. Turning to a new language, I was rejecting not the language of Avakkum, Pushkin, Tolstoy—or Ivanov, or of Russian journalism—in a word, not the common language, but my own, individual dialect. My longtime habit of expressing myself in my own way did not allow me to be satisfied with clichés in my newly chosen language." Further, Nabokov, who was intolerant only of the criticism of others, judges himself severely, speaking of "intolerable flaws" in one of his English-language novels, of sentences that stand out hideously, of gaps and unnecessary explanations that appeared in the course of translating the language of *Conclusive Evidence* into the language of *Drugie berega*. There were certainly unsuccessful moments; these are especially evident if we compare identical texts such as, for instance, the English- and Russian-language versions of *Lolita*. But these are extremely rare exceptions. I believe John Updike—he certainly knows what he's talking about—when he calls Nabokov a "virtuoso in a language" which was not originally his own, "one of those few writers who showed what can be done in literature by means of language, its possibilities."

So, there is language. But not only language.

If we can say that the Russian theme permeates Nabokov's work, there is no less ground for asserting that the American theme holds an important place there.

It is obvious that we must start with *Lolita*, the novel that earned its author world recognition. Many critical essays are devoted to *Lolita*; its literary biography has been minutely traced and the history of its publication described. The latter somewhat resembles the classic examples: the litigation that surrounded *Madame Bovary*; the long struggle against the censorship of *Ulysses*.

The dispute was mostly, of course, over the novel's bearing on ideas of morality. Was this the description of a clinical case, a challenge to hypocrisy, a literary exercise in Freudianism (although Nabokov denigrated Freud in every way, calling him nothing less than the Viennese charlatan)—or a sad book about loneliness and love?

The temptation is great to enter into this ongoing debate. But I will resist and turn only to the novel's content. This, of course, impoverishes it terribly, but what can be done? I have my own subject, my own goal.

The love story that is built into *Lolita*'s subject matter unfolds against the dense backdrop of postwar America. Sameness, depressing sameness—of roads, homes, words, actions, feeling—this is what surrounds the thirty-year-old immigrant intellectual Humbert Humbert (the novel is written in the form of a confession; the hero, accused of murdering a man who abducted his underage step-daughter/lover, awaits the verdict). The character—or rather, the characterlessness, of Mrs. Haze, Lolita's mother (she "clearly belonged to that class of women whose polished words could reflect a ladies' tea or bridge club, but could not reflect the soul")—seems to duplicate the evident lack of taste in their domestic circumstances: "The entrance hall was decorated with a cluster of doorbells, a white-eyed wooden monster made in Mexico for tourists, and a painting by Van Gogh, the banal favorite of the pretentious middle class." Here, the world of ideas is replaced by the world of things, education with a code of practical instruction ("It is certainly necessary to know the precise positions of the planets, but knowing the most expedient place in the kitchen for the refrigerator is perhaps even more important for a future young housewife"). Art is replaced by a trade, in which the playwright, Humbert's lucky rival in the struggle for Lolita, and his victim, is quite successful; memory with imitation ("a completely modern cabin, boldly imitating that former cabin in which Lincoln was born"), people with mannequins: ". . . a modest little soldier . . . a schoolboy who wants to go two blocks; a murderer who wants to go two thousand miles; a mysterious, nervous, elderly gentleman with a new suitcase and a trimmed mustache"—all are cut from the same cloth, all have the same name as those people are called in America who vote in the streets. The heroine of the title is herself drawn into the circle: "It was to her the advertisements were speaking, it was she who was the ideal consumer, the subject and object of every vulgar poster."

Two years after *Lolita*, Nabokov wrote *Pnin* (1957), and the same picture of spiritual impoverishment opened before the reader: the eccentric professor, whose name titles the book, just cannot manage to fall into the rhythm of American life, in which artists wish to give automobile parts immortality on canvas, people in bookstores have never heard of Jack London, and philologists working in universities "don't love literature and don't know the language." Timofey Pavlovich is unable to find a position in a French department precisely because he knows the language. This, he is made to understand, is not only unnecessary, it is even undesirable.

More than anything, Nabokov despised the ordinary, vulgarity, *poshlost'* (a word for which he was unable to find a worthy equivalent, and which he tried unsuccessfully simply to introduce, transliterated, into English). All of this, in a sharply concentrated form, combines in the image of American mass culture, which Nabokov depicts with the full force of his characteristic sarcasm.

Recalling a few examples of native, so to speak, American literature— works by Updike and Cheever, Heller and Bellow—we can easily affirm that artistically they are close to *Lolita* and *Pnin*. This is beyond dispute. Equally beyond dispute is that Nabokov liked a great deal about his new homeland (he received American citizenship in 1945). For example, he nearly decided that here were the best conditions for free creative work. At first he liked it, then he stopped liking it, so much that he left America.

Both the sympathy and the antipathy that replaced it were that of an outsider. The subjects, heroes, and conflicts may have been the same; but Nabokov never became an American writer in the essential sense, whatever many critics—or, frequently, he himself—may have said. On the other hand, he sometimes showed appropriate caution. If he spent his Cambridge years attempting to become a Russian writer, then, as he says in the preface to *Lolita*, "I chose American motels instead of Swiss hotels and French inns only because I am *trying* [emphasis mine] to be an American writer."

Nabokov had a remarkable eye. He was able to describe his object so that it became tangible and visible. But too often his images lose their physical outlines, and a weightlessness, an airiness, appears, which is altogether absent from the classics of the last two centuries: Cooper and Melville, Twain and Whitman, Faulkner and Thomas Wolfe. In this sense, Nabokov is closer to Henry James, who is very much a European writer.

Nabokov has no place on the vast map of America that he can call his own—as the author of *Huckleberry Finn* could say of Missouri, Fizgerald and Dos Passos of New York, Sandberg of Chicago, Anderson of the towns of Ohio, and Faulkner of Mississippi. Even Hemingway, despite all his love for France and Spain, had a complete right to say "in Michigan, where I come from." Nabokov had no such right, nor did he seek it.

Most important, he was entirely uninterested in the theme of the unattainable—at first shining, later dimmed—American dream, that same American dream which has long nourished America's social and artistic consciousness and without which there would be no American literature.

So, where is the writer Vladimir Nabokov's home?

Nowhere—and everywhere. The first to recognize this was that "pet of the European bourgeoisie," Sartre. In a review of the novel *Otchizna* (1936), he wrote: "There is a certain similarity between the author and his hero. Both are victims of war and emigration. . . . There now exists a strange literature of Russian and other emigrés who have *no roots*. Nabokov's rootlessness, like that of Karlovich (the name of the novel's hero), is total. He ties himself to no society, he even rebels against it, as he belongs to none."

Twenty years later, Berberova expressed the same thought: "Nabokov is the only Russian author (either in Russia or in emigration) who belongs to the *whole* Western world (or to the world in general), not only to Russia. Fealty to one nationality or one language does not, in essence, play a large role for such as him. . . . For Kafka, Joyce, Ionesco, Beckett, Jorge Borges, and Nabokov, language has ceased to be what it was, in the narrow nationalistic sense, eighty and a hundred years ago. In our time, linguistic effects and national psychology, *supported by nothing else*, are no longer a necessity for either the author or the reader."

As far as linguistic effects are concerned (national psychology is more doubtful), this is true, as the author himself attests. He calls himself "an American writer, native to Russia, educated in England where he studied French literature before going to Germany for fifteen years." And he firmly states: "[The] nationality [of any good writer] is of secondary importance." The lectures on Russian literature are eloquently titled: "Lermontov as a Western European Writer," "So and So as a Western European Writer," "Pushkin as a Western European Writer." "Russianness" (or—it makes no difference—"Englishness" or "Frenchness") has nothing to do with true art.

In a word, Vladimir Nabokov stands in 20th-century literature as the most prominent representative of an extremely small group of cosmopolitan writers. It is sad that to this day that term is used in a disparaging sense; behind it looms the spectre of "rootlessness." But it would seem we could finally free ourselves from its judgmental chill or belligerence and simply call things by their names.

I will permit myself one more reference.

Reading and thinking about Nabokov, I always recall words from Faulkner's *Light in August*. Referring to a man, a literary hero of an entirely different sort, they characterize with unexpected accuracy the author of the Russian-language *The Defense* and the English-language *Ada*: ". . . homelessness emanated from him, as if he had no city, or hometown, or street, or plot of land. And he carried the awareness of this like a banner, with an independent, cruel, almost proud expression."

That sense of homelessness, hidden for a time, was familiar to Nabokov from childhood. In *Drugie berega*, he calls himself a "five-year-old exile," then adds: ". . . the theme of homelessness is a vague preface to later, far harsher, wanderings." One of his poems speaks of his "passportless soul."

These admissions breathe with an inescapable sadness, but there is also proud aloofness. The soul registered at no address has supreme freedom; it desires to rise above the world and plunge into its own depths. A refuge for such a soul was found long ago, and Nabokov, softening his words with his customary irony, is prepared to join his predecessors. It is the "ivory tower so despised by all, yet which is equipped with a telephone and elevator in case one feels like going down for the evening paper or inviting an acquaintance over for a game of chess." We understand that the view from the tower is peculiar; its windows are too high and too narrow.

Exactly the same age as the century, Vladimir Nabokov witnessed its unprecedented tragedies and its magnificent flights. But all of this—wars, revolutions, and atomic explosions—is only dimly guessed at in his books. Where and when does the action of *The Defense* take place? First in prerevolutionary Russia, then in Germany, apparently in the second half of the 1920s. But time as a material—a social category, time as a receptacle of events that change the fate of millions of people—is here reduced. There is vague mention of "civil chaos"; it is mentioned and immediately forgotten as all that is merely "a vulgar mess," which has no relation to the inner world of a brilliant chess player.

Where and when does the action of *The Gift* take place? Also in Germany and at the same time, or perhaps a little later—in the 1930s. We are forced to guess, however, because everything we know about the country at that time—from historians, commentators, and writers (Thomas and Heinrich Mann, Feikhtwanger, Thomas Wolfe, and many others)—is left out of Nabokov's novel. Even Russian emigré existence is presented fleetingly and, on the whole, openly polemically. The reality of life is replaced by the reality of fantasy, the object with its shadow, which is described with great zeal. Say the hero, going out for a walk, meets the only person he feels close to—his fellow Russian literary exile, Koncheyev. They begin a conversation about art, the artist's lot, spirituality. But near the end, we discover that this is only a monologue; Koncheyev is not there; he has been called forth by the strength of imagination. In fact, Godunov-Cherdyntsev is addressing some chance burgher who answers with disgustingly banal comments ("Today the weather is beautiful, but tomorrow it will probably rain"). Godunov-Cherdyntsev—and with him, of course, Vladimir Nabokov—preserves and develops this ability to put the settled in motion, to bring mirages to life, as his most precious gift. Everything else is unimportant ("so-called politics [that whole foolish alternation of pacts, conflicts, increases in tension, frictions . . .]")—all the rest is lies and impediments. "Now, fifteen years later," reasons the father of the hero of *The Defense*, an author writing a book about his *wunderkind* son,

> those war years have turned out to be an irritating impediment. It was some kind of infringement on freedom of creativity, since in every book where the gradual development of a specific human individual was described, it was necessary somehow to mention the war, and even the death of the hero at a young age was no way out. . . . It was even worse with the revolution. In the general opinion, it affected the life of every Russian; you could not pass your hero through it without burning him, it was inescapable. This was a genuine forcing of the writer's will.

All of this concerns fictitious heroes, and the elder Luzhin never wrote his book. But Vladimir Nabokov left a biography; it presents a fifty-year-long road—prerevolutionary Russia, Russia during the revolution, Germany, France. What was preserved in his memory, and what did he deem it important to tell? As a child, the author met, in his father's office, General Kuropatkin, who had just been named commander-in-chief of the Far Eastern army (this was during the Russo-Japanese War). Nabokov recalled not the appointment but a pattern the general laid out in matches. This is easy to understand: a child's perceptions. Nearly fifteen years go by; Nabokov is in the Crimea with his family just before his emigration. They meet an old man who asks for a smoke and breaks the matches. By the man's nervous movements, Nabokov recognizes him as Kuropatkin. This is nearly all that remains in the book from those severe, critical years: "What is interesting to me here is the logical development of the theme of matches . . . to discover and trace over the course of one's whole life the development of such thematic patterns is, I think, the main task of the memoirist." In 1940, Nabokov lived in Paris; but he tells not of the fascist invasion, not of the Resistance, but of an elegant chess problem he thought up just at that time. Such is his confession—the confession of an outsider.

Why, then, is Nabokov of interest? Why is he studied and read?

He was, of course, an incomparable, inimitable writer. Flaubert, at one time, dreamed of writing a book that would rest on the strength of style alone; Nabokov came close to achieving this. He once remarked that it was necessary to harden the muse's muscles. His muse attains nearly classical perfection. Opening any of his works, whether written in Russian or in English, and reading the very first lines, we see that Nabokov is a complete stranger to banality, to the slightest vagueness. Under his pen, both elusive human feelings and the most ordinary existence—which loses, under his pen, its ordinariness, becoming full of mysterious meaning—gain astonishing authenticity. This can seem a paradox: Hating all materiality, Nabokov the stylist strives for precisely that. But there is no paradox here; it is, on the contrary, the natural order of things. If reality involves so much vulgarity, if all is lost—spiritual purity, poetry, love (and the writer had no doubt of this)—then it follows that the emptiness must be filled with the substance of words. A different, true reality must be created: the reality of literature. This is, of course, aestheticism, but aestheticism on what a level!

Many have attempted to re-create the creative process itself—few have succeeded in this as Nabokov did in *The Gift*. We see and feel how, in the hero's consciousness, the first vague sketches of verses attain solid completion in poetic form.

In *Drugie berega* the weightlessness of dry snow remarkably is transformed into the weightlessness of time: "Everything is quiet, everything is enchanted by the bright sphere over the Russian desert of my past. Snow is real to touch, and when I bend to take it in my hand, half a century of life falls through my fingers in a frosty powder."

Nabokov doesn't describe; he doesn't express a mood. He creates it. Sometimes he does so with chains of words and sounds: the boat (*lodka*), the swan (*lebed'*), the light ripple on the surface of the pond near Lausanne (*legkaia volna na poverkhnosti pruda pod Lozannoi*) by themselves convey the inner state of the hero of *Drugie berega*; sometimes with a sudden pointedness of detail: the pawn on the chessboard "was knocked down like a tooth"—this comparison alone becomes a sign of unrest, of spiritual confusion (*The Defense*). And sometimes a chapter title itself, such as "Cloud, Lake, Tower" contains the poetic code of a whole work.

"I note with pleasure the higher achievements of Mnemosina: the skill with which she combines disconnected parts of the basic melody, gathering the lily-of-the-valley stems of notes hanging here and there over the whole rough score of the past" (*Drugie berega*). How beautifully said, how freely, how seemingly effortlessly does the word extend its limits, gathering life's moments into its length. In language, nothing was impossible for Nabokov. His sentence is light, his imagination inexhaustible, his alliteration dazzles with its brilliance. What's more, Nabokov, creating a new world of words, easily enters into the universe already created, taking his place there not as one invited but as one called. His books contain many concealed quotations that take on new meanings. He "converses" with Shakespeare and Tolstoy, Poe and Flaubert, Gogol and Chekhov, Stern and Joyce.

So, then, are Nabokov's books, to use Jean Ricardieu's well-known expression, an adventure in writing, an indispensable aid for gaining literary skill, food for gourmets? Partly. It is no surprise, incidentally, that Nabokov, who was quite successful in the area of chess composition, never became a strong practical player. Imagination alone is not enough for this; it requires psychology, even, as Lasker said, philosophy; it requires general ideas. So literature was for Nabokov, not least of all, an exercise in difficulty, as the French say. This is particularly noticeable in his English-language prose.

Nabokov's status as a living classic was secured with *Lolita* and *Ada*, novels in which the author, it might seem, strove, like Joyce, to create a universal myth of reality. Here, as in *Ulysses*, everything is reflected in everything; the action embraces the entire globe, embodied in geographical concepts of worlds and antiworlds; the hero, Van, writes on "The Texture of Time" and reads *Hamlet* in a Russian tavern; the clay soil of the state of Utah preserves the imprint of Leo Tolstoy's foot; and so on. But the author himself quickly destroys the illusion of life's plentitude, becoming captivated—and attempting to captivate the reader—with virtuosic play. The first sentence of the novel is the beginning of *Anna Karenina*, turned upside down: "All unhappy families resemble one another, but each happy family is happy in its own way." Then comes Chekhov's turn: Tuzenbach's name is lengthened (Tuzenbach-Krone-Altschauer); Olga, Masha, and Irina are joined by a certain nun by the name of Barbara, turning the "three sisters" into four. Here and there, the title of F. Scott Fitzgerald's novel is modified: In place of *The Beautiful and the Damned*, we have "the young and the damned."

Entire genre forms become the object of parody. The very shape of *Ada*, with its intentionally distorted proportions, with its perpetual, unmotivated digressions and chaotic whirl of action, is a comic lowering, a self-destruction of the epos—as, I repeat, the author's glance embraces centuries and continents—to external appearances, an epic sweep. Next is a parody of the love novel: Tragedy and the fate of love are constantly and comically turned inside out. At the end, exhausted by the incestuous passion they have carried through their entire long lives (Van and Ada are blood relatives), the heroes are peacefully united—just like Daphnis and Chloe, Philemon and Baucis. Nor does Nabokov neglect the devices, prevalent at that time (the novel was written in the 1960s), of documentary narrative. At a certain point, the book takes the form of Van's journal with Ada's commentary. Having made fun of literature, however, the author turns to philosophical concepts; ironic comments addressed to Bergson are placed on the hero's lips, although Van's own theory of time adheres to the spirit of Bergsonian subjectivism. This entire travesty is constantly accompanied by plays on the word itself—the novel is saturated with various palindromes, ciphers, "crosswords" as the author liked to call them.

All the same, thank God, Nabokov's illuminations are not merely the illuminations of an engineer who has found a flawless technical solution. Yes, he drew patterns masterfully; but they are held together not only by verbal threads but by unity of theme and spiritual problems. These are the problems that are painfully close both to the heart of the Western intelligentsia and to the literature of Europe and America. As we have now finally realized, and openly admitted to ourselves and others, they are far from alien to us as well.

Making unskillful use of Nabokov's style, the main conflict in his work could be expressed thus: gift versus the crowd (*dar/riad*). This juxtaposition of the creatively gifted, extraordinarily brilliant individual to the mob, which thoughtlessly but savagely encroaches upon his freedom, runs through all of Nabokov's books.

From his most tender years the hero of *The Defense* is separated from the external world by a blind wall of incomprehension, which will only grow and strengthen over the years. In school he becomes the object of "hate" and "mocking curiosity" from his fellow pupils. Then the "mob" is gathered into a single image—a certain Valentinov, a successful manager and a devourer of talent, after milking public interest in the *wunderkind*, abandons Luzhin in order later to snare him again, tempting him with a part in some Hollywood film. In Berlin the hero is once more the victim of philistines who are roused only to mockery and contempt by his awkward manners, strange speech, and, above all, full inner concentration on his art. Even his wife—the only person close to him, who dimly senses something deep and extraordinary behind his absurd exterior—turns out to be alien to him. She keeps trying to divert Luzhin from chess, to return him to normal life: an overly orderly house, walks, Swiss resorts. In the end, the entire world appears to the hero to be an enormous chessboard, its inhabitants a combination designed to attack and checkmate him, which must be fought off at any cost.

Equally solitary is Godunov-Cherdyntsev, who cannot find a common language with anybody—not with the emigré milieu, much less with Berlin, oppressive with the gray weight of its buildings, cheerless rain, and petty interests.

Nabokov's English-language prose develops the same theme. Much in *Pale Fire* is purely literary play. In fact, the entire book is a sort of parody of his own translation of *Eugene Onegin*, in which the correlation between Pushkin's text and Nabokov's commentary is about the same. But it has meaning as well; this is revealed by a comparison of the book's two parts. They are united, more often than not, not formally (the notes lose their connection to the text of the poem) but by the principle of counterpoint. The poet—whose fate in the world is revealed by his very name (Shade), endowed with a secret inner life—finds no place in the surrounding world, with its intrigues, vulgarity, and persecution of beauty. At times, the incompatibility breaks through in words: "The regular vulgarian, I daresay, / Is happier: he sees the Milky Way / Only when making water."

In *Lolita*, there is no such sharply expressed polarity. Humbert Humbert—separating himself from the flat, one-dimensional (as they say today) people who surround him—is himself morally deformed. At the same time, the atmosphere in this novel is thick with an especially concentrated sense of moral decay. Nabokov himself, in the afterword, addressed this to the Russian edition of *Lolita*, emphasizing, by the way, his completely random choice of the American landscape. "I needed inspiring circumstances. There is nothing in the world more inspiring than Philistine vulgarity. But in terms of Philistine vulgarity there is no radical difference between life in the Old World and life in the New. Any worker from Chicago can be just as bourgeois (in the Flaubertian sense) as any English lord."

The deadly force of vulgarity—not only in the metaphorical but in the literal sense, as well—is embodied extremely powerfully in the novel which the author thought his most significant work: *Invitation to a Beheading* (1938). It is often seen to contain a concealed opposition to fascism. This view is probably well founded, especially if we recall that the book was written during the accursed years of Hitler's triumph. All the same, the undisguised parable form of the novel makes any excessively concrete interpretation doubtful.

Whatever the author may have said, *Invitation* clearly recalls Kafka and Huxley and anticipates Orwell and Vonnegut. The novel presents a deathly picture: Man as an individual being, endowed with the gift of consciousness and feeling, has dissolved into the reigning, furious impersonality around him. Rebellion is punished swiftly and cruelly. Or not even rebellion. After all, Cincinnatus, the novel's main hero, makes no attempt to threaten the established order of life. This small man, wrapped to his head in a Gogolian overcoat, does not venture any active deed. For what is he sentenced to death? Because he is not transparent; that is, he preserves some personal secret. This is his crime, as the required condition for life among the inhabitants of this fantastical city is full penetrability, that is, interchangability.

This is a kingdom of twins and doubles. The lawyer differs in no way from the prosecutor: "The law required them to be half-brothers, but this was not always possible, and then they would change their appearance." According to custom, the victim and the executioner must become friends, and M'sieur Pierre, who is to carry out the sentence, comes in as Cincinnatus's cellmate. The director of the jail is the same as the doctor; the lawyer is the executioner's assistant. Roles are always changing.

The world of *Invitation to a Beheading* is an artificial, imaginary world. A spider hanging in the cell is made of brass. The clock in the jail has a face but no hands. The fate of Emmie, the director's daughter, is predicted by a photohoroscope. The tears shed by the hero's lascivious wife are neither salty nor sweet, but "simply drops of water."

It is also an openly grotesque world. Everything is as if in a fun house. Objects and figures now shrink, now grow to appalling size; faces—the white faces of clowns—bare their teeth in a terrible grin. Anybody who has seen the Antonioni film *Blow Up* will recall the scene in which a tennis game is played *without a ball*—an image of senselessness. Thus the situation in Nabokov's novel lacks purpose and rational order.

But what is tragic is that this deformed picture preserves material solidity. With his usual mastery, the author finds words and colors that hold the image on the line between reality and unreality. Of course, the text of the program for the execution sounds barbaric: "Circus subscription stubs will be honored." But it is only its content that is barbaric. The absurdity seems to be removed by the absolute ordinariness of the advertising kiosk. Although the spider is artificial, it scurries about the cell exactly like a live one. And so on.

Poor Cincinnatus is deprived of the strength to resist, the will to self-realization which is generously bestowed upon Godunov-Cherdyntsev and even Luzhin. As has been said, however, he has nothing to realize— he is an ordinary, unremarkable person. If such a person can find no place in a world that has lost all conception of individual values, how would things look for an artist?!

Nabokov is far from the first writer of this century to ask himself that question. We immediately think of the books of Rolland, Dreiser, Thomas Wolfe, Hesse, and especially of Thomas Mann's *Doctor Faustus*. Striving for perfection of form, giving in to the devilish temptations of "the emancipation of art," Adrian Leverkuhn, as we recall, wastes God-given talent and suffers spiritual, then physical death. Music which has lost a human source (too human, in the words of Nietzsche, later repeated by Ortega y Gasset) destroys itself and its devotees. Such is the artistic logic of *Doctor Faustus*.

Nabokov came to a different conclusion: One may preserve one's gift; one may speak true, last words only alone with oneself. But will they reach people? But what business is that of the artist? The hero of *The Gift* answers the admonition of the publisher Vasiliev in this spirit. He is told: "I ask you as a friend, don't try to publish this thing . . . mark my words, everyone will turn away from you." This prospect does not distress

Godunov-Cherdyntsev in the least: "'I prefer the backs of people's heads,' said Fedor Konstantinovoch."

In *Pale Fire*, too, the artist's inner world remains the only sacred reality.

> Often, irritated by the superficial brilliance
> Of ordinariness and discord, I turned inside myself . . .

> I thought on my way home, shouldn't I take the hint
>   and stop investigating my abyss?
> When it suddenly dawned on me that that is
> The whole true meaning, the whole theme of the
>   counterpoint.

What, after all, is human life? What is to be done with civilization's imperfection?

It is easier to say that this problem did not trouble Nabokov, particularly since, as we have seen, he himself constantly tried to convince us of this. "I simply like to write riddles and to accompany them with elegant solutions."

All the same, as soon as Nabokov left that ivory tower he so cherished, he was forced not simply to record with a Mephistophelean laugh the signs of general deterioration, but to seek some moral alternative. He himself, of course, would never have admitted this. But what of that? It seems to me, at least, that for all his cosmic—again, Kafkaesque—pessimism; for all his demonstrative coldness, Nabokov believed that all was not lost. It is quite possible that Dostoevsky's celebrated maxim—beauty will save the world—was secretly close to his heart. In this case, it would be the beauty of the word, the masterful perfection of form.

Tatiana Morozova

Character in American Fiction

Is there any difference between the characters in American literature and those in Russian, French, English, and other literatures? Is there some distinctive trait that infallibly betrays their American origins?

As far as the Russian character is concerned, the West figured it out long ago. "It is the soul that is the chief character in Russian fiction," noted Virginia Woolf in one of her best-known works, "Character in Fiction." Can we not attempt to search out a similar definition of the American hero?

Following Woolf's example, we might formulate such a definition thus: "It is self-reliance that is the chief character in American fiction," as it is indeed self-reliance that appears to be the dominant trait in the American national character. It is no coincidence that this doctrine was advanced by an American philosopher and writer.

He who would understand America must understand Emerson, such is the conclusion one could draw from F. A. Stovall's book, *American Idealism*. It is hard to disagree with this. The heart of Emerson's ethical teaching was the idea of the sovereignty of the individual. "The apotheosis of individualism—such in briefest terms was the gospel of Emerson," wrote Vernon L. Parrington. Emerson himself confessed: "In all my lectures, I have taught one doctrine, namely, the infinitude of the private man." And indeed, the kernel and foundation of American philosophy's ethical system was the new concept of the individual's role in history, place in society, and relationship to others, to the collective, the nation, the government, humankind, world order, to the "over-soul," to God.

In "Historic Notes of Life and Letters in New England," Emerson wrote: "The former generations acted under the belief that a shining social prosperity was the beatitude of man, and sacrificed uniformly the citizen to the state. The modern mind believed that the nation existed for the individual, for the guardianship and education of every man."

The doctrine of self-reliance contains the quintessence of some of the most important traits of the American national character, the foundations of which had already been laid by the end of the 18th century, leaving the interpretation of this phenomenon to philosophy and art. The American national character was formed under the influence of peculiar historical circumstances: the first settlers' isolation from the civilized world, the need to defend one's life in the battle against nature's severity, the habit of counting only on one's own strengths in this battle, and so forth. A handful of Europeans deposited on American shores learned by their own experience that, in their position, the only way to survive was not even to hope for outside help. From the north, west, and south, virtually impassable forests encroached on the tiny settlements; to the east stretched the Atlantic Ocean. In lean years it sometimes happened that nearly all of the colonists died; there was nowhere to borrow a sack of flour and no one to accuse of indifference to neighbors. There were no neighbors anywhere near. The dilemma was so simple it was obvious—either help yourself, or nobody will help you.

Of course, the colonists were in such an extreme situation for a relatively short time; the population grew, the coast was tamed. The situation of the first settlers, however, was more or less repeated on the frontier over the course of nearly 300 years (the frontier, as we know, ceased to exist only on the eve of the 20th century). It was also significant that, as they went deeper into the mainland, the pioneers moved out of the reach of authorities, officials, and the whole colonial—and later, federal—bureaucratic apparatus. In unoccupied territories they were their own masters; nobody watched over them, nobody pestered them. Is it any wonder that such qualities as independence, enterprise, and initiative became the predominant traits of the American character, permeating American flesh and blood?

Even Benjamin Franklin proposed self-help as one of his moral postulates. Emerson's doctrine of self-reliance shares a fair amount with Franklin's idea, continuing and developing it. Franklin is the writer who introduced to the literature of the United States the archetype of the main American literary hero—the self-made man. The hero/author of Franklin's *Autobiography* is a representative of a self-made society in a self-made country, a forefather of the self-made nation. The stormy pressure of all this self-creation is the main drama of the *Autobiography*.

Franklin's life story turned out to be typical of many prominent Americans of later generations. Vernon L. Parrington wrote, truly, that Franklin was surrounded by "thousands of kindred spirits" who "honored such qualities as he possessed." In Parrington's opinion, if Franklin had been an Englishman, he would not have been able to achieve the glowing successes that he did. Defoe, for instance, "remained a Grub Street hack, the servant and not the counselor of aristocratic politicians." Parrington's comparison can be extended to Rousseau in France, Lomonosov in Russia. These great educators and scholars, like Franklin, came from the lower classes and owed their outstanding successes only to their own talent, determination, and hard work. Having brought glory to their names in science and literature, however, they could never dream of approaching the helm of state power. Furthermore, their achievements were seen in their countries as exceptions, something far out of the ordinary, whereas in America, Franklin's life was quickly canonized as an example for general emulation. In the story "The Late Benjamin Franklin," Mark Twain, with his usual humor, accused the great scholar of forever depriving American boys of their "serene childhoods." With Franklin's self-educated example before their eyes, young American citizens had to study with equal diligence the trades, mechanics, and physics and forget about pigeons, stamps, and similar boyhood pleasures.

Franklin was well aware that his life was a lesson for his fellow citizens; the *Autobiography* is intended for the instruction and edification of youth. It is interesting to compare this work with the autobiography of another great thinker, Rousseau, the author of *Confessions*. Rousseau's goal was to place before the reader, for judgment, the history of a human soul; to attempt to do what, as a rule, few succeed at: speak with the utmost honesty, confess with sincerity shocking to "good taste" his base passions and deeds.

Franklin's *Autobiography* is another matter entirely. The book's goal is set forth on the first page: sober, practical, if indubitable usefulness. Explaining his reasons for taking up the quill, the author writes:

> Having emerged from the poverty and obscurity in which I was born and bred, to a state of affluence and some degree of reputation in the world, and having gone so far through life with a considerable share of felicity, the conducing means I made use of, which with the blessing of God so well succeeded, my posterity may like to know, as they may find some of them suitable to their own situations, and therefore fit to be imitated.

The self-made man never dreamed of knightly valor; rather, he trusted in virtues less brilliant but more necessary to everyday life. He made a religion of industriousness. He was endowed with dogged persistence in achieving his chosen goals. He was distinguished by his individualism, his custom of relying on his own strength. In him the most varied qualities were combined; but the most important one—later taken up by the literature of the United States—was an irrepressible striving for success, an unwillingness to accept the lot appointed to him at birth by an ungenerous fate.

Franklin's basic criterion in his self-education was *practical use*. The list he made of thirteen virtues was meant not to help him attain some abstract moral nobility or special spiritual heights; its aim was more modest—learn to avoid errors that would cause damage and to acquire qualities that would be of use. That is why, when we glance at his list, we discover that, indeed, the loftier virtues, those lacking in utilitarian purpose, are few: perhaps only sincerity, justice, and humility. The rest clearly have applied value: Moderation is called upon to protect against gluttony and drunkenness; silence, against the waste of time on empty conversation; order is directed at saving time; frugality at saving money; industry also at saving time.

Along with the hero of the *Autobiography*, Franklin introduced to American literature yet another important figure: Poor Richard, who, in many ways, resembles the former, differing from him most significantly in the scale of his social pretensions. Poor Richard does not strive to rise to the heights of the social pyramid; he is quite satisfied with the independent, provided-for existence at its very bottom. But two basic conditions—independence and sustenance—are of deciding importance for him, just as they are for the hero of the *Autobiography*. Respect for wealth earned by one's own labor is another trait that unites the two heroes. One of Poor Richard's precepts is: "'Tis hard for an empty bag to stand upright." He well knew that, like it or not, to be poor is to be dependent. Poor Richard accepted the custom of judging people according to their material position. In "The Way to Wealth" (1758), he says: "Now I have a sheep and a cow, everybody bids me good morrow."

The descendants of the *Autobiography*'s hero were the myriad characters doggedly and successfully rising to the summit of the social pyramid: Christopher Newman, of James's *The Americans*; Philip Sterling, in Twain's *The Gilded Age*; Silas Lapham, of Howells' novel, *The Rise of Silas Lapham*; Dreiser's Cowperwood. The cheapened, vulgarized version of Franklin's hero was to be Horatio Alger, on whose example more than one generation of Americans was raised. Poor Richard drew after him a long chain of characters—"average Americans," not aiming for the high spheres of big business and big politics but struggling with antlike persistence for a middling material sufficiency. Two hundred years ago, Poor Richard felt himself in the greatest bliss, having attained a "sheep and a cow." With the growth of the average standard of living and the changing standards for winning the respect of others, a sheep and a cow have been replaced by an expensive car, a house in a respectable suburb, vacations in a fashionable resort, and so on. Poor Richard's descendant is Updike's Rabbit.

It is worth mentioning that, with historical development, the attitudes of American writers to the self-made man have changed sharply. From unquestionably positive, they have become mixed, sometimes even sharply negative. This process of reevaluation is noticeable, even at the turn of the century, in the work of Henry James. It is especially clear when one compares Christopher Newman, of *The Americans*, with Chad Newsome and Jim Pocock, of *The Ambassadors*. The difference can be felt even in their names. "Christopher Newman" has the sound of bugles, heralding the approach of something extraordinarily grand: the first name of the discoverer of America is effectively combined with the last name "New Man" (Crevecoeur had written back at the end of the 18th century that the American was a new man on a new land). But what is "Newsome"? The first half of the name is the same: The hero is, as before, a representative of the New World; in this respect, the quality of novelty is preserved in him. But what is behind this novelty? Something unclear, indistinct, is suggested by the ending of this name—*some*. Chad reveals himself only at the end of the novel, and not at all in the best light. The name *Pocock* is simply a parody, farcical; the character does not contradict the impression his name creates.

In *The Ambassadors*, James expresses a negative attitude to that success that once inspired Franklin. When Strether refers to himself as a "complete failure," Maria Gostrey replies: "Thank goodness you're a failure— it's why I so distinguish you! Anything else to-day is too hideous. Look about you—look at the successes. Would you *be* one, on your honor?"

James's apology for, and poeticization of, failure is close to the Russian literary tradition, in which the cult of success is entirely absent; what's more, the very genre of "career novel," so popular in the West, is conspicuously lacking. Perhaps one of the reasons for James's expatriation was the incompatability of his inner nature with the demands made on a person by American society. James ran from the cult of success and, naturally, in Paris became close with Turgenev, who, like all his Russian fellow writers, did not see success as a goal in life or failure as evidence of personal inadequacy.

William Faulkner wasn't very well-disposed to the self-made man either. He censured Thomas Sutpen and, after ridiculing Flem Snopes, deprived him of his life. He considered the Snopes's descent upon the South a natural calamity. Another Southern writer, Robert Penn Warren, also depicted the ascent of a self-made man, Willie Stark, rather unfavorably. This hero marks a peculiar transition: He is a link in the chain of Franklin's heirs and followers. The great educator's *Autobiography* depicts the irreproachable path of an irreproachable person to the irreproachable use of the power he receives. In the course of long evolution, a character is formulated who represents precisely the opposite—a far-from-irreproachable person who achieves power by deeply flawed means, which he uses to satisfy his maniacal political ambition. The peculiarities of the Southern social structure undoubtedly played their part in forming the attitudes of Southern writers to the self-made hero.

At the beginning of the 20th century, characters appeared in American literature who suffered cruel defeat attempting to imitate Franklin's model for achieving success. From self-made, they become self-*ruined* men. Such is Jack London's Martin Eden; Clyde Griffiths, of Dreiser's *An American*

Tragedy, and, of course, Fitzgerald's Gatsby. In European literature we meet such characters much earlier; Stendhal's Julien Sorel can be seen as their forefather. His American brother's "late" entrance on the scene is explained by the fact that for several centuries, the New World had a significant advantage over the Old: To achieve success in America and do away with aristocratic privileges was far easier than in Europe, where the caste system, preserved from the feudal Middle Ages, hindered young, capable people from the "lower" classes from realizing their social ambitions. The gradual equalizing of social structures (in Europe, toward greater social mobility; in the United States toward less) evened the chances for success of young people trying to realize, by any means necessary, their right to the "pursuit of happiness." The appearance of Angry Young Men in England coincided with the appearance of Beatniks in the United States. The former were angry at the rich for not allowing them into their circles, the latter renounced in advance the dream of success, recognizing the insignificance of their chances.

It would be a mistake to suggest that self-reliance found its manifestation only in the individual's social and financial self-assertion. This self-assertion was realized also in the spiritual realm, beginning with the Transcendentalists and continuing right through to our time. The idea of the spiritual autonomy of the individual obsessed the characters of the Romantic writers, as well as those who carried their banner into this century. The most characteristic example is the hero/author of *Walden*. In the fierce defense of her right to the unlimited freedom of solitude, only Emily Dickinson can be compared with Thoreau. The Gullivers of the soul fly from any contact with the Lilliputians, trying to drag them down to the level they see as normal. Thoreau composes hymns to freedom and solitude, speaking with contempt of any social grouping that encroaches upon the sacred rights of the individual. "Nations! What are nations?" he exclaims in "Life Without Principle." "Like insects they swarm. The historian strives in vain to make them memorable. It is for want of a man that there are so many men. It is individuals that populate the world."

The poetry of Emily Dickinson is a declaration of independence of the spirit:

> The Soul unto itself
> Is an imperial friend -
> Or the most agonizing Spy -
> An Enemy could send.

Secure against its own -
No treason it can fear -
Itself—its Sovereign—of itself
The Soul should stand in Awe.

One of the major themes in European literature of the 20th century has been the struggle for a place in the sun. A person strives at any cost to break into the "light," to earn the favor of titled persons, to approach the throne. This is a "European dream" of sorts. It gripped Rastignac, Lucien Chardin, Julien Sorel, Rebecca Sharp, and many similar heroes and heroines. They were prepared to undertake any mean or base feat to attain their cherished goal: to shine in the highest circle, to be favored with the king's attention. Emma Bovary's fate was decided forever during those minutes when, for the first and only time in her life, she danced at a high-society ball. The recollection of that enchanted moment, promising happiness but deceiving her, will burn and torment her forever after, instilling disgust at vulgar provincial life, pushing her into the embraces of "romantic" lovers, and finally leading to her death.

To this practice of ingratiating oneself with the exalted, this thirst for the recognition of society, this bowing before idols of "Vanity Fair," is opposed the idea voiced by Dickinson in one of her programmatic poems:

The Soul selects her own Society -
Then shuts the Door
To her divine Majority
Present no more -
  Unmoved—she notes the chariots—passing
  At her low Gate -
  Unmoved—an Emperor be kneeling
  Upon her mat -
I've known her - from an ample nation
Choose one -
Then—close the Valves of her attention
Like Stone.

This heroine's free, self-reliant, sovereign soul doesn't search for signs of somebody's attention; it gives or refuses them itself. The soul does not favor even an emperor kneeling before it with the honor of beholding it. Here is expressed the typical American idea of the supremacy of the individual, standing above any earthly power.

Walt Whitman, so like Emily Dickinson and yet so unlike her, also sings the praises of the individual, the separate human "I." "Song of Myself," as well as many of Whitman's other works, are a poetic apotheosis of individualism, as are the works of Emerson its philosophical apotheosis. On the other hand, Whitman's poetry, even the title *Leaves of Grass*, contains a certain contradiction. What's more, his poetry points to a hidden danger: For the "good gray poet," the idea of individualism is entirely separate from that of individuality. In a lawn covered with grass, Whitman tries to separate every leaf, securing its right to sovereignty and autonomy. But why do those leaves look so much alike? Why do they meld into one superindividual mass? Why does each one not have a "face of extraordinary expression"?

Here, the paradox of American life is reflected: The pull of individualism lives side by side with the pull of conformism—the willingness to stand for one's "I," with the willingness to adapt, even with a thirst for sincere adaptation to society, whatever that might be. This "American paradox" is the opposite of the Russian paradox. In Russian life—and, correspondingly, Russian literature—the individual, as a rule, doesn't struggle for autonomy; conciliarism, more concerned with the individual's peculiarity and originality, is the ideal. In America, the idea of individualism predominates over the idea of individuality; in Russia it is the opposite: Individuality overrides individualism. That is why such misunderstandings can occur, as when a Soviet translator of Whitman, the well-known poet and literary scholar Kornei Chukovsky, in love with the writer he was translating, nonetheless made a stern accusation against him. Why, he asked, doesn't Whitman's hero have the peculiarity and uniqueness characteristic of the heroes of Gogol and Dostoyevsky? Given such an approach, the Russian perception of Whitman turns out to differ from the American perception; translation must often be not merely from language to language, but from mentality to mentality.

In 20th-century American literature, Whitman's type of hero was revived in Thomas Wolfe's enormous epic, in Kerouac's characters living "on the road," and in other representatives of the Beat Generation. The heathen element raging in this hero also found one-sided (and, in many ways, waning) expression in the works of Henry Miller and William Burroughs.

The present condition of American literature attests to the fact that the traditional American character, with unlimited faith in self-reliance, is in a difficult position. As John Barth correctly observed in "The Literature of Replenishment" (1980), moral pluralism in society and literature can become moral entropy. This means that the result of self-reliance can be a complete disconnectedness of autonomous individuals, as well as the loss of any unified criterion for determining good and evil. Emerson believed that the preservation of the harmony between sovereign individuals was ensured by the supreme power of the oversoul. Does anybody in our time believe in an omnipotent divinity's loving care for the human race? *Can* anybody believe? And if not, what could serve as a defense or guarantee against misuse of the principle of self-reliance? As yet, there is no answer—neither in American literature nor in any other.

TAMARA DENISOVA

In Search of Community

The Individual and Society

in the New American Novel

Every young society intensively goes about creating its history and governmental system; and no less intensively, it mythologizes this process. This inseparable combination of myth and history then forms the foundation on which national self-consciousness is built and develops. So it was with the United States of America; so it was, incidentally, with Russia. Sooner or later, a moment arrives—often due to a crisis situation, and not just once in the history of a state—when it becomes urgently necessary to stop and look around, to ponder and weigh, from the vantage point of time and accumulated experience, those founding principles that have determined the direction of development and the fate of the country, as well as every one of its citizens.

One of these periods—when flaws in the American system broke through to the surface, becoming tangible and visible to many people—was the sixties: Vietnam, the civil rights movement, the rebellion of youth against the establishment, the labor movement and strikes, the New Left, the New New Left, hippies, yippies—all of this rocked American society from top to bottom, clearly illustrating the loss of equilibrium in the system of "individual, society, state" and forcing a reconsideration of the basic principles of the governmental system. The bicentennial served as a fitting occasion for the nation to turn to its own history. There was a torrent of historiography. Side by side with renewed eulogizing of the Founding Fathers and a revival of the national mythology, the so-called "revisionist" theory of history came into fashion, and extremely interesting works appeared, which were, I would venture to say, atypical of American public thought.

The book *Russia and America—A Philosophical Comparison*, by W. J. Gavin and T. J. Blakeley, was published in Boston in 1976. The authors, from the Center for Europe, Russia, and Asia, at Boston College, set out to rethink American tradition in connection with the bicentennial. To do this, they felt, they needed to compare it with something. Tiny Europe, heir to the Renaissance, would not serve. They see Russia as having much in common with America. It had a belated development, a weak Renaissance tradition. "Her land mass is such as to be experimentally infinite in character—not unlike the American frontier," and its social system is not yet completely formed, has not hardened.[1] It is in a stage of development that lays an obligation on the individual, who is forced to be not merely a participant in historical process but its creator. All of this, according to the authors, links Russia and America. The main thread for comparison of the American and Russian traditions is the problem of the individual's relationship to the world. *Russia and America* is an attempt to examine the problem of the relationship between the individual and society, expressed through those philosophical theories most influential to the development of social consciousness. It stresses the contrast between traditional individualism and the search, different in every stage but ever present, for community.

Generally speaking, the individual's relationship to the world is always the central problem for civilization—for the study of culture, for literature, and, in particular, for the novel. This problem can be positively solved neither by the most extreme individualization nor by the dissolution of the individual in the collective. Its optimal solution is yet to be found, and the experience of American social consciousness will undoubtedly play no small role in its discovery. In reconsidering the institution of bourgeois democracy, mobilizing its resources and trying to remove its contradictions, American scientific thought is furthering not only the greater health of the social climate in the United States but the development of criteria for the "new thought," so necessary for the existence of humankind today.

It is generally accepted that the philosophy of individualism and the American dream are the cornerstones of American social consciousness, as well as the country's leading tradition. If Renaissance ideas of humanism American-style are most vividly expressed in Walt Whitman's personalism, they were embodied in the person and fate of Benjamin Franklin.[2] "But an immense and distinctive commonality over our vast and varied area for the first time in history, aggregated real *people* worthy of the name and developed heroic individuals of both sexes." This is America's principal, perhaps only, reason for being. However, Poor Richard, Franklin's literary mask and a character in his posthumously published *Autobiography*, does not represent the unfettered, many-sided man, but the noticeably truncated, not the natural man but the purposeful maker. In Franklin's works the essential contradictions of the Enlightenment are revealed: "The reign of reason" and "common sense" inevitably turn into the spiritually bankrupt reign of capital.[3] A person whose entire life is reduced to "use" is not only regulated but castrated, truncated, and deprived of spiritual wealth, tragedy, and meaningfulness, while at the same time being extremely individualistic. It is precisely for this narrow understanding of the person—as nothing more than a creator of the instruments and objects of labor, lacking that social contact which alone makes a person into an individual—that Marx criticized Franklin.

Emerson makes an attempt to overcome narrow mercantilism and leave the isolation of individualism. On one hand, with the theory of self-reliance, he reaches the apogee of individualism (egalitarian, it is true); on the other, he develops the idea of the "oversoul," joining humanity to the cosmos, to nature, seeing every separate person as an integral part of the universal, the general, which contains the spiritual. "We are now men," proclaimed Emerson, "and must accept in the highest mind the same transcendental destiny; not minors and invalids in a protected corner, not cowards fleeing before a revolution, but guides, redeemers and benefactors, obeying the Almighty effort, and advancing Chaos and Darkness."[4] Pantheism, idealism, deism? Yes, of course; but also an understanding of the fact that, as soon as one leaves the confines of individualism and steps into a certain community, one can realize oneself. From time immemorial, however, the best human minds have been capable of feeling themselves part of nature, of a great and single world in which the living and the nonliving make up a single organism, and the secrets of its union and interaction are far from being discovered. I would digress far from the subject of this essay if I were to delve more deeply into reflection on the theme of "the person and the world." Nonetheless, one cannot avoid this subject when analyzing the main direction of the contemporary American novel, in which I see the desire to integrate the person—every separate individual—into a single whole.

The rational 19th century led humankind along the road to the technocratic explosion of the 20th century—a road, in the final account, based on the mechanistic perception of the universe. Attempts to understand its organic unity, manifested in the work of Charles Darwin, the theory of noosphere, and the work of V. I. Vernadsky have not gained prominence to this day and do not define the world-view and direction of human development. But today, their necessity to life is unquestionable. Emerson's oversoul is among their theories.

Gavin and Blakeley, comparing America and Russia, bring closer—or, rather, equalize—transcendentalism and "sobornost." They see both as confirmation of humanity's involvement with a higher spirit—with, simply speaking, God. Of course, conciliarism is an idealistic concept; but its source was in Russian community as a way of existence, of organization, and, above all, of production and the life based on it—that is, a practical community. There is no analogous, practical foundation in American society. Emerson's theory is an attempt to join humanity to the universe, sidestepping society.

As is well known, in America, the institution of creating associations—community—is traditional. The country itself came into being on the basis of a collective agreement signed by the worthy passengers of the *Mayflower*. The American Dream is not only belief in the possibility of everyone's maximal self-realization, but also the desire to create a blessed land for all (and each). The person, individuality, is the basis of American philosophy, politics, and government. The characteristic American community is essentially different from the Slavic. It is formed voluntarily, by agreement, based on the personal affinities of its members. Gavin and Blakeley pay particular attention to the fact that coauthors W. James and J. Royce understood community as a mysterious, ongoing process, as the individual's intransient demand for human society.

A discussion of the means and forms of the expression of Americans' need for human society could be very fruitful, as it contains the kernel of sociological, cultural, and literary problems—since individuality and the nature of its realization is the main object of social consciousness.

The great body of American literature of the 20th century is, in essence, the story of the solitary man, of his tragic alienation and his attempts to overcome it—through courage, kindness, love, association with a specific group, through a common history and a single consciousness based upon it.

Only the apologists for a mass society of the middle of the century promise the ordinary American the happiness of blending with others, of becoming part of the de-individualized mass, becoming "like everybody." There exists another point of view, one belonging to "highbrow" criticism, according to which the typical American condition is the most insurmountable alienation. What is more, absolute alienation is treated as a condition soon to be experienced by people of other countries. After all, the United States is the avant garde. Many try to overtake it in technology and standard of living, hoping to attain its way of life. On the whole, this view is not unfounded, but with one qualification: It is not the simple establishment of alienation, but the heroic attempts to overcome it, the untiring search for means to join the person to the community, that are the main material of the American writers.

Community may be absolutely concrete (most often, it is the family) or purely abstract, not belonging to the material sphere, in the spirit of Emerson. Religion and art are two forms of spirituality which organically "enlist" a person in a certain magical circle of human society. As a rule, black American artists turn to them. Music provides a connection with the spirit of the people in some of the stories and novels of James Baldwin ("Sonny's Blues," *Another Country*), in the essays of Ralph Ellison, and the novels of Killens. The role of religion is very specific in Baldwin's *Go Tell It on the Mountain*. Attempts to find unity are varied: Beatniks search for it in rebellion, Updike in love, Pynchon in paranoia.

The search for human unity in the social sphere first appeared in the 1930s, in John Steinbeck's *The Grapes of Wrath*, and in other literature about the labor movement. It was short-lived. Even the best American novels on the Second World War (Norman Mailer's *The Naked and the Dead*, James Jones's *From Here to Eternity*) tell of tragic, insurmountable isolation within the army; they are in no way like the novels of the Lost Generation, about brotherhood in the war. William Faulkner, Robert Penn Warren, that is to say, Southerners—for all the complexity and tragedy of the history of their land—positively assert the importance of social experience to the individual, its formative and unifying role.

For Thomas Wolfe, "home" was all of America; nonetheless, his hero's individuality and solitude remained wherever he found himself. For Faulkner, only the South could be such a home. In interviews, Faulkner more than once emphasized that the American South is "the only really authentic region in the United States, because a deep indestructible bond still exists between man and his environment. In the South, above all, there is still a common acceptance of the world, a common view of life, and a common morality." According to Faulkner, only in the South of disconnected, "patchy," broken-up America did commonality of circumstance engender something stable and solid, the main wealth of that region—its people, a people consisting of individuals.[5] On the other hand, Faulkner's community is a society to some degree no less idealistic than Emerson's "over-soul"; that is, it is constructed on an idealization of the patriarchal South.

The world situation changes, however; sooner or later, changes are reflected in national consciousness and literature. In times of intensified popular movements, the link between the individual and society makes itself felt, and works such as *The Grapes of Wrath* are created. A new approach to the problem of the individual—new attempts to join the individual to society—are characteristic as well of the literature expressing the national consciousness that came out of the 1960s. Attempts vary. For instance, the hero of *A Place to Come To*, by Robert Penn Warren, searches for his "small homeland," that piece of land where he feels himself at home, where everything is his own. Where is that for the American whom fate has so often displaced? Where and who is the American's "community"?

In the literature of the 1970s, history enters to take the place of a realizable, indisputable community and a clear, social practice to which the individual is connected.

Gore Vidal is today the most erudite and prolific writer of historical novels. Historians confirm that he is highly accurate in his representation of facts. The novelist's freedom, Vidal says, lies in interpretation. In his novels, the history of life in his native land becomes not only an object of representation and research, but a scale for the evaluation of the whole—the political system of the United States.

Vidal's novels typically include several time shifts and spacial planes—

coexisting, parallel, intersecting, varying in direction; views of various characters on the historical process cross and alternate. A reconstruction of the movement of history takes place. But history's approbation of past heroes, of those who formed the glory of the land, occurs as well. In Aaron Burr's recollections (which the novelist emphasizes in particular), the most important factor in the evaluation of a person is that person's historical-political description and his relationship to the state. Personal traits are secondary, as the value of the individual depends upon political role and social practice.

E. L. Doctorow has a different approach to history and fiction. He actively mixes fact and invention, equalizing them. Because of this approach, history in his novels moves in a distinctive way—it is "essential" history composed of individual fates. In *Ragtime* (1975), the era from the turn of the century to the First World War is re-created in genre scenes, through portraits of real people and through generalized images and symbols, revealing the function of the individual. The author portrays the past as a single unbroken current; he makes no qualitative distinction between designated "points" in time. Distinct moments flow into the current of the past, on which, side by side, ride real historical figures and imagined, "average" heroes: Mother, Father, Child. The general tone of the writing is the author's ironic voice, leveling, uniting, drawing into one the flow of moments, of the many different times of the past. It is the voice of the storyteller distanced by half a century from his subject matter, and thus never becoming part of it.

Retrospection is not history; it is a look back to the past which is gone. The past appears somewhat softened by time—hazy, the corners somewhat smoothed. Most brightly depicted is not what was most essential at the time, but what, by association or contrast, is most connected to today, to today's pain and failure. When all is said, what we are looking at is what is described by the term *retro-novel*. One of its uniting sources is the rhythm of ragtime.

In this interpretation any individual may be illusory, if not set in time, not poured into the current of history. History is like a pointilist's canvas on which a picture is formed from many separate dabs. History—space and time—is a single river uniting the individual, turning even the illusory into reality.

Sophie's Choice, by William Styron, is one of the few works of American literature that links the fate of the United States and the spiritual development of the individual American with world history. The author makes use of the traditional classical-realist technique, combining the European narrative style with the American tendency to depict "innocent Adam" coming in contact with the world. The novel contains several levels of time and events, opening out the picture of America and American society far beyond the confines of one year. It is built as a system of "stories within a story," allowing material to emerge that is unusually important to the author: reflection on the Second World War and American history in the world context.

In describing the heroine's experience in the concentration camp, Styron examines the camps within Western civilization not as something breaking loose monstrously from all human structure, but as the logical "résumé" of a civilization originally based on slavery. In this sense, the concentration camps, according to Styron, are the unique prototype of a possible structure, an organization of human society—slavery taken to the limit of absolute dehumanization—in which people not only dig their own graves but obediently lie in them awaiting death. It is possible that Styron does not pay enough attention to the social conditions that engendered this system. Nonetheless, they, too, are revealed as that social structure in which the sovereignty of each individual is destroyed. Thus fascism is shown as the reason for evil, upheaval, and the destruction of morals—and at the same time as the result of such upheaval.

History and the individual are directly linked in this novel. Moreover, an American is brought into the context of world history, which forms his person and serves as a scale to measure individuality, confirming the responsibility of each for the development of humankind. The entire context of the novel, its whole symbolic system, is constructed in such a way as to prove that nobody can be indifferent to human history, that even independently of any consciously chosen role, a person is caught up in the long, unbroken chain of human history; that one's position, one's social and human value, are defined only in the context of greater history and according to its scale.

I have mentioned novels of the 1970s that have already received the approbation of critics, Soviet critics among them. Many of our Americanists have already noted, quite correctly, an increased realism in the literature of the United States. Also correct are assertions that the very type and structure of the novel are changing. Instead of the laconic, concentrated, "centripetal" novel (D. V. Zatoneky's term; N. A. Anastasiev, using Goethe's maxim, suggests *subjective epic*), which centers on the fate and consciousness of the estranged individual and in which an era is reflected, more and more books are appearing in which the social background widens and the hero is included in it, connected by many threads. In the novels of Gore Vidal, E. L. Doctorow, and William Styron, this "background" is history.

Faulkner, Hemingway, Fitzgerald, and Wolfe wrote in differing styles, but they were united by an epic nature expressed through individual consciousness, psychology, and the behavior of their heroes. The "scale" of the world in which the action occurs is essential. As far as, say, Styron is concerned, his hero-writer is no smaller in range than Quentin Compson—one of Faulkner's most intellectual characters. The difference is not in the range of the subject reflecting consciousness, but in the organization of the whole artistic work, in which the world-view and the perceptions of the artist are reflected. Widening the concrete historical background in these analyzed works, as well as changes in their structure and organization, are due to the fact that the authors, consciously or unconsciously, are searching for a way out of traditional individualism in social practice. That way out is history. In these works, the heroes do not act as bearers of historical consciousness; rather, history is drawn upon as a context for the evaluation of the individual.

Faulkner measured the essence of his characters according to the standards of the Southern myth, John Steinbeck by the Bible, John Updike, in *The Centaur*, with myth. The list could be continued. These were attempts to place individuality among the ranks of the epic. For writers of the seventies, history serves the same end. The product of history is still the individual, the single person. That person's fate, life, consciousness, and behavior are the subject of the novelist's investigation, just as they always were in American literature. In this respect, the tradition has not been broken. But the real "distribution of strength" in the United States has influenced the nature of aesthetic choices. In the American novel of the 1970s, the endeavor to join the individual to a specific concrete human society, to test it through social practice, makes itself felt with urgency. In this is felt, undoubtedly, not only the experience of two centuries and their vital missions (the need for an escape from the tragic solitude of the alienated individual deprived of support in the surrounding world), but also the specific dramas of American society in the sixties. Searches for ways to link the individual and the state, the person and society, become more and more urgent, varied, and tangible.

In this cacophony of dissonant voices, in which the dominant notes are the most aggressive ones, we may single out the work of John Gardner as characteristic of the striving to proclaim and reinforce positive values. To some degree, this striving coincides with the spirit of neoconservatism, which is fairly stable in the politics of the nation, as it rests on the entirely logical desire of the masses for permanence, stability, and confidence in their existence. This is true only to a degree, only as far as neoconservatism coincides with people's yearning for peace, stability, and security about tomorrow. The main theme of Gardner's work is the search for positive sources. His peculiarity lies in the fact that he searches neither in invention nor in introspection, but in the very people, in their particularly American foundation—the farm—for that which is worthy of revival and continuation, that which can strengthen and support the moral and spiritual life of Americans. This support, the foundation of the country, is the WASP—the white Anglo-Saxon Protestant—the perpetual hero of Gardner's novels.

The heroes of *October Light*, the Page family, are 100 percent Americans. These are not blacks, Mexicans, Jews, or Irish, but WASPs whose ancestors arrived in America in the 17th century.

Everything in the novel is strictly localized, designated, limited. The action occurs over a few October days—no more than four—in a small area of the state of Vermont. The time is the bicentennial of the formation of the independent American state, that is, the end of the seventies. The heroes are Vermont farmers. With this narrow material, Gardner was able to create a novel-meditation on that which is most important for his homeland, on the illness that is gnawing at his country from inside, inexorably making its contemporary citizens unhappy and insignificant. It is a luminous book, complex and poetic.

The novel seems to have one main hero: James Page. There is no doubt that this seventy-three-year-old, bent, constipated, toothless old man is intentionally contrasted with the American superman, the cowboy-style hero. It is strange and absurd that it is this cantankerous, aggressive old man (throughout the entire course of the book, Page is almost never parted from his shotgun, using it not to chase skunks and foxes but his friends and relatives) whom the author makes his positive hero. What's more: Like a true artist, Gardner even convinces the reader that James Page is the foundation of American democracy (although James himself hates the word); Page is not an average sort, but an individual—bright and unique, real, "hard-rock," a preserved, true, Puritan settler who came to this continent with the desire to work and create a good life for himself through honest labor alone, a patriot always ready to defend his homeland, a man of hard rules and unshakable convictions.

A few words of digression. In an article, Saul Bellow says that history is whatever "happens" to his hero. He exists on his own and is always a victim of history. Gardner's hero, though simple and insufficiently educated—and, unlike Bellow's, unaccustomed to philosophizing—is himself the creator of history, the creator of his country and its laws; and he feels responsible for everything that happens in it.

This is, so to speak, the pathetic level of *October Light*, on which the author's voice settles in the first chapter. The novel ends on this same dramatic note. Gardner's description of the feelings of the farmer who is "drawn" to the earth repeats almost verbatim the end of *The Mansion*, in which Faulkner describes how the dying Mink Snopes goes "into the ground." In general, Gardner's dialogue with Faulkner is evident: It is announced at the beginning in the author's monologue and at the end of the novel, when the old bear leaves alive with James's honeycombs—an event which, of course, is polemical with the death of Faulkner's bear, symbolizing the death of nature and the old, natural way of life. Gardner's state, Vermont, is similar, in essence, to legendary Yoknapatawpha, William Faulkner's "postage stamp."

The dramatic plane is only one of the planes created by Gardner in *October Light*. The contemporary "intellectual" detective inserted into the novel is a foreign body, deliberately removed from the organism, seemingly entirely alien in a contemporary novel, set apart sharply from it in both style and content. It is an entirely different plane of the narrative.

Just as the "classical" section of the novel is post–Faulkner and post–Wolfe, so its entertaining, "modern" section is post–Burroughs, post–Beckett, post–Bellow. Into a typical Burroughs-style, "narcotic" situation is placed an intellectual, introspective, Bellowesque hero incapable of action, who collides with a transformed Beckett-style "cripple" and with parodied existentialist counterculture characters. Not for nothing is Richard Wagner always lost in literary reminiscence. The grotesque, parody, farce—all is openly mingled, nakedly conjuring up the unattractive; everything is turned upside down. The problem of racism and the struggle against drugs, reflection on free will, "the shadows of great forebears." Before us—with cuts emphasizing all the more its absurdity (truly, as promised in the ad for "The Smugglers of Lost Souls' Rock")—passes that same, sick America at which James Page shoots.

All the poetry of this well-wrought novel is directed at solving its "higher task": the search for foundations capable of re-creating American "community"—the hard-working farmer's America. The external conflict is carried on, unnoticed, on many levels. The main development of the plot occurs on a purely everyday, even a slightly caricatured, level (only on October days, relatively free from stressful household cares, is the rise of such a conflict possible). But by means of historical epigraphs—albeit humorous—the conflict takes on a national character and, at the same time, a national size. The contriving of the "trashy book" allows the everyday situation to be correlated in various ways, most often ironically, with the abstract, creating a multilevel juxtaposition of the personal, general, and abstract.

The conflict goes through the stages of personal reactions and Gardner attempts a collective resolution, allowing the creation of deep psychological portraits as well as a collective portrait of the true American, the salt of the nation.

People of various generations take part in it, from the deceased "iron-concrete" Puritan Uncle Ira, to James's precociously sober-thinking grandson. (The scene in the first chapter between James and Dickey, in which it becomes clear that it is the grandfather who has a romantic view of the world and the grandson a prosaic one, is beautifully wrought.) Generations are constantly juxtaposed, contrasted for various reasons, in various ways, but always purposefully and subtly. The weakening of character, from Ira to Richard, is stressed repeatedly by their approaches to the main question: having their way in the most important matter of all—the matter of life and death.

Once again emphasizing the simplicity of the subject, it is necessary to stress the high level of the book's organization, to which its structure and composition are directed. If the subject is a straight line, the composition is woven of the parallels and intersections. It is a Hawthornesque–Jamesian "system of mirrors" and crosscurrents through which passes not only the contemporary individual but the contemporary American. The author takes this individual through various aesthetic levels: tragic, dramatic, comical, farcical. He combines symbolism with precise, realistic description, fantasy with the tangible smells and colors of a Vermont autumn. He skillfully uses the possibilities of realism, creating a counterpoint of two novels, alternating intermezzos with moments of dramatic stress, daily life with entertainment, bringing in "percussive" episodes (the entire party at the Pages', almost a hundred pages, is never interrupted by the thriller), and, most important, masterfully spotlights his fundamental question.

Yes, before us is the real America. Reconstruction of reality is not the author's goal, however. His purpose is its aesthetic consideration via the solution of his main problem, that of the individual, on whom depend both the present and the future of the country, the government, the world.

Critics stress the dialogue form as the main peculiarity of Gardner's art. The dialogue form of reflection—making impossible one-dimensional, flat representation—allows the creation of various images. When an artist has no stable world-view based upon the real life of the people, reflection in the form of dialogue most often leads to a mosaic quality. The picture is fragmented (Thomas Pynchon is an example). Gardner's dialogue allows him to reconstruct reality on many levels, making it possible to reflect its most important laws of normality and interconnections and create a three-dimensional model. In the center of this model, an infinite number of times, of a multitude of points, the problem illuminated is that of the individual. The optimism of Gardner's novel, emphasized at the end on both real and symbolic levels, rests on its positive, concrete-historical solution, in the foundation of which are laid two traditional American qualities—diligence and personal responsibility for one's actions—which cement the American people as a community, in the widest sense of the word.

What is extraordinarily interesting is that the author himself was not reassured. He was not satisfied that the problem of the relationship between the individual and society was fully solved by the proposal contained in *October Light*.

Gardner's next work, *Mickelsson's Ghosts*, appeared in 1982. With this novel, remarkably different from *October Light*, the author seems to confirm that solitude is ruinous, even to the highly educated, creative person. The word *community* becomes of utmost importance, because only in association with others can one remain a complete human being.

For American literature, which has advocated individualism from the first, this is an unusual position. It signals a new stage in the development of Americans' national consciousness. In this way, Gardner juxtaposes his hero with the multitude of characters in the mid-century and contemporary literature of the United States, in which alienation is considered an eternal, unchanging, primordial, practically organic American trait. Gardner's hero is a philosopher. Philosophy is organic to his life; it is in everything. It is not ornamentation or affectation, but essence, raison d'etre. It is existential philosophy. Peter Mickelsson is hotly concerned with the political and social life of his country and tries to comprehend its historical-philosophical content. He is troubled by the presidential election, the condition of democratic rights in the nation, the level of students' conscience, and the problem of preserving humanity and life on earth. Twenty-year-old Mark, Mickelsson's son, devotes his life to the struggle against the nuclear bomb. He tells his father:

> Nobody's got a life if things continue as they're going. I'm not sure you understand or, OK, agree; but it's all or nothing. I think it really is. I might be wrong. People like me have been wrong before. But if I'm right, I have no choice—you know, Dad? Look, I'm not a terrorist. I'd never hurt a fly. But they have to be stopped, people have to see what's really happening, and I'm not sure it's possible to stop them in the way I'd approve of. They're too big, the whole federal government wrapped around them like eggwhite, feeding 'em. I think, well, it's a war for life.

Mickelsson is proud of the boy, and his arrival (real or dreamed) brings his father great relief at a difficult moment, returning him to life and activity.

As we see, Gardner's novel is a meditation on the complicated, pressing problems of contemporary American life. But what of the visions—ghosts—present even in the novel's title, which occasionally appear (or "materialize") on its pages? They could be as much the fruit of the professor's disordered state of mind as of the local folklore. But there is still more to the "devilry" that populates the novel. Just as the "visions" never leave the American philosopher's consciousness, so the "spirits" of Nietzsche, Plato, Luther, Wittgenstein and many others never leave the book's pages; without their thoughts, imaginings, works, and generalizations, Western culture could not be presented. The professor lives, breathes and works in their company, in polemic with them. If his family, colleagues, neighbors, and students are community, human society in the present day ("sliced horizontally"), then the "visions" are his spiritual past ("sliced vertically"), which has prepared the way for this "today"; concrete image grows into metaphor, history and tradition "materialize"

in visions and apparitions. Gardner masterfully uses symbol and metaphor, the arsenal of the romance. Strictly speaking, *October Light* is a
hymn to the basic principles of American democracy, to its foundation,
the farmers who created the nation and its intransient values. *Mickelsson's
Ghosts* is a call for human association ("God blesses community, any association," the hero thinks at a difficult moment), without which the human
individual cannot exist.

In speaking of "community," however, Gardner, like other Americans,
is not referring to the collective; his consciousness has been formed by
America, by its spirit and past, its way of life. In this context, an appeal to
the idea of community in no way means that the writer is an enemy of
capitalism; he merely wants to improve it, to resurrect its democratic
nature.

John Gardner is not alone among his American contemporaries in populating his last novel with spirits and visions. The later in the 1980s one
looks, the more often one finds miracles on the pages of novels, mystical
events that cannot be explained rationally. At the end of 1980, the *New
York Times Book Review* asked some of the most prominent prose writers in
the country to describe their feelings as they entered the new decade.
Among those responding to the questions was Joyce Carol Oates, who
spoke fairly optimistically about the prospects for the novel in the
eighties. If we consider the golden age of the novel to be that period when
the writer is limited by no canon, she says, then that time has arrived, as,
from the point of view of technique, the creator now has complete freedom. Oates makes use of freedom to one end—she tries to insert into her
usual canvas elements of the Gothic romance. In a review published on
Bellefleur, John Gardner notes that Oates works in the Gothic tradition
but is herself a realist, with images serving only as symbols. This is under-
scored by the title of Oates's next book: *A Bloodsmoor Romance*. Her hero,
John Quincy Zinn, is a typical American Yankee who, as a convinced
follower of Emerson, wholeheartedly devotes his life to the search for a
physical expression of the idea of unity—of the world, material and spiritual, of nature and humanity. Zinn wants to understand the mechanism
of the transformation of living and inanimate material, to catch the moment of metamorphosis.

In his prime, Zinn appears to a six-year-old girl he meets in the woods
as a kind, wonderful, cheerful giant. A reclusive life in poverty and, most
important, concentration not on human problems but on inhuman in-

vention, robs him of his charm, assurance, kindness, sense of self-worth, and—simply—beauty. By the age of seventy, he has become a corpulent, unkempt old man with a disheveled beard and absent glance. An individual who once was brilliantly fulfilled has exhausted himself. John Quincy Zinn's death arrives on December 31, 1899—on the eve of the new century, the new era, the new man. In the nation's history, the only memory of him is the electric chair, invented by order of the government.

Not in vain does Oates call her book a "romance": It possesses all of the external and internal attributes of the genre. It is a Romantic love story written in an unhurried rhythm characteristic of the idyllic 19th century (according to national legend). The pace of the narrative itself is not entirely consistent. It does not yet have the nervous rhythm of the 20th century; but the spirit of the Gilded Age is felt in its fragmentation, chronological breaks, and asymmetrical structure. As is to be expected in a romance, the novel contains much that is mysterious and inexplicable: spirits, visions, miraculous transformations, and simple hoaxes.

In the last section the author admits "that *A Bloodsmoor Romance* presents itself, with humility and hope, as an allegorical—indeed, an exemplary—narrative, I should be very foolish to wish to deny; that its numerous personages are instructively enjoined as to most clearly lend themselves to *moral interpretation*, I can but affirm. In so doing, however, I am not conscious of having betrayed the individuals who discover themselves herein—and make my plea to them that the capacities of readers, no less than authors, being resolutely finite, I am obliged to continue with my general favoring of *contour*." In creating interesting, unusual, individualized, unique characters, Oates stretches each character into a symbol, the embodiment of a specific side of her "higher task": to show us the fate of Emerson's teaching on the unity of man and the universe. In Oates's treatment the search for a "point of union" of living and inanimate material is fruitless. It is impossible to direct the process; the theory of an organic mixing of the individual with the transcendental is groundless. The man who has built his life on this idea dies alone and ruined.

The three heroines of John Updike's *The Witches of Eastwick* (1984) create their own peculiar community—a closed society. Before a year has passed, this "isosceles triangle," the foundation of their universe, collapses on its component straight lines, which no longer intersect.

Witches was long on the best-seller list. Critics called it strange and terrible and placed it in the tradition of "baroque realism." The well-known Canadian writer Margaret Atwood wrote an article on it in which she attempts to prove that Updike intended to illustrate the unity of humanity and nature ("higher forces"). Although, as Atwood writes, nature is portrayed as an evil force, we are nonetheless a part of it. We carry within ourselves its devilish spirit. I bring in Atwood's evaluation here not by chance; it must be addressed, as it accentuates one of the most essential points of Updike's novel: the nature of the search for unity between the person and the world. This problem was solved in its way in *The Centaur* (by turning to myth as a store of unshakable moral criteria and ideas common to all humankind), in *Of the Farm* (in which only by mowing a meadow can the hero feel himself a complete person), in *Marry Me* (in which only the woman, as a symbol and personification of life, provides any sense of the stability or dependability of one's place in the world). In *Witches*, Atwood interprets witchcraft as a link with nature. Yes, nature, which in the three sections of the novel completes a full cycle and draws the heroes into its orbit—especially the most romantic character, Alexandra. She is in her element in rain and storm. Not for nothing does she, like the Lord God, sculpt people out of clay. It is Alexandra who casts spells—Jane and Suki are merely her accomplices. This theme is reinforced by the sermon read in church by the new parishioner, the chemist Van Horne. He tells the congregation of the unity of living and inanimate nature. The search for oneness with nature is characteristic among Americans as the search for a defined foundation, a balance point, some unification of Each with All. It springs up during transitional moments in the country's history; its appearance in the work of the barometer of American social consciousness, John Updike, gives evidence to a great deal. It tells of trouble, of a clear disharmony of reason and spirit, of the clarity of the threat to the world brought about by technocracy uncontrolled by humaneness; it is symptomatic in its own way.

"Witchcraft," Atwood says, is one of the main motifs in the book. But for an educated person of the 20th century well prepared for reading literature—above all, for an American—this theme enlivens and colors the story through its associations with national history and with the realities of the native land. The very location (Narragansett Bay) says a great deal. The women/witches call up in the reader's consciousness the Salem trials. All the (at first glance) absurd rites the contemporary witches perform resonate with the system of the Puritan tradition, in which such a huge role is played by symbolism. Then the witchcraft of the three women sounds in a different key. In an especially modern provincial American town (Updike is a master of his subject; his details are tangible, and the action takes place during the Vietnam War), apparitions appear in the shadows, which try to tie the present to the past, to bring into this story of today a certain epic depth.

The end of the narrative, written in the spirit of Hawthorne, is also significant, as it confirms the proposed reading of the book: Someone leaves a mark in people's lives, thus becoming part of the world, and on the basis of this is united with nature. This thought combines realism, breathing life into baroque poetics, with the psychological novel, finding expression in the book as much in naturalistic scenes as in Gothic episodes.

In an essay, Norman Mailer recalls a winter he spent in Provincetown, Massachusetts, at the end of the 1950s. In it, he says: "I thought of writing a novel that would be so full of horror that for many years I just couldn't start it." In *Tough Guys Don't Dance*, where the spirits of dead captains wander, voices of whores who inhabited the town in the last century ring out, and the wind which sweeps the dunes seems to urge one to murder and suicide on this piece of "devastated land," Mailer has finally realized his idea.

The novel is constructed and carried out in the classical "romance" style: it has an opening in which the terrible and mysterious appear; there is action equally full of horror and mystery; and there is an epilogue, which preserves the secret. Inveterate scoundrels and supermen play roles, and in decisive moments "voices" are heard which suggest things that no one could know.

Mailer's Gothic has its distinctly marked setting: the United States in the second half of the 20th century. It is in both the content and the form of the novel: tough reality, in which violence, murder, and sadism are common—the policeman himself is trained in murder and mafiosa, having been schooled as a Green Beret in American atrocities in Asia. Pornography, drugs, and sexual license are the norm. One of Tim's friends is nicknamed Stoodie because in youth his favorite activity was stealing Studebakers. Tim himself grows, keeps, sells, and uses "grass" and has served three years for dealing cocaine. It is not surprising that he just can't manage to write his novel, "In Our World—Studies Among the Sane."

"In Our World" is a title that clearly calls to mind Hemingway's *In Our Time*. Similarly, Mailer's *Tough Guys* is, in his opinion, the logical continuation of Hemingway's *Men Without Women*. Finally, Patty Lareine, Tim's wife—who has left him in order to buy, with money swindled from her former husband, an old mansion on a mountain, convert it into a fashionable hotel, become its hostess and a high-society lady, and reign in her kingdom of beautiful life—quite consciously and persistently strives to attain the status of Daisy and Gatsby simultaneously, to overtake the "American dream." The symbolic downfall of the "blonde rogue" is described extremely realistically, with a relishing, I would even say, of naturalistic details: murder, cutting off heads, and so on. All of this is tough reality, formulated in the Gothic style. To a great extent, this Gothic collection could already be felt in Mailer's *An American Dream* and *Why Are We in Vietnam?*. As I have already pointed out, however, *Tough Guys* contains the mystical as well, which, it would seem, long ago disappeared forever from realistic literature and which until the last decade babbled only on the pages of cheap, mass-reading material—"voices," table-turning, mysticism, apparitions.

Yes, of course, not by chance did this give rise to a discussion of Mailer. He loves shock value and is subject to the influence of trends. To some extent, that explains the Gothic quality of the novel. Unquestionably, the author's irony is felt throughout the book. But it would seem that there are still other reasons why mysterious voices sound on his pages. These are the voices of the past; they create the extent and continuity of the American tradition, the tradition of strong, cruel, tough guys, those bandit-superheroes capable of standing up for themselves. Not for nothing are houses in Provincetown built of remnants of old ones: "Something of a perished Klondike of whores and smugglers, and whalers . . . lived in our walls."

Tough Guys can hardly be counted among Norman Mailer's most successful works. The evil in it is very "baroque"—with American-style forcefulness, "arrant" and traditional, sucking one in like a swamp. But Mailer has achieved his goal: With the help of the Gothic, the shady underworld is convincingly drawn. In this context, the Gothic attains content, fulfills the function of an epic source, an epic past, helping to join the modern American with the national community, with the spirit of the nation.

Only a few works have been analyzed here, in all of which Gothic tendencies were clearly revealed. Today, there is no wall between "high" and "mass" culture; it fell down long ago and everything got mixed up, even in modernism, which was once the elite culture, or at least laid claim to that title. Of course, there are no guarantees that the spirits of talented realists came into their imaginations without first doing time among the brigades of popular heroes. Most likely the relationship is indisputable, especially in the United States, where striving for entertainment cannot be accidental or brought about by high aesthetics alone—it is also necessarily dictated by the desire to attract the reader, to print large editions, to do business. But another thing is equally doubtless: romance and Gothic, just like historical approach, are adapted to the task of including the individual in the human community within the conditions of today's reality.

The reality of the end of the 20th century—What is its most important feature? Where is it moving? What does it take with it? What is it preparing for humanity in the future? How to evaluate it, and how to survive it? Everybody ponders this—scholars and writers, rulers and housewives, farmers and children, in Asia and Africa, in the Soviet Union and in the United States. . . . In the face of nuclear technocracy, everything is leveled. The most important question is that of the life and death of the planet and of humankind. Hamlet's "To be or not to be" gains not only unexpected philosophical meaning, but a truly universal scope as well. Of course, one should not modernize Shakespeare. His thoughts are no smaller in scope and philosophical depth than are those of our contemporaries, but his "eternity" differs from ours: It is abstract; our nonexistence is absolutely concrete. Nevertheless, the person remains the main character both in Shakespeare's universe and in the reality of the end of the 20th century. Today, Hamlet's question must be decided by each and all, for oneself and for humankind, in which we are all specks of dust.

In its June 1986 issue, *Harper's* published an article by Walker Percy entitled "The Diagnostic Novel: On the Uses of Modern Fiction." It is a characteristic article—expressing the humanistic spirit which more and more penetrates democratic America. Percy's main idea is that the world stands on the brink of catastrophe and must be saved, and that it can be saved only by humankind returning to humanistic criteria, once again regarding the person as of highest value. And in this, nobody and nothing can replace literature, which, by its nature, can be nothing if not the study of people. For confirmation of his ideas, examples, and proof, Percy turns to his favorite Russian classics, which he has studied deeply—to Chekhov

(Percy himself was a doctor and, like Chekhov, saw himself as society's diagnostician), Dostoevsky, Tolstoy. All in all, Percy puts forth the humanistic credo we all know and share, which has nourished us and which we will share and advocate to the end of our days. There is one aspect of Percy's article, a nuance that could characterize the thoughts of the modern person, someone perhaps who is inspired by the end of the 20th century: doubt in the omnipotence of science. According to Percy, we are accustomed to the idea that science is capable of anything, that, with the aid of science and reason, any accident, any catastrophe, can be eliminated. This has engendered in us a philosophy of consumption (we agree with the American writer that there is a large element of truth in this). The nuclear-technocratic reality at the end of the 20th century has shown us that science is far from omnipotent, and what's more, that reason—in the sense that it has been established in human consciousness as an exact science based on mathematical computation—eventually may prove powerless in its most important task.

In advancing his ideas in "The Diagnostic Article," Percy is not the brilliant cat's cradle about the same topic. Nor is Kurt Vonnegut in his later work, right through *Galapagos* (1985), in which the passengers of a modern Noah's ark are described as the survivors of atomic disaster. Vonnegut is indeed a canary in a coal mine; he has designed his own arsenal of poetics with which to sound a loud warning of the coming catastrophe. His active enemy is raging technocracy, reason cut loose from its master—humanity.

As we see, something else occurs in literature as well, something paradoxical and improbable. It is an age of unheard-of scientific-technological achievements by humankind, visions, apparitions, spirits come to life. What is this? A splash of obscurantism? What calls contemporary Gothic to life if not the same force that causes to hang in the air a sense of a growing rift between people and nature, reason and spirituality, of such absolute alienation that it leads inevitably to estrangement from oneself, to the disintegration of the individual? Every honest writer in this situation searches for his or her path; they express their understanding of and engagement with the situation. The artists whose work has been discussed above—all very different from each other, all developed, vivid, well-known individuals—turned to the Gothic and the Romantic as a means of aesthetic generalization. In this way, they attempt to restore balance, to harmonize the idea of "the person" as being endowed with both reason and intuition, a member of society but also a part of nature, of the universe, living in the present time but carrying inside them the past—his or her own, as well as that of all humanity.

Hawthorne once complained: "No shadows, no mystery." A century and a half later, on the sites of the first settlements, America's own shadows and mysteries have appeared. The hero of such a work necessarily is far higher than the ordinary human individual. The plot is always suspenseful, dynamic. The time and place are localized, but the narrative, in no way, turns into a fairy tale or ordinary mystery story. As we have noted, it is the inner tragic tension that dominates. The attributes, cares, and problems of the era are not merely present, they are accentuated both in the outer world and in the consciousness of the characters.

Even in the most lyrical romance, one seemingly as subjective as possible, we find a striving for objectification and generalization. Henry James looked for ways to attain objectification and generalization—extolling Turgenev for the civilized nature of his prose, which openly expressed the epic nature, and formulated the remarkable device of, "intersecting consciousnesses"—but found no distinctive criterion for social practice for his writing. Our contemporaries use visions toward this end. Is this good or bad? This question cannot be answered simply, nor need it be. It is clear only that this is very "American." It comes from Emerson, who had such a great influence on the formation of the national consciousness. For this reason, there is no doubt that the "introduction" of romance enriches the genre of the novel and allows its release from flat, linear parameters. A redistribution is taking place—in comparison with the midcentury—of objective and subjective categories, toward greater objectification through the introduction of Gothic as a means of sublimating the social consciousness, that is, the joining of the individual to a community.

Of course, in the epic framework, concrete history or scientific research of society as a means of objectification is more familiar, dependable, and, finally, simpler. But so unusual a means as the introduction of the Gothic in the contemporary novel also aids in solving the problem of the individual and human society, in helping "vertically" (as does reference to history) and symbolically to reconstruct national self-knowledge and join the individual to it.

The search for community as a necessary condition for the existence of the individual becomes the stable characteristic of the American novel of the last few decades. The new forms that it takes correspond to the spirit of the times, giving witness to the striving to restore the fullness of the human individual on a universal scale.

MAYA TUGUSHEVA

The Soviet View of American Feminism with a Side Look at Our Native Antifeminism

How did this begin? What aroused my interest in American "women's literature"? It must have started with my childhood acquaintance with Harriet Beecher Stowe's *Uncle Tom's Cabin*. Of course, at that time I could never have thought that this novel would become for me not only the disturbing story of the sufferings and steadfastness of a martyr, but a great work of world literature written by a woman. Nor could I foresee that under the influence of that literary fact, I would, in 1973, complete *The American Woman and Literature*, which would be rejected by every one of our publishing houses because the subject was "insubstantial" and "not serious."

Yes, failure was bitter; I felt humiliated and insulted. "Do you really think one can seriously talk about women's literature?" I was asked in condescending tones. "But that's not what I'm writing about," I vainly protested. "I'm saying that you can't divide literature into male and female dioceses! I'm writing about the contribution women have made to the common treasury of world culture." I was unable to convince anyone. "It's interesting, of course; but still, it's strange—women and literature.

American women, what's more. Now maybe if you'd written about our own women."

What could I say to that? Well, at least that I am moved by a professional interest and that the American woman began to enter her native literature two hundred years before I wrote my book, whereas, until the middle of the last century, Soviet women writers could be counted on one's fingers. American women took very seriously child-rearing and the education of youth, both boys and girls. Not for nothing did Jane Addams proclaim, "Only an educated woman can become the mother of heroes and philosophers." More and more often, women themselves strove to be active figures, both in life and in literature, creating more than just didactic works and guides to home economics for young housewives. One of the first novels written by a woman appeared in the 1830s. The author even takes on social themes, this despite society's strong opposition, opposition to the primordial quest to free one's consciousness and affirm one's role in society. The obstacles were serious; above all, they were constitutional. One is reminded of Mrs. Carter's sarcastic response to Alcuin's question (Charles Brockden Brown, *Alcuin*, 1792–1808) and her political convictions. Mrs. Carter's political views and her whole life are regulated by the "limitations" of her sex; after all, she is a "representative, altogether, of half the American population, whose political rights have been abolished by the Constitution . . . that is, recent immigrants, poor people, and blacks."

Alexis de Tocqueville wrote: "American women are not allowed to engage in activities outside their families or to take part in political life."[1] Two Englishwomen, Frances Trollope and Harriet Martineau, traveling in America in the late 1820s and mid-1830s, would be shocked by this inequality. Trollope wrote in her book, *Domestic Manners of the Americans* (1832), that the difference in status of men and women in society compromised the essence of that nation's ideals and values, and that, until women took their due place in society, America would be unable to rival Europe in its level of culture and civilization. The subordinate "domestic" position of American women limited the nation's potential for progress and development.

Trollope is particularly critical of the "domestic servitude," which was the lot of female citizens in the country of the free and equal, noting that housework is the most exhausting and thankless kind of labor. This was a response to Elizabeth Stanford's claim, which was popular in America at the time: "Her heart must belong to the home. She must find both pleasure, and constant activity in the area for which she is destined. The Apostle Paul knew what was best for woman when he counselled her to be a domestic creature. He knew that the home was the safest place for her, that that was where she belonged."[2] Trollope could not agree with this conservative opinion, so spiritually limiting to women. She recalls American women—the wives of pioneers and farmers—exhausted by labor beyond their strength. But they, at least, she reflects, know that they have done something useful for society by conquering wild lands while middle class women lead, in her words, a "useless life." This was followed by a statement that enraged adherents of the religious-domestic philosophy of life "for women": "No, not in this way can woman gain that influence in society which she may attain in Europe, and which philosophers and citizens of the world agree to be so beneficial." Similar, stormy indignation was raised by her criticism of various religious sects. Denied a wide range of public activity by society, she says, American women find an outlet for their unrealized thirst for activity, an escape from the sense of a useless aimless life and from emotional emptiness, in the unhealthy exaltation of religious feelings, in an idolotry of their spiritual pastors, who are not always insensible of such exalted worship on the part of their parishioners. "More than once," she recalls, "did I observe some 'venerable' hand on a girl's neck." This at a time when girls were instilled from childhood with an exaggerated sense of shame concerning the opposite sex, when American ladies fainted at the sight of nude ancient statues. Trollope, in the words of her indignant critics, was attacking the "cult of true femininity," an unforgivable sin. The *Illinois Monthly Review* was particularly savage toward the English writer, insulting her appearance, her "loose" manners, and her "bad taste, so reminiscent of the Indians in our own country." The journal lamented that Trollope's book would have a "ruinous" influence on American women readers, "estranging them from religion and morals." The book was called the product of "spleen and malice" toward everything American. Trollope's discussion of religion and the position of women was "disgusting." She herself lacked "all the feminine virtues" and was an enemy of everything "pure, beautiful, and lofty"—so much ire did her presumptuous claim that women are created "not only to bake cookies and gingerbread, sew shirts, darn socks, and bring presidents into the world" arouse.

On the other hand, Elizabeth Stanford and her book found many supporters among both sexes, both in America and abroad. Thus a literature appeared about women, by women, for women. It was created for the "iron maiden"—the many-million-strong army of women readers wishing to know and read only about how bold, manly, enterprising Charles managed to lead virtuous Susan to the altar.

How Margaret Fuller hated that banal love story, dreaming of the balanced woman of the future—a free, wonderful, fully developed individual. How she battled against that set plot—a cheap, sentimental construct calculated on conservative thinking and undeveloped taste. "They say . . . that these stories are written for seamstresses, but we think that that class, which is already insulted in every way, could receive pleasure from more refined food as well, and could manage with it even after a long day of exhausting labor." Now, however, the magazine industry interferes with "inner growth," and not only the magazines but, for example, the novels of Caroline Lee Hentz, which claim that an independence-loving woman is depraved.

The "iron maiden" was a strict dictator. Louisa May Alcott, her father's daughter, challenges Dickens. His attitude towards women was alien to her. Piqued at the iron maiden and at conservative views on woman's role in the family and society, Louisa wrote her article, "Happy Women." She defended a girl's right to a life devoted to literature, art, and the common good. She praises the ranks of "great American old maids" who dedicated themselves to the struggle for a worthy life for all Americans, whatever their sex or skin color. (In the traditional love story, the old maid was depicted as deeply unhappy, perfidious and envious, all because she had never managed to get married.) How dramatic it is that in her "best book" (*Little Women*), of which she dreamed all her life, Alcott succumbed to the ultimatum laid down by reader and publisher. *Little Women* and *Little Men*, once so popular here in Russia, aimed less to inculcate the highest virtues of human nature—for which the philosopher and neo-platonist Bronson Alcott strove in his Temple School—than to cultivate the best qualities of the future: a well-educated, enlightened (Addams could rest easy) housewife and mother. True, at first, Louisa May Alcott tried to defend her point: A woman could live a worthy, useful life without tying herself to marriage and family. But her young readers protested. Louisa was indignant: "Girls insist that I marry off the 'little women,' as if marriage were the only meaning and goal of a woman's life"; her Jo refused the proposal of her childhood friend, the handsome and charming Laurie. However, her young readers were so distressed by her refusal; and her publisher, fearing a loss of interest in the book—and, thus, lower profits—became so alarmed that Alcott gave in. Is it not in part due to this that, in the history of her native literature, she is now referred to as a "half-forgotten, old-fashioned writer"?

We, too, had our Lee Hentzs and Louisa May Alcotts—inferior to the latter in talent and particularly in freedom of thought. We are, above all, reminded here of the sentimental and conservative Lydia Charskaia and her novel, *Upriamitsa* (The Stubborn Girl), in which the heroine, coming to her senses in time, stops rebelling and docilely marries, not, it's true, a scholarly linguist, as Jo does, but a "dear" soldier.

My interest in American women's literature quickened in the mid-1960s; the books of Katharine Rogers, Betty Friedan, and Kate Millett played a large role in this. I thought, however, that the authors of these interesting, consciousness-raising works forged in vain their interpretation of the well-known hypothesis of the "battle of the sexes," that they were unable to break out of predetermined, self-imposed, literary-historical, sociological, and philosophical limitations. How, for instance, after reading their assertions of the primordial misogynist essence of the works of male writers, was I to regard the novels of Sinclair Lewis, who wrote of the role of American women in society with sympathy and understanding? Indeed, sometimes his heroines (Une Golden, for instance), succeed in defending the right of women to do useful work which brings them joy and to marry for love. On the other hand, the unlucky Carol Kennicott surrenders to bourgeois convention without, however, losing hope in the future. There is no other way to explain the prophetic episode in which Carol leads her husband to their newborn daughter's bed with the words: "Do you see that object on the pillow? Do you know what it is? It's a bomb to blow up smugness. If you Tories were wise, you wouldn't arrest anarchists; you'd arrest all these children. . . . Think what that baby will see and meddle with before she dies in the year 2000!" Through Carol, who dreams of "aeroplanes going to Mars," Lewis predicts not only the scientific-technical revolution in our 20th-century space age, but another, social "explosion": the wide democratic women's movement for civil rights in the 1960s and since.

And what of Ernita Dreiser, who, among the many women in the "red thirties," went to the USSR to take part in building socialism? In those years an entire generation of fervently democratic women grew up— Lillian Helmann tells of them in *Pentimento*—who defended a woman's right to a worthy, intelligent, full, socially useful life.

Ten years later, this mindset had changed fundamentally. In 1945, at the
end of World War II, the little girl in the crib would have reached the age
her mother had been when she was suffocating in the grip of domestic
life. Perhaps she, like Carol, would have sought the wide world of freedom, action, and joy. But there is another possibility—she might have
grown into that comfortable and closed existence and given herself over
only to household concerns—especially as, at this time, the dream of a
better, more just social structure (not without the influence of the tragic
events of the 1930s in our country) appeared impossible and compromised, and writers considered it their duty to preserve people's most
positive image of surrounding reality, frequently, incidentally, advising
them to take refuge from the storms of modern life in the quiet, peaceful
world of the family. Marriage and motherhood in those years were more
and more often extolled as the most important—the only sphere—for a
woman's activity, quite in the spirit of Elizabeth Stanford. D. H. Lawrence's posthumous literary reputation grew once again, as well as his
authority on questions of the sexes. The world would perish should woman reject the role assigned to her by "nature": that of priestess of the
hearth. Men must save civilization by establishing and strengthening their
psychological and emotional power over women. If a woman rebels
against her primordial, "natural" destiny, she is rational and cold, not a
real woman; that is, she is unfeminine (for example, *Lady Chatterly's
Lover*). This admonition brought noticeable results, and in 1956, *Life* magazine confirmed with satisfaction "the American woman's return home."

Thus, at the beginning of the Cold War, Carol Kennicott's grown-up
daughter probably would have had to retreat. Who knows?—perhaps her
own daughter would in no way have differed from the heroine of Patricia
Dizenzo's *An American Girl* (1973). The character, callous and demanding,
is quickly consoled after the death of her older sister by counting the new
blouses she will receive.

Betty Friedan's collection of essays, *The Feminine Mystique*, however,
had already appeared—the manifesto of "neo-feminism," as the press
called the revived women's movement. Friedan's book, of course, is an
attack on the conservative mood expressed most fully in the book *Modern
Woman: The Lost Sex*, by Marynia Farnham and Ferdinand Lundberg—
which maintains, yet again, that only "sexually frustrated" women can
strive for social and political freedom. (Incidentally, these arguments had
some influence. Who wanted to be seen as unfeminine or abnormal?)

Another dissatisfaction gradually arose among women, however: The press began to refer to the housewife's "neurotic syndrome." Conservatives increased their pressure; everything would be fine if it weren't for the false idea of a woman's responsibility to herself and the yearning for socially useful activity outside the home. American housewives would peacefully bring children into the world, not in the least lamenting other buried creative possibilities. They would be eternally feminine and happy with their fates. But the mystical charms of eternal femininity (or "eternal sacrifice," as Charlotte Brontë sarcastically put it) dissipated irretrievably. Recalling Sinclair Lewis's *Main Street*, one could say that Carol Kennicott's daughter, and perhaps her granddaughter, again were faced with the problem that disturbed their foremother: Only the daughter and granddaughter were subjected to the more intense and powerful influence of commercial Romance literature, much of it in the spirit of "retro," the style of Emily James Putnam's *The Lady* (1910), in which every woman aspires to create a "little domestic republic, dependent on male favor, and the qualities by means of which this can be attained are in general not suited to any other goal. A girl . . . must be prepared for the ordinary man like a ready-made dress."

How could an American woman not be outraged at this? How could she not turn her heart and head to the new credo of women's liberation advocated by Friedan, Millett, and Greer? Even when they went overboard, passing the limits of reason, proclaiming, for instance, the advantages of "single-sex love," or proposing that the traditional family be eliminated and the care of children laid on society alone? In her story, "Source," Alice Walker later showed to what absurd extremes this could lead.

Responsibility for attempting to divert the women's movement from its sociopolitical and civil struggles probably lies mostly on the conscience of Germaine Greer, who has claimed that the most important thing is a personal, "restored" female consciousness rather than the restructuring of all social relations on a more humanistic and democratic basis. Also mistaken, in my opinion, is Katharine Rogers' position. In full agreement with Hannah Arendt's theory of violence, Greer maintains that at the root of all social evils lies men's dominating role, which is based on force, and that there is only one solution to the situation: a rebellion of wives and daughters against such domination. This rebellion, incidentally, most often included the idea of a sexual rebellion (or "sexual revolution," as the official press referred to it). The literary cost of advocating such ideas showed up quickly—the traditional love story was brazenly eroticized. The novels of Henry Sutton, Irving Wallace, and, of course, Jacqueline Suzanne, are examples of sexual "emancipation." The latter is most paradoxically compared with Louisa May Alcott by advertisers, who claim that she too was a supporter of women's equality. However, the independent, unfettered woman in Suzanne's novels always dreams of fitting her life into the mold of respectable marriage, something one finds no trace of in Alcott. Probably for this reason, excerpts from Suzanne's *The Love Machine* (1969) appeared in *Ladies' Home Journal*.

Conservative tendencies gained strength during Ronald Reagan's first term. Reagan, who called for the return of the American woman "to the kitchen," influenced Congress against approval of the 27th Amendment. It is true that in January 1983, the world learned that, in light of the upcoming presidential election, two women had received ministerial posts—an important card against the Democratic party, allowing the Republicans to beat Walter Mondale at his own game, since Mondale had not only to promise the office of vice-president to a woman (which certainly alarmed many conservatives, and not all of them men), but to develop a practical plan for achieving equal rights. As is well known, economic inequality leads to civil and political inequality. We see this clearly in our own country, as well; we have no women ministers, and we take inordinate pride in the (single) fact that a woman is honored with the post of ambassador to Switzerland.

Of course, the American woman was, as before, eagerly assigned the task of mending the sociopolitical tear at home. It was her job to cement the family and pass on traditional values, that is, to raise the next generation to believe in those ideals which further her civil inequality. As before, sociology, journalism, literature, and advertising strove to fortify the hold on women of conservative views of her goal in life and her role in society. The place she now occupies is the only one she should look to, it is determined by "nature." The sexual counterrevolution was raised not unsuccessfully in opposition to the ideas of the sexual revolution. The wide, democratic women's movement was squeezed into the narrow confines of feminism and neofeminism; sociopolitical, civil, and antimilitarist consciousness was identified with a certain "raised consciousness," seemingly demanding the abolition of moral restrictions and complete license. The struggle to defend women's human rights and their opportunity to develop their full potential—the dream of Fuller, Alcott, and Lewis—was transformed into a threat to the home, the family, and society. The idea of a free—that is, voluntary—union of man and woman, the legacy of Mary Wollstonecraft (*A Vindication of the Rights of Woman* [1792]) and William Godwin (*Enquiry Concerning Political Justice* [1793]) was replaced in the popular mind by free love—a synonym for moral dissipation.

Unfortunately, such hasty and preconceived judgments are not uncommon in our native criticism either; nor is the uncritical assimilation of evaluative formulas and stereotypes, or of literary, sociological, and other clichés. This shows up in the perception of questions of sexual equality, women's emancipation, feminism, and, in literary criticism, of the question of men's and women's prose. Here, as in the West, the ideal of free, democratic, civil equality is often brought down to frightening images of emancipation as complete sexual license and the weakening of the family. Indeed, a vulgarized, simplistic understanding of the idea of equality of the sexes—the true barometer of a society's morality and humanistic potential—is no rarity here. Is not, for instance, the effort to divide prose into separate men's and women's genres an uncritical acceptance of the ancient idea of a natural hierarchy of the sexes, which considers them endowed with separate "natural gifts"? Indeed, Ella Shcherbanenko's article, published several years ago in the journal *Inostrannaya Literatura* (Foreign Literature), is nothing other than the popularization of this Aristotelian postulate. I see the same basic idea in the ultracontemporary, theoretical debates in American feminist scholarship, such as the collection of essays edited by Elaine Showalter, *The New Feminist Criticism: Essays on Women, Literature, and Theory.* This calls to mind George Henry Lewes (who, incidentally, was much respected and much read, as a founder of positivism, in Russia in the 1860s). It was Lewes who first distinguished women's literature as a separate literary form in, for instance, an article on Charlotte Brontë's novel *Shirley* (1849).[3] This article was essentially disparaging, as Lewes, in 1849, recognized no such equality. Only five to seven years later, he became convinced of the opposite view by the example of his common-law wife, Marian Evans. She, too, however, would become known to the world under a male pseudonym, "George Eliot." (In Victorian society, a man's name on the title page served to guarantee acceptance and sale of a book.) It is true that by "women's literature," Lewes meant something different than did his younger colleague, Arthur Quiller-Couch, who wrote at the turn of the century, and something other than what our critics now call "ladies' stories" and the West refers to as the traditional love story, or romance. Lewes considered raising the question of civil and sociopolitical equality of the sexes to be the most characteristic trait of women's literature. A man, he thought, would not spend his talent and abilities on the propagation of such ideas.

Quiller-Couch, on the other hand, tried to base his distinction between literatures on something else. He assumed that there exist cardinal differences between men's and women's ways of writing and attributed these gender differences in literary style to age-old male and female "natures." The same level of scholarly theorizing often appears in Showalter's collection. Again, we are asked to consider how the sexual difference influences "reading, writing, and literary interpretation." Showalter also maintains that, "unlike structuralists who hark back to the linguistic discoveries of Saussure, psychoanalytic critics loyal to Freud or Lacan, Marxists steeped in *Das Kapital*, or deconstructionists citing Derrida, feminist critics do not look to a Mother of Us All or a single system of thought to provide their fundamental ideas."

They don't? Isn't their theoretical platform that which was proclaimed by their foremothers in the 1960s, known as the "battle of the sexes"? The difference is perhaps only in the fact that today a "specific woman's literary consciousness," represented, according to Showalter, by Adrienne Rich, Marge Piercy, and Alice Walker, is more often extolled. Of course, it is gratifying that, for the most part, feminist critics resist attempts to identify feminism with "lesbian self-awareness" and to trace women's artistic and literary gifts directly from her "lesbian nature." However, many of those for whom the theory of misogynist male literature has been replaced (time, after all, does not stand still) with deep study of "the distinctively female aesthetic" are challenging not oppressive, unjust social institutions but, in large part, fundamental literary, historical, and aesthetic ideas such as that of the "American Renaissance," introduced by F. O. Matthiessen to describe American Romanticism. This, again, for the antiquated reason that such a distinguishing of periods is based on the work of male writers, as though American Romanticism were not the common cultural property of both sexes. Need one be surprised, then, that feminist criticism today sets as its most important task a "revision of the accepted theoretical assumptions about reading and writing that have been based entirely on male literary experiences"? On this is based feminist criticism's "revisionist imperative" regarding paternalistic literature. The claim that the study of gender difference is the key to new vitality in both women's literature and gynocriticism—that is, criticism entirely isolated from "male" theoretical models, which must, above all, reveal that women's literary style derives from the peculiarities of female physiology and anatomy.

Contemporary champions of women's literature, of course, as well as gynocriticism, have moved far from the misogynist theorizing of Quiller-Couch. But his ideas, which come down to us from the times of Philemon and Baucis, of distinctive male and female psychological and emotional characters, are revived quite clearly in some of the postulates of feminist theoretical thought. And what a coincidence! The echo of such assertions can be heard in our own criticism and literature as well. Only, I would say, with an even more pronounced conservative bias, for which reason one reads and hears more often (in an extremely negative context)—about "this" emancipation, about "so called" sexual equality, about *true female* abilities and qualities, about "aggressive Helen of the 20th century." If we turn to critical debates, we also hear about a "specifically female vision" in literature, formulated by A. Latynina in an article on the contemporary "ladies' story."[4] This article indisputably implies that there exists "male prose," which is inherently "sure and sober" in its outlook, and "female prose." The worst variety of the latter, ladies' stories, is characterized by "sentimentality, hackneyed style, and an abundance of melodramatic passion." Occasionally, women write "like men" (that is, with true artistry); but even in the "best examples of this women's prose . . . one senses a sort of suffragist complex, an involuntary attempt to reduce the subject to the problem of woman's social status and external realization." There it is: George Henry Lewes himself could not have expressed his contempt with more irony.

It's a pity, of course, that the author of the article is not pleased with the suffragists, although, as we know, it was they who fought for a woman's right to her own property in case of divorce and for her writing sister's right to her own royalties. As is well known, in England in the mid-19th century, before the suffragist movement, the situation was different. The then celebrated Mrs. Gaskell wrote novels, and her husband, the venerable William Gaskell, neatly tucked the proceeds into his wallet. For Agatha Christie, thanks largely to the stubborn militancy of the suffragists, such discrimination was a thing of the distant past. Furthermore, the suffragists fought for a woman's right to work, to raise her own children in case of marital separation (it is a shame that, in Russia at the time of Anna Karenina, no rumor of this had yet been heard), and for the right to vote, an utter absurdity which greatly amused a young man working in the ministry of foreign affairs by the name of Winston Churchill. Could he have dreamed that his future position would be filled only about thirty years after him by a certain resolute woman? So, the suffragists accomplished a great deal for today's Englishwomen and for the liberation of women's consciousness throughout the world. In any case, the suffragist complex—this includes women's desire to achieve social and personal realization—does not deserve to be regarded with scorn, and certainly not by women.

Old-fashioned feminist zeal is not so very out of place in a world where, according to Latynina, "masculinism" reigns supreme (Millett, Friedan, and Greer informed us of this in the 1960s). Especially touching here is the term *old-fashioned*. No, this zeal has pertinence both in the United States and for us. It is irritating, indeed, to look at the presidiums of our important assemblies, from which women are strikingly absent—the only exception being the yearly celebration of International Woman's Day. Feminism is the burning struggle for equal pay for work, for genuine—political and civil—equality, for the abolition of night shifts and hard physical labor for women, of which there is still plenty in our country, for equal representation in government, and for protection of that "early female potential" which frequently is replaced by neuroses and apathy, including social apathy—the result of being doomed, like a squirrel in a cage, to run in circles around the problems of a bad existence. So that a negative judgment of the complex phenomenon called *feminism* is also, if I may be forgiven, a "masculinized" view—disseminated, unfortunately, by criticism, journalism, and literature—suffice it to recall V. Belov's *Vospitanie po doktoru Spoku* (Upbringing According to Dr. Spock) or, for example, V. Leonovich's story, "*Na rabote i doma. Zapiski rabochego cheloveka*" (At Work and At Home. Notes of a Working Man), with its entirely patriarchal conception of woman's place in the family, its unflattering description of female psychology, and its comparison of the "man's" with the "lady's" mind. One more example: V. Krupin's novel *Spasenie Pogibshikh* (The Salvation of the Dead).[5] Here we have the full Aristotelian—or, rather, the Old Testament—complement: "Why do we need the love of these lying, mercenary creatures when they are the cause of everything—theft and deceit, envy and evildoing?" Or really unforgivable: "Suffragist, curse you!" written as the "revelation" of a contemporary, established "man of eloquence," asking with sincere surprise, "Why should a woman need independence from men?"

It is not surprising that a Swedish woman journalist, according to a story in *Moscow News*, lamented with surprise the conservatism of Soviet men, using as an example the words of a highly visible representative of our press (whom she did not name), in whose opinion true civilization consists in woman's return to the home. Does that remind you of anything? Of course: *Life*, 1956.

Also, ubiquitous in our criticism, literature, and journalism is the call for the "eternal feminine." Shcherbanenko's article, affirming a timeless, "primal" female nature, says, in particular, that "a normal woman looks at the world through the eyes of her husband." It includes fairly categorical advice to the contemporary woman, which would be very much to the liking of our conservative writers, both male and female, concerning her behavior. "Struggle, work, way of life, feelings—all of this must be within the limits of your sex." What a curious echo to Mrs. Carter two centuries later if, of course, we don't consider that Mrs. Carter rejected these oppressive limits.

I think that the interpretation of the "woman question"—which lowers democratic and humanistic ideals of equal rights to the idea of freedom from moral foundations and sexual scruples—complements, not by chance, the theory of the eternal feminine, that mysterious, all-healing grail, and, in literature, the concept of a specifically female vision. It is a thoroughly logical conclusion: If a woman's "struggle, work, way of life, feelings" must be within the limits of her sex, then why shouldn't literature be divided into privatized spheres of men's and women's consciousness, style, and methods—in a word, into men's and women's prose? Logically connected to this is the striving, in counterbalance with the dominant male establishment, to fight that establishment not by means of, for instance, the struggle for civil and social rights, but by introducing "gynocriticism" and a literature created by women in a hermetically isolated, supersocial, specifically women's region. One cannot help recalling, in this instance, Joyce Carol Oates' position, who more than once wrote and spoke with alarm about attempts to drive women's literature into a "ghetto" of unimportance, and condemned old-fashioned (but, as we see, still existing) attempts to divide literature into sexual genres.

It is interesting to note, by the way, that the American scholar Alfred

Habegger, recognizing this division, most surprisingly categorizes the works of W. D. Howells and Henry James as "women's" literature, tracing them to the maternal, women's tradition in American literature, as they are characterized by their edifying nature—in Habegger's opinion, a specifically female quality. What, then, should we make of the proselytizing zeal of Emerson and Thoreau? Habegger does not address this question. It is all too obvious that edification is not necessarily a distinctive trait of women's literature, but, like melodrama and hackneyed style referred to by Latynina, is frequently characteristic of men's prose as well. There is no question that *Uncle Tom's Cabin* is melodramatic, but so are the novels of Dickens. What is important is an author's mastery of melodrama, that is, the ability to touch the deeply hidden nerve of compassion, the most sensitive spot. Far from all writers, classical or contemporary, have that ability.

Margaret Atwood has cleverly debunked the division of literature into various departments, challenging customary limits—in this case, the idea of differing psychological, moral, and stylistic traits of male and female prose. Asked whether she felt that the nature of her work—her choice of subject, syntax, and style—is determined by the fact that she is a woman, Atwood described an experiment conducted by her students. "We took an excerpt from a little-known piece of literature, copied it, and, adding a woman's name, asked a control group to describe the writer's style. The evaluations were 'cloudy,' 'vague,' 'sentimental,' 'limp.' We showed the same piece, with a male name, to a different group of students. The judgments were 'superb,' 'restrained,' 'severe,' 'energetic.' No, I don't think talent and literature depend on whether the author is a man or a woman. I have always been against such determinations, whatever wrapping they are presented in. I reject the categorization which maintains that if you are a woman and give birth to children, the style of your works must proclaim this. I don't like it when men claim this, and I do not agree with women who say the same thing."

The "queen of the mystery," Agatha Christie, made the point even more laconically: "There simply exist various types of mental activity. There are businesslike women, who think with impeccable logic. There are men who think in a confused and chaotic way. Gender concerns only what is directly sexual." And that was in 1938!

Literature can be divided into various compartments only theoretically. In fact, there exist only real literature and pseudo-literature; both can be created by men and women equally. The main distinguishing traits of pseudo-literature are, as a rule, superficial exposition and deep-seated conformism. A typical example is Barbara Gordon's *Defects of the Heart* (1984). The book's heroine is a television director who enjoys public popularity and the attention of her boss. Jessica receives an award for good, talented work, and, of course, she is pleased. At the same time, she is burdened by a vague dissatisfaction with herself. A woman who publicly is awarded for conscientious work has, she feels, something "unnatural," artificial, about her. She is not worthy of the hopes society has invested in her. In the "natural sphere," Jessica has nothing to boast of: She is single and involved with her boss, a married man. By the middle of the book, however, Judge Doug Weber has appeared in her life ("handsome, sullen, with thick curly hair and a decisive jaw"). Together, they expose a large-scale scam involving a "miracle" medicine, and the main criminal, the head of the company, a youth activist in the 1960s. Weber creates intrigues and machinations, but Jessica manages to make and show a film proving his guilt, and the criminal suffers a fiasco. Doug, who has already become "her man," proposes to Jessica, and on Thanksgiving Day they are to marry. Now a new, real life will begin for her: She will be a wife and mother and will raise her children according to traditional American values. The circle is closed.

If we were to remove from the novel all indications of modernity (television, affair with the boss, youth movement of the 1960s against the Vietnam War, or, rather, the memory of the war), how would this narrative—with its happy ending and immutable principles, all secret vices revealed, bad guys punished, the good victorious not only morally but, as our Pushkin put it ("good's reward was the wedding veil")—differ from the traditional love story?

Thus, one of the novel's conclusions is the typical, traditional solution to the "woman question," that is to say, the "kitchen solution"; but the novel also has a political message. Is it mere coincidence that the author leads the generation of the 1980s to regard critically their predecessor who once rebelled against and questioned traditional values? Here we have the result: Rebellion leads to crime. Gordon's novel is not only an example of sentimental entertainment literature with an element of "exposure," it is a conscious tour de force of neoconservative taste.

It remains to be added that the claim of an eternal opposition of the sexes in literature is tantamount to metaphysical assertions of their eternal struggle, as both models replace the concept of sociopolitical and civil struggle with struggle based on type. Is not this the source of the demand by the well-known critic Nina Baym (her essay appears in Showalter's book) that the "literary canon" be reconsidered, as the entire accepted view of classic American literature must be—after all, it is based on a male point of view? Discussing the disparagement and vulgarization of Stowe's politically motivated novel, Jane P. Tompkins, in her interesting article, "Sentimental Power: *Uncle Tom's Cabin* and the Politics of Literary History," maintains that historians of American literature refuse to recognize the book's artistic significance (Carlos Baker is an example) because the author was a woman. But Tompkins herself uses this fact to obscure the novel's sociopolitical content. Leslie Fiedler goes even further in this direction in the book *What Was Literature?* (1982), demoting *Uncle Tom's Cabin* from an abolitionist novel to a family one and glorifying the joys of the domestic hearth—this based on the facts that the word *cabin* (a home, after all) appears in the title and that Stowe herself was a woman and the mother of a large family—a convincing attempt to confirm biological criteria in literature and to confine the interests of a woman writer whose novel had "worldwide" (according to Tolstoy) political significance to the circle (or "limits") of asocial, "kitchen" interests. Is it surprising that as a result of his analysis, Fiedler equates *Uncle Tom's Cabin* with Margaret Mitchell's *Gone With The Wind*, as both, he says, sing hymns to the "paradise" of the home. Never mind that in Mitchell's novel "hymns are sung" to the mansion of rich slaveowners and the plantation on which hundreds of thousands of "Toms" paid for decades with their sweat and blood for the prosperity of their white masters. Thus the specific nature of women's literature is again confirmed. Cultural-historical and sociopolitical criteria are replaced by a biological-psychological, physiological approach; the dependence of a work's artistry or lack thereof; its social content, or lack thereof, on the author's sex is perpetuated—all this in light of the fact that real, true, artistic literature cannot be divided; it is created equally by men and women—"two notes, without which the music of humanity cannot sound," in the words of Giuseppe Madzini. Madzini also said, addressing the male half of humanity: "Love and respect woman. Look to her not only for comfort, but for strength and inspiration. She can double your intellectual and moral resources. Throw away any ideas in your head about male superiority, you don't have it. Man and woman are equal in every way. . . ."

Golden words!

ALEXANDR MULIARCHIK

Neoconservatism

and American Literature

of the 1980s

The swing to the right in the internal politics of the United States, which received rather clear expression in many of the actions of the Reagan administration, pushed to the forefront of intellectual debate in that country the trend referred to as the "new conservatism." As a sociophilosophical doctrine, neoconservatism already had a long history; many aspects of it have been analyzed in detail by Soviet philosophers and sociologists. The sum of their observations is that the effort of the neoconservatives to provoke a shift to the right in all areas of national life is far from consonant with the mood of many segments of the American population. A certain part of the Western press, however, has rushed to overtake events, in hopes of giving them a nudge in one direction. "A process of radical transformation is beginning in American society," Italy's *Panorama* announced to its readers at the beginning of the 1980s. "In America the conservative idea, in various forms, is becoming predominant," seconded the French *Monde Diplomatique*.

"Simple" conservatives had existed in America earlier as well; but only rarely did they venture from the ideological and political margins and attempt to thrust their credo on the majority. The authors of articles on the pages of such extremely right-wing publications as *The National Review* and *American Opinion* do not conceive of any social order other than that which formed in America more than a hundred years ago, during the classical period of "free" capitalism. The new conservatives, however, endeavor to present their views as the "ideology of the future." Although many in the West are accustomed to maintaining that this teaching consists entirely of nuance and innuendo, the basic positions of the neoconservatives are quite clear-cut.

"The aim," writes the editor of *Public Interest* and one of the movement's leading ideologues, Irving Kristol,

> was not to minimize or abolish self-interest as a goad to economic and political activity, but instead to channel that self-interest into the disciplinary context of the marketplace for goods, and into that simulacrum of a "marketplace" for influence and ideas known as representative government. The assumption was that as men improved their material condition through economic activity, and as they gained experience in self-government, they would become more "civil," more enlightened, more gentle and humane in their relations with one another.[1]

Foregoing clever invention, the "old" conservatives divided American society strictly along vertical lines—into employers and hired laborers, including among the latter the many millions who form the working masses. Along with this, denying the class struggle, they were not against building into their sociological plans "corporate pyramids," each of which would take its appropriate place and aid the social organism to function properly. In their way, the neoconservatives, too, battle Marxist theory, maintaining that internal social tensions in the United States are the result not of struggle between the haves and the have-nots, but of conflict between two bourgeoisies.

On one side, they see canny, industrious entrepreneurs and hardened businessmen not inclined to personal extravagance and not afraid of being seen as old-fashioned. These are opposed by a "new class" consisting, for the most part, of highly educated, salaried people who supplement their income in various ways. The new class includes many lawmakers and government officials, college professors, consultants with academic degrees, and workers in mass media. According to the neoconservatives, this "new elite" is more inclined to spend than to save and reinvest money.

As Kristol asserts, it has already succeeded in squandering the national wealth on concessions to blacks and other ethnic minorities, the "professionally unemployed," and similar groups in society's lower echelons.

Such a readiness to see the new class as muddle-headed accomplices of underprivileged America only points to the theoretical nature of this arbitrarily divided society and, at the same time, to the immutability of real class barriers. In their desire to restrain the excessive demands of American workers, neoconservatives are all the more frequently tempted to do away once and for all with the "sacred tablets" of bourgeois democracy: "Solutions [in the area of social relations] must be less and less political, and more and more administrative," proclaimed Senator Daniel Patrick Moynihan.[2] Advancing the catchword *meritocracy*, Moynihan and his associates, comparing poor people to a ball and chain attached to the feet of the American economy, wish to deprive the majority of them of any political role.

There can be no doubting the backwardness of the neoconservatives' socioeconomic movement. "No longer finance activities harmful to the self-preservation of capitalism . . . . Aid those who believe in the preservation of a powerful private sector"—these are typical slogans of the platform advocating full support for big business. Equally one-sided are the foreign-policy aims of neoconservatives, who invariably cry out for a high level of armament, for "unremitting activity" by the United States in many parts of the world and who, in the second half of the 1980s, were able (thanks to the Reagan administration) to point to the real fruits of their policy.

In an attempt to enlist the widest possible support of public opinion, which by the mid-1970s had been forced to admit the defeat of the openly oppositional New Left, neoconservatives, in polemic with the latter, stressed questions of culture, morals, daily conduct, and way of life. The obscurantism in their cries for reduced democratic initiative and religious revival, in their assurance that "reason is not all-powerful and limitless," was evident to many. At the same time, the protests perpetually voiced in the pages of neoconservative publications against "self-destructive hedonism" and "ethical irresponsibility," the raising to the ranks of absolute values the triad of "family, work, ambition" were, in their most general form, fairly close to the democratic forces in American literature, groping in difficult historical circumstances for a balance point for the renewal of their moral creed.

Not understanding this extremely complicated dialectic, the mass media rushed to number among the accomplices of neoconservatism several prominent realist writers, and nearly the entire genre of the "family novel," including the work of such writers, well known both in the United States and abroad, as Richard Price, John Gardner, Toni Morrison, and Anne Tyler. Indeed, neoconservative ideas did not pass by American literature; but it can be affirmed that they received unconditional, full support almost exclusively in the "literary demi-monde," among representatives of that middle zone between real art and unabashed trash.

In his mainly historical novels *Centennial* (1976) and *Chesapeake* (1978), James Michener, relying on a modest talent, substantiated as best he could the main concern of his ideological allies who had an interest in the stability of existing structures. Michener did not conceal the fact that his social philosophy held close and dear "law and order," the slogan of the war against opposition. Slightly softened and "aestheticized," lifted from street confrontation under the banner of belles lettres, this philosophy appears in slightly different guise in Michener's work as "respect for imperishable tradition and authority."

The novels of Arthur Hailey, from *The Money Changers* (1975) to *Strong Medicine* (1984), were a similar response to the socioeconomic problems troubling many Americans. They tell the story of a modern Cinderella named Celia Jordan who, thanks to her personal qualities, travels the road from assistant pharmacist in an impoverished drugstore to manager of a large pharmaceutical company.

Strong Medicine had a certain success in the mid-1980s; but the average reader was much more taken by another work—similar in its ideological premises and nearly the longest book, both in volume and in time spent on its writing, in the history of modern publishing. Helen Hooven Santmyer took more than half a century to write her 1,176-page novel *. . . And the Ladies of the Club*, published when the author was nearly ninety years old. The appearance of this novel—which affirmed, less through artistic mastery than by the number of its pages, "true American values"—was an embellishing chord to the "new patriotism" proclaimed by the Reagan government and supported by a significant portion of public opinion. Conceived as a polemical response to Sinclair Lewis's well-known *Main Street* (1920), Santmyer's novel embraces nearly three quarters of a century of American history, beginning with the years immediately after the Civil War. Like Lewis, the author strove to show the United States "from the inside," refracted through the thoughts, feelings, and moods of American upper-middle-class women. At the age of eighteen, two married women, Anne Alexander and Sally Cochran, join a women's club in the town of Waynesboro, Ohio, remaining members over the course of long decades. The story of the activities of the club—which, like thousands of similar organizations, set as its goal, "to maintain the intellectual and cultural tone of life" in the city—is the main content of the unhurriedly unfolding narrative.

In its ideological spirit, Santmyer's book has much in common with Margaret Mitchell's *Gone With The Wind*, which created a sensation in its time. It is as if the author wanted to say, "This is how I remember 'our America,' which, to a great extent, we have lost." At times, the pages of this work resemble a catalogue informing the reader how Americans dressed and what their interests were in "former times," what their homes were like, their holidays, schools, religion, and social life—all accompanied by a feminist movement and struggles against illiteracy and alcoholism no less militant than today's. Also important to the heroines of the book was the personal and spiritual, thus the topics for discussion at regular club meetings: along with the obligatory Bible and Shakespeare, the historical writings of Herodotus and Thucydides, the philosophy of Marcus Aurelius, and the extremely modern (at that time) poetry of Robert Browning.

Santmyer's enthusiastic hymn to "good old America" does not, however, refer to the whole nation, only to a specific stratum: Americans of white skin, Protestants, well raised, adequately educated. In Santmyer's novel a sort of collective portrait is formed of the forebears of today's "middle Americans," who form, altogether, a solid sociopolitical base for the initiatives of the Republican administration. It is to this influential segment of American society that the aged writer is appealing, insisting that "all is not yet lost, and we must do all we can to keep the happy past from disappearing for good."[3]

That Michener, Hailey, and Santmyer are, at best, second-rate writers of contemporary American prose only emphasizes the opposition of the overwhelming majority of writers to that "swing to the right," on which conservative ideologues have calculated. It is also worth noting that the anticommunism of the foreign-policy aims—uniting, in essence, neoconservatives and traditional liberals—received unconditional support from

Michener in his novel *Poland* (1983) and from Saul Bellow, who, since the late 1960s, has, in this sense, sharply differed from many of his colleagues. Bellow devotes nearly half of the novel *The Dean's December* to life in socialist Eastern Europe. The story is of a Rumanian immigrant who, with her husband, the dean of a Chicago college, travels to Bucharest to visit her dying mother. The unfolding of sad events causes Albert Corde and his wife no little trouble. Under the pressure of the author's will, five swift days are quite enough to allow them, without deeply investigating the country's problems, to refer to it as a "police state."

At the same time, having failed to draw into its course a significant number of influential, responsibly thinking writers of the older generation, the stream of conservative ideology had a depressive influence on the frame of mind of a certain number of young writers. Many of those whose youth coincided with the "ninth wave" of oppositional antibourgeois activity tended to think that the next stage of American history would be marked on the social front by a retreat from borders already attained and, on the psychological, by a spiritual breakdown and disappointment in high ideals. *The Culture of Narcissism*, by the "radical-romantic" Christopher Lasch, added an accent to the ideological chaos by maintaining that the primary characteristic of American social consciousness after the New Left was universal, narrowly egotistical, narcissistic hedonism. It is worth adding that a similar claim—that "nihilistic modernism, irresponsible hedonism, and outrageous extremism are at the center of daily life"— can be found in the writing of the prominent neoconservative Daniel Bell, in the book *The Winding Passage* (1980).

"I don't mean to say that we live in the worst of times, but I have the impression that everything's falling apart around us." This sentence, from Bellow's *Mr. Sammler's Planet*, became a sort of pitch pipe to which a certain part of American prose was tuned for more than a decade. The general tone of books by the gifted writers Mary Gordon and Ann Beattie is set by the spiritual exhaustion of their characters, who, having passed through the enthusiasm of the "leftist revolt," feel uncomfortable with the aimless years that followed. The existence of ordinary Americans belonging to the comparatively well-off section of society is presented as appalling and absurd, wholly given to primitive impulses of acquisition and consumption. When Beattie's eloquently titled *Falling in Place* (1980) was published, critics in the United States asserted that this novel could have the same significance for today's America that J. D. Salinger's *Catcher in the Rye* had in its time: It would become a manifesto for a whole genera-tion. If Salinger stood at the source of an emotional protest, however, the echoes of which long resounded in the United States, Beattie's novel reflected only a "marginal," far-from-typical mood already of the past.

To cheerless defeatism and irresponsible self-admiration, the realist lit-erature of the 1980s was able to juxtapose a sober understanding of its time, shrouded in aesthetic form, which in no way reduces to the flat "sense" of the conservatives' writings. Of course, the level of ideological and spiritual maturity varies, attaining only in a few instances that corre-spondence with true life that is the invariable mark of high artistic work.

The most unambiguous challenge to all shades of conservative thought was presented by the problem of war and peace—the front line of the ideological battle of our time. Ronald Reagan's militaristic foreign-policy declarations in the early years of his term, and particularly his campaign against Nicaragua, received virtually unanimous disapproval from the literary community. Robert Stone's novel *A Flag for Sunrise* and Joan Didion's documentary book *Salvador* (1983), were largely devoted to a discussion of US policy in Latin America. Drawing a parallel between US involvement in the Vietnam War and American interference in the internal affairs of its neighbors to the south, Stone's story points to the conclusion that, of all the characters in the book, the most worthy of the reader's sympathy are the Latin American revolutionaries.

Awareness of the threat of nuclear self-destruction also united many writers of democratic convictions. This concern had nothing in common with the intentional alarmism of such veterans of the tendentious "politi-cal novel" as Allen Drury and John Hackett, who, even in the 1980s, continued to provide the book market with new versions of the "atomic utopia." The main character in Bernard Malamud's humanistic novel-parable, *God's Grace* (1983), along with God and talking animals, is a modern-day Noah by the name of Calvin Cohn, who has managed to survive a thermonuclear disaster. The same theme arises simultaneously in Kurt Vonnegut's *Deadeye Dick* (1982), while in *Galapagos* (1985), the sati-rist-fantasist places the action a million years in the future, when human-kind, presumably, is only just beginning to regain its strength after the nuclear war at the end of the 20th century.

An even more direct response, with biting topical content, is Joyce Carol Oates' satirical novel *Angel of Light* (1981), which touches, perhaps too fleetingly, on many important aspects of American domestic conditions. Oates cites (not without foundation) real instances of interference in the administrative and legislative mechanism of the country by such industrial giants as Lockheed, Kennicott, and Anaconda. Along with the leaders of these companies, in the background pass other "ordinary criminals," including extremely influential figures from governmental circles.

Unfortunately, the topical bite of *Angel of Light* turned out to be an isolated phenomenon in Oates' recent work. In *Mysteries of Winterthurn* (1984), *Solstice* (1985), and *Marya* (1987), she again and again returns to that mix of pseudoromantic Gothic and open affectedness that has predominated in her fiction for a long time. But the example outlined in *Angel of Light*—of active resistance to negative aspects of American life—received support in the works of other writers; particularly worthy of note is John Cheever's *Oh What a Paradise It Seems* (1982), which virtually became its creative legacy. The local—and, it would seem, especially "ecological"— conflict depicted in this work gives its writer the opportunity to move to wider sociophilosophical generalization. What is a loyal person with a civic conscience to do if an injustice takes place before his eyes that will bring detriment not only to him, but to a whole group of his fellow citizens? Cheever endows his hero, the elderly gentleman, Lemuel Sears, with a precious and, in the present day, especially necessary trait: an efficacious interest in everything he comes across in life. Sears works for a computer company and can boast of many foreign business trips. He often crosses the ocean to visit various countries in Western and Eastern Europe. However, the journey that most attracts him is the two-hour trip from New York to the town of Janice, on the outskirts of which is a large pond named for its former owner, Beasley. In a good winter, one can ice skate there to one's heart's content, and educated people with an artistic bent can imagine themselves a figure come to life out of a painting by Brueghel or some other Dutch painter. Imagine Sears' indignation when he learns one fine day that the local authorities, bribed by brazen businessmen, have doomed the beautiful, peaceful spot to become a stinking dump.

The struggle to clean Beasley's Pond grows, for Cheever, into the struggle for the soul of America, and the stakes in this game are high. At the end of the book, Sears is victorious, though in an unexpected way. The battle to save nature is won not by an enlightened liberal appealing to public opinion but by a simple housewife, who threatens in an anonymous letter to poison all the food in the supermarkets if the pond is not left alone. The threat is taken seriously, and the trust exploiting the seemingly bottomless dump fails. Then engineering enters the scene. The water is enriched with oxygen, and within a year it is fit for drinking. The next winter, Beasley's Pond again becomes a great plain of ice, gladdening the hearts of skaters and hockey lovers.

The narrative's ironic denouement does honor to the hero's humanistic feelings; but, at the same time, it emphasizes the obvious vulnerability of Sears' practical struggles, which never stretch beyond the limits of the credo of a bourgeois liberal. Those in the United States at the end of the 1970s and the beginning of the 1980s, who gradually became less convinced by traditional liberalism, associated in the political sphere with the Democratic party, were more and more frequently subjects of artistic analysis by American writers. Joseph Heller's novel *Good as Gold* (1979) is a satire on the inconsistency of government policy under Jimmy Carter. With no less wit, criticism of various shades of liberalism found literary expression in examination of such important spheres of ideological conflict as the present condition of the racial problem.

"He was never petty or grasping, and his political sympathies were distinguished by reason and humaneness." That is how Valerian Street, one of the central characters in black writer Toni Morrison's *Tar Baby* is described. Recently the owner of a major industrial concern and the possessor of a considerable fortune, Street decides upon retirement to search for solitude, in order to savor fully the pleasure of uninterrupted leisure. A gentleman and a liberal, he simply cannot allow himself to throw out an uninvited guest who appears one day at his villa. The dark-skinned "man from nowhere" (named William Green but preferring the nickname "Son") not only remains with Street for an indeterminate time but arouses the genuine interest of his new acquaintances.

To the residents of the estate, Son seems as much an oddity as a being from another planet. "He was a man, but only in the anthropological sense, not the social," writes Morrison of her hero, comparing him to Tar Baby of *The Tales of Uncle Remus* by Joel Harris.

Son's arrival in the Streets' home can only lead to conflict, exposing the sharp line which, as before, divides many Americans on the question of race. The line of demarcation lies between servant-blacks, whom Son represents, and white masters, whose patience and indulgence prove finite. Street's equability turns out to have its limits. At the first hard word spoken by Son, who has been in his good graces, his recent favorite becomes his mortal enemy. Such is the inglorious result of the experiment in erasing racial and social contradictions undertaken by "liberal America" under idealized, nearly laboratory conditions.

While making an ironic statement about white liberals, the black writer is, at the same time, fully conscious of the internal weakness of the modern offshoots of the leftist counterculture, which, with its tawdry splendor and false revolutionary spirit, was at one time able to attract no few enthusiastic admirers. At the beginning of the 1980s, both traditional liberalism and anarchist, leftist radicalism went through an especially difficult period. Immediately after Reagan's election victory, the *Partisan Review* grieved: "The present moment looks . . . exceptionally unpromising for any initiative from the left." A few years later, authoritative Soviet researchers stressed that "in recent years liberalism [in the United States] has entered a time of serious ideological and organizational hardships."[4] It stands to reason that this shift did not escape the attention of the literary community, receiving interpretation in various genres of literary work.

Disappointment in the programmatic goals of the Democratic party colors *America in Search of Itself* (1982), by the veteran of liberal thought, Theodore White, the concluding volume of White's brilliant series depicting American presidential campaigns. According to general opinion, the "epitaph of the leftist movement in the US" is *A Margin of Hope* (1982), the "intellectual autobiography" of Irving Howe, editor of the journal *Dissent*. Howe's longtime comrade in the "old left," William Phillips, announced at about the same time in *Partisan Review* (of which he was editor), that "neither I nor Irving Howe . . . were scared to become neo-conservatives . . . [we] have been critical of neo-conservatism on political and cultural grounds, though we grant that they are right in some matters."[5]

At times, the sense of a crisis of liberal ideas spontaneously penetrates the fabric of artistic work, not only becoming one of a book's component ideological concepts, but dominating the author's position. In E. L. Doctorow's *Loon Lake* (1980), one can trace evident connections to the "proletarian literature" of the 1930s. Indeed, the very setting of the book coincides with the "red decade." At its conclusion, however, Joe, the hero and a "voluntary wanderer," is overcome by a sense of confusion, shown through an abundance of deliberately mythologized, "strangified" symbolic choices. Doctorow's next book, *Lives of the Poets* (1985), confirms the movement of the author's thinking toward acceptance of an apolitical "oscillating" existence. In its pictures of New York's bohemian life, there is not that deadening triviality one finds on the pages of works by Beattie and Gordon. Still, in essence, the observations of the renowned master and the young writers meld into one plane.

"We hear endless calls for, and occasional sightings of, a new liberalism . . . but, so far at least, the content of the new liberalism remains obscure. Much of it comes down to a Democratic version of the old Republican theme of 'me-tooism'. . . . Today the Democrats promise they will do the same as Reagan, only more humanely."[6] In such expressions, unflattering yet not devoid of truth, the neoconservative press describes the pretensions of those bourgeois ideologists who proclaim themselves neoliberals. A great deal has been written in the United States about neoliberalism and its ideological leaders and about the contradictory nature of its socioeconomic postulates—especially during the 1984 presidential campaign, when Senator Gary Hart attempted to compete for leadership of the Democratic party with Walter Mondale, considered an adherent of more traditional liberalism. However, the efforts of representatives of the party to draw to their side the majority of American voters ended in their painful defeat in the 1984 presidential election. It so happened that this decline in liberal stocks, so to speak, was recorded almost simultaneously on the dial of a sensitive literary barometer.

The general characteristics of the politics of the left wing of the Democratic party—represented by such figures as George McGovern, Edward Kennedy, and Gary Hart—are described by Joan Didion in her novel *Democracy* (1984). The love story in the foreground of the work does not conceal—rather, it accentuates—the strong underlying ideological question of the novel, which leads to rather unexpected conclusions. The career of Harry Victor, one of the book's central characters, embraces important landmarks in recent American history, including antiracist protest marches, strikes by farm workers, and clashes with police on city streets. By showing support to oppositional positions, Victor gains a fair amount of political capital; but his successes in the public sphere are devalued, in his eyes, by the lack of mutual understanding within his family. The first clouds appeared on his marital horizon long ago; since then, more and more have arisen, many in connection with his wife Inez's increasing affection for her longtime platonic admirer, Jack Lovett.

Although the author never speaks directly on this point, we may assume, without great risk of being mistaken, that Lovett is one of those who, thanks to Graham Greene, had thirty years earlier begun to be referred to as a "quiet American." Lovett works for one of the "special services" created to carry out special tasks. Reviewers of Didion's book in US journals have plainly called Lovett a CIA agent. What is most interesting, however, is that a man with such an occupation, involved in counterespionage, whose job it is to protect and strengthen the national interests of the United States in Southeast Asia and the Pacific Basin, not only gradually moves to the foreground of the novel, but enjoys the growing favor of both the novel's heroine and the author herself.

Lovett's acquaintance with the Victor family lasts no less than twenty years, by the end of which the contrast between husband and admirer has become especially vivid. On one side are the empty words of the liberal, latching onto any opportunity to remain in the public eye and, to his own wife's displeasure, accommodating himself unscrupulously to circumstances. On the other is the quiet assurance of a man of action, who, time after time, finds the opportunity to prove his devotion to Inez. Jack Lovett is, first of all, a professional, an organizer, both analytical and practical, although the details of his many missions are not set forth in the novel. He is also the hero-lover who, for long years, yearns for the fair lady of his dreams and who wins her full favor when he returns to Inez her eighteen-year-old daughter, thought to have disappeared forever.

The concluding chapters of the novel, which tell of Lovett's sudden death, are deeply emotional. At that point, the book loses the tone of intellectual irony typical of Didion's style. Lovett dies in Inez's arms, his life's goal achieved. He is finally together with his beloved, and there is no longer a need for him to make sacrifices, to run back and forth over thousand-mile distances, to argue with emptyheaded word-mongers, all the while methodically carrying on his own work. Inez buries Lovett in the military cemetery in Honolulu, in the shade of the jacaranda, adding yet another touching moment to the story of male constancy which does not remain unrewarded.

It must be reiterated: Jack Lovett is not merely a modern "knight without fear or reproach," but the personification of a certain policy which, by the mid-1980s, enjoyed much more support in the United States than it had previously. It cannot be said that responsibly thinking American writers seriously yielded to the now-popular "new patriotism" in its particular semiofficial interpretation dictated by the neoconservatives. Nonetheless, the contents of Didion's novel, emphatically starting with its title, give witness to an accumulating dissatisfaction, a wearing-thin of customary ideological stereotypes. The choice—to be a starry-eyed impotent liberal, or a faithful "new" conservative who fully supports the Washington administration—is to many today unsatisfactory; therefore, it is not surprising that there arose on the American literary landscape analysts of contemporary social and spiritual conditions to whom, for lack of a more precise definition, we may refer as "alternativists."

As a strengthening, ideological tendency, alternativism in the United States during the 1980s was characteristic, above all, of the educated, "mature" layers of society. A description of this movement centers, first of all, on cultural-ideological and moral-ethical ideas. Summarizing everything the alternativists stand for and against, one may conclude that their views are a sort of amalgam of elements drawn both from the New Left and from those whom, at the beginning of the 1970s, the well-known sociologist Robert Heilbroner designated "radical conservatives," all of which categorically break with primitive political retrogression:

> It will be a matter of returning to the problems of primordial human essence, [of] human nature, of overcoming misguidedness in favor of peace and progress . . . the goal of our questions and doubts is to improve the human condition, to renew and revive eternal humanistic ideals.[7]

Like the New Left, the alternativists speak out against self-interested consumerism, the capitalist orientation toward maximum "self-financing" profit and the struggle to win life's battle at any cost. Just like the critics of primitive egalitarianism, alternativists condemn bureaucratic dependence, placing a high value on labor, the principle of competition, and economic initiative. Not without foundation, the alternativists see in them the basis for the well-being of any society. If faithful conservatives openly make use of moral questions for especially opportunistic goals, to the alternativists, the idea of converting humanistic values into the small change of commonplace political intrigue is organically alien. The radical approach of breaking with cheap demagoguery is marked, in particular, by the idea that familiar everyday ideas—family, work, personal relations—are taken in broad perspective as if overflowing into the more extended transcendental categories of spirituality, self-realization, and creation.

If one inspects the concepts of alternativism along hard logical lines, it is easy not only to reveal a long string of contradictions, but to place in doubt the overall justifiability of alternativism. Alternativists do not simply pass over in silence, or fail to answer convincingly, many pressing socioeconomic questions in the United States. The very nature of their views could be called eclectic, naively romantic, and, finally, utopian. As we know, however, not everything born of swift-flowing reality is immediately graced with adequate theoretical generalization. Weighty confirmation that such views exist in the United States—that, in the final account, they grow out of the long traditions of American democracy, that they have lately managed to penetrate deep into the national spirit— is provided by a long stream of extraordinary literary works. At the source of this current stands John Gardner's *October Light*, published in 1976.

The scope of the author's design, which strives to characterize the leading tendencies in American spirituality, is reflected even in the book's composition. It could be said that *October Light* is not one but two novels under a single cover. The main, "framing" narrative depicts the traditional farming lifestyle, with its roots deep in America's past. Parallel to this, Gardner places another, "inserted" story depicting a relatively recent America, an America of heartrending screams and narcotic euphorias, a country hurtling swiftly toward an unknown goal, in its frenzy, burning the spiritual legacy bequeathed to it by its founders.

The ideological-aesthetic plan of *October Light* centers on a problem that invariably attracts writers with a realistic bent. The subject is the struggle between, on one hand, tendentious and organic perceptions of life, the conflict between all that is contrived and in decline and, on the other, what is natural and healthy. Constantly juxtaposing the two planes, alternating scenes of unhurried farm existence with grotesquely exaggerated passions and exploits, the author creates two inherently opposed philosophical-ethical models of reality. To the chaotic, convulsive universe that arises from the pages of the "trashy book," Gardner contrasts the solid forms of human community and moral foundations which resist the degenerative influence of swaggering "outlaws."

Although Gardner chooses in favor of firm and sensible ideas, relying on the good traditions of working America, he fully understands the complexity of their consistent application to existing reality. Unlike some of his earlier books, *October Light* is free of conventional pastoral tones. The threat coming from the hedonistic counterculture, and the reckless revolutionary spirit behind it, is, finally, not all that great. Far more dangerous to the American future are the conflicts from within. The quarrel in the farmer's home between the brother and the sister is an expression of the divergences between the strictly conservative approach and the consistently democratic one, between ancient male supremism and the struggle, characteristic of the 1970s and 80s, for women's rights. In the general philosophical scheme, it is a rift between the doctrinaire attitude, inflexible and laying claim to absolute truth, and the wide humanistic concept of harmonious interaction between the individual and society.

At the beginning, the theoretical interpretation of the shoots of a new belief system (in this case, alternativism) tends to be vague. It is another matter when these currents take form in the symbolic substance of an artistic work, embodying life in generalized, aestheticized forms. A telling example of constant attention to the sociopsychological evolution of the United States is the work of John Updike. Updike's novel, *Rabbit Is Rich* (1982), is undoubtedly a major work of American literature of the 1980s. Once again, the author brings out onto the literary stage the central character of his earlier novels, *Rabbit, Run* (1960) and *Rabbit Redux* (1971). In the image of our contemporary Harry Angstrom, nicknamed Rabbit, Updike attempts to embody the characteristic traits of that person who is often (and not entirely appropriately) referred to in everyday usage as the "simple American," as the "man on the street." More precisely, the object of the author's description—*working America*, that social sphere which, sometimes combining in a surprising way good sense and resistance to change, its narrow views and vital energy—in many ways determines the social consciousness and practical development of the American nation.

Middle America, the description of which Updike has remained faithful to throughout his literary career, cannot be called taciturn. Gathering around the dinner table at somebody's home or settled on a day off by the side of the swimming pool at the city club, Rabbit's friends and acquaintances heatedly discuss the latest news. Their political views reflect convictions and prejudices in keeping with their social stratum. But, along with the character's recognized limitations, this American author tries to underline the rightness of his vital instinct. This is what is usually known as goodwill or, in more elevated and abstract terms, humanism, although the latter word is difficult to find in Harry Angstrom's vocabulary. Updike's hero has read few books; nor has he acquired the habit of engaging in penetrating analysis. Instead, Harry simply "loves"—he loves nature, although he barely knows the name of a single tree or plant. He loves people, people like himself: men of few words, with prominent bellies and suntanned heads. As a working man, Harry values money. He rises every morning at 6:00 to begin the twelve-hour workday of a small-business owner; knowing nothing of political economy, he is forced to live under the Damoclean sword of market unpredictability.

Less one-sided is the psychological portrait of Rabbit's son, Nelson, a college dropout with special meaning for the understanding of certain segments of a "young America" trying to find a place for themselves as they enter the 1980s. "Listen, Nelson," Harry says, "maybe I didn't always do the right thing in my life, it's very possible. But I didn't fall into the very worst sin. I didn't fold my wings and start to prepare for death . . . to give in is against nature: whatever happens you mustn't let life die in you." In this uncharacteristically long speech, Rabbit/Angstrom, for the first time in the reader's acquaintance with him, boldly sets forth his general views. And Nelson does not remain indifferent to this proclamation, which rests on a convincing, concrete example. Along with his father, he rejects high-flown slogans and empty words, both in their pseudointellectual guise and in their deliberately folksy form. Both men, enjoying the clear though not insistent support of the author, stand for a strengthening of those foundations that have proved reliable among the breaking waves of postwar history. Among these buttresses are the family, modernized in light of the United States' famous "moral revolution," but not having lost its significance; persistent and able work, as opposed to empty experiments and unabashed dependence; and, finally, in keeping with the ideal of material abundance and spiritual generosity, the concept of the uninhibited development of the individual, as if borrowed from the visionaries of the past and only at the end of the 20th century receiving significant chance of embodiment.

The determining ethical message of the novels of Gardner and Updike—the demand for greater responsibility and a serious attitude toward civic obligations in the approaching "age of decreasing possibilities"— received the support of an entire cohort of writers of a younger generation. Of those who have already gained wide recognition, three have distinguished themselves: John Irving, Anne Tyler, and Alice Walker. All of these writers had already published, but by the beginning of the 1980s, the work of each showed symptomatic changes.

After winning acclaim for his novel *The World According to Garp* (1978), Irving, in his next book, did not avoid naturalistic, or even Freudian, layering. The story of the Berry family's struggle to maintain a hotel, first in the United States and then, for seven more years, in the Austrian capital, abounds in sometimes humorous, sometimes dramatic, intentionally exaggerated situations. As the author stresses, however, his *Hotel New Hampshire* (1981) is less a chronicle than a realistic parable whose characters are at once real and symbolic. Only a fairy tale, says Irving, is capable of dealing with all of life's horror and filth; we must admit that there is more than enough of this "filth"—shocking, most candid, worldly details—in the novel. At the same time, unlike writers of an apocalyptic or, on the other hand, apologetic bent, Irving sees strengths capable of opposing these centrifugal tendencies and defending healthier norms of human society. "The way the world is cannot be grounds for complete cynicism or infantile despair." These words, spoken by one of the book's characters, summarize an important moral idea, one that quickly gained citizenship rights in the literature of the United States.

Next to Irving's novel can be placed several works by Tyler (*Dinner at the Homesick Restaurant*, 1982; *The Accidental Tourist*, 1986) and Alice Walker (*The Color Purple*, 1982). It is significant that the inherent tendency of these works toward "collecting pebbles," as well as their calls for a unification of humanistic aspirations, which invariably have informed high moral thought, are echoed by a number of talented young writers. "I think this generation of novelists is technically far superior to the generation before it," wrote John Gardner not long before his death. "The question that remains is whether that technique is accompanied by a vision—a vision that will endure."[8] Many of those to whom these words referred followed in the footsteps of the author of *October Light*. Among them, along with those just mentioned, we can single out Jay McInerney (*Bright Lights, Big City*, 1984), Jayne Anne Phillips (*Machine Dreams*, 1984), and, above all, Bobbie Ann Mason (*In Country*, 1985) and Mary Morris (*Crossroads*, 1983). Realistic social criticism does not allow these writers of the "post-Vietnam generation" to ignore the influence of those who remain in the power of blind, class self-interest, ignorance, and ingrained prejudices; at the same time, at the center of their works' artistic-emotional world is found, by rights, a deep, sincere humaneness.

The title of Mason's novel is ambiguous. A literal interpretation, "in the country," suggests, above all, "deep in the heart of the United States," which generally is well founded, as the action of the book rarely leaves the small Kentucky town of Hopewell, typical in many ways of "one storey America." But in the context of the narrative, we find indications of another, also fully justifiable, interpretation. "In Country," thus unspecified, is a term often used by Vietnam veterans to refer to that place where they were cast in the 1960s and 70s by the pride of official Washington. The war in Vietnam, and its ruinous results for various generations of today's Americans, is the central theme of this young author's first major work.

The novel's heroine, Samantha Hughes, is all of seventeen years old, and her interests are in many ways those of her peers. She has a boyfriend by the name of Lonnie; in accordance with the custom of our time, their relations have gone fairly far. Samantha dreams of having her own car so she can go see Florida's Disneyworld and perhaps remain there to work. In the fall there will be an election, and the future will somehow be decided; but meanwhile, in these summer months of 1984, Samantha, like millions of her fellow citizens, prefers to spend nearly all her free time in front of the television in the company of "Uncle Emmet," an inveterate bachelor and stay-at-home.

The emphasized closeness of this not entirely usual, even somehow absurd, pair is reminiscent of the vivid description, common in American 20th-century literature, of human "grotesques," drawn in stressed opposition to their surroundings. Traces of that tradition are noticeable in the novel; but, unlike the somewhat abstract-existentialist treatment of the phenomenon of alienation and superfluousness in the works of Carson McCullers or Truman Capote, the reasons for the situation are distinctly revealed by Mason. What mainly draws Samantha close to her dead father's brother is the thought of the war in the jungles of Indochina and the still unhealed wounds it inflicted.

Although nearly ten years have passed since the infamous American evacuation of Vietnam, Emmet's health and that of other demobilized soldiers has not returned to normal. Yet mass America has hurried to close its eyes to what occurred; given the economic upswing and the "new patriotism" of the 1980s, few venture to stir up the past. Samantha is of a different sort. Her ability for deeper reflection and her conviction that "the present flows out of the past" bring a sharp dissonance to the measured and, on the whole, tranquil life of her family.

Lack of writing experience and the sharply didactic quality of the book's central thesis prevent the author from creating a full, psychologically convincing portrait of her heroine. The fixated way in which Samantha again and again returns to thoughts of Vietnam suggests something nearly maniacal. She interrogates Emmet, becomes close to others like him (also veterans who have not fully recovered), and, most of all, never misses a single episode of the television series M*A*S*H. "What we and Uncle Emmet watch on TV is completely made up," Lonnie tries to reason with her. "It's not realistic, it's exaggerated. And everything's different now, we live a completely different life." Her mother, her best friend, neighbors, and acquaintances, including some who served in Vietnam, try to convince Samantha of the same thing; but the heroine's moral maximalism remains deaf to common sense, which she finds too banal.

At the same time, it is precisely this approach that predominates in the American "country." Mason's novel contains several vignettes reflecting the reigning spirit of the times. The majority of those who participated in the war have organically entered everyday life, with all its cares and amusements. Over the years much has changed in America: "Plastic money" has appeared, as well as VCRs and video games; and many, especially among the young, are euphorically mastering these new mindless pastimes. Nonetheless, as the writer asserts, despite yet another upsurge of consumerism, a serious, troubled note still sounds among the many voices of the public mood.

Independently, Mary Morris reaches similar conclusions in the novel *Crossroads*. Her characters are not Kentucky provincials but people who seem to have been picked at random from the motley crowd filling the streets of New York, San Francisco, and other large American cities. They are modern both in their behavior and in their occupations, which, not long ago, would probably not have found corresponding spheres of application. The novel abounds in signs of psychological reality characteristic of the "new" America, but which do not lie on the surface and are therefore inaccessible to the outsider's eye, becoming fully visible only upon continued attentive observation. These are the excessive readiness for ever new human contact, for the easy relations so captivating at first, but, as a rule, replaced by complete indifference upon a second meeting. They are the almost reflex, obligatory laughter in conversation, which has nearly everywhere supplanted a much more meaningful, though also "traditional," American tendency to smile. Behind these external signs is concealed something larger and more alarming, showing itself in a most important peculiarity of the spiritual climate. What concerns the writer can be called the striking *disconnectedness* of American society, felt especially keenly in the sphere of personal, intimate relations.

The development of the love relationship of the central couple, Deborah and Sean, is like the well-known fable of the fox and the crane, who just couldn't manage to work things out between them. Morris attributes the layer of psychological obstacles interfering with a fast, happy denouement to the heroine's inner mentality; but, at the same time, what is generally meant by the "spirit of the times" stamps the actions of the characters and the movement of the plot. Love in contemporary Manhattan is no more than one element in a featureless routine, introduced alongside other components in a neatly marked scheme. The general impression is that Deborah and Sean become lovers—if not under compulsion, then purely out of boredom. The very feeling that brings them together—and, from time to time, to bed—can hardly be called love unless, of course, the meaning of the word is amended to fit the modern, exclusively Americanized, "instrumental" variation.

All the same, Deborah, with her fairly obstinate personality and her occasional womanly inconsistency, seeks a more integral, meaningful life. This constant, though not necessarily clearly conscious, search for "spiritual firmness" forms the work's central ideological axis. Morris's novel does not contain all that many crossroads, in the sense of the strict necessity of choice between mutually exclusive alternatives; the writer simply takes her heroine from one everyday situation to another, telling the story of her relations, over the course of about a year and a half, with about ten people, of whom Sean, Deborah's parents, her brother Zap, and two or three friends are singled out. Always introspective, trying to draw a moral lesson from her personal experience, Deborah constructs from scratch a prototype of moral guiding principles, the significance of which, we must assume, goes beyond separate concrete events.

Working in New York's Center for Urban Advancement, Deborah is driven by the desire to transform the wretched life of the residents of the South Bronx and other regions of the huge metropolis. The slums must be eliminated; in their place, through the efforts of architects, urban planners, and traffic specialists, new regions will spring up, where people will be able to live freely and work productively. Such dreams have little room in which to grow in this world; but gradually, without excessive delay, they become tangible, and the sense of participation in this movement, not swift but steady, helps the heroine to heal the wounds of her heart.

"We were born too late. It was a lot more fun in the '60s," Samantha

Hughes sighs, not just once but twice; it is hard, however, for the reader of Mason's book to agree with this overly pessimistic evaluation. The most important points in the work, the very fact of its appearance in the world, suggest that young America has not turned its back on the troubling pages of its recent past. After suffering once again from the "childhood illness of leftism," democratic forces have not allowed the country to swerve too far to the Right. They have not given themselves up to fruitless self-flagellation; they have not come under the spell of the tempting truths of neoconservatism; they have unhurriedly, in a focused way, undertaken sober analysis, separating unfounded but superficially attractive fantasy from desirable and, in principle, attainable priorities.

The ending of Morris's novel is in line with these aspirations. Her heroine, together with a close friend, finds hope of continuing her much-loved, useful work. Accentuating the positive role of the family—social activism, cooperation, and the spiritual legacy of the classics—the writers of the 1980s both join their voices to what has been said on this matter by humanist artists of the recent past and add something new. This connection can be called as much typological as it can genetic. In other words, the works discussed in the concluding pages of this essay are joined to a solid tradition and are, at the same time, called forth by fully objective sociocultural circumstances.

Humanistic spirituality, not superficially imposed but arising from a study of reality, is the moving force behind the most fruitful and viable part of American literature. In recent years, the consistency of this ideological-aesthetic position has not been shaken by the irascible dogmatism of the ultraright, the unfounded illusions of liberals, or the "new synthesis" of the neoconservatives. The idea, consonant with so much in the democratic tradition, of preserving respect for "undying values," of drawing from both past and present experience necessary lessons for moral and, presumably, political guidance, is receiving, it appears, wider and wider public support. In the course of prolonged ideological battles (far from concluded), this call has seized the minds of many American writers. As far as one can judge, it opens out onto the rapids of their ideological quests.

ALEKSEI ZVEREV

The Prose of the 1980s

Three New Names

The "criticism boom" has pretty much passed by contemporary prose, which remains, for the most part, the domain of newspaper reviews. Attempts to systematize and classify this literature are isolated. The matter is most often left at the interpretation of works by single writers or, more frequently, of single works.

This is not a new situation. It is easy to explain, above all, by the subject's lack of prestige. Contemporary prose did not enter the field of interest of academic criticism for a long time. In *The Literary History of the United States*, for instance, chapters on the most recent literature appeared only in the fourth edition and, on the whole, are merely compilations.

Today, the situation is slowly changing for the better. Specific difficulties immediately arise, however. How, for instance, are we to define the very concept of "contemporary literature"? Should it include only works of the most recent years or, say, the literature of the last two or three decades, or perhaps everything written after the Second World War? What criteria must define the new period?

The question is not as rhetorical as it may seem to be. Strictly speaking, criteria allowing us to assign the work of one or another writer to contemporary literature do not exist. Instead, we have the division of literature by decades—the literature of the 60s, the 70s, the 80s. This is very much a matter of convention, however, for the boundaries of literary epochs are marked by entirely different lines than are those of the calendar.

From this point of view, is it possible to speak of the literature of the 1980s as literature of an independent period? In all probability, no. The last decade has observed neither an appreciable change in basic literary trends nor genre forms that are truly new, nor innovative artistic ideas, to herald a new literature. At first, the decade seems pretty colorless. A sense of a lull, even of a certain creative impasse, is prevalent in the few reviews devoted to literary life of this time. Upon a second look, however, this impression is somewhat deceptive, as the 1980s had their indisputable artistic accomplishments. Given such a many-sided, dynamic literature as that of the United States, any discussion of a crisis or of creative stagnation will always have an abstract quality. Such generalizations are easily refuted by facts testifying to the opposite—to the intensity of a literary movement with all its attendant complexity.

The matter at hand is not a summing up of anything; it is not a general evaluation of the literature of the 1980s. Criticism has not yet sufficiently assimilated the literature. Not enough time has passed for the necessary distance to be attained. The point here is simply that which can be verified today: that future historians will find it extremely difficult to distinguish this decade as an independent period in the development of literature, if they are guided not merely by the calendar.

However, it does not follow from this that the 1980s in no way marked any new currents in literature, much less that they revealed no notable new names. Such currents and names did appear in this decade. Although it remains hard to say definitively that a new trend specific to the literature of the most recent years has appeared, apparently certain preconditions for this have come to be. This is what we will attempt to demonstrate, turning to the books of three literary newcomers of the 1980s.

Having won recognition with *Ransom* (1985) and *Bright Lights, Big City* (1986), Jay McInerney is now considered perhaps the most promising prose writer among his contemporaries—writers in their thirties. Constantly compared to Salinger and Kerouac, he too is perceived as the spokesman for the young generation. Echoes in McInerney's work of

Salinger and Kerouac are, indeed, easy to find—in his choice of characters, style, and tone. In essence, his main conflict is the same as that of his
two closest predecessors: the psychological and spiritual incompatibility
of the older and younger generations, which, though living side by side,
seem to speak different languages.

McInerney always narrates in the first person. He needs the spontaneity
of monologue, in which intonation tells more about the character than
words themselves. McInerney's prose is sprinkled with symbols that contain intimate meaning for the hero and his or her contemporaries. This is
more than the jargon of a certain milieu. Before us is a kind of code for
relating—in which every specific linguistic error takes on a particular
content and function—allowing the reader to feel the world in a certain
way. The resonance of McInerney's books is caused, above all, by the fact
that, in them, the young generation of the 1980s seems to have found its
own voice.

McInerney's characters are easily recognizable. The situations in which
they find themselves are taken nearly verbatim from the prose of the
Beatniks. His plots are loose; the ordinary is emphasized; a few days
seized from everyday life is trivial in its monotony. The stories boil down
to ordinary tales of betrayed illusions, disappointments, disorder, and
loneliness. Psychological introspection is altogether absent.

Events themselves are not important to McInerney, only their spiritual
consequences for his characters. Heroes are emphatically representational.
Remaining largely impersonal, they, for the most part, personify the generalized type of contemporary rebel; everything that happens to them is
easily predictable.

In McInerney's best novel, *Bright Lights, Big City*, such indistinguish-
ability of the hero/narrator against the background of his young milieu
creates a memorable artistic effect, as the hero himself is relatively unusual
for contemporary prose. Despite easily identifiable literary echoes—from
Salinger to Joseph Heller's *Something Happened*—the novel draws us in
by the authenticity with which it conveys the character's sense of being
lost in the surrounding world of clichéd ideas, extremely formal human
relations, and universal impersonality. Even with this book, however, it
was possible to predict the complications that would arise for McInerney
in the future. His orientation to long since mastered motifs and artistic
methods, and the very style of constant reminiscence, seem to suggest an
element of aesthetic reiteration, if not outright imitation.

In *Story of My Life* (1988), this derivativeness and too-easy recognizability (both of the characters and of the plot) result in the narrative, against the author's wishes, beginning to resemble nearly a parody of Salinger. McInerney tells of the fate of a New York City student, meant to illustrate the eternal similarity of conflicts between fathers and children. Alison, a rebel against the hypocrisy, indifference, and moral degradation that distinguish her parents, walks the familiar road of all such seekers of life's true values in the world of complete indifference to all but immediate pleasure. Rebellion quickly grows into cynicism, serving as a convenient justification for the dissipation that becomes her lifestyle. Alison is convinced that the world consists of egotists, liars, and bad guys. Reality presents no other evidence.

From such experience beliefs are born which are shocking to those uninitiated in the ethics of the rebel. Here, the rebel takes the shape of the "postmodern girl," as the heroine is called by one of her lovers. Perhaps this term itself will become, thanks to McInerney's book, as popular as the concept of the Beatnik did because of Kerouac. An overly sober understanding of the true motives behind people's behavior, and a too-early indifference to everything—these traits define McInerney's characters' feelings about the world. On second look, their very cynicism is merely a misshapen form of self-protection in a world in which they feel their own superfluity acutely.

McInerney is able to convey such a mindset expressively and with talent worthy of his readers' attention. With each of his books, however, it becomes more evident that he has already exhausted the role of chronicler of today's rebellions and the disappointments of the young generation. He needs a new creative stimulus if he is to avoid the self-repetition and stereotypes quickly taking root in his prose.

Jayne Anne Phillips' ascent was not as swift as McInerney's, but it can be said today with certainty that she *has* won recognition. This was brought about by two collections of her stories—*Black Tickets* (1979) and *Fast Lanes* (1987)—but also, above all, by *Machine Dreams* (1984), which Robert Stone has called "one of the most outstanding books of the decade." Reviews by Anne Tyler, Tillie Olsen, and Raymond Carver have been no less complimentary.

Machine Dreams is an entirely traditional novel. A family epic of sorts, it tells the history of a family from West Virginia, traced over forty-plus

years, from the end of the 1930s to the beginning of the 80s. The traditional nature of this novel is deceptive, however. Phillips' narrative is a
chain of episodes divided at times by decades. Immediate action is interrupted by recollection, documents, and letters arranged with no commentary by the author. The narrator varies. At times, the author takes on the
role, but more often, it is the heroes themselves who do the talking.
Altogether, we have the history of two generations: Mitch and Jean,
people of the 1930s, and their children, Danner and Billy, formed in the
spiritual and social climate of the 1960s. The typicality of conflicts, situations, and fates in such a construction does not at all resemble a formal
device. It contains within itself a clear idea: the ties between different
times, understood as the age-old repetition of human experience.

Reflection of the moods that marked the 1980s is everywhere discernible in Phillips' work, but above all in the intonation of the story—
intentionally impassive and resigned. In an interview given at the time of
the book's publication, Phillips said that today one doesn't see a trace of
resistance even when people fear for their lives. This passivity becomes a
leitmotif of the novel. Characters exist in the flow of time, mechanically
assimilating its ideas, values, tastes, and ethical prescriptions. Spiritual
numbness and the standardization of the individual become a truly inescapable drama. *Machine Dreams* is a book about lack of will, about being
locked into a system of banal ideas, about the inability for genuine moral
independence.

The emphasized triteness of the story Phillips tells contrasts sharply
with its inner dramatic tension, with the constant theme of the fate that
never happened. The mechanical rhythms of reality enslave Phillips' heroes, who find themselves facing the fact of their spiritual bankruptcy, as
well as the fact that they cannot understand how they arrived at such a
condition.

The machine dreams that give the novel its title are not only a metaphor
for such an existence, but another leitmotif of the story, this time a poetic
one. Phillips, in fact, has many dreams; all of them bring a feeling of some
disaster that has occurred almost unnoticed. The living of life has been
replaced by mechanical ritual, which gradually deadens the will to self-
actualization. Slow, humdrum, day-to-day existence is the lot of these
spiritually broken people.

This "dreary story"—to borrow the phrase from Chekhov—happens
to the older generation of Phillips' heroes and repeats with the younger,

only even more cruelly, as Billy will die in Vietnam. Billy's letters from the army are a direct echo of his father's letters from the military camps and fronts of World War II, from which the father returned irreparably traumatized by the cruelty he had witnessed. The idea of a closed circle, important to the novel's composition, is pointed out with utmost clarity by the echo.

Shaken by what has happened to her brother, Danner loses faith in all values. Although almost nothing tied her to Billy, she dissipates herself in casual liaisons with other veterans as she tries artificially to awaken in herself a feeling of closeness to the dead. She is oppressed by the feeling, familiar to everyone in the family described by Phillips, of the senselessness of mechanical, everyday life. The motif of spiritual vacuum is so persistent for Phillips that it drowns out everything else.

Like several other books of this period, Phillips' novel shows how much the state of mind in the 1980s was determined by the "Vietnam syndrome." This is one of the most frequent themes in recent prose by young Americans. However, what is essential is not in itself the presence of the Vietnam experience in the spiritual atmosphere of the decade (and, in any case, not its direct and evident echoes), but rather that view of daily life formed under the unquestionable influence of the still-remembered disaster that concluded that war. Phillips' idea of existence by inertia as the main feature of present social psychology is organic to the prose that took root in the 1980s. Perhaps it is in just such a perception of everyday life that the trauma of consciousness that is the direct, long-term result of the Vietnam War can be recognized most distinctly.

This impression is strengthened upon acquaintance with the books of Bobbie Ann Mason, probably the most striking writer of the new generation. Mason has come to be discussed seriously only in recent years, although *Shiloh* (1982), a collection of her stories, was noted earlier by critics. Nonetheless, she owes her recognition to books that appeared toward the end of the last decade. These are the novel *In Country* (1985), the short work *Spence and Lila* (1988), and the collection, *Love Life* (1989).

Mason quickly found her own theme and style—even her own geography. The small towns and farms of Kentucky, where the action always occurs, become a special artistic reality under Mason's pen. It is recognizable as the world of the country: monotonous, boring, ordinary. At the same time, this recognizability does not obscure the peculiar foreshorten-ing with which daily life is shown on Mason's pages.

Critics who have written about Mason confidently assign her to mini-malism—a movement that strives to illustrate psychological monotony and the extreme standardization of life by means of an intentionally mea-ger palette, sketchiness of psychological portraits, and abundance of clichés in the language of the narrative. Despite their apparent per-suasiveness, such analogies are, nonetheless, fairly superficial. Mason's prose is, indeed, distinguished by a poverty of illustrative methods, and often by the emphasized, even defiant banality of situations, weak emo-tional tension, and abundance of everything conventional and trite, not only in the life she re-creates, but in the consciousnesses of her characters, as well. Their lives bring nothing extraordinary; the stamp of anemia lies on their entire spiritual existence. The passive moods so typical of mini-malists, however, are not at all characteristic of Mason's books. For her—unlike, for example, Mary Gordon—reality gives evidence not only of petrification but of deadness, too. The problem of moral choice in Ma-son's stories is not at all removed by today's social order of things. Behind the apparent lack of events in her books, a longing shows through for genuine freedom of spiritual self-definition. Her characters strive for this, even though they are mostly convinced of their own helplessness before fate.

A lyrical intonation entirely alien to the style of minimalism appears natural in Mason's work, as she doesn't consider her characters worthy of indifferent description alone. Behind coarseness and insensitivity, some-thing else is revealed: a search for their own place in the chain of their spiritual inheritance, and a stable sense of their roots, which allows them to stand their ground at life's dramatic moments.

Mason is interested in a type of character who is too absorbed in worldly problems to ponder the meaning of his or her existence on earth. Almost all her characters experience a moment when the irretrievability of losses suffered in the eternal battle with unyielding, clinging dullness is revealed to them with great clarity. This is always the culminating mo-ment in the conflicts on which Mason's narrative is focused.

Sociological interpretation of such conflicts is barely sufficient. In this case, the very nature of the narrative refutes all the usual blueprints. Not only paragraphs but sentences are often unconnected. An invisible dis-tance is preserved between them; they seem to run off into emptiness, leading to no logical development. Or they might repeat in a way that appears unexpected but that creates the necessary rhythm which reflects not only the reality of the surrounding world, full of such disconnectedness and emptinesses, but, above all, the reality of the characters' perception of the world. For Mason, they are all to some degree victims of conformity, which has deeply penetrated even the intimate spheres of human existence and deprived the individual of the ability to take things in, to make sense of phenomena lying outside the limits of stereotype. These phenomena are either deformed—to fit a prepared image which obscures reality, simplifying and formalizing its connections—or which simply pass by the person, who is unable to put them into his or her conceptual store.

It is difficult for such a character to perceive fully the atypical and nonstandard. Essentially, reality exists for this character only to the extent that he or she can recognize it. The gaps and breaks in perception that Mason's style expresses become inescapable, given such involuntary, selective vision. But it is from selectivity and unreceptiveness that her dramas are born.

It cannot be overlooked what a large role is played in Mason's prose by the television screen. Nearly every character has his or her favorite program, which plays a much greater role in determining the tastes and ideas of characters than does anything that actually happens to them. It seems that their view of reality itself is a view through a TV camera. Although seeming to have full scope, this view is strictly selective, subject to determined regulations, designed as a certain kind of model for behavior, even for one's psychological reactions. The characters are not aware of their lack of freedom, although it makes itself known time after time in situations where choice is required and fates are decided.

Reviewers of the collection *Love Life* wrote that the stories contain "the quintessence of everyday America." This is true in the most general sense: Mason's sphere of observation is daily life, with its banal situations and problems: family breakdown, listless adultery, the petty burdens of life. Turns of plot, however, are unimportant; what matters are the systems of feelings and ideas the characters possess. The key word with which this can be described is *anemia*. Although the characters' dissatisfaction with their lot may even become acute, it cannot break through their passivity. There remain only empty dreams before the TV set and uncommitted reflections on the "kaleidoscope of possibilities" open to everybody.

The artistic effect is created not by the novelty of the material but the uniqueness of the material's artistic organization. While conveying the sense of everyday life, this method is capable of expressing both the type of thinking and the attitude toward life most typical of mass consciousness. In this sense, Mason's prose, though nearly devoid of introspection, can be seen as a continuation of the lessons of Henry James. The two writers share a basic creative goal: to embody not so much reality itself as its image buried in consciousness, and in this way to express their time.

For this reason, James's perceptible influence on Mason's books, especially on her novel, is not surprising. If we limit ourselves to the plot, we must also ascribe her work to the body of prose dealing specifically with the Vietnam syndrome. Mason's novel, however, is unusual against that background as well. The action takes place many years after the war. The central episode is the trip the Vietnam veteran Emmet takes with his niece to Washington, where the name of Samantha's father is inscribed on the memorial—among fifty thousand-odd others.

The main theme of the book involves the 17-year-old Samantha, who has never seen her father and has virtually grown up motherless. Shadows of the past burden the world, which is still taking shape for her, with the dramas and traumas that marked Vietnam for the previous generation. On the other hand, the experience of that generation is perceived and realized by the adolescent, capable of recognizing truths to which her elders try to close themselves off as they search for various extenuating circumstances and explanations to take away their feeling of guilt.

Particularly Jamesian is the approach of reconstructing reality through the consciousness of a teenager able to see reality more clearly and sharply than the people who have adjusted all too well to life around them. No less essential in Mason's book is the fact that it is overfilled with echoes of subculture and, above all, of television, which plays as important a role in the formation of the heroine as do Emmet's fragmentary confessions or her dead father's journals from Vietnam. All of this information is as if preformed for Samantha by the versions presented to her by rock music, television, and cinema—all of which have interpreted and explained the war in their way. Breaking through these explanations to reality is extremely hard for Samantha, however obvious the truth may appear to be. The trip to Washington becomes an encounter with truth, taking on a symbolic meaning.

Everything that precedes the trip could be fit into the framework of a typical story by Mason, in which the dominant theme is apathy. Samantha's Kentucky hometown is the embodiment of spiritual provinciality. Only Emmet's presence brings a note of disquiet into that measured life. Emmet is unable to step beyond what he has experienced in Vietnam. He has immersed himself in everyday life, convincing himself that he is answerable for nothing and to no one. Living in his own impenetrable world, he frightens away the local inhabitants, who create numerous legends about his past: as a corruptor of minors, a drug dealer, a butcher who shot Vietnamese children. None of this is true. Emmet, like many others, carried out orders without considering their meaning. He simply tried to survive, but the spiritual wound that was the result of his military service in Vietnam is deep and cannot be healed fully. In Emmet's consciousness are mixed remorse, self-pity, hatred of contented and colorless daily life, and, at times, even longing for his days as a soldier.

In her contact with Emmet, Samantha tries to understand the experience of her father's generation, to restore a tie severed too early. It is as if she were returning to her roots. Her self-knowledge, hampered from childhood by the accepted myths of the TV screen and Emmet's psychological wound, is the true subject of Mason's novel.

Behind the ordinary story in this book, we find the themes of social psychology and the deterioration of the social consciousness. The typical form of defense against this pain is an artificially fostered amnesia which avenges itself with the emptiness and dullness of comfortable daily life. Mason's heroine attempts to relive former experience; her awakened consciousness of this inheritance becomes the deciding step in her formation.

Mason expresses the state of spiritual petrification with an artistic accuracy not yet attained by other writers of her generation. More important, however, is the fact that Mason also finds ways of overcoming that petrification. This gives us reason to predict that her future as a writer is very promising.

There is probably no sense in drawing any conclusions from these first observations of the prose that appeared in the 1980s. The literature itself is still in the making; it is not yet clearly enough defined. The choice of the three writers who have been discussed is, of course, subjective. Certainly, other representative names could have been presented.

Nevertheless, some characteristics of this generation of writers are solid enough to make some generalization possible. For instance, none of them is drawn to refinement or unusual narrative methods. This does not mean that complicated methods of illustration are unattainable to them; on the contrary, the architectonics of their works, despite apparent artlessness, is very skillful. Sometimes this is openly demonstrated, as in Phillips' *Machine Dreams*, which forms a collage in which narrative times, and narrators themselves, frequently are changed. However, they display no emphasized striving for experimentation, for anything artistically unusual.

In fact, all three writers—Mason, McInerney, and Phillips—remain fairly traditional writers, in the sense that they strive to fully embrace the social environment depicted, with its types and peculiarities of social behavior. Each writer has created his or her own sort of topos, intended to convey a particular social microcosm with the utmost authenticity. Mason's country, Phillips' farm in the middle of nowhere, McInerney's city with its anonymous and impersonal life—each is a topos, combining the detail of factual description with a certain symbolic meaning, as each time a distinct image of existence is created, not merely a picture of society, however complete it might appear.

This type of illustration is associated primarily with Henry James. In a certain sense, the prose of the 1980s can be described as a revival of the tradition that began with him. What is essential, however, is not so much the name *James*, as it is the conscious orientation to traditional narrative methods. The reasons for this cooling off toward experimentation and the partiality for forms that were solidly mastered by literature at the turn of the century remain to be explained. For now, we will simply register the fact; it is important in order to perceive the trend in American prose in recent years.

It is natural to expect the criticism that this conscious old-fashionedness, which seems to have become the creative position of this young literature, has no future. We should not rush to such conclusions, however. The weaknesses of this prose are obvious, the main one being its passion for a fairly one-dimensional description of events, something with limited literary possibilities. Clearly, this passion is excessive. The writers themselves are aware of it, as they try (though so far without particular success) to compensate in one way or another for the flaws of such a style, about which James himself was well aware, as he tirelessly reminded himself: "Dramatize! Dramatize!" In fact, dramatization is the weakest side of the books just discussed. They are capable of re-creating precisely an atmosphere of everyday life, but they have not yet achieved the effect of literature that touches on the existential questions of being.

Let us not forget that these are the books of writers who are still far from having spoken their last word. The artistic merits of such books may be evaluated variously; but as documents of their time, they doubtless will remain in the history of the American postwar novel.

NOTES

The Formation of the Secular Literary Tradition
in Colonial America   EKATERINA STETSENKO

1. Louis B. Wright, *The Elizabethan's America: A Collection of Early Reports by Englishmen on the New World*, Cambridge, Mass.: Harvard Univ. Press, 1965, p. 10.

2. J. K. Piercy, *Studies in Literary Types in Seventeenth-Century America, 1607–1710*, New Haven, Conn.: Yale Univ. Press, 1939, p. 9.

3. Carl Holliday, *A History of Southern Literature*, 1906, Port Washington, N.Y.: Kennikat Press, 1969.

4. Daniel Boorstin, *The Americans: The Colonial Experience*, New York: Random House, 1959, p. 150.

5. Robert E. Spiller, *Literary History of the United States*, 3d ed. rev., New York: Macmillan, 1963, p. 9.

6. Moses Coit Tyler, *A History of American Literature, 1607–1783*, 1878, Chicago: Univ. of Chicago Press, 1967, p. 97.

7. *Travels and Works of Captain John Smith, President of Virginia and Admiral of New England, 1580–1631*, Edinburgh, 1910, p. 407.

8. Everett H. Emerson, *Captain John Smith*, New York: Twayne Publishers, 1971, p. 121.

9. Michael T. Gilmore, ed., *Early American Literature: A Collection of Critical Essays*, Englewood Cliffs, N.J.: Prentice-Hall, 1980, p. 16.

10. N. S. Grabo, "The Veiled Vision: The Role of Aesthetics in Early American Intellectual History," in Sacvan Bercovitch, comp., *The American Puritan Imagination—Essays in Revaluation*, New York: Cambridge Univ. Press, 1974, p. 24.

11. Emerson, *Captain John Smith*, p. 124.

12. Charles Angoff, *A Literary History of the American People*, New York: Knopf, 1931, 1:5.

13. Howard Mumford Jones; *Literature of Virginia in the Seventeenth Century*, Charlottesville: Univ. Press of Virginia, 1968, p. 17.

14. Boorstin, *The Americans*, p. 5.

15. Larzer Ziff, *Puritanism in America: New Culture in a New World*, New York: Viking, 1973, pp. 9–10.

16. Ibid., p. 26.

17. J. Rosenmeier, "'With My Owne Eyes': William Bradford's *History of Plymouth Plantation*," in Bercovitch, comp., *The American Puritan Imagination—Essays in Revaluation*, New York: Cambridge Univ. Press, 1974, p. 90.

18. Ibid., p. 9.

19. William Bradford, *The History of Plymouth Plantation*, New York: Knopf, 1952, p. 13.

20. Ibid.

21. Ibid., p. 61.

22. Ibid., p. 62.

23. Ibid., p. 63.

24. S. Bercovitch and A. A. Dolinin have written about the Puritan use of the desert as a symbol for wilderness and chaos. See Bercovitch, "The American Puritan Imagination: An Introduction," in Bercovitch, comp., *The American Puritan Imagination—Essays in Revaluation*, New York: Cambridge Univ. Press, 1974.

25. A. A. Dolonin, "At the Source of American Culture: The Picture of the World in the Literature of New England Colonies in the 17th Century," in *The Origins and Formation of American National Literature, 17th–18th Centuries*, Moscow, 1985.

26. Bradford, *Plymouth Plantation*, p. 282.

27. Ibid., p. 303.

28. Ibid.

29. Ibid., p. 316.

30. Ibid., p. 296.

31. *Pioneer Literature, In Colonial Prose and Poetry*, New York, 1903, p. 139.

32. Ibid., p. 153.

33. Bradford, *Plymouth Plantation*, p. 120.

34. Ibid., pp. 120–21.

35. Ibid., p. 121.

36. Ibid., p. 46.

37. *Problems of Formation of American Literature*, Moscow, 1981, p. 52.

38. D. F. Connors, *Thomas Morton*, New York: Twayne Publishers, 1969, p. 60.

39. *Selections from Early American Writers, 1607–1800*, New York, 1909, p. 62.

40. Ibid., p. 45.

41. K. B. Murdock, *Literature and Theology in Colonial New England*, Cambridge, Mass.: Harvard Univ. Press, 1949.

42. *American Literary Survey: Colonial and Federal to 1800*, 1968, p. 52.

43. Ibid., p. 51.

44. *Formation of American Literature*, p. 45.

45. R. E. Spiller, *The Roots of National Culture: American Literature to 1830*, New York: Macmillan, 1949, p. 84.

46. *Selections from Early American Writers*, pp. 226–27.

47. Ibid., p. 198.

48. Ibid., p. 197.

49. Richard Slotkin, *Israel in Babylon: The Archetype of the Captivity Narrative, in Early American Literature—A Collection of Critical Essays*, 1980.

50. R. B. Nye, *American Literary History, 1607–1830*, New York: Knopf, 1970, p. 55.

51. *Sea L. Filosophiya amerikanskoy istorii* (Philosophy of American History), Moscow, 1984, p. 148.

52. *Istoriya Literature Latïnskoy Ameriki* (History of the Literatures of Latin America), Moscow, 1984, 1:1985.

The Romantic Poetics of Hawthorne   MAYA KORENEVA

1. *Hawthorne: The Critical Heritage*, ed. J. Donald Crowley, London: Routledge & Kegan Paul, 1970, p. 514.

2. Nathaniel Hawthorne, *The House of the Seven Gables*, New York: New American Library, 1961, p. viii.

3. In *Strich F. Deutsche Klassik und Romantik, oder Vollendung und Unendlichkeit*, Ein Vergleich, III Auflage, Munchen, 1928, S.75.

4. The author's concern, Hawthorne explains, "is merely to establish a theatre, a little removed from the highway of ordinary travel, where the creatures of his brain may play their phantasmagorical antics, without exposing them to too close a comparison with the actual events of real lives. In the old countries, with which fiction has long been conversant, a certain conventional privilege seems to be awarded to the romancer; his work is not put exactly side by side with nature; and he is allowed a license with regard to every-day probability, in view of the improved effects which he is bound to produce thereby. Among ourselves, on the contrary, there is as yet no such Faery Land, so like the real world, that, in a suitable remoteness, one cannot well tell the difference, but with an atmosphere of strange enchantment, beheld through which the inhabitants have a propriety of their own. This atmosphere is what the American romancer needs. In its absence, the beings of imagination are compelled to show themselves in the same category as actually living mortals; a necessity that generally renders the paint and pasteboard of their composition but too painfully discernible." Hawthorne, *Blithedale Romance*, New York: Dell, 1960, pp. 21–22.

5. Hawthorne, *The Scarlet Letter*, New York, Signet Classics, p. 45.

6. Hawthorne, *Twice-Told Tales*, Boston: Houghton Mifflin Riverside Literature Series, 1907, pp. 486–87.

7. Ibid., p. 487.

8. Ibid., p. 34.

9. Ibid., p. 36.

10. Ibid., p. 39.

11. Henry James, *Hawthorne*, Ithaca, N.Y.: Cornell Univ. Press (orig. published in England in 1879), pp. 94–95.

12. Nathaniel Hawthorne, *The American Notebooks*, ed. R. Stewart, New Haven: Yale Univ. Press, 1932, p. 107.

13. Ibid., p. 89.

14. Ibid., p. 121.

15. P. Miller, *Errand into the Wilderness*, New York: Harper & Row, 1964, p. ix.

16. *The Works of Nathaniel Hawthorne*, 15 vols., Cambridge, Mass.: Houghton Mifflin, 1883, 3:449.

17. Hugo, *Notre-Dame de Paris 1482, Les Travailleurs de la mer*, Paris: Gallimard, 1975, p. 229.

18. *Works of Hawthorne*, vol. 3, p. 460.

19. Richard Brodhead, *Hawthorne, Melville, and the Novel*, Chicago: Univ. of Chicago Press, 1977, p. 16.

20. Ibid., p. 20.

21. Y. V. Mann, *Poetica russkogo romantisma*, Moscow, 1976, pp. 15, 16.

22. James, *Hawthorne*, p. 98.

23. *Hawthorne: A Collection of Critical Essays*, ed. A. N. Kaul, Englewood Cliffs, N.J.: Prentice-Hall, 1966, p. 21.

24. *Works of Hawthorne*, vol. 8, p. 386.

25. *Works of Hawthorne*, vol. 7, pp. 18–19; emphasis mine.

The Limits of Herman Melville's Universe   Yuri Kovalev

1. Later, in the forties and fifties, such works appeared as well—for example, Cooper's *The Crater*, Hawthorne's *Blithedale Romance*, Thoreau's *Walden*, and so forth.

2. The interested reader will find a detailed analysis of the structure of Mardi in my work, "The Four Books of Mardi," in *American Literature: Problems of Romanticism and Realism,* 2d issue (1973), pp. 16–33.

Mark Twain's Autobiography *as an Aesthetic Problem*   Pavel Balditzin

1. As did Twain's first biographer and literary executor, Albert P. Paine cites the author's wishes in his *Mark Twain: A Biography: The Personal and Literary Life of Samuel Langhorne Clemens*, 2 vols., New York: Harper Bros., 1924.

2. In further references to these publications within the text, their titles will be abbreviated as follows: Paine, MTA: DeVoto, MTE; Nider, AMT. The volume will be indicated by roman numerals, page by arabic.

3. G. Gusdorf, "Conditions and Limits of Autobiography," in *Autobiography: Essays Theoretical and Critical*, Princeton, N.J.: Princeton Univ. Press, 1980, p. 36.

The Russian Man at Russell Square: Reflections on the Critical Conception of T. S. Eliot   Dmitry Urnov

1. John Gross, *The Rise and Fall of the Man of Letters*, New York: Macmillan, 1969, p. 259.

2. Ibid., p. 256.

3. Such was the conclusion R. P. Blackmur drew in his article published in 1951, "In the Hope of Straightening Things Out." T. S. Eliot, *A Collection of Critical Essays*, ed. Hugh Kenner, Englewood Cliffs, N.J.: Prentice-Hall, 1962, p. 141.

4. T. S. Eliot, *Ulysses, Order and Myth*, New York: Dial, 1923, 1942, p. 269.

5. I. A. Richards, *Principles of Literary Criticism*, London: Kegan Paul, 1924, 1963, p. 46.

6. T. S. Eliot, *The Use of Poetry and the Use of Criticism*, London: Faber and Faber, 1932, 1964, p. 123.

7. Percy Lubbock, "How the Book Is Made," in *The Craft of Fiction*, New York: Cape and Smith, 1921, 1957, p. 274.

8. *A Selection from "Scrutiny,"* comp. F. R. Leavis, Cambridge: Cambridge Univ. Press, 1968, vol. I, p. 25.

9. This book "is aimed . . . at giving the reader a fairly complete idea, by instance and example, of achievement as poet and dramatist. There will be no attempt to impose on the reader general estimates or vague appreciations. The best and worst in Jonson shall be offered, and those who disagree with the views submitted will here find the material they need for a confutation." John Palmer, *Ben Johnson*, 2, 1934, p. xi.

10. Eliot, *The Sacred Wood*, London: Methuen, 1920, p. 104.

11. Eliot, *Sacred Wood*, p. 114.

12. Eliot, *Sacred Wood*, p. 117.

13. Peter Conrad, "The Grab Street and the Dreaming Spires," *Times Literary Supplement*, March 22, 1974, p. 285.

14. Richards, *Principles of Literary Criticism*, p. 144.

15. Richards, *Principles of Literary Criticism*, pp. 144–45.

16. Ibid.

17. This nuance of Tolstoy's theory of "infection" was unnoticed also by L. Vygotsky in whose interpretation it looked as though, for Tolstoy, the capacity of the ordinary feeling to "infect" and that of the creative feeling were alike in nature. Compare L. Vygotsky, *Psykhologiya iskusstva* (Psychology of Art), Moscow, 1968, pp. 305–306). There is a good deal of similarity in the views of I. A. Richards and Vygotsky, who were active during the same period. There are even exact textual parallels in their phrasing and main formulations, which, evidently, may be accounted for by use of the same sources.

18. Richards, *Principles*, p. 165.

19. A chapter of Tolstoy's essay, "What Is Art?" is referred to.

Eugene O'Neill and the Ways of American Drama   MAYA KORENEVA

1. *American Playwrights on Drama*, ed. H. Frenz, New York: Hill and Wang, 1965, p. 2.

2. Arthur Miller, *Timebends: A Life*, New York: Grove Press, 1987, pp. 228–29.

3. Harold Clurman, *The Naked Image: Observations on the Modern Theatre*, New York: Macmillan, 1966, pp. 160–61.

4. Joseph Wood Krutch, intro. to *Eugene O'Neill—Nine Plays*, New York: Modern Library, 1959, p. xvii.

5. John Gassner, intro. to M. Himelstein, *Drama Was a Weapon*, New Brunswick, N.J.: Rutgers Univ. Press, 1963, p. viii.

6. A. S. Romm, *Amerikanskaia dramaturuiia pervoi poloviny XX v.* (American Playwriting of the First Half of the 20th Century), Leningrad, 1978, p. 130.

7. *Best American Plays, 1918–1958*, supp. vol., ed. John Gassner, New York: Crown, 1961, p. 527.

8. Eugene O'Neill, *Thirst and Other One-Act Plays*, 1914, p. 43.

9. O'Neill, *Nine Plays*, New York: Random House, 1954, p. 132.

10. Tennessee Williams, *The Night of the Iguana*, New York: New American Library, 1964, pp. 59–60.

11. Edward Albee, *The American Dream, and The Zoo Story*, New York: New American Library, p. 35.

The Metaphor of History in the Work of F. Scott Fitzgerald
V. M. TOLMATCHOFF

1. *F. S. Fitzgerald in His Own Time: A Miscellany*, ed. Matthew Bruccoli, New York, Popular Library, 1971, p. 176.

2. *The Notebooks of F. Scott Fitzgerald*, ed. Matthew Bruccoli, New York: Harcourt Brace Jovanovich/Bruccoli/Clark, 1978, p. viii.

3. Carlos Baker, *Hemingway: The Writer as Artist*, Princeton, N.J.: Princeton Univ. Press, 1972, p. 79.

4. *The Letters of F. Scott Fitzgerald*, ed. A. Turnbull, New York: Scribner's, 1963, p. 251.

5. Bruccoli, ed., *Notebooks*, p. 159.

6. Bruccoli, ed., *Fitzgerald*, p. 299.

7. Letter to Fitzgerald, May 28, 1934. See also, Bruccoli et al., *The Authority of Failure and the Authority of Success*, Carbondale, Ill.: Southern Illinois Univ. Press, 1978, p. 113.

8. Bruccoli, ed., *Notebooks*, p. 147.

9. *The Correspondence of F. Scott Fitzgerald*, ed. Bruccoli and Duggan, New York: Random House, 1980, p. 139.

10. Ibid.

11. See Fitzgerald's letter to John Hibben, June 3, 1920, in which he admits to the relationship between his world-view and that of Conrad and Dreiser.

12. In a letter to M. Mann, October 1925, Fitzgerald quite seriously refers to himself as a Schopenhauerist.

13. Bruccoli, ed., *Fitzgerald*, p. 244.

14. Turnbull, ed., *Letters of Fitzgerald*, p. 96.

15. *Fitzgerald in His Own Time*, p. 265.

16. Letter, November 16, 1926; *Ernest Hemingway: The Selected Letters*, ed. Carlos Baker, New York: Scribner's, 1981, pp. 225–26.

17. Turnbull, ed., *Letters of Fitzgerald*, pp. 509, 358.

18. Bruccoli, ed., *Notebooks of Fitzgerald*, pp. 159, 299.

19. Bruccoli, ed., *Correspondence of Fitzgerald*, p. 145.

20. Bruccoli, ed., *Notebooks of Fitzgerald*, p. 113.

21. Letter, October 1925, Turnbull, ed., *Letters of Fitzgerald*, p. 488.

22. *Fitzgerald in His Own Time*, p. 199.

23. Ibid., p. 271.

24. Bruccoli, ed., *Notebooks of Fitzgerald*, p. 189.

25. Turnbull, ed., *Letters of Fitzgerald*, pp. 85–86.

26. Bruccoli, ed., *Notebooks of Fitzgerald*, p. 158.

27. Wells G. D. - *Sobrannye sochineniia v 15–ti tt.* (H. G. Wells, Collected Works), 15 vols., Moscow: Pravda, 1964, 8:412.

28. For a recent treatment of this problem, see Joyce A. Rowe, *Equivocal Endings in Classic American Novels*, New York: Cambridge Univ. Press, 1988, pp. 118–22.

29. Turnbull, ed., *Letters of Fitzgerald*, p. 482.

30. *The Portable Conrad*, ed. with intro. M. D. Zabel, New York: Viking, 1976, p. 493.

31. *The Bodley Head Scott Fitzgerald*, Bodley Head, 1958, 1:123–69. Further references to this text are followed by the volume and page number in parentheses.

32. *Editor to Author: The Letters of Maxwell Perkins*, ed. J. H. Wheelock, New York: Scribner's, 1979, p. 59.

33. Boris Pasternak, *Doktor Zhivago*, Novy mir, 1988, no. 4, p. 107, part 16, epilogue, 5.

Ernest Hemingway: The Road to Literary Craft   NATALIA YAKIMENKO

1. L. H. Cohn, *A Bibliography of the Works of Ernest Hemingway*, New York: Random House, 1931, p. 112.

2. Ernest Hemingway, *Selected Letters, 1917–1961*, New York: Scribner's, 1981, p. 805.

3. Ibid., p. 787.

4. *Anything Can Happen: Interviews with Contemporary American Novelists*, cond. and ed. by T. LeClair and L. McCaffery, Urbana: Univ. of Illinois Press, 1983, p. 35.

5. M. Reynolds, *The Young Hemingway*, London: Basil Blackwell, 1986, p. 186.

6. Hemingway, *Selected Letters*, p. 765.

7. Ernest Hemingway, *By-Line: Selected Articles and Dispatches of Four Decades*, ed. W. White, New York: Scribner's, 1967, pp. 179–80.

8. Hemingway, *Selected Letters*, p. 774.

9. C. A. Fenton, *The Apprenticeship of Ernest Hemingway*, London: Vision Press and Peter Owen, 1954, p. 43.

10. *Ernest Hemingway, Cub Reporter: Kansas City Star Stories*, ed. Matthew Bruccoli, Pittsburgh, Pa.: Univ. of Pittsburgh Press, 1970, p. 28.

11. Ibid., p. 32.

12. Ibid., p. 51.

13. Ibid., p. 15.

14. Reynolds, *Young Hemingway*, chs. 2, 4.

15. Ernest Hemingway, *Dateline: Toronto. The Complete Toronto Star Dispatches, 1920–1924*, ed. W. White, New York: Scribner's, 1985, p. 5. Further quotations from this source are followed by the page number in parentheses.

16. R. O. Stephens, *Hemingway's Non-Fiction: The Public Voice*, Chapel Hill: Univ. of North Carolina Press, 1968, p. 49.

17. Ibid., p. 363.

18. Fenton, *Apprenticeship of Hemingway*, pp. 229–36; I. A. Kashkin, *Ernest Hemingway: Kritiko-biograficheskii ocherk* (Ernest Hemingway: A Critical Biographical Sketch), 1966, pp. 59–62; J. F. Kobler, *Ernest Hemingway: Journalist and Artist*, Ann Arbor, Mich.: UMI Research Press, 1985, pp. 9–16.

19. Reynolds, *Young Hemingway*, pp. 39, 91–92ff.

20. Ernest Hemingway, *In Our Time*, New York: Scribner's, 1958, pp. 89–90.

21. *E. Hemingway, sobranie Sochinenii: V 4 Tomakh* (Hemingway: Collected Works in Four Volumes) Moscow, 1968, 2:163.

22. Rudyard Kipling, *Rudyard Kipling's Verse*, inclusive edition, 1885–1932, London: Hodder and Stoughton, 1934, pp. 453–54.

23. Hemingway, *In Our Time*, p. 90.

24. Ibid., p. 94.

25. Ibid., p. 98.

26. R. W. Lewis, "Hemingway's Concept of Sport and 'Soldier's Home'," in *The Short Stories of Ernest Hemingway: Critical Essays*, ed. Jackson J. Benson, Durham, N.C.: Duke Univ. Press, 1975, pp. 170–80.

27. Hemingway, *In Our Time*, p. 101.

28. Ernest Hemingway, "Notes on Life and Letters," *Esquire* 3 (January 1935).

29. Hemingway, *In Our Time*, p. 134.

30. *E. Hemingway, Izbrannye Proizvedeniia: V 2 Tomakh* (Hemingway: Selected Works in Two Volumes), Moscow, 1959, 2:188.

31. Hemingway, *In Our Time*, p. 197.

32. M. Bakhtin, *Voprosy Literatury i Estetiki*, Moscow, 1975, p. 30.

33. Hemingway, *In Our Time*, p. 92.

34. Reynolds, *Young Hemingway*, p. 191.

35. W. E. H. Lecky, *History of European Morals, From Augustus to Charlemagne*, London: Longman, Green, 1911, pp. 271–90.

36. Ibid., pp. 208, 185, 195, 196.

37. Ibid., p. 206.

38. *E. Hemingway, Izbrannye Proizvedeniia: V 2 Tomakh*, 2:173.

39. P. Young, *Ernest Hemingway: A Reconsideration*, University Park, Pa.: Pennsylvania State Univ. Press, 1966.

40. T. S. Eliot, *The Sacred Wood: Essays on Poetry and Criticism*, London: Methuen, 1934, p. 15.

41. U. Fokner, *stat'i, rechi, interv'iu, pic'ma* (W. Faulkner: Essays, Speeches, Interviews, Letters), Moscow, 1985, p. 164.

42. Ibid., pp. 155–56.

43. Ernest Hemingway, "Monologue to the Maestro: A High Seas Letter," in *By-Line*, p. 215.

44. Sherwood Anderson, *Winesburg, Ohio*, New York: Penguin, 1983, p. 163.

45. Ernest Hemingway, "On Writing," in *The Nick Adams Stories*, ed. P. Young, New York: Scribner's, 1972, pp. 238–39.

46. *Sherwood Anderson's Notebook*, New York: Boni and Liveright, 1926, p. 53.

47. Ibid., p. 185.

48. *Ernest Hemingway: The Writer in Context*, ed. J. Nagel, Madison: Univ. of Wisconsin Press, 1984, p. 218.

49. Hemingway, *Selected Letters, 1917–1961*, pp. 264, 802.

50. Ibid., p. 378.

51. Ezra Pound, *The Literary Essays of Ezra Pound*, ed. T. S. Eliot, London: Faber & Faber, 1954, p. 45.

52. Eliot, *Sacred Wood*, p. iii.

53. Pound, *Literary Essays*, p. 44.

54. Eliot, *Sacred Wood*, p. 150.

55. K. S. Lynn, *Hemingway*, London: Simon & Schuster, 1987, p. 187.

56. J. Tavernier-Courbin, "Ernest Hemingway and Ezra Pound," in *Ernest Hemingway: The Writer in Context*, p. 184.

57. Stephens, *Hemingway's Non-Fiction*, p. 207.

58. J. J. Benson, "Ernest Hemingway as Short Story Writer," in *The Short Stories of Ernest Hemingway: Critical Essays*, pp. 273–83.

"The Whole History of the Human Heart on the Head of a Pin": Toward Faulkner's Philosophy of Composition   SERGEI CHAKOVSKY

1. *Lion in the Garden: Interviews with William Faulkner, 1926–1962*, ed. James B. Meriwether and Michael Millgate, Lincoln: Univ. of Nebraska Press, 1980, 1968. Hereafter, abbreviated LIG.

2. I agree with John T. Matthews' pointed remark that Faulkner's silence is a "worded silence," not "the blank space at the center of Addie's section." (*A Play of Faulkner's Language*, Ithaca, N.Y.: Cornell Univ. Press, 1982, p. 41). However, my view is less linguo-philosophically and more pragmatically oriented. This "brand" of silence is achieved through the affected redundancy of, for example, Mr. Compson's speech in chapters 3 and 4 of *Absalom, Absalom!* to make Wash Jones's matter-of-fact remark on the killing of Charles Bon sound deafeningly loud. For my further purposes, it is relevant to point out that the immutability of the non-linguistic reality (thus made dramatically vivid) clearly is important to Faulkner's poetics, whatever Jacques Derrida might have had to say about this.

3. P. V. Palievsky, rightly, holds Faulkner's outwardly "nonartistic" statement as an "integral part of his work . . . an extension of what he had always done—another way of achieving his main goal." In "Faulkner's View of Literature," *New Directions in Faulkner Studies*, ed. Doreen Fowler and Ann J. Abadie, Jackson: Univ. Press of Mississippi, 1984, p. 270.

4. *Faulkner in the University: Class Conferences at the University of Virginia, 1957–1958*, ed. Frederic L. Gwynn and Joseph L. Blotner, Charlottesville: Univ. Press of Virginia, 1959, p. 243. Hereafter cited as FU.

5. *Selected Letters of William Faulkner*, ed. Joseph Blotner, New York: Vintage Books, 1978, p. 391; *Faulkner: A Comprehensive Guide to the Brodsky Collection*, vol. 2: Letters, Jackson: Univ. Press of Mississippi, 1984, pp. 189–90.

6. V. Shklovsky, *Tekhnika pisatelskogo remesla*, Moscow, 1927, pp. 7, 13.

7. Arthur F. Kinney, *Faulkner's Narrative Poetics: Style as Vision*, Amherst: Univ. of Massachusetts Press, 1978.

8. Quoted in Joseph Blotner, introd., William Faulkner, *Helen, A Courtship, and Mississippi Poems*, Oxford, Miss.: Yoknapatawpha Press, 1981, p. 137.

9. René Wellek and Austin Warren, *Theory of Literature*, New York: Harcourt Brace & World, 1956, p. 156.

10. Ibid., p. 241.

11. Ibid., p. 25.

12. Malcolm Cowley, *The Faulkner-Cowley File: Letters and Memories, 1944–1962*, New York: Viking, 1966, p. 14.

13. *Soldiers' Pay*, Great Britain: Penguin Modern Classics, in association with Chatto & Windus, 1970, 7. Hereafter cited as SP.

14. William Faulkner, *Absalom, Absalom!: The Corrected Text*, New York: Random House, 1986, p. 157. Hereafter cited as AA.

15. William Faulkner, *Mosquitoes*, New York: Liveright, 1927 (1955), p. 210.

16. O. G. Drobnizkyj, *Mir ozhivshikh predmetov. Problema tsen-nosti i Marksistskaya filosofiya*, Moscow, 1967, p. 54.

17. *Faulkner: A Comprehensive Guide to the Brodsky Collection*, 2:75.

18. William Faulkner, "Address upon Receiving the Nobel Prize for Literature," in *William Faulkner: Essays, Speeches, and Public Letters*, ed. James B. Meriwether, New York: Random House, 1966, 1965, p. 119.

In Search of Community: The Individual and Society in the New American Novel   TAMARA DENISOVA

1. W. J. Gavin and T. J. Blakeley, *Russia and America—A Philosophical Comparison: Development and Change of Outlook from the 19th to the 20th Centuries*, Boston: Reidel, 1976, p. vii.

2. Walt Whitman, *Complete Prose Works*, New York, 1891, p. 316.

3. I. Iljin, *The American Enlightenment: The American Age of Reason*. Moscow, 1977, p. 11.

4. *Lion in the Garden: Interviews with William Faulkner, 1926–1962*, ed. James B. Meriwether and Michael Millgate, New York: Random House, 1968, p. 72.

5. See Faulkner's article "On Privacy," in which he defends individualism as an American tradition.

The Soviet View of American Feminism with a Side Look at Our Native Antifeminism   MAYA TUGUSHEVA

1. Alexis De Tocqueville, *Democracy in America*, London: Saunders & Otley, 1835.

2. Elizabeth Stanford, *On the Domestic and Social Role of Woman*, 1831.

3. "Intellectual Equality of the Sexes? Women's Literature," *Edinburgh Review*, 1849.

4. *Literaturnaya Gazeta* (Literary Gazette), June 27, 1984.

5. *Novyi Mir* (New World), no. 11 (1988), pp. 77, 80.

Neoconservatism and American Literature of the 1980s
ALEXANDR MULIARCHIK

1. I. Kristol, *Reflections of a Neoconservative: Looking Back, Looking Ahead*, New York: Basic Books, 1983, p. xi.

2. Daniel Patrick Moynihan, *Reflections on America's Future*, New York: Harcourt Brace Jovanovich, 1980.

3. Helen Santmyer, . . . *And Ladies of the Club*, Columbus: Ohio State Univ. Press, 1982.

4. E. I. Batalov and B. V. Mikhailov, "Americanskii Liberalizm: Poiski Novykh Putei" (American Liberalism: A Search for New Routes), in *S.Sh.A.: Economika, Politika, Ideologiia*, United States: Economics, Politics, Ideology, 1984, no. 9, p. 16.

5. *Partisan Review*, no. 3 (1982), pp. 330–31.

6. *Commentary*, September 1982, p. 38.

7. *New York Review of Books*, Oct. 6, 1972, p. 19.

8. *New York Times Book Review*, June 8, 1980, p. 38.

Notes on Contributors

Nikolai Anastasiev graduated from Moscow State University where he is currently a professor. He is the author of *William Faulkner: Life and Letters* (1975), *The Novels of Ernest Hemingway* (1981), *Tradition and Movement* (1984), and *The Owner of Yoknapatawpha* (1991).

Pavel Balditzin graduated from Kuban State University and is currently associate professor at the School of Journalism at Moscow State University. He has published many articles and reviews on Mark Twain, John Cheever, Russian symbolism, and comparative studies.

Sergei Chakovsky graduated from Moscow State University and is currently a researcher at A. M. Gorky Institute of World Literature. He has published widely on Faulkner, black American literature, and literary theory. Since 1982 he has lectured at six Faulkner and Yoknapatawpha Conferences and served as visiting Fulbright professor at the University of Mississippi in 1991.

Tamara Denisova graduated from Kiev State University and is currently a chief researcher at Shevchenko Institute of Literature, Ukranian Academy of Sciences. She is the author of *The Novel and the Problems of Its Structure* (1968), *The Modern American Novel* (1976), and *Existentialism and the Modern American Novel* (1977).

Maya Koreneva graduated from Moscow State University and is currently a senior researcher at A. M. Gorky Institute of World Literature. She is the author of *Franklin's Autobiography* (1989) and *Eugene O'Neill and the Development of American Drama* (1990), editor of six books of scholarship, and a contributor to many books on American literature published by A. M. Gorky Institute.

Yuri Kovalev is a graduate of Leningrad State University and taught there from 1956 until his retirement in 1989. He is the author of *Young America* (1971), *Herman Melville and American Romanticism* (1972), and *Edgar Poe—A Short Story Writer and Poet* (1984).

Tatiana Morozova graduated from Moscow State University and is currently a researcher at A. M. Gorky Institute of World Literature. She is the author of *The Image of Young Americans in the Literature of the U. S. A.* (1990), *Debate on Man in America* (1990), and numerous essays on Russian authors and comparative studies.

Alexandr Muliarchik is a senior research fellow at the A. M. Gorky Institute of World Literature and chair of the World Literature Department of Moscow Pedagogical University. He is author of *In the Center of Dispute is Man: On American Literature in the Second Part of the Twentieth Century* (1985), *The Contemporary Realistic American Novel in the United States* (1988), and *Listening to Each Other: On the Contemporary Cultural and Literary Times Between Russia and the United States* (1991).

Ekaterina Stetsenko graduated from Kiev State University and is currently a researcher at A. M. Gorky Institute of World Literature. She is the author of *The Fate of America in the U. S. A. Novel* and numerous articles on various southern writers, Mark Twain, and American documentary prose.

V. M. Tolmatchoff graduated from Moscow State University and is currently an associate professor at the School of Philology there. He is the author of *American Novel of the 1920s* (1992) and numerous articles on American and modern Western culture.

Maya Tugusheva graduated from Moscow State University and has held a number of scholarly and editorial positions. She is the author of *Life and Work of Charlotte Bronte* (1982), *Uncle Tom's Cabin by Harriet Beecher Stowe* (1985), and *The Hopes of Truth and Kindness: The Portraits of Women Writers of the 19th Century* (1991).

Dmitry Urnov graduated from Moscow State University and is currently head of the literary criticism department at A. M. Gorky Institute of World Literature and editor-in-chief of *Problems of Literature* at the Institute. He is the author of *Defoe: Life Story* (1978), *Literature and the Progress of Time* (1978), *A Work of Literature as Evaluated by the Anglo-American "New Criticism"* (1982), and *Borodino Battle Cup* (1983).

Natalia Yakimenko was graduated from Moscow State University. She is a researcher at the A. M. Gorky Institute of World Literature.

Aleksei Zverev graduated from Moscow State University and is currently a chief researcher at A. M. Gorky Institute of World Literature. He is the author of *American Modernists: Ezra Pound to John Barth* (1979), *American Novel Between Two Wars* (1982), and *The Novel in the 20th Century* (1989).

INDEX